The MCSE Windows® 2000 Professional Cram Sheet

This Cram Sheet contains the distilled, key facts about Windows 2000 Professional. Review this information last thing before you enter the test room, paying special attention to those areas where you feel you need the most review. You can transfer any of these facts from your head onto a blank sheet of paper immediately before beginning the exam.

ADMINISTERING RESOURCES

1. Hidden or administrative shares are share names with a dollar sign ($) appended to their names. Administrative shares are created automatically for the root of each drive letter. Hidden shares do not display in the network browse list.
2. You can allow or deny share permissions of Full Control, Change, or Read for each shared folder. The default for new shares is Everyone, Allow, Full Control. If share permissions conflict with NTFS permissions, the *most restrictive* permissions take precedence.
3. NTFS permissions are cumulative for all permissions assigned to users and groups. When you combine NTFS permissions based on users and their group memberships, the *least restrictive* permissions take precedence. However, explicit Deny entries *always override* Allow entries.
4. By default, NTFS permissions are inherited from the parent folder. Permissions that are not inherited are referred to as *explicit*. Explicit permissions always override inherited permissions—an explicit Allow will even override an inherited Deny permission.
5. To change NTFS permissions on a file or folder, you must be the owner, or have the Change Permissions permission, which itself is part of Full Control. NTFS permissions are transferred when you move or copy files, as shown in Table 1.
6. NTFS for Windows 2000 supports both file compression and data encryption. Encryption is implemented via Encrypting File System (EFS). You can compress or encrypt a file, but not both.
7. Windows 2000 print server computers automatically download the correct printer drivers for client computers running Windows as long as the correct drivers have been installed on the print server.
8. Windows 2000 Professional computers can connect to printers that are attached to Windows 2000 print servers through a Web browser. You can enter one of the following URLs into your Web browser:
   - **http://print_server_name/printers**
   - **http://print_server_name/printer_share_name**

Table 1 Transferring NTFS permissions.

Type of Transfer	Effective Permissions after Move or Copy
Moving to another folder within the same NTFS volume	Files and folders retain their explicit permissions and inherit propagated permissions from the destination folder.
Moving to a different NTFS volume	Files and folders inherit their permissions from the destination folder.
Copying within the same NTFS volume	Files and folders inherit their permissions from the destination folder.
Copying to a different NTFS volume	Files and folders inherit their permissions from the destination folder.

USER AND GROUP ACCOUNTS

9. Local user and group accounts can be granted privileges and permissions to resources on the same system only. They cannot access resources on other systems.
10. Local user accounts can belong to local groups on the same system only. They cannot belong to any other group type or to groups on any other system. A local group cannot be a member of any other group. Domain user accounts can belong to global groups in the domain, universal groups, domain local groups, and machine local groups.

11. Renaming an account maintains all group memberships, permissions, and privileges of the account. Copying a user account maintains group memberships, permissions, and privileges assigned to its groups, but doing so does not retain permissions associated with the original user account. Deleting and re-creating an account with the same name loses all group memberships and permissions.

12. The most powerful group on a system is its local Administrators group. Removing users from this group and putting them in groups such as Power Users and Backup Operators gives these users broad control of a system but less power.

13. Organizational Units (OUs) in Active Directory create a hierarchical structure of containers for other objects, such as users, groups, and computers. Objects inherit attributes of their parent objects.

14. You can remember the application of group policy as LSDOU (local, site, domain, OU). The "closer" a policy is to a user or computer, the more it "wins" over higher-level policies when a conflict occurs.

15. Incremental security templates for Windows 2000 can be applied to systems using the Security Configuration And Analysis snap-in, as shown in Table 2.

Table 2 Incremental security templates for Windows 2000.

Template	File Name	Description
Compatibility	compatws.inf	Also referred to as the basic template; configures permissions of the local Users group so that legacy programs are more likely to run.
Secure	securews.inf	Increases security through Account Policy and Auditing settings. All members are removed from the Power Users group.
High security	hisecws.inf	Requires all network communications to be digitally signed and encrypted. Because Windows 9x and NT do not function on the network under this requirement, you should not use this template in environments with down-level Windows clients.

INSTALLATION AND CONFIGURATION

16. Know all the following processes for unattended and Remote Installation Service (RIS) installations:
    - *winnt.sif*—Used to automate CD-ROM-based installs.
    - *sysprep.inf*—The answer file for System Preparation (Sysprep) installs.
    - *winnt.exe with the /u, /s, and /udf switches*—Used for unattended installations.
    - *winnt32.exe and unattend.txt*—Automate an upgrade to Windows 2000.
    - *Requirements for RIS*—Active Directory, DNS, and DHCP.

17. **winnt32.exe** and **checkupgradeonly** are used to verify hardware and software compatibility.

18. Upgrade packs (or migration DLLs) are used during an upgrade to ensure that applications will run after the upgrade to Windows 2000 has completed.

19. **rbfg.exe** is used to create remote boot disks for RIS clients if computers don't have network adapters with Pre-boot Execution Environment (PXE) boot ROM.

20. **riprep.exe** is used to create images of Windows 2000 Professional and applications for an RIS server.

21. **risetup.exe** is used to configure RIS.

22. **update.exe /s** is used to apply a service pack to a distribution share in slipstream mode.

CONFIGURING THE USER AND SYSTEM ENVIRONMENT

23. Know the purpose and configuration of all the accessibility features: StickyKeys, FilterKeys Narrator, Magnifier, and On-Screen Keyboard.

24. The Accessibility Wizard is an easy way to turn on accessibility features. The resulting settings can be saved with an .acw file extension. By default, this file is accessible only by the user who created the file, and the administrator.

25. The Regional Options applet controls user and input locales. It can also be used to add new language groups. Also, use this applet to pair input locales with a specific keyboard layout when a user needs to type in different languages.

26. Use the Fax Service Management console to configure the fax modem to receive faxes. By default, only an administrator can configure the fax service options.

27. The Fax applet appears only if a fax device has been installed.

28. Applications can be deployed to users via a Group Policy. Applications can be either published or assigned. Install published applications via the Add/Remove Programs applet. Assigned applications have shortcuts in the Start menu, which will launch installation on first use.

29. Typically, only applications compiled as an MSI file can be deployed via a Group Policy. However, non MSI applications can use a ZAP file to tell Group Policy how to install the application.

EXAM CRAM™

MCSE™ Windows® 2000 Professional

Dan Balter
Dan Holme
Todd Logan
Laurie Salmon

CORIOLIS™

MCSE™ Windows® 2000 Professional Exam Cram

The Coriolis Group, LLC
14455 N. Hayden Road
Suite 220
Scottsdale, Arizona 85260

(480)483-0192
FAX (480)483-0193
www.coriolis.com

Library of Congress Cataloging-in-Publication Data
Holme, Dan [et al.]
MCSE Windows 2000 professional exam cram: Microsoft certified systems engineer
p. cm.
Includes index.
ISBN 1-57610-712-4
1. Electronic data processing personnel--Certification. 2. Microsoft software--Examinations--Study guides. 3. Microsoft Windows (Computer file) I. Holme, Dan II. Series.
QA76.3.M3285 2000
005.4'4769--dc21 00-058960
CIP

Printed in the United States of America
10 9 8 7 6 5 4 3 2 1

President and CEO
Keith Weiskamp

Publisher
Steve Sayre

Acquisitions Editor
Shari Jo Hehr

Marketing Specialist
Brett Woolley

Project Editor
Greg Balas

Technical Reviewer
James Randall

Production Coordinator
Carla J. Schuder

Cover Designer
Jesse Dunn

Layout Designer
April Nielsen

CORIOLIS™

The Coriolis Group, LLC • 14455 North Hayden Road, Suite 220 • Scottsdale, Arizona 85260

ExamCram.com Connects You to the Ultimate Study Center!

Our goal has always been to provide you with the best study tools on the planet to help you achieve your certification in record time. Time is so valuable these days that none of us can afford to waste a second of it, especially when it comes to exam preparation.

Over the past few years, we've created an extensive line of *Exam Cram* and *Exam Prep* study guides, practice exams, and interactive training. To help you study even better, we have now created an e-learning and certification destination called **ExamCram.com**. (You can access the site at **www.examcram.com**.) Now, with every study product you purchase from us, you'll be connected to a large community of people like yourself who are actively studying for their certifications, developing their careers, seeking advice, and sharing their insights and stories.

I believe that the future is all about collaborative learning. Our **ExamCram.com** destination is our approach to creating a highly interactive, easily accessible collaborative environment, where you can take practice exams and discuss your experiences with others, sign up for features like "Questions of the Day," plan your certifications using our interactive planners, create your own personal study pages, and keep up with all of the latest study tips and techniques.

I hope that whatever study products you purchase from us—*Exam Cram* or *Exam Prep* study guides, *Personal Trainers*, *Personal Test Centers*, or one of our interactive Web courses—will make your studying fun and productive. Our commitment is to build the kind of learning tools that will allow you to study the way you want to, whenever you want to.

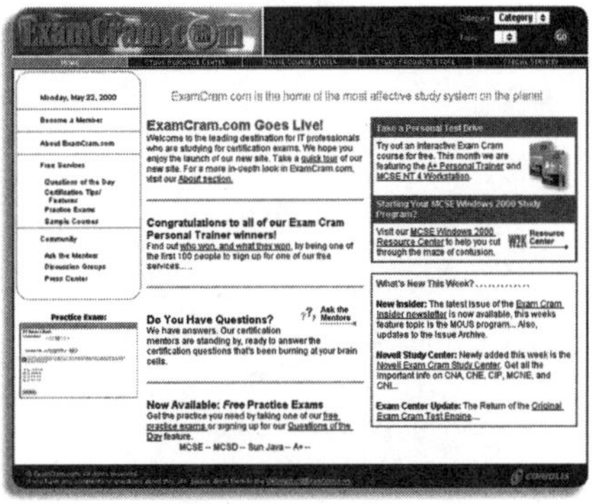

Visit ExamCram.com now to enhance your study program.

Help us continue to provide the very best certification study materials possible. Write us or email us at **learn@examcram.com** and let us know how our study products have helped you study. Tell us about new features that you'd like us to add. Send us a story about how we've helped you. We're listening!

Good luck with your certification exam and your career. Thank you for allowing us to help you achieve your goals.

Keith Weiskamp

Keith Weiskamp
President and CEO

Look for these other products from The Coriolis Group:

Exam Prep

MCSE Windows 2000 Accelerated Exam Prep
By Lance Cockcroft, Erik Eckel, and Ron Kauffman

MCSE Windows 2000 Server Exam Prep
By David Johnson and Dawn Rader

MCSE Windows 2000 Professional Exam Prep
By Michael D. Stewart, James Bloomingdale, and Neall Alcott

MCSE Windows 2000 Network Exam Prep
By Tammy Smith and Sandra Smeeton

MCSE Windows 2000 Directory Services Exam Prep
By David V. Watts, Will Willis, and Tillman Strahan

MCSE Windows 2000 Security Design Exam Prep
By Richard Alan McMahon and Glen Bicking

MCSE Windows 2000 Network Design Exam Prep
By Geoffrey Alexander, Anoop Jalan, and Joseph Alexander

MCSE Migrating from NT 4 to Windows 2000 Exam Prep
By Glen Bergen, Graham Leach, and David Baldwin

MCSE Windows 2000 Directory Services Design Exam Prep
By J. Peter Bruzzese and Wayne Dipchan

MCSE Windows 2000 Core Four Exam Prep Pack

Exam Cram

MCSE Windows 2000 Server Exam Cram
By Natasha Knight

MCSE Windows 2000 Network Exam Cram
By Hank Carbeck, Derek Melber, and Richard Taylor

MCSE Windows 2000 Directory Services Exam Cram
By Will Willis, David V. Watts, and J. Peter Bruzzese

MCSE Windows 2000 Security Design Exam Cram
By Phillip G. Schein

MCSE Windows 2000 Network Design Exam Cram
By Kim Simmons, Jarret W. Buse, and Todd B. Halpin

MCSE Windows 2000 Directory Services Design Exam Cram
By Dennis Scheil and Diana Bartley

MCSE Windows 2000 Core Four Exam Cram Pack

and...
MCSE Windows 2000 Foundations
By James Michael Stewart and Lee Scales

About the Authors

Dan Balter is a senior partner of *Marina Consulting Group LLC*, a Microsoft Certified Solution Provider firm located in Westlake Village, California. Dan works as an independent consultant and trainer for both corporate and government clients specializing in integrating messaging and scheduling software to improve organizational productivity. MCG provides consulting services, training, and custom application development.

A graduate of U.S.C.'s School of Business in 1983, Dan has authored more than 250 computer training courses on video and CD-ROM for KeyStone Learning Systems Corporation. Throughout his 15-year career, Dan has worked with numerous network operating systems, and achieved a long list of credentials and certifications. He regularly speaks at computer conferences throughout North America on Windows NT, Windows 2000, and other Microsoft BackOffice solutions. In addition, he is a contributing author for three books on the Windows NT 4 network operating system. Dan Balter can be reached at **dan@pcvideos.com**.

Dan Holme is President and CEO of *trainAbility,* a global, integrated IT training company based in Scottsdale, Arizona. The company's independent, solutions-focused curricula, and proprietary technologies allow it to deliver extremely customized solutions that bridge the gap between consulting and training. Dan spearheads the company's efforts to provide advanced, intensive ConsulTraining that meets 21st century clients' needs for cost- and time-efficient knowledge transfer.

Dan comes armed with a Bachelor's degree from Yale, a Master of International Management from Thunderbird, and 12 years of international training, public speaking, and management experience. If he's not buried in work or catching some big air on his snowboard, Dan can be reached at **dan.holme@trainability.com**.

Todd Logan has been training people how to actually use computers instead of throwing them out the window in frustration since 1992, back when the new thing was called "e-mail." Todd's wife took him away from his consulting business and the constant rain of Vancouver, British Columbia to sunny Phoenix, Arizona where he has been a technical trainer for ExecuTrain, Mastering Computers, and now works as a ConsulTrainer at *trainAbility,* where he is known for his penchant for ferreting out extraordinary solutions for clients the likes of Compaq, Hewlett-Packard, Sprint, and Microsoft. In between his never-ending quest for the truth of Windows and the pursuit of the ultimate tofu cookbook, you can reach Todd at **todd.logan@trainability.com**.

Laurie Salmon is a full-time technical consultant with *trainAbility* in Scottsdale, Arizona. Laurie has built a stellar eight-year track record in the computer business providing technical training and consulting services on Windows NT, Microsoft Back Office, Internet Information Server, and Windows 2000. Microsoft asked Laurie to be a keynote speaker for the Windows 95 Launch series touring Texas in April of 1995. Courseware for Windows 95/98, NT, and Windows 2000 that Laurie has written or co-authored is in use at many companies around the world. Laurie has been an MCT and MCSE since 1994, and has taught fast-paced and entertaining technical workshops all over the U.S. Laurie can be reached at **laurie.salmon@trainability.com**.

Acknowledgments

Writing a book is never an easy task; writing a technical book for certification on a new software product is especially daunting and challenging. First of all, I want to express my gratitude to my awe-inspiring wife of more than ten years now, Alison Balter, for teaching me how to really be an effective trainer and author. I also appreciate her putting up with me during the time that I was writing the chapters for this book. I love you, honey—happy tenth anniversary! I also want to acknowledge my two darling kids—Alexis and Brendan, ages 4 and 1 respectively, for just being so loving and fun to be around. Thanks for being so understanding of mom and dad's long hours—I love you both very, very much!

An incredible amount of appreciation also goes to Sonia Aguilar, her husband, Hugo and their children Claudia, Gabby, and little Hugo. Thank you for your incessant love, support, and unparalleled care for our children when we're attending to business matters. Sonia, you're the best.

A big tip of the hat goes to Dan Holme of trainAbility, Inc. (**www.trainability.com**), the finest team leader in the universe and one of the smartest men in the world (at least in my opinion). Congratulations on pulling all of us together and really making this project happen! Thanks for including me in this book and for hanging in there with me when deadlines were looming imminently overhead!

Huge thanks also go out to Greggory Peck and Clint Argyle of KeyStone Learning Systems (**www.keystonetraining.com**). Thank you both for giving me the opportunity to become a trainer using video-based and CD-ROM-based technology. Jeremy Moskowitz and Alan Sugano are also always there whenever I have a burning question—thank you both. Finally, to Charlotte and Bob Roman (my in-laws)—thank you both for everything that you do for us, all the time! To my Mom and Dad—thanks for emphasizing reading and writing, among other things. These skills sure come in handy for the IT industry!

—Dan Balter

It was a thrill indeed to contribute to the continued success of the *Exam Cram* series and my thanks go to the whole team at The Coriolis Group, especially Keith Weiskamp, Shari Jo Hehr, Greg Balas, and Carla Schuder for their cooperation, support, and vision. I would also like to thank Bonnie Trenga and Jim

Randall for copyediting and tech reviewing the text. Also, thanks to Andea Stonelook and Jack Lutgen for proofreading, and Christine Karpeles for indexing.

The excellence required was more than met by my stellar colleagues on this project: Dan Balter, thank you, thank you! Todd and Laurie, I cannot begin to express how proud I am to count you as peers and friends at trainAbility—your professionalism, talent, and gusto are indeed the best in the training business! I hope that all of you reading these acknowledgments someday are honored by an opportunity to work with the likes of these folks, Hank, Thom, and the entire extraordinary trainAbility team.

None of *my* work would be possible without the decades of support from my family. Mom, Dad, Bob, Joni, I love you with all my heart and I promise I will *try* to sleep when this page is submitted! Finally, to my beautiful Einstein, for bringing me lunch when I wouldn't have eaten and making the world a fabulous place to return to when the Shut Down command is finally clicked…thank you.

—Dan Holme

I would like to thank my coauthor Dan Holme for bringing me on board to help write this book. Dan, you are an inspiration to everyone at trainAbility and a true leader! A thanks also goes to Hank Carbeck for putting up with me while I have been working on this book. Hank, you've been a true friend to my family and me! I would also like to thank my co-authors Dan Balter and Laurie Salmon for their invaluable contributions to this book.

A special thanks goes to my wife Gladys and my son Seth for giving me the time and space to work on this book. I would not have been able to finish this project without your constant love and support. For this I thank you from the bottom of my heart, and I promise we will go on vacation soon!

—Todd Logan

Thanks to my loving husband, Scot, who patiently listens to my rants without laughing—I love you, and you are my rock. Chloe, Sasha, and Maggie would pursue certification if they had opposable thumbs—but I love them anyway! I would like to thank my family and friends for their unconditional, unwavering support. Dan—thanks for your constant support and for including me in this project! Hank—thanks for the flowers and for always making me smile! Cindy, Leslie, Gwen, Melany, and Holly—thanks for motivating and inspiring me, and keeping me on track!

—Laurie Salmon

Contents at a Glance

Chapter 1 Microsoft Certification Exams 1

Chapter 2 Implementing and Administering Resources 23

Chapter 3 Implementing, Monitoring, and Troubleshooting Security Accounts and Policies 75

Chapter 4 Configuring and Troubleshooting the User Experience 101

Chapter 5 Configuring and Troubleshooting System Services and Desktop Environment 125

Chapter 6 Installing Windows 2000 Professional 145

Chapter 7 Implementing, Managing, and Troubleshooting Hardware Devices and Drivers 169

Chapter 8 Implementing, Managing, and Troubleshooting Disk Drives and Volumes 203

Chapter 9 Implementing, Managing, and Troubleshooting Network Protocols and Services 233

Chapter 10 Monitoring and Optimizing Performance Reliability 263

Chapter 11 Sample Test 293

Chapter 12 Answer Key 315

Table of Contents

Introduction xix

Self-Assessment xxxi

Chapter 1
Microsoft Certification Exams 1

Assessing Exam-Readiness 2
The Exam Situation 3
Exam Layout and Design 4
Multiple-Choice Question Formats 5
Build-List-and-Reorder Question Format 6
Create-a-Tree Question Format 8
Drag-and-Connect Question Format 10
Select-and-Place Question Format 11
Microsoft's Testing Formats 13
Strategies for Different Testing Formats 14
The Case Study Exam Strategy 15
The Fixed-Length and Short-Form Exam Strategy 16
The Adaptive Exam Strategy 17
Question-Handling Strategies 18
Mastering the Inner Game 19
Additional Resources 20

Chapter 2
Implementing and Administering Resources 23

Managing Access to Shared Folders 24
Connecting to Shared Resources on a Windows Network 25
Using Automatically Generated Hidden Shares 26
Controlling Access to Shared Folders 27
Monitoring, Managing, and Troubleshooting Access to Shared Files and Folders Under NTFS 29
NTFS Security: Users and Groups 30

Monitoring, Managing, and Troubleshooting Access to Files and Folders 42
Configuring, Managing, and Troubleshooting NTFS File and Folder Compression 42
Controlling Access to Files and Folders by Using Permissions 46
Optimizing Access to Files and Folders 48
Auditing System Access 50
Keeping Data Private with Encrypting File System (EFS) 53
Managing and Troubleshooting Web Server Resources 56
SystemRoot Console Administering the Default Web and FTP Sites 58
Troubleshooting IIS 58
Managing Local and Network Print Devices 59
Connecting to Local and Network Printers 60
Configuring Printer Properties 63
Managing Printers and Print Jobs 65
Using Internet Printing Protocol (IPP) 66
Practice Questions 67
Need to Know More? 73

Chapter 3
Implementing, Monitoring, and Troubleshooting Security Accounts and Policies 75
User and Group Accounts 76
Local and Domain Accounts 76
Managing Local User and Group Accounts 77
Managing Domain User Accounts 83
Authentication 85
Understanding Active Directory 86
Understanding and Implementing Policy 89
Local Policy 89
Group Policy 92
Practice Questions 95
Need to Know More? 100

Chapter 4
Configuring and Troubleshooting the User Experience 101
Configuring and Managing User Profiles 102
User Profiles 102
Roaming User Profiles 103

Using Offline Files and Folders 104
Setting Up Offline Files and Folders 105
Making Files and Folders Available Offline 106
Synchronizing Offline Files and Folders 107
Accessing Offline Files and Folders 108
Managing Offline Files and Folders 108
Configuring and Troubleshooting Desktop Settings 109
Keyboard Applet 109
Display Applet 109
Mouse Applet 110
Sound Applet 110
Personalized Start Menu 110
Quick Launch Pad 111
Toolbars 111
Windows Installer Service Packages 112
Installing Packages 113
Publishing MSI Packages 114
Practice Questions 117
Need to Know More? 124

Chapter 5
Configuring and Troubleshooting System Services and Desktop Environment 125
Multiple Location and Language Support 126
Language Options 126
Locales 126
Multilanguage Support 128
Multilanguage Version of Windows 2000 128
Accessibility Options 129
Accessibility Options Applet 129
Accessibility Wizard 131
Additional Accessibility Features 132
Fax Features 132
Configuring the Fax Service 132
Managing the Fax Service Management Console 133
Task Scheduler 134
Creating a Task 135

Practice Questions 137
Need to Know More? 144

Chapter 6
Installing Windows 2000 Professional 145
Performing Attended Installations of Windows 2000 Professional 146
Installation Methods 146
Automating the Installation of Windows 2000 Professional 147
Using Setup Manager to Create an Unattended Installation 148
Using the System Preparation Tool 151
Using Remote Installation Services (RIS) 153
Upgrading to Windows 2000 Professional 157
Pre-Upgrade Checklist 158
Deploying Service Packs (SPs) 159
Slipstreaming SPs 159
Applying SPs after Installing Windows 2000 159
Troubleshooting Failed Installations 159
Practice Questions 161
Need to Know More? 167

Chapter 7
Implementing, Managing, and Troubleshooting Hardware Devices and Drivers 169
Implementing, Managing, and Troubleshooting Hardware 170
Installing, Configuring, and Managing Hardware 170
Driver Updates 172
Updating Individual Drivers 172
Updating Your System Files Using Windows Update 172
Managing and Troubleshooting Device Conflicts 173
Managing and Troubleshooting Driver Signing 173
Managing and Troubleshooting I/O Devices 174
Using Printers 175
Using Keyboards and Mice 176
Using Smart Cards and Smart Card Readers 176
Mobile User 177
Using Cameras and Other Multimedia Hardware 178
Using Modems 179
Supporting Faxes 181

Using Infrared Data Association (IrDA) Devices and Wireless Devices 181
Using Network Adapters 184
Internet Connection Sharing (ICS) 184
Managing and Troubleshooting Display Devices 186
Display Settings 186
Configuring Multiple-Display Support 186
Installing, Configuring, and Supporting a Video Adapter 189
Mobile Computer Hardware 189
Managing Hardware Profiles 189
APM 190
ACPI 190
Managing Battery Power on a Portable Computer 192
Using a Portable Computer on an Airplane 192
Managing Power When Installing a Plug and Play Device 192
Monitoring and Configuring Multiple Processors 193
Installing Support for Multiple CPUs 193
Practice Questions 195
Need to Know More? 202

Chapter 8
Implementing, Managing, and Troubleshooting Disk Drives and Volumes 203

Hard Disk Management 204
Basic Disks 204
Dynamic Disks 204
Comparing Basic Disks to Dynamic Disks 205
Upgrading Disks 206
Moving Disks to Another Computer 207
Reactivating a Missing or Offline Disk 208
Basic Volumes 208
Spanned Volumes on Basic Disks 208
Striped Volumes on Basic Disks 208
Partitions and Logical Drives on Basic Disks 209

Dynamic Volumes 210
Simple Volumes 210
Spanned Volumes 210
Striped Volumes 212
RAID-5 Volumes 212
Limitations of Dynamic Disks and Dynamic Volumes 212
Troubleshooting Disks and Volumes 213
Diagnosing Problems 213
Monitoring Disk Performance 213
Detecting and Repairing Disk Errors 214
Using Disk Defragmenter 215
Understanding Why Files Are Not Moved to the Beginning of NTFS Volumes 215
Using the Disk Cleanup Wizard 216
File Systems Supported in Windows 2000 216
FAT and FAT32 216
The New Flavor of NTFS: Windows 2000's NTFS 5 File System 216
Converting from One File System to Another 217
Assigning, Changing, or Removing a Drive Letter 218
Mounted Drives 219
Creating a Mounted Drive 219
The Logical Drives Tool 220
Viewing Drive Properties, Changing Drive Labels, and Changing Security Settings 220
Disk Quotas 220
NTFS Compression 221
Moving and Copying Compressed Files and Folders 221
Managing Tape Devices 222
Configuring and Managing DVD Devices 222
Practice Questions 224
Need to Know More? 232

Chapter 9
Implementing, Managing, and Troubleshooting Network Protocols and Services 233
Configuring and Troubleshooting Transmission Control Protocol/Internet Protocol (TCP/IP) 234
Deciphering the TCP/IP Protocol Suite for Windows 2000 234

Understanding TCP/IP Computer Addresses: It's All about Numbers 237
Configuring TCP/IP 238
Troubleshooting TCP/IP 239
Connecting to Remote Computers Using Dial-up Connections 242
New Authentication Protocols 242
Connecting to Remote Access Servers 245
Setting up and Configuring VPN Connections 248
Connecting to the Internet Using Dial-up Connections 249
Configuring and Troubleshooting ICS 250
Practice Questions 254
Need to Know More? 262

Chapter 10
Monitoring and Optimizing Performance Reliability 263
Backing Up and Restoring Data 264
Using Windows Backup 264
Permissions and Rights 264
Backup Types 265
Configuring File and Folder Backup 266
Backing up the System State 267
Scheduling Backup Jobs 267
Restoring Files and Folders 268
Troubleshooting and Repairing a Windows 2000 System 268
Safe Mode and Other Advanced Startup Options 268
Specifying Windows 2000 Behavior if the System Stops Unexpectedly 270
The Recovery Console 271
Emergency Repair Disks (ERDs) and the Emergency Repair Process 274
Optimizing and Troubleshooting Performance 276
System Monitor 276
Performance Logs And Alerts 277
Managing Performance 278
Task Manager 284
Practice Questions 285
Need to Know More? 292

Chapter 11
Sample Test 293

Chapter 12
Answer Key 315

Glossary 327

Index 351

Introduction

Welcome to *MCSE Windows 2000 Professional Exam Cram*! Whether this is your first or your fifteenth *Exam Cram* book, you'll find information here and in Chapter 1 that will help ensure your success as you pursue knowledge, experience, and certification. This book aims to help you get ready to take—and pass—the Microsoft certification Exam 70-210, titled "Installing, Configuring and Administering Microsoft Windows 2000 Professional." This Introduction explains Microsoft's certification programs in general and talks about how the *Exam Cram* series can help you prepare for Microsoft's Windows 2000 certification exams.

Exam Cram books help you understand and appreciate the subjects and materials you need to pass Microsoft certification exams. *Exam Cram* books are aimed strictly at test preparation and review. They do not teach you everything you need to know about a topic. Instead, we (the authors) present and dissect the questions and problems we've found that you're likely to encounter on a test. We've worked to bring together as much information as possible about Microsoft certification exams.

Nevertheless, to completely prepare yourself for any Microsoft test, we recommend that you begin by taking the Self-Assessment included in this book immediately following this Introduction. This tool will help you evaluate your knowledge base against the requirements for an MCSE under both ideal and real circumstances.

Based on what you learn from that exercise, you might decide to begin your studies with some classroom training or some background reading. On the other hand, you might decide to pick up and read one of the many study guides available from Microsoft or third-party vendors on certain topics, including The Coriolis Group's *Exam Prep* series. We also recommend that you supplement your study program with visits to **ExamCram.com** to receive additional practice questions, get advice, and track the Windows 2000 MCSE program.

We also strongly recommend that you install, configure, and fool around with the software that you'll be tested on, because nothing beats hands-on experience and familiarity when it comes to understanding the questions you're likely to encounter on a certification test. Book learning is essential, but hands-on experience is the best teacher of all!

The Microsoft Certified Professional (MCP) Program

The MCP Program currently includes the following separate tracks, each of which boasts its own special acronym (as a certification candidate, you need to have a high tolerance for alphabet soup of all kinds):

- *MCP (Microsoft Certified Professional)*—This is the least prestigious of all the certification tracks from Microsoft. Passing one of the major Microsoft exams qualifies an individual for the MCP credential. Individuals can demonstrate proficiency with additional Microsoft products by passing additional certification exams.

- *MCP+SB (Microsoft Certified Professional + Site Building)*—This certification program is designed for individuals who are planning, building, managing, and maintaining Web sites. Individuals with the MCP+SB credential will have demonstrated the ability to develop Web sites that include multimedia and searchable content and Web sites that connect to and communicate with a back-end database. It requires one MCP exam, plus two of these three exams: "70-055: Designing and Implementing Web Sites with Microsoft FrontPage 98," "70-057: Designing and Implementing Commerce Solutions with Microsoft Site Server 3.0, Commerce Edition," and "70-152: Designing and Implementing Web Solutions with Microsoft Visual InterDev 6.0."

- *MCSE (Microsoft Certified Systems Engineer)*—Anyone who has a current MCSE is warranted to possess a high level of networking expertise with Microsoft operating systems and products. This credential is designed to prepare individuals to plan, implement, maintain, and support information systems, networks, and internetworks built around Microsoft Windows 2000 and its BackOffice Server 2000 family of products.

  To obtain an MCSE, an individual must pass four core operating system exams, one optional core exam, and two elective exams. The operating system exams require individuals to prove their competence with desktop and server operating systems and networking/internetworking components.

  For Windows NT 4 MCSEs, the Accelerated exam, "70-240: Microsoft Windows 2000 Accelerated Exam for MCPs Certified on Microsoft Windows NT 4.0," is an option. This free exam covers all of the material tested in the Core Four exams. The hitch in this plan is that you can take the test only once. If you fail, you must take all four core exams to recertify. The Core Four exams are: "70-210: Installing, Configuring and Administering Microsoft Windows 2000 Professional," "70-215: Installing, Configuring and Administering Microsoft Windows 2000 Server," "70-216: Implementing and Administering a Microsoft

Windows 2000 Network Infrastructure," and "70-217: Implementing and Administering a Microsoft Windows 2000 Directory Services Infrastructure."

To fulfill the fifth core exam requirement, you can choose from three design exams: "70-219: Designing a Microsoft Windows 2000 Directory Services Infrastructure," "70-220: Designing Security for a Microsoft Windows 2000 Network," or "70-221: Designing a Microsoft Windows 2000 Network Infrastructure." You are also required to take two elective exams. An elective exam can fall in any number of subject or product areas, primarily BackOffice Server 2000 components. The two design exams that you don't select as your fifth core exam also qualify as electives. If you are on your way to becoming an MCSE and have already taken some exams, visit **www.microsoft.com/trainingandservices/** for information about how to complete your MCSE certification.

In September 1999, Microsoft announced its Windows 2000 track for MCSE and also announced retirement of Windows NT 4.0 MCSE core exams on 12/31/2000. Individuals who wish to remain certified MCSEs after 12/31/2001 must "upgrade" their certifications on or before 12/31/2001. For more detailed information than is included here, visit **www.microsoft.com/trainingandservices/**.

New MCSE candidates must pass seven tests to meet the MCSE requirements. It's not uncommon for the entire process to take a year or so, and many individuals find that they must take a test more than once to pass. The primary goal of the *Exam Prep* series and the *Exam Cram* series, our test preparation books, is to make it possible, given proper study and preparation, to pass all Microsoft certification tests on the first try. Table 1 shows the required and elective exams for the Windows 2000 MCSE certification.

- *MCSD (Microsoft Certified Solution Developer)*—The MCSD credential reflects the skills required to create multitier, distributed, and COM-based solutions, in addition to desktop and Internet applications, using new technologies. To obtain an MCSD, an individual must demonstrate the ability to analyze and interpret user requirements; select and integrate products, platforms, tools, and technologies; design and implement code, and customize applications; and perform necessary software tests and quality assurance operations.

  To become an MCSD, you must pass a total of four exams: three core exams and one elective exam. Each candidate must choose one of these three desktop application exams—"70-016: Designing and Implementing Desktop Applications with Microsoft Visual C++ 6.0," "70-156: Designing and Implementing Desktop Applications with Microsoft Visual FoxPro 6.0," or "70-176: Designing and Implementing Desktop Applications with Microsoft

Table 1 MCSE Windows 2000 Requirements

Core

If you have not passed these 3 Windows NT 4 exams	
Exam 70-067	Implementing and Supporting Microsoft Windows NT Server 4.0
Exam 70-068	Implementing and Supporting Microsoft Windows NT Server 4.0 in the Enterprise
Exam 70-073	Microsoft Windows NT Workstation 4.0
then you must take these 4 exams	
Exam 70-210	Installing, Configuring and Administering Microsoft Windows 2000 Professional
Exam 70-215	Installing, Configuring and Administering Microsoft Windows 2000 Server
Exam 70-216	Implementing and Administering a Microsoft Windows 2000 Network Infrastructure
Exam 70-217	Implementing and Administering a Microsoft Windows 2000 Directory Services Infrastructure
If you have already passed exams 70-067, 70-068, and 70-073, you may take this exam	
Exam 70-240	Microsoft Windows 2000 Accelerated Exam for MCPs Certified on Microsoft Windows NT 4.0

5th Core Option

Choose 1 from this group	
Exam 70-219*	Designing a Microsoft Windows 2000 Directory Services Infrastructure
Exam 70-220*	Designing Security for a Microsoft Windows 2000 Network
Exam 70-221*	Designing a Microsoft Windows 2000 Network Infrastructure

Elective

Choose 2 from this group	
Exam 70-019	Designing and Implementing Data Warehouse with Microsoft SQL Server 7.0
Exam 70-219*	Designing a Microsoft Windows 2000 Directory Services Infrastructure
Exam 70-220*	Designing Security for a Microsoft Windows 2000 Network
Exam 70-221*	Designing a Microsoft Windows 2000 Network Infrastructure
Exam 70-222	Migrating from Microsoft Windows NT 4.0 to Microsoft Windows 2000
Exam 70-028	Administering Microsoft SQL Server 7.0
Exam 70-029	Designing and Implementing Databases on Microsoft SQL Server 7.0
Exam 70-080	Implementing and Supporting Microsoft Internet Explorer 5.0 by Using the Internet Explorer Administration Kit
Exam 70-081	Implementing and Supporting Microsoft Exchange Server 5.5
Exam 70-085	Implementing and Supporting Microsoft SNA Server 4.0
Exam 70-086	Implementing and Supporting Microsoft Systems Management Server 2.0
Exam 70-088	Implementing and Supporting Microsoft Proxy Server 2.0

This is not a complete listing—you can still be tested on some earlier versions of these products. However, we have included mainly the most recent versions so that you may test on these versions and thus be certified longer. We have not included any tests that are scheduled to be retired.

* The 5th Core Option exam does not double as an elective.

Visual Basic 6.0"—*plus* one of these three distributed application exams—"70-015: Designing and Implementing Distributed Applications with Microsoft Visual C++ 6.0," "70-155: Designing and Implementing Distributed Applications with Microsoft Visual FoxPro 6.0," or "70-175: Designing and Implementing Distributed Applications with Microsoft Visual Basic 6.0." The third core exam is "70-100: Analyzing Requirements and Defining Solution Architectures." Elective exams cover specific Microsoft applications and languages, including Visual Basic, C++, the Microsoft Foundation Classes, Access, SQL Server, Excel, and more.

- *MCDBA (Microsoft Certified Database Administrator)*—The MCDBA credential reflects the skills required to implement and administer Microsoft SQL Server databases. To obtain an MCDBA, an individual must demonstrate the ability to derive physical database designs, develop logical data models, create physical databases, create data services by using Transact-SQL, manage and maintain databases, configure and manage security, monitor and optimize databases, and install and configure Microsoft SQL Server.

  To become an MCDBA, you must pass a total of three core exams and one elective exam. The required core exams are "70-028: Administering Microsoft SQL Server 7.0," "70-029: Designing and Implementing Databases with Microsoft SQL Server 7.0," and "70-215: Installing, Configuring and Administering Microsoft Windows 2000 Server."

  The elective exams that you can choose from cover specific uses of SQL Server and include "70-015: Designing and Implementing Distributed Applications with Microsoft Visual C++ 6.0," "70-019: Designing and Implementing Data Warehouses with Microsoft SQL Server 7.0," "70-155: Designing and Implementing Distributed Applications with Microsoft Visual FoxPro 6.0," "70-175: Designing and Implementing Distributed Applications with Microsoft Visual Basic 6.0," and two exams that relate to Windows 2000: "70-216: Implementing and Administering a Microsoft Windows 2000 Network Infrastructure," and "70-087: Implementing and Supporting Microsoft Internet Information Server 4.0."

  If you have taken the three core Windows NT 4 exams on your path to becoming an MCSE, you qualify for the Accelerated exam (it replaces the Network Infrastructure exam requirement). The Accelerated exam covers the objectives of all four of the Windows 2000 core exams. In addition to taking the Accelerated exam, you must take only the two SQL exams—Administering and Database Design.

- *MCT (Microsoft Certified Trainer)*—Microsoft Certified Trainers are deemed able to deliver elements of the official Microsoft curriculum, based on technical knowledge and instructional ability. Thus, it is necessary for an individual seeking MCT credentials (which are granted on a course-by-course basis) to pass the related certification exam for a course and complete the official Microsoft training in the subject area, and to demonstrate an ability to teach.

  This teaching skill criterion may be satisfied by proving that one has already attained training certification from Novell, Banyan, Lotus, the Santa Cruz Operation, or Cisco, or by taking a Microsoft-sanctioned workshop on instruction. Microsoft makes it clear that MCTs are important cogs in the Microsoft training channels. Instructors must be MCTs before Microsoft will allow them to teach in any of its official training channels, including Microsoft's affiliated Certified Technical Education Centers (CTECs) and its online training partner network. As of January 1, 2001, MCT candidates must also possess a current MCSE.

Microsoft has announced that the MCP+I and MCSE+I credentials will not be continued when the MCSE exams for Windows 2000 are in full swing because the skill set for the Internet portion of the program has been included in the new MCSE program. Therefore, details on these tracks are not provided here; go to **www.microsoft.com/trainingandservices/** if you need more information.

Once a Microsoft product becomes obsolete, MCPs typically have to recertify on current versions. (If individuals do not recertify, their certifications become invalid.) Because technology keeps changing and new products continually supplant old ones, this should come as no surprise. This explains why Microsoft has announced that MCSEs have 12 months past the scheduled retirement date for the Windows NT 4 exams to recertify on Windows 2000 topics. (Note that this means taking at least two exams, if not more.)

The best place to keep tabs on the MCP program and its related certifications is on the Web. The URL for the MCP program is **www.microsoft.com/trainingandservices/**. But Microsoft's Web site changes often, so if this URL doesn't work, try using the Search tool on Microsoft's site with either "MCP" or the quoted phrase "Microsoft Certified Professional" as a search string. This will help you find the latest and most accurate information about Microsoft's certification programs.

Taking a Certification Exam

Once you've prepared for your exam, you need to register with a testing center. Each computer-based MCP exam costs $100, and if you don't pass, you may retest for an additional $100 for each additional try. In the United States and

Canada, tests are administered by Prometric and by Virtual University Enterprises (VUE). Here's how you can contact them:

- *Prometric*—You can sign up for a test through the company's Web site at **www.prometric.com**. Or, you can register by phone at 800-755-3926 (within the United States or Canada) or at 410-843-8000 (outside the United States and Canada).
- *Virtual University Enterprises*—You can sign up for a test or get the phone numbers for local testing centers through the Web page at **www.vue.com/ms/**.

To sign up for a test, you must possess a valid credit card, or contact either company for mailing instructions to send them a check (in the U.S.). Only when payment is verified, or a check has cleared, can you actually register for a test.

To schedule an exam, call the number or visit either of the Web pages at least one day in advance. To cancel or reschedule an exam, you must call before 7 P.M. pacific standard time the day before the scheduled test time (or you may be charged, even if you don't appear to take the test). When you want to schedule a test, have the following information ready:

- Your name, organization, and mailing address.
- Your Microsoft Test ID. (Inside the United States, this means your Social Security number; citizens of other nations should call ahead to find out what type of identification number is required to register for a test.)
- The name and number of the exam you wish to take.
- A method of payment. (As we've already mentioned, a credit card is the most convenient method, but alternate means can be arranged in advance, if necessary.)

Once you sign up for a test, you'll be informed as to when and where the test is scheduled. Try to arrive at least 15 minutes early. You must supply two forms of identification—one of which must be a photo ID—to be admitted into the testing room.

All exams are completely closed-book. In fact, you will not be permitted to take anything with you into the testing area, but you will be furnished with a blank sheet of paper and a pen or, in some cases, an erasable plastic sheet and an erasable pen. We suggest that you immediately write down on that sheet of paper all the information you've memorized for the test. In *Exam Cram* books, this information appears on a tear-out sheet inside the front cover of each book. You will have some time to compose yourself and to record this information.

When you complete a Microsoft certification exam, the software will tell you whether you've passed or failed.

If you need to retake an exam, you'll have to schedule a new test with Prometric or VUE and pay another $100.

The first time you fail a test, you can retake the test the next day. However, if you fail a second time, you must wait 14 days before retaking that test. The 14-day waiting period remains in effect for all retakes after the second failure.

Tracking MCP Status

As soon as you pass any Microsoft exam (except Networking Essentials), you'll attain Microsoft Certified Professional (MCP) status. Microsoft also generates transcripts that indicate which exams you have passed. You can view a copy of your transcript at any time by going to the MCP secured site and selecting Transcript Tool. This tool will allow you to print a copy of your current transcript and confirm your certification status.

Once you pass the necessary set of exams, you'll be certified. Official certification normally takes anywhere from six to eight weeks, so don't expect to get your credentials overnight. When the package for a qualified certification arrives, it includes a Welcome Kit that contains a number of elements (see Microsoft's Web site for other benefits of specific certifications):

- A certificate suitable for framing, along with a wallet card and lapel pin.
- A license to use the MCP logo, thereby allowing you to use the logo in advertisements, promotions, and documents, and on letterhead, business cards, and so on. Along with the license comes an MCP logo sheet, which includes camera-ready artwork. (Note: Before using any of the artwork, individuals must sign and return a licensing agreement that indicates they'll abide by its terms and conditions.)
- A subscription to *Microsoft Certified Professional Magazine*, which provides ongoing data about testing and certification activities, requirements, and changes to the program.

Many people believe that the benefits of MCP certification go well beyond the perks that Microsoft provides to newly anointed members of this elite group. We're starting to see more job listings that request or require applicants to have an MCP, MCSE, and so on, and many individuals who complete the program can qualify for increases in pay and/or responsibility. As an official recognition of hard work and broad knowledge, one of the MCP credentials is a badge of honor in many IT organizations.

How to Prepare for an Exam

Preparing for any Windows 2000 related test (including "Installing, Configuring and Administering Microsoft® Windows® 2000 Professional") requires that you obtain and study materials designed to provide comprehensive information about the product and its capabilities that will appear on the specific exam for which you are preparing. The following list of materials will help you study and prepare:

- The Windows 2000 Professional product CD includes comprehensive online documentation and related materials; it should be a primary resource when you are preparing for the test.
- The exam preparation materials, practice tests, and self-assessment exams on the Microsoft Training & Services page at **www.microsoft.com/trainingandservices/default.asp?PageID=mcp**. The Testing Innovations link offers samples of the new question types found on the Windows 2000 MCSE exams. Find the materials, download them, and use them!
- The exam preparation advice, practice tests, questions of the day, and discussion groups on the **ExamCram.com** e-learning and certification destination Web site (**www.examcram.com**).

In addition, you'll probably find any or all of the following materials useful in your quest for Windows 2000 Professional expertise:

- *Microsoft training kits*—Microsoft Press offers a training kit that specifically targets Exam 70-210. For more information, visit: **http://mspress. microsoft.com/prod/books/1963.htm**. This training kit contains information that you will find useful in preparing for the test.
- *Microsoft TechNet CD*—This monthly CD-based publication delivers numerous electronic titles that include coverage of Directory Services Design and related topics on the Technical Information (TechNet) CD. Its offerings include product facts, technical notes, tools and utilities, and information on how to access the Seminars Online training materials for Windows 2000 Professional. A subscription to TechNet costs $299 per year, but it is well worth the price. Visit **www.microsoft.com/technet/** and check out the information under the "TechNet Subscription" menu entry for more details.

- *Study guides*—Several publishers—including The Coriolis Group—offer Windows 2000 titles. The Coriolis Group series includes the following:
  - *The Exam Cram series*—These books give you information about the material you need to know to pass the tests.
  - *The Exam Prep series*—These books provide a greater level of detail than the *Exam Cram* books and are designed to teach you everything you need to know from an exam perspective. Each book comes with a CD that contains interactive practice exams in a variety of testing formats.

  Together, the two series make a perfect pair.
- *Multimedia*—These Coriolis Group materials are designed to support learners of all types—whether you learn best by reading or doing:
  - *The Exam Cram Personal Trainer*—Offers a unique, personalized self-paced training course based on the exam.
  - *The Exam Cram Personal Test Center*—Features multiple test options that simulate the actual exam, including Fixed-Length, Random, Review, and Test All. Explanations of correct and incorrect answers reinforce concepts learned.
- *Classroom training*—CTECs, online partners, and third-party training companies (like Wave Technologies, Learning Tree, Data-Tech, and others) all offer classroom training on Windows 2000. These companies aim to help you prepare to pass Exam 70-210. Although such training runs upwards of $350 per day in class, most of the individuals lucky enough to partake find it to be quite worthwhile.
- *Other publications*—There's no shortage of materials available about Windows 2000 Professional. The resource sections at the end of each chapter should give you an idea of where we think you should look for further discussion.

By far, this set of required and recommended materials represents a nonpareil collection of sources and resources for Windows 2000 Professional and related topics. We anticipate that you'll find that this book belongs in this company

About this Book

Each topical *Exam Cram* chapter follows a regular structure, along with graphical cues about important or useful information. Here's the structure of a typical chapter:

- *Opening hotlists*—Each chapter begins with a list of the terms, tools, and techniques that you must learn and understand before you can be fully conversant with that chapter's subject matter. We follow the hotlists with one or two introductory paragraphs to set the stage for the rest of the chapter.

- *Topical coverage*—After the opening hotlists, each chapter covers a series of topics related to the chapter's subject title. Throughout this section, we highlight topics or concepts likely to appear on a test using a special Exam Alert layout, like this:

> This is what an Exam Alert looks like. Normally, an Exam Alert stresses concepts, terms, software, or activities that are likely to relate to one or more certification test questions. For that reason, we think any information found offset in Exam Alert format is worthy of unusual attentiveness on your part. Indeed, most of the information that appears on The Cram Sheet appears as Exam Alerts within the text.

Pay close attention to material flagged as an Exam Alert; although all the information in this book pertains to what you need to know to pass the exam, we flag certain items that are really important. You'll find what appears in the meat of each chapter to be worth knowing, too, when preparing for the test. Because this book's material is very condensed, we recommend that you use this book along with other resources to achieve the maximum benefit.

In addition to the Exam Alerts, we have provided tips that will help you build a better foundation for Windows 2000 Professional knowledge. Although the information may not be on the exam, it is certainly related and will help you become a better test-taker.

> This is how tips are formatted. Keep your eyes open for these, and you'll become a Windows 2000 Professional guru in no time!

- *Practice questions*—Although we talk about test questions and topics throughout the book, a section at the end of each chapter presents a series of mock test questions and explanations of both correct and incorrect answers.

- *Details and resources*—Every chapter ends with a section titled "Need to Know More?". This section provides direct pointers to Microsoft and third-party resources offering more details on the chapter's subject. In addition, this section tries to rank or at least rate the quality and thoroughness of the topic's coverage by each resource. If you find a resource you like in this collection, use it, but don't feel compelled to use all the resources. On the other hand, we recommend only resources we use on a regular basis, so none of our recommendations will be a waste of your time or money (but purchasing them all at once probably represents an expense that many network administrators and would-be MCPs and MCSEs might find hard to justify).

The bulk of the book follows this chapter structure slavishly, but there are a few other elements that we'd like to point out. Chapter 11 includes a sample test that provides a good review of the material presented throughout the book to ensure you're ready for the exam. Chapter 12 is an answer key to the sample test that appears in Chapter 11. In addition, you'll find a handy glossary and an index.

Finally, the tear-out Cram Sheet attached next to the inside front cover of this *Exam Cram* book represents a condensed and compiled collection of facts and tips that we think you should memorize before taking the test. Because you can dump this information out of your head onto a piece of paper before taking the exam, you can master this information by brute force—you need to remember it only long enough to write it down when you walk into the test room. You might even want to look at it in the car or in the lobby of the testing center just before you walk in to take the test.

How to Use this Book

We've structured the topics in this book to build on one another. Therefore, some topics in later chapters make more sense after you've read earlier chapters. That's why we suggest you read this book from front to back for your initial test preparation. If you need to brush up on a topic or you have to bone up for a second try, use the index or table of contents to go straight to the topics and questions that you need to study. Beyond helping you prepare for the test, we think you'll find this book useful as a tightly focused reference to some of the most important aspects of Windows 2000 Professional.

Given all the book's elements and its specialized focus, we've tried to create a tool that will help you prepare for—and pass—Microsoft Exam 70-210. Please share your feedback on the book with us, especially if you have ideas about how we can improve it for future test-takers. We'll consider everything you say carefully, and we'll respond to all suggestions.

Send your questions or comments to us at **learn@examcram.com**. Please remember to include the title of the book in your message; otherwise, we'll be forced to guess which book you're writing about. And we don't like to guess—we want to *know*! Also, be sure to check out the Web pages at **www.examcram.com**, where you'll find information updates, commentary, and certification information.

Thanks, and enjoy the book!

Self-Assessment

The reason we included a Self-Assessment in this *Exam Cram* book is to help you evaluate your readiness to tackle MCSE certification. It should also help you understand what you need to know to master the topic of this book—namely, Exam 70-210, "Installing, Configuring and Administering Microsoft Windows 2000 Professional." But before you tackle this Self-Assessment, let's talk about concerns you may face when pursuing an MCSE for Windows 2000, and what an ideal MCSE candidate might look like.

MCSEs in the Real World

In the next section, we describe an ideal MCSE candidate, knowing full well that only a few real candidates will meet this ideal. In fact, our description of that ideal candidate might seem downright scary, especially with the changes that have been made to the program to support Windows 2000. But take heart: Although the requirements to obtain an MCSE may seem formidable, they are by no means impossible to meet. However, be keenly aware that it does take time, involves some expense, and requires real effort to get through the process.

Increasing numbers of people are attaining Microsoft certifications, so the goal is within reach. You can get all the real-world motivation you need from knowing that many others have gone before, so you will be able to follow in their footsteps. If you're willing to tackle the process seriously and do what it takes to obtain the necessary experience and knowledge, you can take—and pass—all the certification tests involved in obtaining an MCSE. In fact, we've designed *Exam Preps*, the companion *Exam Crams*, *Exam Cram Personal Trainers*, and *Exam Cram Personal Test Centers* to make it as easy on you as possible to prepare for these exams. We've also greatly expanded our Web site, **www.examcram.com**, to provide a host of resources to help you prepare for the complexities of Windows 2000.

Besides MCSE, other Microsoft certifications include the following:

- MCSD, which is aimed at software developers and requires one specific exam, two more exams on client and distributed topics, plus a fourth elective exam drawn from a different, but limited, pool of options.

- Other Microsoft certifications, whose requirements range from one test (MCP) to several tests (MCP+SB, MCDBA).

The Ideal Windows 2000 MCSE Candidate

Just to give you some idea of what an ideal MCSE candidate is like, here are some relevant statistics about the background and experience such an individual might have. Don't worry if you don't meet these qualifications, or don't come that close—this is a far from ideal world, and where you fall short is simply where you'll have more work to do.

- Academic or professional training in network theory, concepts, and operations. This includes everything from networking media and transmission techniques through network operating systems, services, and applications.
- Three-plus years of professional networking experience, including experience with Ethernet, token ring, modems, and other networking media. This must include installation, configuration, upgrade, and troubleshooting experience.

Note: *The Windows 2000 MCSE program is much more rigorous than the previous NT MCSE program; therefore, you'll really need some hands-on experience. Some of the exams require you to solve real-world case studies and network design issues, so the more hands-on experience you have, the better.*

- Two-plus years in a networked environment that includes hands-on experience with Windows 2000 Server, Windows 2000 Professional, Windows NT Server, Windows NT Workstation, and Windows 95 or Windows 98. A solid understanding of each system's architecture, installation, configuration, maintenance, and troubleshooting is also essential.
- Knowledge of the various methods for installing Windows 2000, including manual and unattended installations.
- A thorough understanding of key networking protocols, addressing, and name resolution, including TCP/IP, IPX/SPX, and NetBEUI.
- A thorough understanding of NetBIOS naming, browsing, and file and print services.
- Familiarity with key Windows 2000-based TCP/IP-based services, including HTTP (Web servers), DHCP, WINS, DNS, plus familiarity with one or more of the following: Internet Information Server (IIS), Index Server, and Proxy Server.

- An understanding of how to implement security for key network data in a Windows 2000 environment.
- Working knowledge of NetWare 3.x and 4.x, including IPX/SPX frame formats, NetWare file, print, and directory services, and both Novell and Microsoft client software. Working knowledge of Microsoft's Client Service For NetWare (CSNW), Gateway Service For NetWare (GSNW), the NetWare Migration Tool (NWCONV), and the NetWare Client For Windows (NT, 95, and 98) is essential.
- A good working understanding of Active Directory. The more you work with Windows 2000, the more you'll realize that this new operating system is quite different than Windows NT. New technologies like Active Directory have really changed the way that Windows is configured and used. We recommend that you find out as much as you can about Active Directory and acquire as much experience using this technology as possible. The time you take learning about Active Directory will be time very well spent!

Fundamentally, this boils down to a bachelor's degree in computer science, plus three years' experience working in a position involving network design, installation, configuration, and maintenance. We believe that well under half of all certification candidates meet these requirements, and that, in fact, most meet less than half of these requirements—at least, when they begin the certification process. But because all the people who already have been certified have survived this ordeal, you can survive it too—especially if you heed what our Self-Assessment can tell you about what you already know and what you need to learn.

Put Yourself to the Test

The following series of questions and observations is designed to help you figure out how much work you must do to pursue Microsoft certification and what kinds of resources you may consult on your quest. Be absolutely honest in your answers, or you'll end up wasting money on exams you're not yet ready to take. There are no right or wrong answers, only steps along the path to certification. Only you can decide where you really belong in the broad spectrum of aspiring candidates.

Two things should be clear from the outset, however:

- Even a modest background in computer science will be helpful.
- Hands-on experience with Microsoft products and technologies is an essential ingredient to certification success.

Educational Background

1. Have you ever taken any computer-related classes? [Yes or No]

   If Yes, proceed to question 2; if No, proceed to question 4.

2. Have you taken any classes on computer operating systems? [Yes or No]

   If Yes, you will probably be able to handle Microsoft's architecture and system component discussions. If you're rusty, brush up on basic operating system concepts, especially virtual memory, multitasking regimes, user mode versus kernel mode operation, and general computer security topics.

   If No, consider some basic reading in this area. We strongly recommend a good general operating systems book, such as *Operating System Concepts, 5th Edition*, by Abraham Silberschatz and Peter Baer Galvin (John Wiley & Sons, 1998, ISBN 0-471-36414-2). If this title doesn't appeal to you, check out reviews for other, similar titles at your favorite online bookstore.

3. Have you taken any networking concepts or technologies classes? [Yes or No]

   If Yes, you will probably be able to handle Microsoft's networking terminology, concepts, and technologies (brace yourself for frequent departures from normal usage). If you're rusty, brush up on basic networking concepts and terminology, especially networking media, transmission types, the OSI Reference Model, and networking technologies such as Ethernet, token ring, FDDI, and WAN links.

   If No, you might want to read one or two books in this topic area. The two best books that we know of are *Computer Networks, 3rd Edition*, by Andrew S. Tanenbaum (Prentice-Hall, 1996, ISBN 0-13-349945-6) and *Computer Networks and Internets, 2nd Edition*, by Douglas E. Comer (Prentice-Hall, 1998, ISBN 0-130-83617-6).

   Skip to the next section, "Hands-on Experience."

4. Have you done any reading on operating systems or networks? [Yes or No]

   If Yes, review the requirements stated in the first paragraphs after questions 2 and 3. If you meet those requirements, move on to the next section. If No, consult the recommended reading for both topics. A strong background will help you prepare for the Microsoft exams better than just about anything else.

Hands-on Experience

The most important key to success on all of the Microsoft tests is hands-on experience, especially with Windows 2000 Server and Professional, plus the many add-on services and BackOffice components around which so many of the Microsoft certification exams revolve. If we leave you with only one realization after taking this Self-Assessment, it should be that there's no substitute for time spent installing, configuring, and using the various Microsoft products upon which you'll be tested repeatedly and in depth.

5. Have you installed, configured, and worked with:

   - Windows 2000 Server? [Yes or No]

     If Yes, make sure you understand basic concepts as covered in Exam 70-215. You should also study the TCP/IP interfaces, utilities, and services for Exam 70-216, plus implementing security features for Exam 70-220.

> TIP: You can download objectives, practice exams, and other data about Microsoft exams from the Training and Certification page at **www.Microsoft.com/trainingandservices/default.asp?PageID=mcp/**. Use the "Exams" link to obtain specific exam information.

     If you haven't worked with Windows 2000 Server, you must obtain one or two machines and a copy of Windows 2000 Server. Then, learn the operating system and whatever other software components on which you'll also be tested.

     In fact, we recommend that you obtain two computers, each with a network interface, and set up a two-node network on which to practice. With decent Windows 2000-capable computers selling for about $500 to $600 apiece these days, this shouldn't be too much of a financial hardship. You may have to scrounge to come up with the necessary software, but if you scour the Microsoft Web site you can usually find low-cost options to obtain evaluation copies of most of the software that you'll need.

   - Windows 2000 Professional? [Yes or No]

     If Yes, make sure you understand the concepts covered in Exam 70-210.

     If No, you will want to obtain a copy of Windows 2000 Professional and learn how to install, configure, and maintain it. You can use *MCSE Windows 2000 Professional Exam Cram* to guide your activities and studies, or work straight from Microsoft's test objectives if you prefer.

TIP

For any and all of these Microsoft exams, the Resource Kits for the topics involved are a good study resource. You can purchase softcover Resource Kits from Microsoft Press (search for them at **http://mspress.microsoft.com/**), but they also appear on the TechNet CDs (**www.microsoft.com/technet**). Along with *Exam Crams* and *Exam Preps*, we believe that Resource Kits are among the best tools you can use to prepare for Microsoft exams.

6. For any specific Microsoft product that is not itself an operating system (for example, SQL Server), have you installed, configured, used, and upgraded this software? [Yes or No]

   If the answer is Yes, skip to the next section. If it's No, you must get some experience. Read on for suggestions on how to do this.

   Experience is a must with any Microsoft product exam, be it something as simple as FrontPage 2000 or as challenging as SQL Server 7.0. For trial copies of other software, search Microsoft's Web site using the name of the product as your search term. Also, search for bundles like "BackOffice" or "Small Business Server."

TIP

If you have the funds, or your employer will pay your way, consider taking a class at a Certified Training and Education Center (CTEC) or at an Authorized Academic Training Partner (AATP). In addition to classroom exposure to the topic of your choice, you get a copy of the software that is the focus of your course, along with a trial version of whatever operating system it needs, with the training materials for that class.

   Before you even think about taking any Microsoft exam, make sure you've spent enough time with the related software to understand how it may be installed and configured, how to maintain such an installation, and how to troubleshoot that software when things go wrong. This will help you in the exam, and in real life!

Testing Your Exam-Readiness

Whether you attend a formal class on a specific topic to get ready for an exam or use written materials to study on your own, some preparation for the Microsoft certification exams is essential. At $100 a try, pass or fail, you want to do everything you can to pass on your first try. That's where studying comes in.

We have included a practice exam in this book, so if you don't score that well on the test, you can study more and then tackle the test again. We also have exams that you can take online through the **ExamCram.com** Web site at **www.examcram.com**. If you still don't hit a score of at least 80 percent after these tests, you'll want to investigate the other practice test resources we mention in this section.

For any given subject, consider taking a class if you've tackled self-study materials, taken the test, and failed anyway. The opportunity to interact with an instructor and fellow students can make all the difference in the world, if you can afford that privilege. For information about Microsoft classes, visit the Training and Certification page at **www.microsoft.com/education/partners/ctec.asp** for Microsoft Certified Education Centers or **www.microsoft.com/aatp/default.htm** for Microsoft Authorized Training Providers.

If you can't afford to take a class, visit the Training and Certification page anyway, because it also includes pointers to free practice exams and to Microsoft Certified Professional Approved Study Guides and other self-study tools. And even if you can't afford to spend much at all, you should still invest in some low-cost practice exams from commercial vendors.

7. Have you taken a practice exam on your chosen test subject? [Yes or No]

   If Yes, and you scored 70 percent or better, you're probably ready to tackle the real thing. If your score isn't above that threshold, keep at it until you break that barrier.

   If No, obtain all the free and low-budget practice tests you can find and get to work. Keep at it until you can break the passing threshold comfortably.

TIP

When it comes to assessing your test readiness, there is no better way than to take a good-quality practice exam and pass with a score of 80 percent or better. When we're preparing ourselves, we shoot for 85-plus percent, just to leave room for the "weirdness factor" that sometimes shows up on Microsoft exams.

Assessing Readiness for Exam 70-210

In addition to the general exam-readiness information in the previous section, there are several things you can do to prepare for the Installing, Configuring and Administering Microsoft Windows 2000 Professional exam. As you're getting ready for Exam 70-210, visit the Exam Cram Windows 2000 Resource Center at **www.examcram.com/studyresource/w2kresource/**. Another valuable resource is the Exam Cram Insider newsletter. Sign up at **www.examcram.com** or send a blank email message to **subscribe-ec@mars.coriolis.com**. We also suggest that you join an active MCSE mailing list. One of the better ones is managed by Sunbelt Software. Sign up at **www.sunbelt-software.com** (look for the Subscribe button).

You can also cruise the Web looking for "braindumps" (recollections of test topics and experiences recorded by others) to help you anticipate topics you're likely to encounter on the test. The MCSE mailing list is a good place to ask where the useful braindumps are, or you can check Shawn Gamble's list at **www.commandcentral.com**.

> TIP: You can't be sure that a braindump's author can provide correct answers. Thus, use the questions to guide your studies, but don't rely on the answers in a braindump to lead you to the truth. Double-check everything you find in any braindump.

Microsoft exam mavens also recommend checking the Microsoft Knowledge Base (available on its own CD as part of the TechNet collection, or on the Microsoft Web site at **http://support.microsoft.com/support/**) for "meaningful technical support issues" that relate to your exam's topics. Although we're not sure exactly what the quoted phrase means, we have also noticed some overlap between technical support questions on particular products and troubleshooting questions on the exams for those products.

Onward, through the Fog!

Once you've assessed your readiness, undertaken the right background studies, obtained the hands-on experience that will help you understand the products and technologies at work, and reviewed the many sources of information to help you prepare for a test, you'll be ready to take a round of practice tests. When your scores come back positive enough to get you through the exam, you're ready to go after the real thing. If you follow our assessment regime, you'll not only know what you need to study, but when you're ready to make a test date at Prometric or VUE. Good luck!

1

Microsoft Certification Exams

Terms you'll need to understand:

- ✓ Case study
- ✓ Multiple-choice question formats
- ✓ Build-list-and-reorder question format
- ✓ Create-a-tree question format
- ✓ Drag-and-connect question format
- ✓ Select-and-place question format
- ✓ Fixed-length tests
- ✓ Simulations
- ✓ Adaptive tests
- ✓ Short-form tests

Techniques you'll need to master:

- ✓ Assessing your exam-readiness
- ✓ Answering Microsoft's varying question types
- ✓ Altering your test strategy depending on the exam format
- ✓ Practicing (to make perfect)
- ✓ Making the best use of the testing software
- ✓ Budgeting your time
- ✓ Guessing (as a last resort)

Exam taking is not something that most people anticipate eagerly, no matter how well prepared they may be. In most cases, familiarity helps offset test anxiety. In plain English, this means you probably won't be as nervous when you take your fourth or fifth Microsoft certification exam, as you'll be when you take your first one.

Whether it's your first exam or your tenth, understanding the details of taking the new exams (how much time to spend on questions, the environment you'll be in, and so on) and the new exam software will help you concentrate on the material rather than on the setting. Likewise, mastering a few basic exam-taking skills should help you recognize—and perhaps even outfox—some of the tricks and snares you're bound to find in some exam questions.

This chapter, besides explaining the exam environment and software, describes some proven exam-taking strategies that you should be able to use to your advantage.

Assessing Exam-Readiness

We strongly recommend that you read through and take the Self-Assessment included with this book (it appears just before this chapter, in fact). This will help you compare your knowledge base to the requirements for obtaining an MCSE, and it will also help you identify parts of your background or experience that may be in need of improvement, enhancement, or further learning. If you get the right set of basics under your belt, obtaining Microsoft certification will be that much easier.

Once you've gone through the Self-Assessment, you can remedy those topical areas where your background or experience may not measure up to an ideal certification candidate. But you can also tackle subject matter for individual tests at the same time, so you can continue making progress while you're catching up in some areas.

Once you've worked through an *Exam Cram*, have read the supplementary materials, and have taken the practice test, you'll have a pretty clear idea of when you should be ready to take the real exam. Although we strongly recommend that you keep practicing until your scores top the 75 percent mark, 80 percent would be a good goal to give yourself some margin for error in a real exam situation (where stress will play more of a role than when you practice). Once you hit that point, you should be ready to go. But if you get through the practice exam in this book without attaining that score, you should keep taking practice tests and studying the materials until you get there. You'll find more pointers on how to study and prepare in the Self-Assessment. But now, on to the exam itself!

The Exam Situation

When you arrive at the testing center where you scheduled your exam, you'll need to sign in with an exam coordinator. He or she will ask you to show two forms of identification, one of which must be a photo ID. After you've signed in and your time slot arrives, you'll be asked to deposit any books, bags, or other items you brought with you. Then, you'll be escorted into a closed room.

All exams are completely closed book. In fact, you will not be permitted to take anything with you into the testing area, but you will be furnished with a blank sheet of paper and a pen or, in some cases, an erasable plastic sheet and an erasable pen. Before the exam, you should memorize as much of the important material as you can, so you can write that information on the blank sheet as soon as you are seated in front of the computer. You can refer to this piece of paper anytime you like during the test, but you'll have to surrender the sheet when you leave the room. You will have some time to compose yourself, and record this information, before you begin the exam.

Typically, the room will be furnished with anywhere from one to half a dozen computers, and each workstation will be separated from the others by dividers designed to keep you from seeing what's happening on someone else's computer. Most test rooms feature a wall with a large picture window. This permits the exam coordinator to monitor the room, to prevent exam-takers from talking to one another, and to observe anything out of the ordinary that might go on. The exam coordinator will have preloaded the appropriate Microsoft certification exam—for this book, that's Exam 70-210—and you'll be permitted to start as soon as you're seated in front of the computer.

All Microsoft certification exams allow a certain maximum amount of time in which to complete your work (this time is indicated on the exam by an on-screen counter/clock, so you can check the time remaining whenever you like). All Microsoft certification exams are computer generated. In addition to multiple choice, you'll encounter select and place (drag and drop), create a tree (categorization and prioritization), drag and connect, and build list and reorder (list prioritization) on most exams. Although this may sound quite simple, the questions are constructed not only to check your mastery of basic facts and figures about Windows 2000 Professional, but they also require you to evaluate one or more sets of circumstances or requirements. Often, you'll be asked to give more than one answer to a question. Likewise, you might be asked to select the best or most effective solution to a problem from a range of choices, all of which technically are correct. Taking the exam is quite an adventure, and it involves real thinking. This book shows you what to expect and how to deal with the potential problems, puzzles, and predicaments.

In the next section, you'll learn more about how Microsoft test questions look and how they must be answered.

Exam Layout and Design

The format of Microsoft's Windows 2000 exams is different from that of its previous exams. For the design exams (70-219, 70-220, 70-221), each exam consists entirely of a series of case studies, and the questions can be of six types. For the Core Four exams (70-210, 70-215, 70-216, 70-217), the same six types of questions can appear, but you are not likely to encounter complex multiquestion case studies.

For design exams, each case study or "testlet" presents a detailed problem that you must read and analyze. Figure 1.1 shows an example of what a case study looks like. You must select the different tabs in the case study to view the entire case.

Following each case study is a set of questions related to the case study; these questions can be one of six types (which are discussed next). Careful attention to details provided in the case study is the key to success. Be prepared to toggle frequently between the case study and the questions as you work. Some of the case studies also include diagrams, which are called *exhibits*, that you'll need to examine closely to understand how to answer the questions.

Once you complete a case study, you can review all the questions and your answers. However, once you move on to the next case study, you may not be able to return to the previous case study and make any changes.

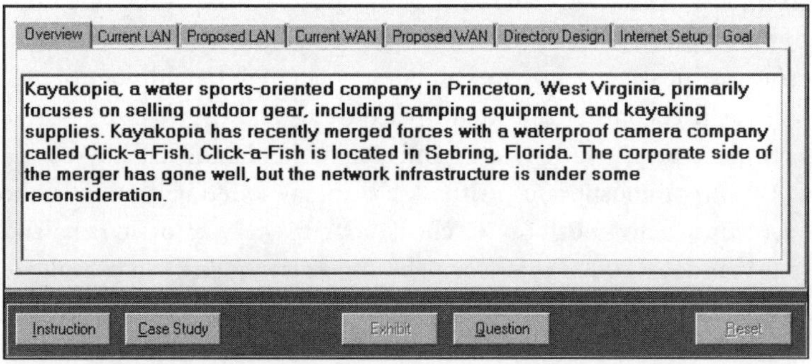

Figure 1.1 This is how case studies appear.

The six types of question formats are:

- Multiple choice, single answer
- Multiple choice, multiple answers
- Build list and reorder (list prioritization)
- Create a tree
- Drag and connect
- Select and place (drag and drop)

Note: *Exam formats may vary by test center location. You may want to call the test center or visit ExamCram.com to see if you can find out which type of test you'll encounter.*

Multiple-Choice Question Formats

Some exam questions require you to select a single answer, whereas others ask you to select multiple correct answers. The following multiple-choice question requires you to select a single correct answer. Following the question is a brief summary of each potential answer and why it is either right or wrong.

Question 1

You are installing Windows 2000 on a system with a blank hard drive. You boot the system with a DOS bootable floppy containing CD-ROM drivers. What must you do to launch the installation of Windows 2000 Professional?

❍ a. Run winnt32 from the i386 directory.

❍ b. Run setup.exe.

❍ c. Run winnt from the i386 directory.

❍ d. Run setup.exe from the i386 directory.

The correct answer is c because that is the only command that runs under DOS and launches an installation of Windows 2000. The other answers (a, b, d) are misleading because they name commands that do not run under DOS (a), or do not exist (b, d), but sound like valid setup commands.

This sample question format corresponds closely to the Microsoft certification exam format—the only difference on the exam is that questions are not followed by answer keys. To select an answer, you would position the cursor over the radio button next to the answer. Then, click the mouse button to select the answer.

Let's examine a question where one or more answers are possible. This type of question provides checkboxes rather than radio buttons for marking all appropriate selections.

Question 2

How can you launch installation of Windows 2000 on a system with a blank hard drive? [Check all correct answers]

- ❑ a. Boot with the Windows 2000 CD-ROM.
- ❑ b. Boot using a DOS-bootable floppy and run i386\winnt.
- ❑ c. Boot using a DOS-bootable floppy then insert the Windows 2000 CD-ROM and wait for AutoRun to launch.
- ❑ d. Boot using a DOS-bootable floppy and run i386\winnt32.

Answers a and b are correct. Both are options to launch an installation of Windows 2000. AutoRun does not function under DOS, and winnt32 does not work in DOS, therefore answers c and d are incorrect.

For this particular question, two answers are required. Microsoft sometimes gives partial credit for partially correct answers. For Question 2, you have to check the boxes next to items a and b to obtain credit for a correct answer. Notice that picking the right answers also means knowing why the other answers are wrong!

Build-List-and-Reorder Question Format

Questions in the build-list-and-reorder format present two lists of items—one on the left and one on the right. To answer the question, you must move items from the list on the right to the list on the left. The final list must then be reordered into a specific order.

These questions can best be characterized as "From the following list of choices, pick the choices that answer the question. Arrange the list in a certain order." To give you practice with this type of question, some questions of this type are included in this study guide. Here's an example of how they appear in this book; for a sample of how they appear on the test, see Figure 1.2.

Question 3

From the following list of famous people, pick those that have been elected President of the United States. Arrange the list in the order that they served.

Thomas Jefferson

Ben Franklin

Abe Lincoln

George Washington

Andrew Jackson

Paul Revere

The correct answer is:

George Washington

Thomas Jefferson

Andrew Jackson

Abe Lincoln

On an actual exam, the entire list of famous people would initially appear in the list on the right. You would move the four correct answers to the list on the left, and then reorder the list on the left. Notice that the answer to the question did not include all items from the initial list. However, this may not always be the case.

To move an item from the right list to the left list, first select the item by clicking on it, and then click on the Add button (left arrow). Once you move an item from one list to the other, you can move the item back by first selecting the item and then clicking on the appropriate button (either the Add button or the Remove button). Once items have been moved to the left list, you can reorder an item by selecting the item and clicking on the up or down button.

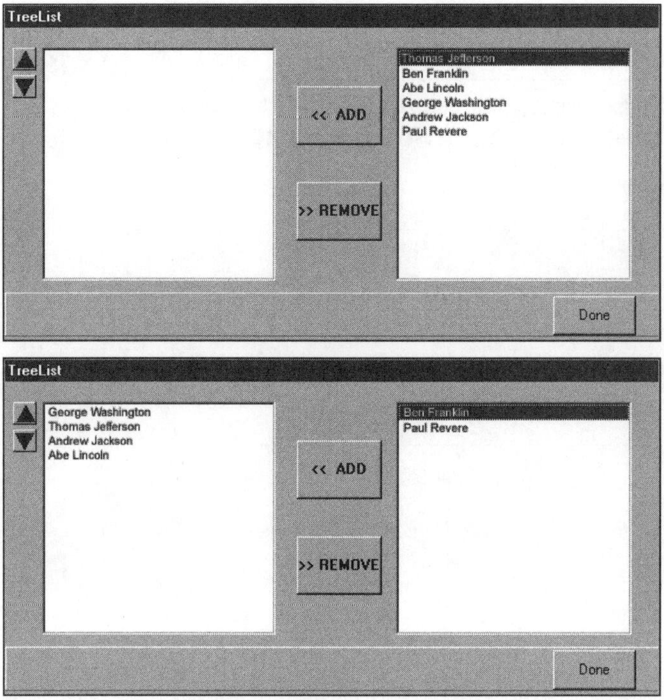

Figure 1.2 This is how build-list-and-reorder questions appear.

Create-a-Tree Question Format

Questions in the create-a-tree format also present two lists—one on the left side of the screen and one on the right side of the screen. The list on the right consists of individual items, and the list on the left consists of nodes in a tree. To answer the question, you must move items from the list on the right to the appropriate node in the tree.

These questions can best be characterized as simply a matching exercise. Items from the list on the right are placed under the appropriate category in the list on the left. Here's an example of how they appear in this book; for a sample of how they appear on the test, see Figure 1.3.

Question 4

The calendar year is divided into four seasons:

Winter

Spring

Summer

Fall

Identify the season when each of the following holidays occurs:

Christmas

Fourth of July

Labor Day

Flag Day

Memorial Day

Washington's Birthday

Thanksgiving

Easter

The correct answer is:

- Winter
  - Christmas
  - Washington's Birthday
- Spring
  - Flag Day
  - Memorial Day
  - Easter
- Summer
  - Fourth of July
  - Labor Day
- Fall
  - Thanksgiving

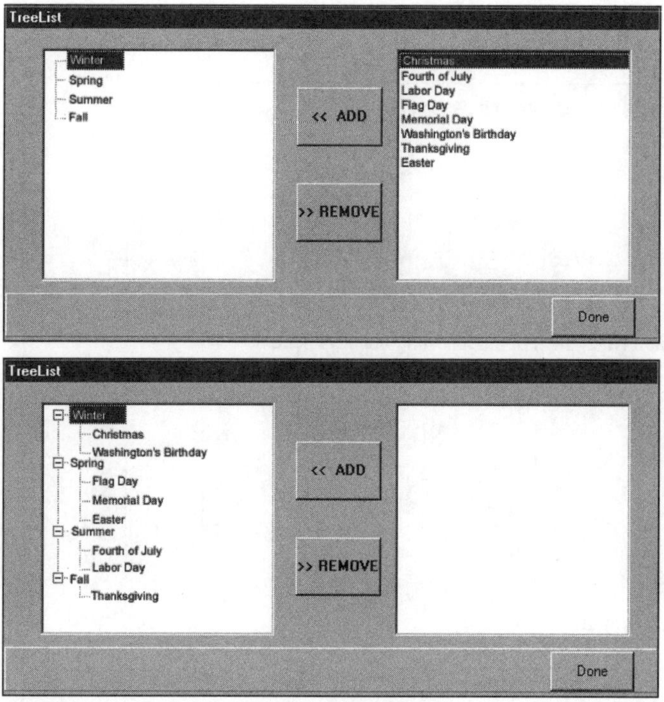

Figure 1.3 This is how create-a-tree questions appear.

In this case, all the items in the list were used. However, this may not always be the case.

To move an item from the right list to its appropriate location in the tree, you must first select the appropriate tree node by clicking on it. Then, you select the item to be moved and click on the Add button. If one or more items have been added to a tree node, the node will be displayed with a "+" icon to the left of the node name. You can click on this icon to expand the node and view the item(s) that have been added. If any item has been added to the wrong tree node, you can remove it by selecting it and clicking on the Remove button.

Drag-and-Connect Question Format

Questions in the drag-and-connect format present a group of objects and a list of "connections." To answer the question, you must move the appropriate connections between the objects.

This type of question is best described using graphics. Here's an example.

Question 5

The following objects represent the different states of water:

Ice | Water Vapor | Water | Steam

Use items from the following list to connect the objects so that they are scientifically correct.

Sublimates to form

Freezes to form

Evaporates to form

Boils to form

Condenses to form

Melts to form

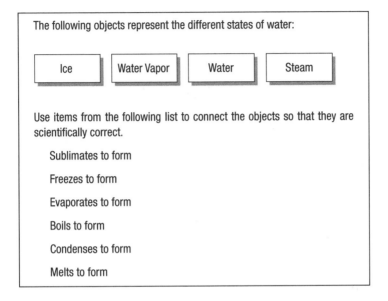

The correct answer is:

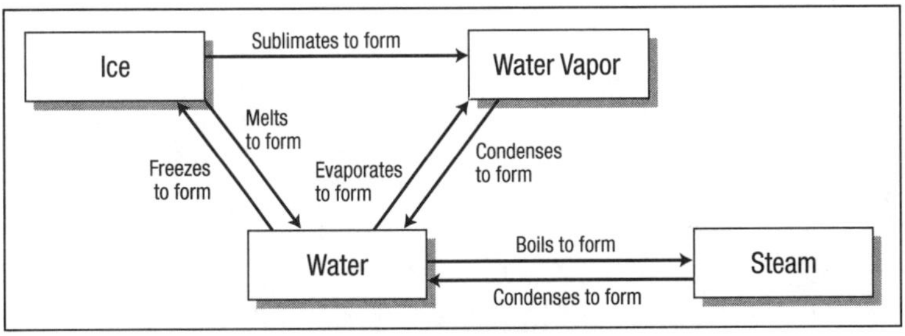

For this type of question, it's not necessary to use every object, and each connection can be used multiple times.

Select-and-Place Question Format

Questions in the select-and-place (drag-and-drop) format present a diagram with blank boxes, and a list of labels that need to be dragged to correctly fill in the blank boxes. To answer the question, you must move the labels to their appropriate positions on the diagram.

This type of question is best described using graphics. Here's an example.

Question 6

Place the items in their proper order, by number, on the following flowchart. Some items may be used more than once, and some items may not be used at all.

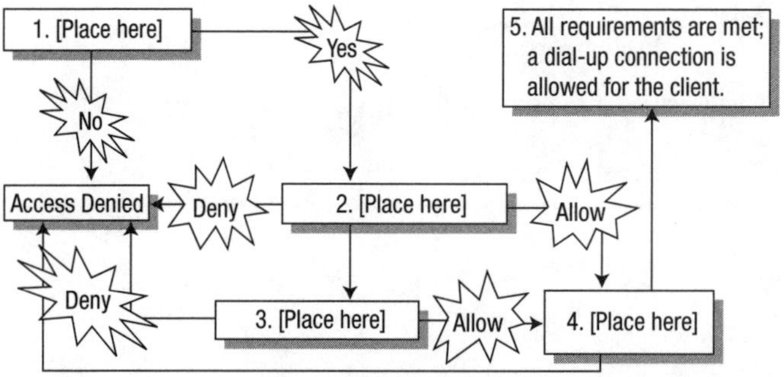

Policy Conditions	Account Conditions
Policy Permissions	Account Profile
Account Permissions	Policy Profile

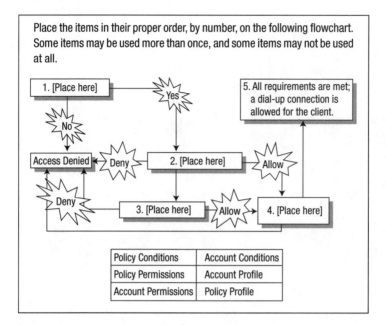

The correct answer is:

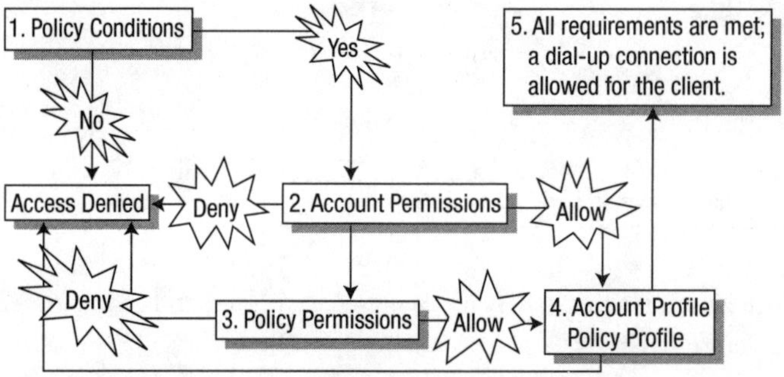

Microsoft's Testing Formats

Currently, Microsoft uses four different testing formats:

- Case study
- Fixed length
- Adaptive
- Short form

As we mentioned earlier, the case study approach is used with Microsoft's design exams, 70-219, 70-220, and 70-221. These exams consist of a set of case studies that you must analyze to enable you to answer questions related to the case studies. Such exams include one or more case studies (tabbed topic areas), each of which is followed by 4 to 10 questions. The question types for design exams and for Core Four Windows 2000 exams are multiple choice, build list and reorder, create a tree, drag and connect, and select and place. Depending on the test topic, some exams are totally case-based, whereas others are not.

Other Microsoft exams employ advanced testing capabilities that might not be immediately apparent. Although the questions that appear are primarily multiple choice, the logic that drives them is more complex than older Microsoft tests, which use a fixed sequence of questions, called a *fixed-length test*. Some questions employ a sophisticated user interface, which Microsoft calls a *simulation*, to test your knowledge of the software and systems under consideration in a more or less "live" environment that behaves just like the original. The Testing Innovations link at **www.microsoft.com/trainingandservices/default.asp?PageID=mcp** includes a downloadable practice simulation.

For some exams, Microsoft has turned to a well-known technique, called *adaptive testing*, to establish a test-taker's level of knowledge and product competence. Adaptive exams look the same as fixed-length exams, but they discover the level of difficulty at which an individual test-taker can correctly answer questions. Test-takers with differing levels of knowledge or ability therefore see different sets of questions; individuals with high levels of knowledge or ability are presented with a smaller set of more difficult questions, whereas individuals with lower levels of knowledge are presented with a larger set of easier questions. Two individuals may answer the same percentage of questions correctly, but the test-taker with a higher knowledge or ability level will score higher because his or her questions are worth more.

Also, the lower-level test-taker will probably answer more questions than his or her more-knowledgeable colleague. This explains why adaptive tests use ranges of values to define the number of questions and the amount of time it takes to complete the test.

Adaptive tests work by evaluating the test-taker's most recent answer. A correct answer leads to a more difficult question (and the test software's estimate of the test-taker's knowledge and ability level is raised). An incorrect answer leads to a less difficult question (and the test software's estimate of the test-taker's knowledge and ability level is lowered). This process continues until the test targets the test-taker's true ability level. The exam ends when the test-taker's level of accuracy meets a statistically acceptable value (in other words, when his or her performance demonstrates an acceptable level of knowledge and ability), or when the maximum number of items has been presented (in which case, the test-taker is almost certain to fail).

Microsoft also introduced a short-form test for its most popular tests. This test delivers 25 to 30 questions to its takers, giving them exactly 60 minutes to complete the exam. This type of exam is similar to a fixed-length test, in that it allows readers to jump ahead or return to earlier questions, and to cycle through the questions until the test is done. Microsoft does not use adaptive logic in this test, but claims that statistical analysis of the question pool is such that the 25 to 30 questions delivered during a short-form exam conclusively measure a test-taker's knowledge of the subject matter in much the same way as an adaptive test. You can think of the short-form test as a kind of "greatest hits exam" (that is, the most important questions are covered) version of an adaptive exam on the same topic.

Note: *Some of the Microsoft exams can appear as a combination of adaptive and fixed-length questions.*

Microsoft tests can come in any one of these forms. Whatever you encounter, you must take the test in whichever form it appears; you can't choose one form over another. If anything, it pays more to prepare thoroughly for an adaptive exam than for a fixed-length or a short-form exam: The penalties for answering incorrectly are built into the test itself on an adaptive exam, whereas the layout remains the same for a fixed-length or short-form test, no matter how many questions you answer incorrectly.

TIP

The biggest difference between an adaptive test and a fixed-length or short-form test is that on a fixed-length or short-form test, you can revisit questions after you've read them over one or more times. On an adaptive test, you must answer the question when it's presented and will have no opportunities to revisit that question thereafter.

Strategies for Different Testing Formats

Before you choose a test-taking strategy, you must know if your test is case study based, fixed length, short form, or adaptive. When you begin your exam, you'll know right away if the test is based on case studies. The interface will consist of a tabbed window that allows you to easily navigate through the sections of the case.

If you are taking a test that is not based on case studies, the software will tell you that the test is adaptive, if in fact the version you're taking is an adaptive test. If your introductory materials fail to mention this, you're probably taking a fixed-length test (50 to 70 questions). If the total number of questions involved is 25 to 30, you're taking a short-form test. Some tests announce themselves by indicating that they will start with a set of adaptive questions, followed by fixed-length questions.

> TIP
>
> You'll be able to tell for sure if you are taking an adaptive, fixed-length, or short-form test by the first question. If it includes a checkbox that lets you mark the question for later review, you're taking a fixed-length or short-form test. If the total number of questions is 25 to 30, it's a short-form test; if more than 30, it's a fixed-length test. Adaptive test questions can be visited (and answered) only once, and they include no such checkbox.

The Case Study Exam Strategy

Most test-takers find that the case study type of test used for the design exams (70-219, 70-220, and 70-221) is the most difficult to master. When it comes to studying for a case study test, your best bet is to approach each case study as a standalone test. The biggest challenge you'll encounter is that you'll feel that you won't have enough time to get through all of the cases that are presented.

> TIP
>
> Each case provides a lot of material that you'll need to read and study before you can effectively answer the questions that follow. The trick to taking a case study exam is to first scan the case study to get the highlights. Make sure you read the overview section of the case so that you understand the context of the problem at hand. Then, quickly move on and scan the questions.
>
> As you are scanning the questions, make mental notes to yourself so that you'll remember which sections of the case study you should focus on. Some case studies may provide a fair amount of extra information that you don't really need to answer the questions. The goal with our scanning approach is to avoid having to study and analyze material that is not completely relevant.

When studying a case, carefully read the tabbed information. It is important to answer each and every question. You will be able to toggle back and forth from case to questions, and from question to question within a case testlet. However, once you leave the case and move on, you may not be able to return to it. You may want to take notes while reading useful information so you can refer to them when you tackle the test questions. It's hard to go wrong with this strategy when taking any kind of Microsoft certification test.

The Fixed-Length and Short-Form Exam Strategy

A well-known principle when taking fixed-length or short-form exams is to first read over the entire exam from start to finish while answering only those questions you feel absolutely sure of. On subsequent passes, you can dive into more complex questions more deeply, knowing how many such questions you have left.

Fortunately, the Microsoft exam software for fixed-length and short-form tests makes the multiple-visit approach easy to implement. At the top-left corner of each question is a checkbox that permits you to mark that question for a later visit.

***Note:** Marking questions makes review easier, but you can return to any question by clicking the Forward or Back button repeatedly.*

As you read each question, if you answer only those you're sure of and mark for review those that you're not sure of, you can keep working through a decreasing list of questions as you answer the trickier ones in order.

> TIP: There's at least one potential benefit to reading the exam over completely before answering the trickier questions: Sometimes, information supplied in later questions sheds more light on earlier questions. At other times, information you read in later questions might jog your memory about Windows 2000 Professional facts, figures, or behavior that helps you answer earlier questions. Either way, you'll come out ahead if you defer those questions about which you're not absolutely sure.

Here are some question-handling strategies that apply to fixed-length and short-form tests. Use them if you have the chance:

- When returning to a question after your initial read-through, read every word again—otherwise, your mind can fall quickly into a rut. Sometimes, revisiting a question after turning your attention elsewhere lets you see something you missed, but the strong tendency is to see what you've seen before. Try to avoid that tendency at all costs.
- If you return to a question more than twice, try to articulate to yourself what you don't understand about the question, why answers don't appear to make

sense, or what appears to be missing. If you chew on the subject awhile, your subconscious might provide the details you lack, or you might notice a "trick" that points to the right answer.

As you work your way through the exam, another counter that Microsoft provides will come in handy—the number of questions completed and questions outstanding. For fixed-length and short-form tests, it's wise to budget your time by making sure that you've completed one-quarter of the questions one-quarter of the way through the exam period, and three-quarters of the questions three-quarters of the way through.

If you're not finished when only five minutes remain, use that time to guess your way through any remaining questions. Remember, guessing is potentially more valuable than not answering, because blank answers are always wrong, but a guess may turn out to be right. If you don't have a clue about any of the remaining questions, pick answers at random, or choose all a's, b's, and so on. The important thing is to submit an exam for scoring that has an answer for every question.

TIP At the very end of your exam period, you're better off guessing than leaving questions unanswered.

The Adaptive Exam Strategy

If there's one principle that applies to taking an adaptive test, it could be summed up as "Get it right the first time." You cannot elect to skip a question and move on to the next one when taking an adaptive test, because the testing software uses your answer to the current question to select whatever question it plans to present next. Nor can you return to a question once you've moved on, because the software gives you only one chance to answer the question. You can, however, take notes, because sometimes information supplied in earlier questions will shed more light on later questions.

Also, when you answer a question correctly, you are presented with a more difficult question next, to help the software gauge your level of skill and ability. When you answer a question incorrectly, you are presented with a less difficult question, and the software lowers its current estimate of your skill and ability. This continues until the program settles into a reasonably accurate estimate of what you know and can do, and takes you on average through somewhere between 15 and 30 questions as you complete the test.

The good news is that if you know your stuff, you'll probably finish most adaptive tests in 30 minutes or so. The bad news is that you must really, really know your stuff to do your best on an adaptive test. That's because some questions are so convoluted, complex, or hard to follow that you're bound to miss one or two, at a minimum, even if you do know your stuff. So the more you know, the better you'll do on an adaptive test, even accounting for the occasionally weird or unfathomable questions that appear on these exams.

> **TIP** Because you can't always tell in advance if a test is fixed length, short form, or adaptive, you will be best served by preparing for the exam as if it were adaptive. That way, you should be prepared to pass no matter what kind of test you take. But if you do take a fixed-length or short-form test, remember our tips from the preceding section. They should help you improve on what you could do on an adaptive test.

If you encounter a question on an adaptive test that you can't answer, you must guess an answer immediately. Because of how the software works, you may suffer for your guess on the next question if you guess right, because you'll get a more difficult question next!

Question-Handling Strategies

For those questions that take only a single answer, usually two or three of the answers will be obviously incorrect, and two of the answers will be plausible—of course, only one can be correct. Unless the answer leaps out at you (if it does, reread the question to look for a trick; sometimes those are the ones you're most likely to get wrong), begin the process of answering by eliminating those answers that are most obviously wrong.

Almost always, at least one answer out of the possible choices for a question can be eliminated immediately because it matches one of these conditions:

- The answer does not apply to the situation.
- The answer describes a nonexistent issue, an invalid option, or an imaginary state.

After you eliminate all answers that are obviously wrong, you can apply your retained knowledge to eliminate further answers. Look for items that sound correct but refer to actions, commands, or features that are not present or not available in the situation that the question describes.

If you're still faced with a blind guess among two or more potentially correct answers, reread the question. Try to picture how each of the possible remaining answers would alter the situation. Be especially sensitive to terminology; sometimes the choice of words ("remove" instead of "disable") can make the difference between a right answer and a wrong one.

Only when you've exhausted your ability to eliminate answers, but remain unclear about which of the remaining possibilities is correct, should you guess at an answer. An unanswered question offers you no points, but guessing gives you at least some chance of getting a question right; just don't be too hasty when making a blind guess.

Note: *If you're taking a fixed-length or a short-form test, you can wait until the last round of reviewing marked questions (just as you're about to run out of time, or out of unanswered questions) before you start making guesses. You will have the same option within each case study testlet (but once you leave a testlet, you may not be allowed to return to it). If you're taking an adaptive test, you'll have to guess to move on to the next question if you can't figure out an answer some other way. Either way, guessing should be your technique of last resort!*

Numerous questions assume that the default behavior of a particular utility is in effect. If you know the defaults and understand what they mean, this knowledge will help you cut through many Gordian knots.

Mastering the Inner Game

In the final analysis, knowledge breeds confidence, and confidence breeds success. If you study the materials in this book carefully and review all the practice questions at the end of each chapter, you should become aware of those areas where additional learning and study are required.

After you've worked your way through the book, take the practice exam in the back of the book. Taking this test will provide a reality check and help you identify areas to study further. Make sure you follow up and review materials related to the questions you miss on the practice exam before scheduling a real exam. Only when you've covered that ground and feel comfortable with the whole scope of the practice exam should you set an exam appointment. Only if you score 80 percent or better should you proceed to the real thing (otherwise, obtain some additional practice tests so you can keep trying until you hit this magic number).

TIP

If you take a practice exam and don't score at least 80 to 85 percent correct, you'll want to practice further. Microsoft provides links to practice exam providers and also offers self-assessment exams at **www.microsoft.com/trainingandservices/**. You should also check out **ExamCram.com** for downloadable practice questions.

Armed with the information in this book and with the determination to augment your knowledge, you should be able to pass the certification exam. However, you need to work at it, or you'll spend the exam fee more than once before you finally pass. If you prepare seriously, you should do well. We are confident that you can do it!

The next section covers the sources you can use to prepare for the Microsoft certification exams.

Additional Resources

A good source of information about Microsoft certification exams comes from Microsoft itself. Because its products and technologies—and the exams that go with them—change frequently, the best place to go for exam-related information is online.

If you haven't already visited the Microsoft Certified Professional site, do so right now. The MCP home page resides at **www.microsoft.com/trainingandservices/** (see Figure 1.4).

Note: This page might not be there by the time you read this, or may be replaced by something new and different, because things change regularly on the Microsoft site. Should this happen, please read the sidebar titled "Coping with Change on the Web."

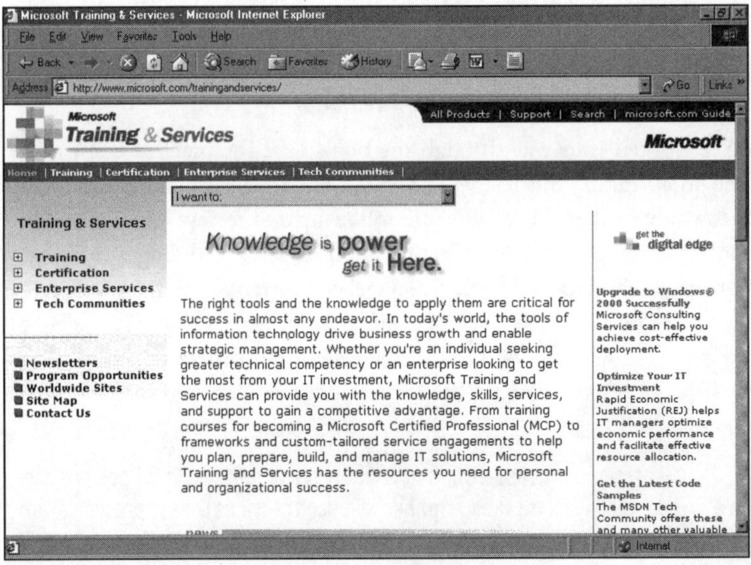

Figure 1.4 The Microsoft Certified Professional home page.

Coping with Change on the Web

Sooner or later, all the information we've shared with you about the Microsoft Certified Professional pages and the other Web-based resources mentioned throughout the rest of this book will go stale or be replaced by newer information. In some cases, the URLs you find here might lead you to their replacements; in other cases, the URLs will go nowhere, leaving you with the dreaded "404 File not found" error message. When that happens, don't give up.

There's always a way to find what you want on the Web if you're willing to invest some time and energy. Most large or complex Web sites—and Microsoft's qualifies on both counts—offer a search engine. On all of Microsoft's Web pages, a Search button appears along the top edge of the page. As long as you can get to Microsoft's site (it should stay at **www.microsoft.com** for a long time), use this tool to help you find what you need.

The more focused you can make a search request, the more likely the results will include information you can use. For example, you can search for the string

```
"training and certification"
```

to produce a lot of data about the subject in general, but if you're looking for the preparation guide for Exam 70-210, "Windows 2000 Professional," you'll be more likely to get there quickly if you use a search string similar to the following:

```
"Exam 70-210" AND "preparation guide"
```

Likewise, if you want to find the Training and Certification downloads, try a search string such as this:

```
"training and certification" AND "download page"
```

Finally, feel free to use general search tools—such as **www.search.com**, **www.altavista.com**, and **www.excite.com**—to look for related information. Although Microsoft offers great information about its certification exams online, there are plenty of third-party sources of information and assistance that need not follow Microsoft's party line. Therefore, if you can't find something where the book says it lives, intensify your search.

2

Implementing and Administering Resources

Terms you'll need to understand:

- ✓ Shared folders
- ✓ Hidden shares
- ✓ Offline files/client-side caching
- ✓ Share permissions
- ✓ NT File System (NTFS)
- ✓ NTFS permissions
- ✓ User rights
- ✓ Access control list (ACL)
- ✓ NTFS compression
- ✓ Taking ownership of objects
- ✓ Auditing
- ✓ NTFS Encrypting File System (EFS)
- ✓ Printer ports
- ✓ Internet Printing Protocol (IPP)

Techniques you'll need to master:

- ✓ Creating network shares
- ✓ Configuring share permissions
- ✓ Configuring options for offline files
- ✓ Setting basic and advanced NTFS permissions
- ✓ Enabling/disabling NTFS data compression
- ✓ Learning how to turn on auditing
- ✓ Working with EFS
- ✓ Connecting to printers over the Internet

Why do we have computer networks anyway? Well, they empower us to collaborate on projects and share information with others. If you're working on a Windows 2000 Professional system that is connected to a network, you can share one or more of that system's folders with other computers and users on that network. Drive volumes and folders are not automatically shared for all users in Windows 2000 Professional. Members of the Administrators group and the Power Users group, discussed later in this chapter, retain the rights to create shared network folders.

Managing Access to Shared Folders

To share a folder with the network, follow these steps:

1. Open a window in either My Computer or Windows Explorer.
2. Right-click the folder that you want to share and then select Sharing from the pop-up menu.
3. Click the Share This Folder radio button, as shown in Figure 2.1.
4. Type in a Share Name or accept the default one. Windows 2000 uses the actual folder name as the default Share Name.
5. Type in a Comment, if you desire. Comments appear in the Browse list when users search for network resources. Comments can help them to locate the proper network shares.
6. Specify the User Limit: Maximum Allowed or Allow x number of Users. Windows 2000 Professional permits a maximum of 10 concurrent network connec-

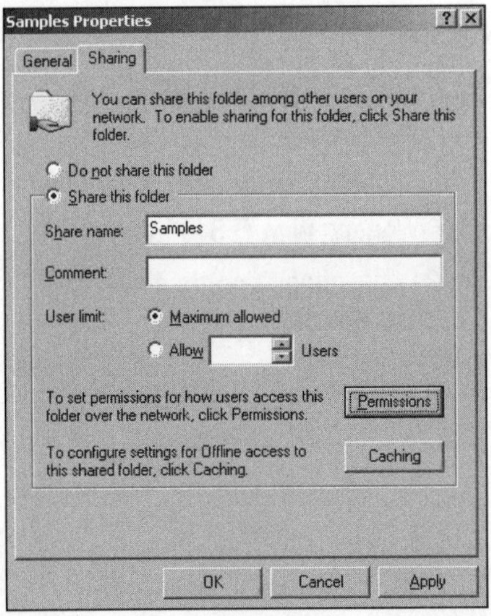

Figure 2.1 You create a network share by accessing the Sharing tab of a folder's Properties sheet.

tions per share. Specify the Allow x number of Users option only if you need to limit the number of concurrent users for this share to fewer than 10 users.

7. Click OK to create the shared folder. The folder now becomes available to others on your network.

Note: *To remove a network share, right-click the shared folder and choose the Sharing option. Click the Do Not Share This Folder radio button and click OK. The folder will no longer be shared with the network.*

Connecting to Shared Resources on a Windows Network

Users and network administrators have several options available to them for connecting to shared network resources. These options include the following:

- Typing in a Universal Naming Convention (UNC) path from the Start|Run dialog box in the format **\\servername\sharename**.
- Navigating to the share from the My Network Places window.
- Employing the **net use** command from a command prompt window.

If you want to connect to a shared folder named "samples" that resides on a Windows computer named "7800pro", click Start|Run. Next, type **\\7800pro\samples** and click OK. At this point, you are connected to that shared resource, provided you possess the required security permissions needed to access the shared folder.

Connecting to Network Resources with the My Network Places Window

You can connect to a network share from My Network Places. Double-click the My Network Places icon on the Windows 2000 desktop. Double-click the Add Network Place icon, which reveals the Add Network Place Wizard, as shown in Figure 2.2. Enter the location of the network place, or click Browse to locate the

Figure 2.2 You can easily connect to shared network folders with the Add Network Place Wizard.

network share by viewing the available network resources. Click Next to enter a name for the network place or accept the default name. Click Finish to establish the connection to the shared folder, provided that you have the proper permissions. A list of network resources to which you have already connected is then displayed within the My Network Places window.

For Command Line Junkies: The net use Command

You also have the option of connecting to network shares via the **net use** command. For help with the various options and syntax of the **net use** command, type **net use /?** at the command prompt. To connect to a remote resource from the command line, follow these steps:

1. Open a command prompt window (Start|Programs|Accessories|Command Prompt).
2. At the command prompt, type **net use X: \\7800pro\samples** and press Enter, where **X:** is a drive letter that you designate. If you possess the appropriate permissions for that network share, you should see the message The Command Completed Successfully displayed in your command prompt window.

Using Automatically Generated Hidden Shares

Windows 2000 Professional automatically creates shared folders by default each and every time the computer is started. These default shares are often referred to as *hidden* or *administrative* because a dollar sign ($) is appended to their share names. The dollar sign at the end of a share name prevents the shared folder from being displayed on the network Browse list; users cannot easily discover that these shares exist. When users browse through the My Network Places window, for example, they cannot see that such hidden shares even exist; Microsoft Windows Networking does not allow hidden shares to be displayed. These hidden network shares include the following:

- *C$, D$, E$, and so on*—One share gets created for the root of each available hard drive volume on the system.
- *ADMIN$*—This shares the systemroot folder with the network (e.g., C:\WINNT).
- *IPC$*—This share is used for InterProcess Communications (IPCs). IPCs support communications between objects on different computers over a network by manipulating the low-level details of network transport protocols. InterProcess Communications enable the use of distributed application programs that combine multiple processes working together to accomplish a single task.

Although you can temporarily disable hidden shares, you cannot delete them without modifying the registry (which is not recommended) because they get re-created on each restart. You can connect to a hidden share, but only if you provide a user account with administrative privileges along with the appropriate password for that user account. Administrators can create their own custom administrative (hidden) shares simply by adding a dollar sign to the share name of any shared folder. Administrators can view all the hidden shares that exist on a Windows 2000 Professional system by accessing the Shares folder within the System Tools/Shared Folders container of the Computer Management console.

Controlling Access to Shared Folders

When you, as a network administrator, grant access to shared resources over the network, the shared data files become very vulnerable to unintentional as well as intentional destruction or deletion by others. This is why network administrators must be vigilant in controlling data access security permissions. If access permissions to shared folders are too lenient, shared data may become compromised. On the other hand, if access permissions are set too stringently, the users who need to access and manipulate the data may not be able to do their jobs. Managing access control for shared resources can be quite challenging.

Revisiting a Shared Folder's Properties

By right-clicking on a shared folder and selecting Sharing, you can modify some of the shared folder's properties. You can specify whether network users can cache shared data files on their local workstations. To configure offline access settings for the shared folder, click the Caching button. If you allow caching of files for a shared folder, you must choose from three options in the Caching Settings dialog box:

- *Automatic Caching For Documents*—This option relies on the workstation and server computers to automatically download and make available offline any opened files from the shared folder. Older copies of files are automatically updated.

- *Automatic Caching For Programs*—This setting is recommended for folders that contain read-only data or for application programs that have been configured to be run from the network. This option is not designed for sharing data files, and file sharing in this mode is not guaranteed.

- *Manual Caching For Documents*—This is the default caching setting. This setting requires network users to manually specify any files they want available when working offline. This setting is recommended for folders that contain user documents.

Click OK on the Caching Settings dialog box after making any configuration changes for offline access to the shared folder.

If you do not want files within the shared folder to be cached locally on workstations, you must deselect the Allow Caching Of Files In This Shared Folder checkbox, as shown in Figure 2.3.

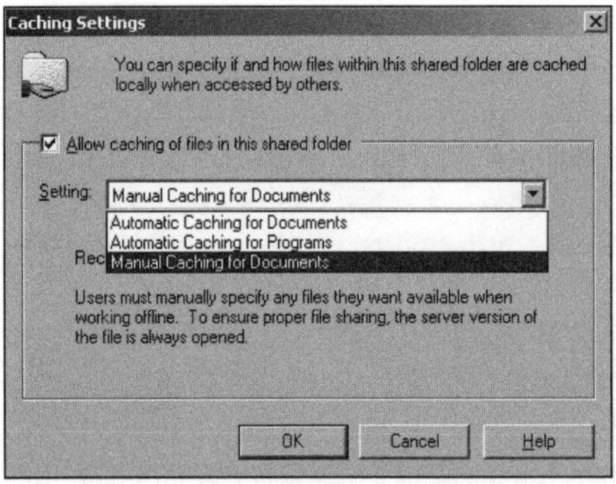

Figure 2.3 The Caching Settings dialog box with Manual Caching For Documents selected.

Note: *The default cache size is configured as 10 percent of the client computer's available disk space. You can change this setting by selecting Tools|Folder Options from the menu bar from any My Computer or Windows Explorer window. The Offline Files tab of the Folder Options dialog box displays the system's offline files settings, as shown in Figure 2.4.*

Note: *The Offline Files feature is also known as Client-Side Caching (CSC). The default location on Windows 2000 computers for storage of offline files is System-Root\CSC (e.g., C:\WINNT\CSC). You can use the* ***Cachemov.exe*** *tool from the Windows 2000 Professional Resource Kit and the Windows 2000 Server Resource*

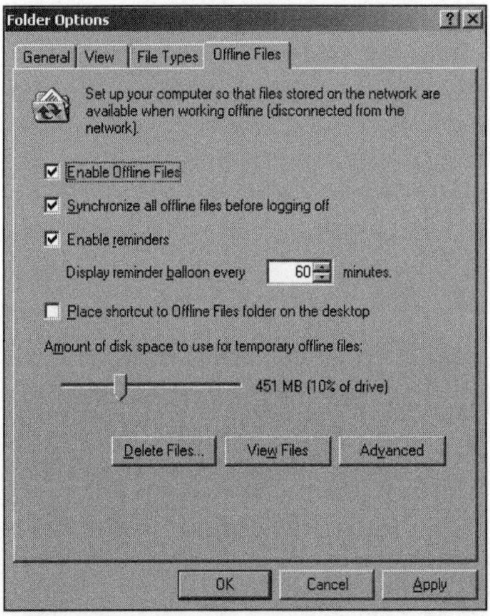

Figure 2.4 The Offline Files tab of the Folder Options dialog box.

Kit to relocate the CSC folder onto a different drive volume. The ***Cachemov.exe*** *utility moves the CSC folder to the root of the drive volume that is specified. After the CSC folder has been moved from its default location, all subsequent moves place it in the root of the drive volume.* ***Cachemov.exe*** *never returns the folder to its original default location.*

Network Share Permissions

In addition to the Caching button, located at the bottom of the Sharing tab of a shared folder's Properties sheet, is the Permissions button. The caption next to this button reads To Set Permissions For How Users Access This Folder Over The Network, Click Permissions. However, these "share" permissions are intended solely for backward-compatibility purposes; you should actually avoid such permissions unless a share resides on a file allocation table (FAT) or FAT32 drive volume, which provides no file system security. In most circumstances, you should store all data and applications on NT File System (NTFS) drive volumes. In fact, as a general rule, you should configure all system drive volumes in NTFS. With the availability of third-party tools as well as the native Windows 2000 Recovery Console, which permit command line access to NTFS drives (even if the system won't boot), it's difficult to argue against NTFS for all drives in Windows 2000.

Network share permissions have their roots back in the days of Windows for Workgroups 3.1x, before Windows NT and NTFS. Share permissions provided a way for administrators to control access to files for network users. Only three permissions are available: Full Control, Change, or Read. These three permissions can be explicitly allowed or denied. The default is Allow Full Control for the Everyone group. For shared folders that reside on FAT or FAT32 drives, share permissions do offer some degree of access control for network users. They provide *no security* for *local access*! Share permissions apply only to access over the network; these permissions have absolutely nothing to do with the underlying file system.

Monitoring, Managing, and Troubleshooting Access to Shared Files and Folders Under NTFS

Although you can somewhat control access to shared network folders by managing share permissions, Windows 2000 NTFS provides a very robust access control solution. In addition to offering administrators more granularity of security access control over files and folders than network share permissions, NTFS permissions reside at the file system level, which allows administrators to manage only one set of access control settings for both network users and local users.

NTFS Security: Users and Groups

You can apply NTFS security permissions to resources like files, folders, and printers for specific users or groups of users. Windows 2000 Professional installs two local users by default: Administrator and Guest. The Guest user is disabled by default. The Administrator user account is all powerful on the local machine and cannot be deleted, although it can be renamed. Six local groups are installed automatically: Administrators, Backup Operators, Guests, Power Users, Replicator, and Users. The Power Users group is not present in any edition of Windows 2000 Server; it exists only as a local group in Windows 2000 Professional. The Administrators account is all powerful because it is a member of the Administrators group, and, you cannot remove the Administrator from membership in the Administrators group. Table 2.1 outlines the local groups that are installed by default when you first install Windows 2000 Professional.

Table 2.2 displays the special built-in groups that are present in the Windows 2000 Professional network operating system (NOS). The primary purpose of the

Table 2.1 Local groups installed by default in Windows 2000 Professional.

Local Group	Role
Administrators	Group members possess full administrative control for managing the local system, local users, and local groups.
Backup Operators	Group members have the rights to back up and restore files and folders on the local system.
Guests	Group members can't make permanent alterations to their desktop settings. The default Guest account is automatically a member of this group. By default, group members possess no specific rights or permissions on objects. If the local computer joins a Windows NT Server or Windows 2000 Server domain, the global Domain Guests group automatically becomes a member of the local Guests group.
Power Users	Group members can add new local user accounts and change existing local user accounts. Members can also create shared folders and shared printers on the network.
Replicator	This group supports file replication within a Windows 2000 domain context.
Users	Group members can perform tasks only after an administrator has specifically granted them rights to do so. They can access resources on only those that an administrator has granted them permissions. When user accounts get created, each new user automatically becomes a member of the local Users group. If the local computer becomes a member of a Windows NT Server or Windows 2000 Server domain, the global Domain Users group automatically becomes a member of the local Users group.

Table 2.2 Built-in system groups installed by default in Windows 2000 Professional.	
Built-in Group	**Role**
Everyone	Group members include all users who access the computer. The best practice is to avoid using this group. If you enable the Guest account, any user can become authorized to access the system, and the user inherits the rights and permissions assigned to the Everyone group.
Authenticated Users	Group members have valid user accounts on the local system, or they possess a valid user account within the domain of which the system is a member. It is preferable that you use this group over the Everyone group for preventing anonymous access to resources.
Creator Owner	A user becomes a member of this built-in group by creating or taking ownership of a resource. Whenever a member of the Administrators group creates an object, the Administrators group is listed as the owner of that resource in lieu of the actual name of the user who created it.
Network	Group members include any user accounts from a remote computer that access the local computer via a current network connection.
Interactive	This group includes the user account for the locally logged on user.
Anonymous Logon	Group members include any user accounts that Windows 2000 did not validate or authorize.
Dialup	Group members include any user accounts that are currently connected via Dial-up Networking.

groups listed in Tables 2.1 and 2.2 is to facilitate managing access control settings (especially in NTFS) by allowing administrators to assign security permissions to groups of users rather than having to assign and maintain security permissions on resources to *hundreds or thousands* of individual users. Special built-in groups also exist under Windows 2000 Professional. These built-in groups include the groups that appear in Table 2.2.

Setting NTFS Security Permissions

Because share permissions apply to network access only, they can serve only to complicate and possibly confuse access control settings when you apply them on top of NTFS security permissions, which take effect at the file system level. If share permissions and NTFS permissions conflict, the *most restrictive* permissions apply. For example, let's say that you set share permissions on the shared folder named C:\Samples. Suppose you have set the share permissions for the Users group to Read. At the same time, let's suppose that you also have NTFS permissions set on that folder. Let's say that you've applied the Change permission for the Users group on that folder in NTFS. So now, you have conflicting permissions: Read at the share level and Change at the NTFS level. The net result is that members of the Users group are granted only the ability to Read the files within that folder; they cannot make any changes to those files because the most restrictive permissions always win.

As you can see, conflicting permissions may make it difficult to decipher which permissions users are granted when they are accessing files over the network. Therefore, the best practice is to place all shared network data and applications on NTFS drive volumes and set the appropriate security permissions for users and groups at the NTFS level. Do not change the default shared folder permissions; leave them at Full Control for the Everyone group. The most restrictive permissions apply, so all NTFS permissions "flow through" the network share. NTFS security settings can then apply equally to both local users and network users, and administrators have to manage only one set of permissions.

Local Accounts vs. Domain Accounts

In Windows NT and Windows 2000 environments, user accounts and group accounts always participate in one of two security contexts: workgroup security (also known as *peer-to-peer networking*) and domain security. Workgroup security is the default security context for individual and networked Windows NT Workstation 4 and Windows 2000 Professional computers that *are not members* of a Windows NT Server or Windows 2000 Server domain. Workgroups are logical groupings of computers that do *not* share a centrally managed user and group database. Local users and groups are managed from each computer's Local Users And Groups folder within the Computer Management console. You must maintain users and groups separately on each computer. No centralized management scheme exists within a workgroup environment; duplicate user and group accounts must exist on each computer to grant and control access permissions on each workstation's individual resources. User and group accounts are stored within a local database on each Windows 2000 Professional computer.

In a Windows NT Server/Windows 2000 Server domain network environment, on the other hand, the domain acts as a central administration point for managing users, groups, and security permissions. A *domain* is simply a logical grouping of computers that share a centrally managed database. Duplicate user and group accounts are unnecessary and unwarranted within the domain security context. Users simply log on to the domain from any domain member computer and their domain group memberships, along with their user rights, follow them wherever they travel throughout the domain.

A Windows 2000 Server Active Directory domain maintains a domain-wide database of users and groups that is referred to as the *directory*. The Active Directory database is physically stored on domain controller computers. The Active Directory can contain much detailed information about its users. The Active Directory database is *replicated* and *synchronized* with all the other domain controllers within a domain. For Windows NT Server domains, domain group memberships can travel with users across domains, provided that the proper trust relationships have been established among domains. For Windows 2000 Server Active Directory domains, group memberships can travel with users throughout the entire forest.

The Windows 2000 Logon Process

When a Windows 2000 Professional computer initially boots, the boot process ends with the system displaying the Welcome To Windows dialog box. The Ctrl+Alt+Delete keystroke sequence invokes the Winlogon process, which runs as a service in the background on Windows 2000 machines, unless you, as an administrator, have set up an automatic logon procedure, or if you have removed the Windows 2000 Professional requirement for users to press Ctrl+Alt+Delete to log on to the system. This keystroke combination advances you to the Log On To Windows dialog box, where you are prompted for a valid User Name and Password. By clicking on the Options button, you can log on using a Dial-Up Networking connection. Another option, if the computer is a member of a domain, is that you can select to log on to a domain or to log on to the local system by using the Log On To drop-down list.

After you enter your logon credentials and click OK, the Winlogon process passes this information to the Windows 2000 Local Security Authority (LSA) subsystem, which compares the information you entered with the user information stored within the local security database for the system. When you are logging on to a domain, the Winlogon process forwards the user logon information that was entered to the LSA, which then forwards the information to the Netlogon process. The Netlogon process locates a domain controller computer, where the information gets compared to the domain's directory database of valid users and passwords. Once the user and password information gets processed and the results are returned, if the Winlogon process can confirm that the user's logon credentials are valid, an *access token* is generated for the user and the user is permitted to log on.

Once the user has been allowed to log on to the system, the Windows 2000 operating system shell (Windows Explorer) launches to provide the user's desktop. The user's access token that gets generated is like a *passport with various admission tickets* attached. The access token is similar to a passport in that users "carry" it with them wherever they go. The admission tickets that come with the passport consist of a list of objects and resources that users can access. In Windows 2000, users are granted two types of access control settings:

- *Rights*—Windows 2000 user rights determine what privileges the user has to interact with the operating system (e.g., shut down the system, install software, log on locally, log on over the network, and so on). Administrators for Windows 2000 Professional computers can modify the default rights for users through the Local Security Settings snap-in of the Microsoft Management Console (MMC), shown in Figure 2.5.

- *Permissions*—Windows 2000 permissions pertain to what the user can do to objects (e.g., permissions for reading, creating, modifying, or deleting files, folders, or printers). Windows 2000 objects include a wide variety of items in addition to files, folders, and printers, including processes, threads, ports, and devices.

Access Control Lists (ACLs)

Every object within Windows 2000 Professional has various properties associated with it. One of those properties is the ACL. The ACL for an object delineates the specific users and groups that have been granted access to the object, along with the particular security permissions that have been granted to each one of those listed users and groups. To view the ACL for an object, like a folder or a file, right-click the object, click Properties, and then click the Security tab, shown

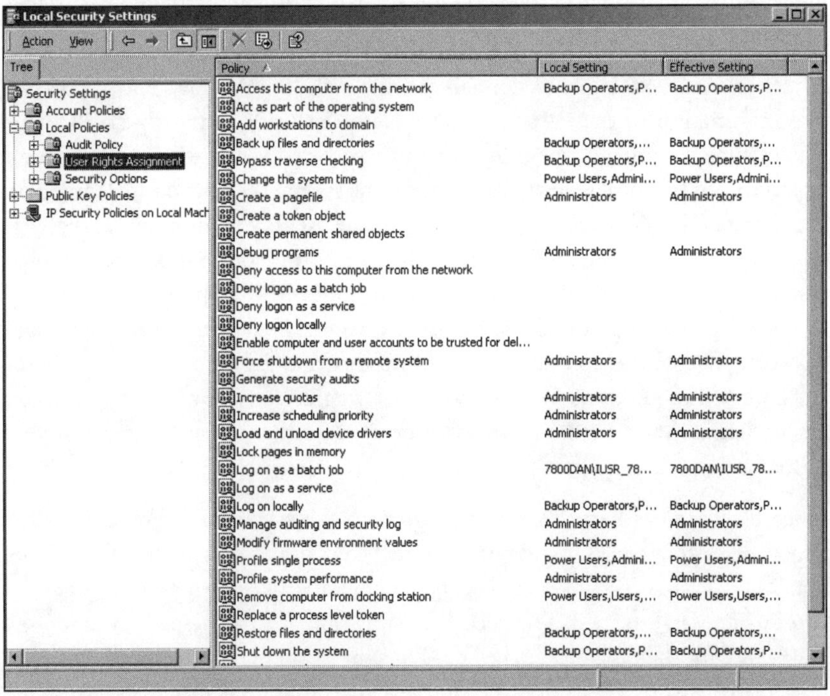

Figure 2.5 User Rights Assignment is highlighted in the Local Security Settings snap-in.

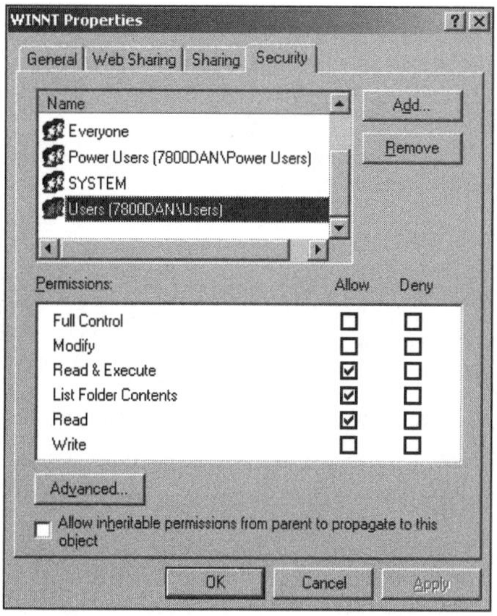

Figure 2.6 The Security tab of WINNT Properties.

in Figure 2.6. NTFS uses the information stored within ACLs to allow or deny access permissions on files and folders to users.

Another way to view and modify the ACL for a file or folder is by employing the command line tool **CACLS.exe**, shown in Figure 2.7.
Here's the **CACLS.exe** command syntax, which is explained in Table 2.3:

```
CACLS filename [/T] [/E] [/C] [/G user:perm] [/R user [...]]
[/P user:perm [...]] [/D user [...]]
```

You can use wildcard characters (* or ?) to specify more than one file or folder for a given command as well as specify more than one user in a command. ACLs are broken down into basic and advanced security permission entries.

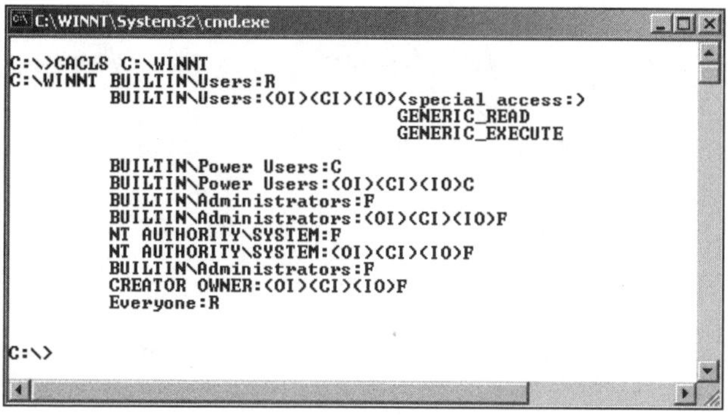

Figure 2.7 Viewing an object's Access Control List using **CACLS.exe**.

Table 2.3 Command line options for the CACLS.exe utility.

Option	Description
filename	Displays ACLs for the specified file or folder.
/t	Changes ACLs of specified files in the current directory and all subdirectories.
/e	Edits the ACL instead of replacing it.
/c	Continues to change ACLs and ignores errors.
/g user:perm	Grants specified user access rights. The permission can be Read (R), Write (W), Change (write) (C), and Full Control (F).
/r user	Revokes a specified user's access rights (valid only with **/e**).
/p user:perm	Replaces a specified user's access rights. The permission can be: None (N), Read (R), Write (W), Change (write) (C), and Full Control (F).
/d user	Denies access to the specified user.

Basic Permissions

Basic permissions are actually comprised of predefined advanced NTFS permissions and are applied per user and per group. Individual file permissions differ slightly from the permissions that apply to folders. Table 2.4 highlights the basic permissions available for files, whereas Table 2.5 outlines the basic permissions available for folders.

Note: *The List Folder Contents permission is inherited by folders but not files, and it should appear only when you view folder permissions. Read & Execute is inherited by both files and folders and is always present when you view file or folder permissions.*

Table 2.4 Basic NTFS security permissions for files for specified users and groups.

Permission	Description
Full Control	Allows/denies full access to the file. Includes the ability to read, write, delete, modify, change permissions, and take ownership of the file.
Modify	Allows/denies the ability to read, write, delete, modify, and read permissions for the file.
Read & Execute	Allows/denies specified users and groups the ability to execute the file and read its contents, read the file's attributes and extended attributes, and read the file's permissions.
Read	Allows/denies the same permissions as Read & Execute except for Execute File.
Write	Allows/denies the ability to write data to the file, create files and append data, and write attributes and extended attributes.

Table 2.5 Basic NTFS security permissions for folders for specified users and groups.

Permission	Description
Full Control	Allows/denies full access to objects within the folder. Includes the ability to read, write, delete, modify, change permissions, and take ownership of the folder.
Modify	Allows/denies the ability to read, write, delete, modify, and read permissions for the folder.
Read & Execute	Allows/denies specified users and groups the ability to traverse the folder, execute files within the folder, list its contents, read its contents, read the folder's attributes and extended attributes, and read the folder's permissions.
List Folder Contents	Allows/denies essentially the same permissions as Read & Execute. Allows/denies the ability to display files and subfolders, but this permission does not affect a user's ability to run (execute) an application program as the Read & Execute permission does.
Read	Allows/denies the same permissions as List Folder Contents except for Traverse Folder and Execute File.
Write	Allows/denies the ability to create files and write data, create folders and append data, and write attributes and extended attributes.

By default, NTFS security permissions are inherited from an object's parent. An administrator can manually override the default inheritance and can explicitly configure ACL settings. To disable permission inheritance, deselect the Allow Inheritable Permissions From Parent To Propagate To This Object checkbox on the Security tab of the folder's Properties sheet. As soon as you uncheck this box, the Security message box, shown in Figure 2.8, appears. It prompts you to either copy the existing permissions or remove them entirely.

Advanced Permissions

NTFS advanced permissions are the building blocks for basic permissions. In Windows 2000, advanced permissions allow administrators to have very granular

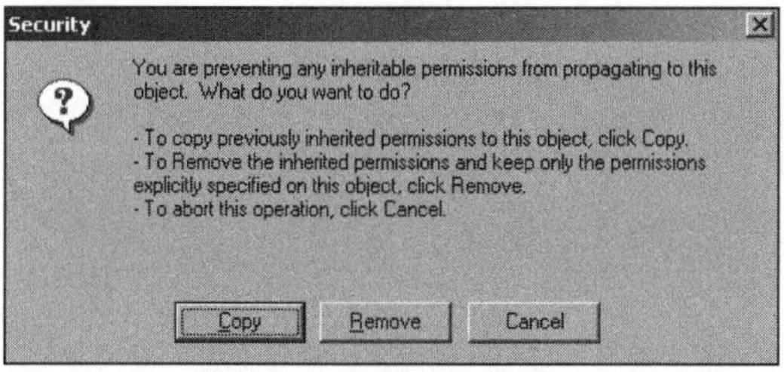

Figure 2.8 The Security message box.

control over exactly what types of access users can have over files and folders. Advanced permissions are somewhat hidden from view. They allow administrators to fine-tune ACL (security) settings. The Security tab in a file or folder's Properties sheet notifies you when advanced permissions are present. Click the Advanced button to view, add, modify, or remove advanced permissions. Figure 2.9 shows you how Windows 2000 notifies you that more than just basic permissions exist for an object. At the bottom of the Security tab, the system displays a text message notification just to the right of the Advanced button that says Additional Permissions Are Present But Not Viewable Here. Press Advanced To See Them.

After you click Advanced, you see the Access Control Settings dialog box, which shows each access control setting that has been applied per user and per group. To view individual advanced permission entries, click one of the users or groups listed and then click the View/Edit button. The Permission Entry dialog box, shown in Figure 2.10, appears. It gives administrators very fine control over individual users' and groups' abilities to manipulate data and program files that are stored on NTFS drive volumes.

From this dialog box, you can:

1. Change the Name so that this permission entry applies to some other user or group.
2. Modify the Apply Onto drop-down list to specify exactly where these advanced permissions should apply.
3. Alter the actual permission entries themselves by marking or clearing the Allow or Deny checkbox for each permission that you want to affect.

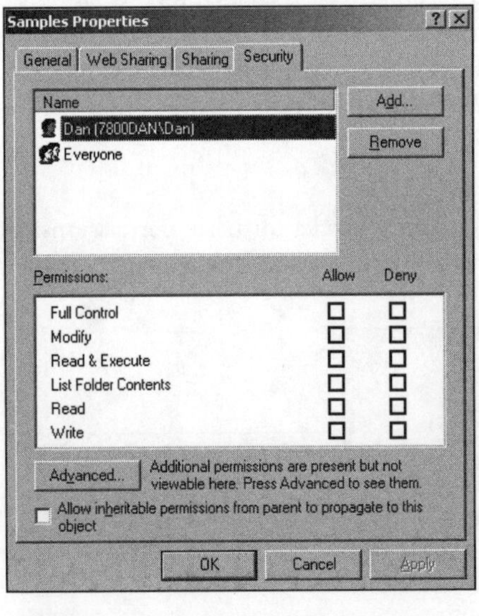

Figure 2.9 The Security tab of Samples Properties.

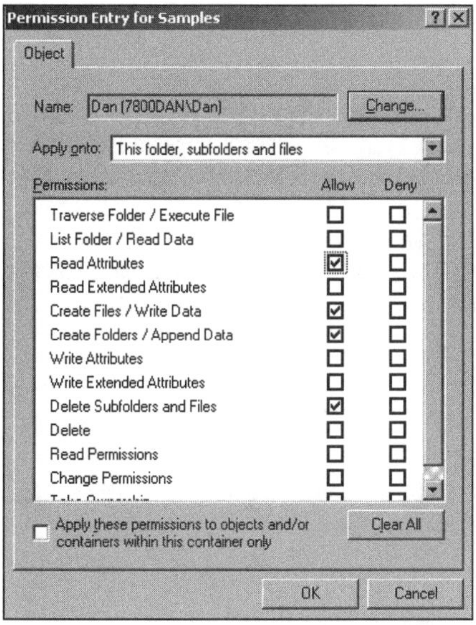

Figure 2.10 The Object tab of Permission Entry For Samples.

TIP

To change NTFS security permissions, you must be the owner of the file or folder whose permissions you want to modify, or the owner must grant you permission to make modifications to the object's security settings. Groups or users who are granted Full Control for a folder can delete files and subfolders *within* that folder *regardless* of the permissions protecting those files and subfolders. If the checkboxes for the Security tab under Permissions are *shaded*, the file or folder has *inherited* the permissions from the parent folder. By cleaning the Allow inheritable permissions from parent to propagate to this object checkbox, you can copy those inherited permissions and turn them into explicit permissions, or you can remove them entirely and manually establish new explicit permissions.

Table 2.6 concisely defines Windows 2000 advanced permissions.

TIP

NTFS security permissions are *cumulative*. Users obtain permissions by having them assigned directly to their user accounts in addition to attaining permissions via group memberships. Users retain all permissions as they are assigned. If a user named Dan has the Allow Read permission for the Graphics folder and if Dan is a member of the Users group, which has been assigned Allow Write for the same folder, Dan has both the Allow Read and Allow Write permissions. Permissions continue to accumulate. However, Deny entries always override Allow entries for the same permission type (Read, Modify, Write, and so on).

Table 2.6 Advanced NTFS security permission entries for files and folders.	
Permission	**Description**
Traverse Folder/Execute File	Allows or denies moving through folders to reach other files or folders, even if the user has no permissions for the traversed folders (applies to folders only). Traverse Folder takes effect only when the group or user is not granted the *Bypass traverse checking* user right in the Group Policy snap-in. (By default, the Everyone group is given the *Bypass traverse checking* user right.)
Execute File	Allows or denies running application program files. Setting the Traverse Folder permission on a folder does not automatically set the Execute File permission on all files within that folder.
List Folder/Read Data	Allows or denies viewing file names and subfolder names within the folder.
Read Data	Allows or denies viewing data in files.
Read Attributes	Allows or denies viewing the attributes—such as read only, hidden, and archive—of a file or folder.
Read Extended Attributes	Allows or denies viewing the extended attributes of a file or folder. Some extended attributes are defined by application programs and can vary by application. The NTFS compression and encryption attributes are considered extended (or advanced) attributes.
Create Files/Write Data	Allows or denies creating files within a folder (applies to folders only).
Write Data	Allows or denies making changes to a file and overwriting the existing data (applies to files only).
Write Attributes	Allows or denies changing the attributes—such as read-only or hidden—of a file or folder.
Write Extended Attributes	Allows or denies changing the extended attributes of a file or folder. Extended attributes are defined by programs and may vary by program. Some extended attributes are defined by application programs and can vary by application. The NTFS compression and encryption attributes are considered extended (or advanced) attributes.
Delete Subfolders and Files	Allows or denies deleting subfolders and files, even if the Delete permission has not been granted on the subfolder or file.
Delete	Allows or denies deleting the file or folder. If you don't have the Delete permission on a file or folder, you can still delete it if you have been granted Delete Subfolders and Files on the parent folder.

(continued)

Table 2.6 Advanced NTFS security permission entries for files and folders *(continued)*.

Permission	Description
Read Permissions	Allows or denies reading permissions of the file or folder.
Change Permissions	Allows or denies changing permissions—such as Full Control, Read, and Modify—of the file or folder.
Take Ownership	Allows or denies taking ownership of a file or folder. The owner of a file or folder can always change permissions on it, regardless of any other permissions that have been assigned to protect the file or folder.
Create Folders/Append Data	Allows or denies creating folders within a folder.
Append Data	Allows or denies making changes to the end of a file, but not changing, deleting, or overwriting existing data (applies to files only).

Default NTFS Security Permissions

By default, all NTFS-formatted drive volumes are assigned the Allow Full Control permission for the Everyone group for the root of each drive. Folders and subfolders within each drive volume automatically inherit this default permission setting. Unfortunately, this setting leaves your Windows 2000 systems very vulnerable. By default, any user who can log on to the system, either locally or over the network, can modify or delete some or all of the files and folders that reside on the system! As a best practice, you should remove the Everyone group's permissions entry from all drive volumes, except from the systemroot drive, where the Windows 2000 system files are stored. When you install Windows 2000 Professional on an NTFS volume, the systemroot folder (e.g., C:\WINNT) is automatically assigned special default security permissions for the following groups: Administrators, Creator Owner, Everyone, Power Users, System, and Users.

The Everyone group's permissions are assigned *no Allows* and *no Denies* for the systemroot folder by default. Users must be granted permission to access a file or a folder with the type of access specified (Read, Modify, Full Control, and so on). If the user's account, or one of the groups that the user is a member of, is not specifically granted or denied permission, the user cannot access the file or folder. This is known as an *implied* or *implicit* Deny.

TIP

You should not change the default security settings for the systemroot folder and its subfolders. Modifying the default permissions for the Windows 2000 Professional system files can have very adverse effects on the system. In addition to not changing its default permissions, you should never attempt to compress or encrypt the systemroot folder or any of its subfolders. Compression or encryption placed on the system folders can render Windows 2000 Professional unstable or possibly unbootable.

NTFS Permission Conflicts

Obviously, a user may be a member of several different groups. You can apply NTFS permissions to both users and groups for access control on resources such as files and folders. For security permissions assigned to a user that conflict with other security permissions that have been granted to groups of which the user is also a member, the most *liberal* permissions take precedence for that user. The one *overriding* exception is any explicit Deny permission entry. Deny permissions always take precedence over Allow permissions.

TIP

Just as Deny permissions always take precedence over Allow permissions, explicit permissions always override inherited permissions.

Monitoring, Managing, and Troubleshooting Access to Files and Folders

NTFS for Windows 2000 Professional offers several accessibility features that help administrators maintain and safeguard applications and data. In addition to providing local and network access control permissions, NTFS offers native data compression to save disk space. Folders that do not implement NTFS data compression can take advantage of native data encryption to help protect the confidentiality of data. For troubleshooting resource access, you can enable auditing for folders and files housed on NTFS volumes.

Configuring, Managing, and Troubleshooting NTFS File and Folder Compression

Unlike previous data compression schemes like DoubleSpace or DriveSpace for the Windows 9x platform (where you had to compress entire drive volumes), Windows 2000 NTFS data compression works folder by folder (or even file by file). NTFS compression is simply an advanced (or extended) file system attribute that you can apply to files and folders. NTFS data compression enables you to compress individual files or folders. You can compress individual files within uncompressed folders; compressed files and folders are identified by being displayed in blue.

NTFS Compression for Files

To enable compression for a specific file, follow these steps:

1. Right-click the file from Windows Explorer or My Computer.
2. Click Properties.
3. Click the Advanced button in the Compress Or Encrypt Attributes section of the Advanced Attributes dialog box, shown in Figure 2.11. This dialog box gives you mutually exclusive options to either Compress Contents To Save Disk Space or Encrypt Contents To Secure Data.
4. Click the Compress Contents To Save Disk Space checkbox.
5. Click OK in the Advanced Attributes dialog box.
6. Click OK in the file's Properties sheet.

The file name that gets compressed will be displayed in the color blue, indicating that it is now a compressed file. Figure 2.12 shows uncompressed files.

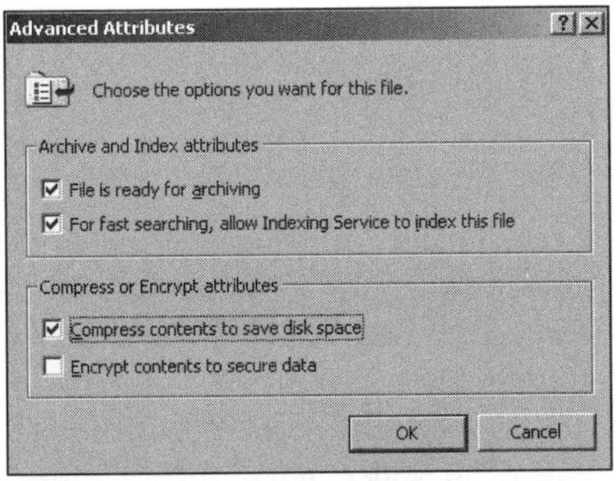

Figure 2.11 The Advanced Attributes dialog box.

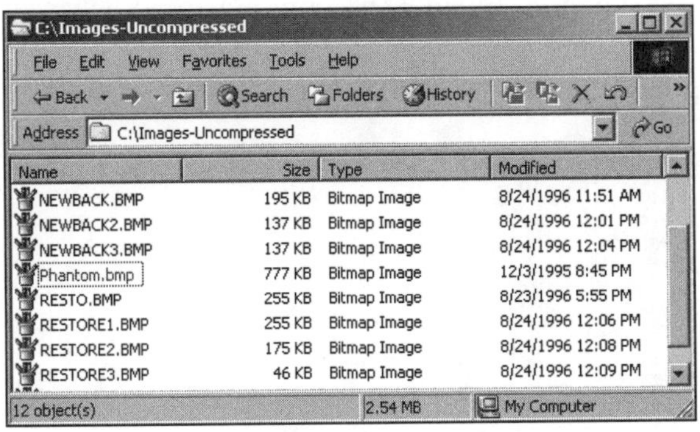

Figure 2.12 Uncompressed files.

To uncompress a specific file, be sure that sufficient disk space exists for the uncompressed size of the file, and then follow these steps:

1. Right-click the file from Windows Explorer or My Computer.
2. Click Properties.
3. Click the Advanced button in the Attributes section.
4. Deselect the Compress Contents To Save Disk Space checkbox.
5. Click OK in the Advanced Attributes dialog box.
6. Click OK in the file's Properties sheet.

NTFS Compression for Folders

You turn on compression for NTFS folders in the same manner as for files:

1. Right-click the folder from Windows Explorer or My Computer.
2. Click Properties.
3. Click the Advanced button in the Attributes section.
4. Select the Compress Contents To Save Disk Space checkbox.
5. Click OK in the Advanced Attributes dialog box.
6. You are attempting to compress an entire folder, not just a single file, so the Confirm Attribute Changes dialog box, shown in Figure 2.13, appears. It prompts the user to specify which files and/or folders compression is applied to. If you click Cancel, you can abort the data compression process. In our case, however, we don't want to do this. Therefore, click one of the two available options—either Apply Changes To This Folder Only or Apply Changes To This Folder, Subfolders And Files.
7. Click OK after you have chosen an option. The Confirm Attribute Changes dialog box closes, and the compression attributes are applied to the files and any subfolders you specified.

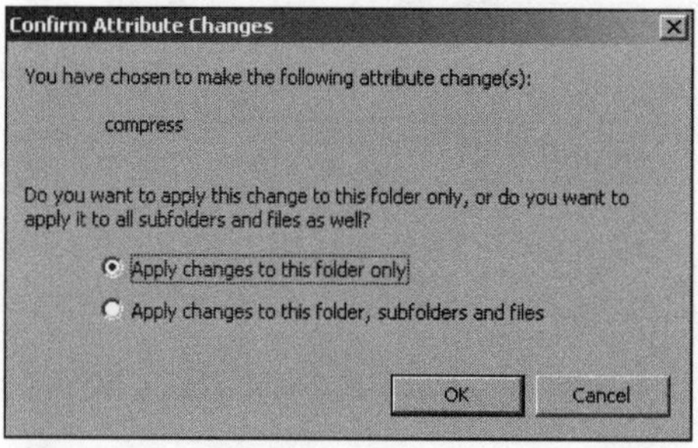

Figure 2.13 The Confirm Attribute Changes dialog box.

Figure 2.14 illustrates the significant difference that compression can make on saving valuable disk storage space. By right-clicking a folder and selecting Properties, you can determine the folder's actual physical size on the disk, as shown under Size On Disk. By comparing folders with identical contents, one compressed and the other uncompressed, you can readily assess the impact that compression can make.

To uncompress a folder, first make sure that enough disk space is available to accommodate the *uncompressed* size of the folder. Next, simply reverse the previously outlined procedure.

Moving and Copying Compressed Files and Folders

Moving or copying compressed files and folders to non-NTFS drive volumes results in those objects being stored in their uncompressed state for the destination drive volume. If you *move* a compressed file or folder into an *uncompressed* folder, the object *retains* its compressed attribute; it remains compressed. If you *copy* a compressed file or folder into an *uncompressed* folder, the object *inherits* its attribute from the destination folder; it loses its compression attribute and becomes uncompressed within the target folder. Of course, the original file or folder that is copied remains unchanged; it stays compressed.

If you *move* an *uncompressed* file or folder into a *compressed* folder located on the same drive volume, the object *retains* its *uncompressed* attribute; it remains *uncompressed*. If you *move* an *uncompressed* file or folder into a *compressed* folder located on a different drive volume, or from a non-NTFS volume, the object

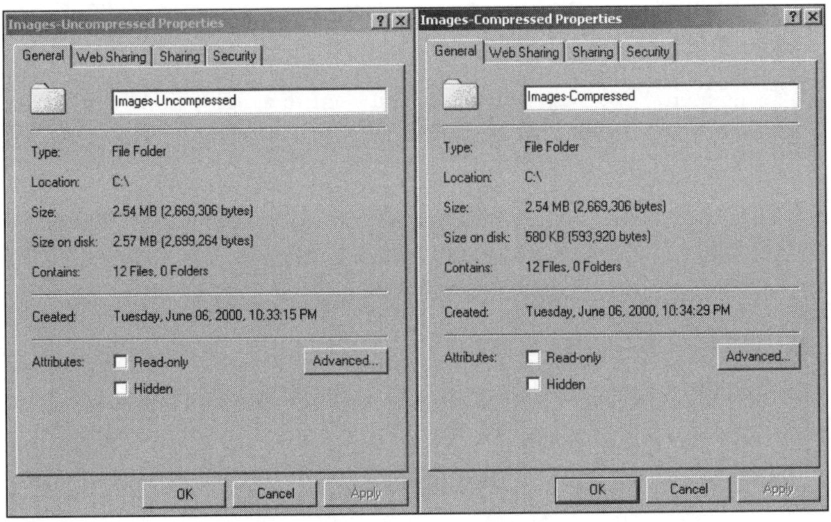

Figure 2.14 Comparing compressed and uncompressed sizes of files and folders.

inherits the compression. If you *copy* an *uncompressed* file or folder into a *compressed* folder, the object *inherits* its attribute from the destination folder; it gains the compression attribute and becomes compressed within the target folder. Of course, the original file or folder that is copied remains unchanged; it stays uncompressed.

TIP: Compressed files and folders still require NTFS security permission settings to ensure data integrity.

Controlling Access to Files and Folders by Using Permissions

Users attain access to NTFS files and folders by virtue of being granted explicit or implicit (inherited) permissions for those resources directly to their user account or through access permissions granted to groups to which the users belong. To assign Read Only security permissions to a user or a group for a specific folder, follow these steps:

1. Right-click the folder on which you wish to apply permissions and select Properties.
2. Click the Security tab.
3. If permissions are being inherited for the user and/or group that you want to work with, deselect the Allow Inheritable Permissions From Parent To Propagate To This Object checkbox.
4. If the user(s) or group(s) to which you want to assign permissions do not currently appear, click the Add button.
5. From the Select Users, Computers, Or Groups dialog box, shown in Figure 2.15, select the group or user to which you want to assign permissions. This dialog box lets you choose from available users and groups for assigning NTFS security permissions onto files and folders.
6. Click the Add button.
7. Click OK to return to the Security tab of the folder's Properties sheet.
8. Verify that the Allow checkboxes are marked for the Read And Execute, List Folder Contents, and Read permissions.
9. Click OK to accept your settings.

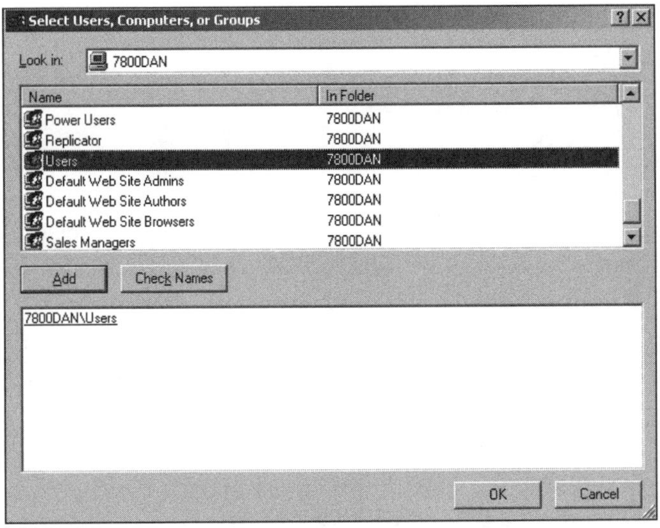

Figure 2.15 The Select Users, Computers, Or Groups dialog box.

Denying Access to a Resource

Deny permissions always override Allow permissions, so you can be assured that once you establish Deny permissions for a particular user or group on a resource, no other combination of Allow permissions through group memberships can circumvent the Deny. To assign Deny security permissions to a user or a group for a specific folder, follow these steps:

1. Right-click the folder on which you wish to apply permissions and select Properties.
2. Click the Security tab.
3. If permissions are being inherited for the user and/or group that you want to work with, deselect the Allow Inheritable Permissions From Parent To Propagate To This Object checkbox.
4. If the user(s) or group(s) to which you want to assign permissions do not currently appear, click the Add button.
5. Select the group or user that you want to assign permissions to from the Select Users, Computers, Or Groups dialog box.
6. Click the Add button.
7. Click OK to be returned to the Security tab of the folder's Properties sheet.

8. Click the Deny checkbox for each permission that you wish to explicitly disallow.
9. Click OK to accept your settings.

If you deny the Read permission for a group on a particular folder, any member of that group is denied the ability to read the contents of that folder. When you assign Deny permissions for a user or a group on a file or folder, as soon as you click OK in the Properties sheet, a Security message box, shown in Figure 2.16, appears. It reminds you that Deny permissions take precedence over Allow permissions.

Click Yes in the Security message box to have the new Deny permissions take effect. When users who are members of the group that was assigned Deny permissions for reading the folder attempt to gain access to that folder, they are greeted by an Access Is Denied message box, shown in Figure 2.17.

Optimizing Access to Files and Folders

The best practice is to always assign NTFS security permissions to groups rather than to individual users. You should place users into appropriate groups and set NTFS permissions on those groups. In this manner, permissions are easier to assign and maintain.

NTFS Permissions: Moving and Copying Files and Folders

Moving or copying files and folders from an NTFS drive volume to network drives or other media that are non-NTFS volumes results in the *loss of all NTFS security permission settings* for the objects moved or copied. The result of moving or copying NTFS files and folders to different NTFS folders varies depending upon whether the objects are being moved or copied, and depending upon the destination drive volume. Table 2.7 shows the different effects on NTFS permissions when copying files and folders versus moving files and folders.

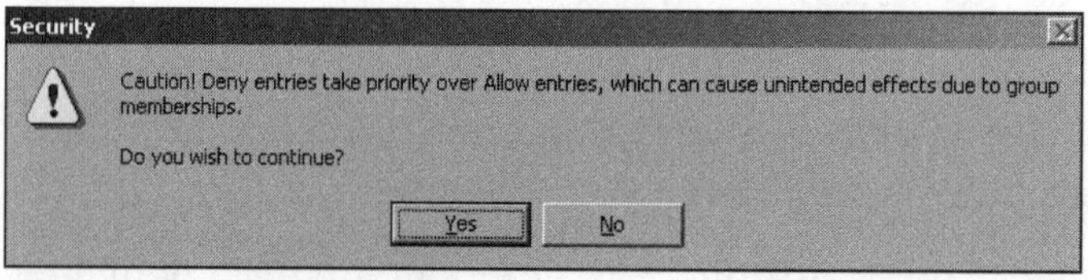

Figure 2.16 A Security message box.

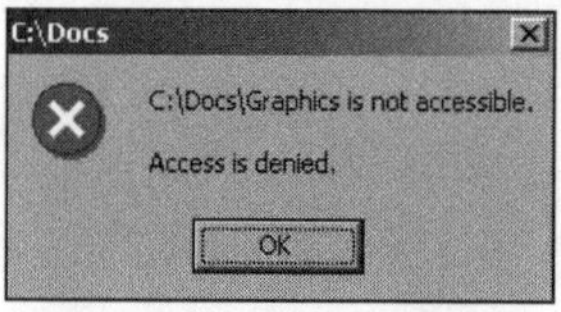

Figure 2.17 The Access Is Denied message.

Table 2.7 NTFS permissions that are retained or inherited when you move and copy files and folders.

Type of Transfer	Effective Permissions after Move or Copy
Moving within the same NTFS volume	Files and folders that are moved retain their permissions from the source folder.
Moving to a different NTFS volume	Files and folders that are moved inherit their permissions from the destination folder.
Copying within the same NTFS volume	Files and folders that are copied inherit their permissions from the destination folder.
Copying to a different NTFS volume	Files and folders that are copied inherit their permissions from the destination folder.

The standard Windows 2000 **xcopy.exe** command line utility offers **-O** and **-X** options that retain an object's NTFS permissions in addition to inheriting the destination folder's permissions. The **-X** switch also retains any auditing settings (which are discussed later in this chapter). To retain only an object's source permissions without inheriting any permissions from the destination folder, use the **scopy.exe** tool or the **robocopy.exe** tool from the *Windows 2000 Professional Resource Kit* or the *Windows 2000 Server Resource Kit*.

Taking Ownership of Files and Folders

A user who has ownership of a file or folder can transfer ownership of it to a different user or to a group. Administrators can grant users the ability to take ownership of specified files and folders. In addition, administrators have the authority to take ownership of any file or folder for themselves. Object ownership cannot be assigned to others; a user must have permission to take ownership of an object.

Changing ownership of files and folders can become necessary when someone who is responsible for certain files and folders leaves an organization without granting any other users permissions to them. To take ownership of a folder as an administrator, follow these steps:

1. Log on to the system as the administrator or an equivalent user.
2. Right-click the folder from Windows Explorer or My Computer and select Properties.
3. Click the Security tab.
4. Click the Advanced button.
5. Click the Owner tab in the Access Control Settings dialog box.

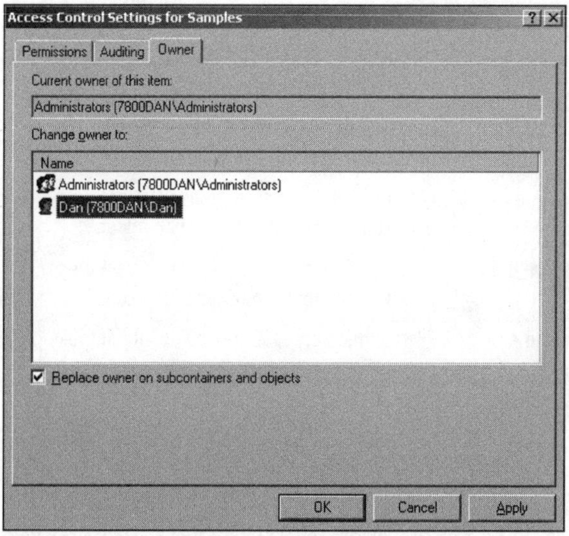

Figure 2.18 Changing the ownership of a file or folder.

6. Click the name of the person in the Change Owner To section to change the folder's ownership, as shown in Figure 2.18.
7. If you also want the ownership to change for the subfolders and files, click the Replace Owner On Subcontainers And Objects checkbox.
8. Click OK in the Access Control Settings dialog box.
9. Click OK in the Properties sheet.

Auditing System Access

Windows 2000 Professional allows administrators to audit both user and system events using the auditing feature. When auditing is enabled for specific events, the occurrence of the events triggers a log entry in the Windows 2000 Professional Security Log. You view the security log with the Event Viewer snap-in of the MMC. By default, auditing is turned off. Before you enable auditing, you should formulate an audit policy to determine which workstations will be audited and which events audited on them. When planning the events to audit, you also need to decide whether you will audit successes and/or failures for each event.

Auditing for the local Windows 2000 system is enabled through the Local Security Settings snap-in of the MMC, shown in Figure 2.19. You must initially turn on auditing from the Local Security Settings console for each type of event that you want to monitor.

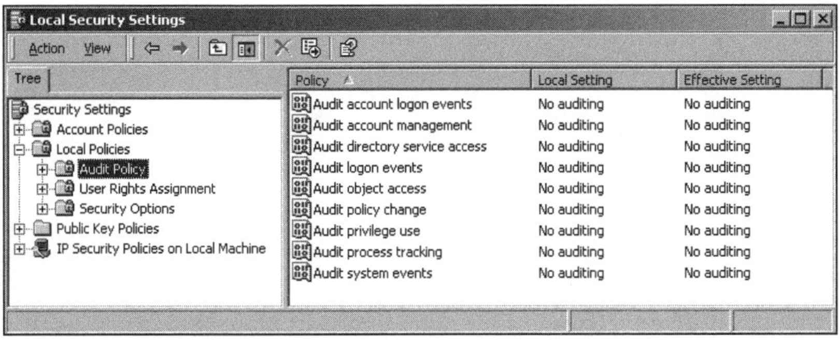

Figure 2.19 The Local Security Settings console.

You can audit several types of events, such as:

- File and folder access
- Logons and logoffs
- System shutdowns and restarts
- Changes to user and group accounts
- Changes attempted on Active Directory objects if the Windows 2000 Professional computer is a member of a Windows 2000 Server domain

When you track successful events, you can gauge the how often different resources are used. This information can be useful when you are planning for future resource allocation. By tracking failed events, you can become aware of possible security intrusions. Unsuccessful logon attempts, attempts to change security permissions, or efforts to take ownership of files or folders can all point to someone trying to gain unauthorized access to the system or the network. If such attempts occur at odd hours, these events take on an even more suspicious tone. To enable auditing on a Windows 2000 Professional system, follow these steps:

1. Launch the Local Security Policy MMC snap-in from the Start|Programs|Administrative Tools folder.
2. At the Local Security Settings console, expand the Local Policies folder and then click Audit Policy.
3. Double-click the event policy to choose which one you want to enable and to display the Local Security Policy Setting dialog box, shown in Figure 2.20. To enable object access auditing, double-click the Audit Object Access policy (refer back to Figure 2.19).

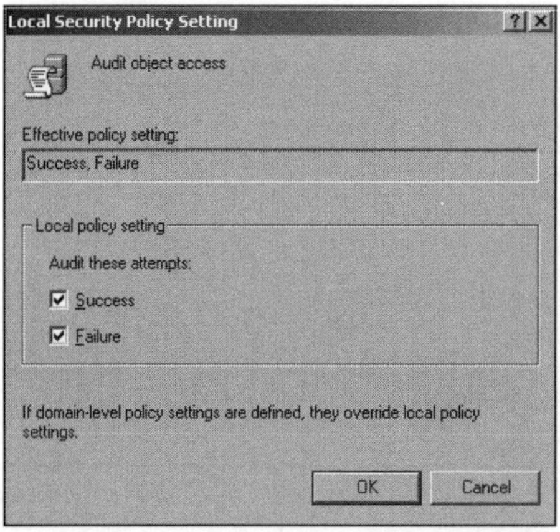

Figure 2.20 The Local Security Policy Setting dialog box for the Audit Object Access event.

4. Click the Success checkbox, the Failure checkbox, or both checkboxes.
5. Click OK.
6. Close the Local Security Settings console and restart the computer.

Once you have turned on audit tracking for object access events, you need to specify which files and folders you want to audit. You should be fairly selective about which ones you choose to audit. If you have enabled auditing for successes as well as failures, the system's Security Event log may become filled very quickly if you are auditing heavily used files and folders. To enable audit logging for specific files and folders, follow these steps:

1. Log on to the system as the administrator or an equivalent user.
2. Right-click the file or folder from Windows Explorer or My Computer and select Properties.
3. Click the Security tab.
4. Click the Advanced button.
5. Click the Auditing tab in the Access Control Settings dialog box.
6. Click the Add button.
7. Click the user or group that you want to track for access to the file or folder and click OK. The Auditing Entry dialog box, shown in Figure 2.21, appears.
8. Select each access event that you want to track by marking each event's associated Successful checkbox, Failed checkbox, or both.
9. By default, audit settings apply to the current folder, subfolders, and files. You can change this behavior by clicking on the Apply Onto drop-down list.

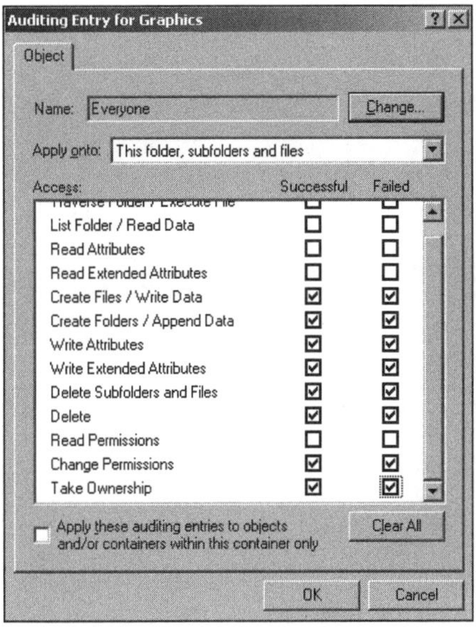

Figure 2.21 The Auditing Entry dialog box.

10. Click OK in the Auditing Entry dialog box.
11. Click OK in the Access Control Settings dialog box.
12. Click OK in the Properties sheet.

After you have properly set up auditing, all events that meet your auditing criteria are logged into the system's Event Viewer Security Log. You access the Event Viewer console from Start|Administrative Tools|Event Viewer or by right-clicking on the My Computer desktop icon and selecting Manage. You'll find the Event Viewer beneath the System Tools folder in the Computer Management console. By selecting the Security Log, you can view all of the auditing events that the system has recorded based on the parameters you have set. If a user deletes an object, for example, that event is listed with all the pertinent information in the security log, shown in Figure 2.22. Double-clicking on an event in the log displays the detailed information.

Keeping Data Private with Encrypting File System (EFS)

Microsoft designed the new EFS for Windows 2000 to ensure the confidentiality of sensitive data. EFS employs public key/private key-based cryptography. EFS works only in the Windows 2000 NTFS 5. Its use is transparent to users. You can either compress or encrypt files and folders, but you can't do both. Files that are encrypted using EFS remain encrypted even if you move or rename them. Encrypted files that are backed up or copied also retain their encryption attributes as long as they reside on NTFS-formatted drive volumes. EFS leaves

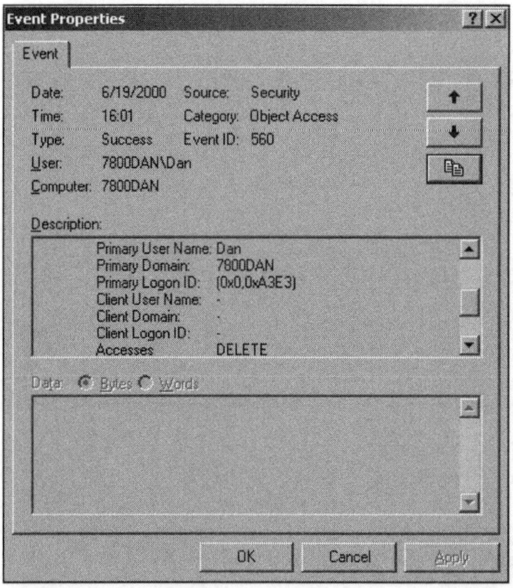

Figure 2.22 An Event Properties window from the Event Viewer security log.

no file remnants behind because it modifies an encrypted file, nor does it leave any traces of decrypted data from encrypted files in temporary files or in the Windows 2000 pagefile. You can encrypt and decrypt files and folders from the graphical user interface (GUI) using Windows Explorer as well as from the command line using the **cipher.exe** tool.

The best practice for using encryption is to first encrypt a folder and then move files into the encrypted folder. Folders do not actually become encrypted; folders get marked with the encryption attribute. The files contained within an encrypted folder are the objects that actually become encrypted. You can also individually encrypt files without their having to reside within a folder that is marked for encryption. To encrypt and decrypt files physically located on a Windows 2000 server over the network, that server must be trusted for delegation. By definition, domain controllers are already trusted for delegation. Member servers require this Trust for Delegation. To encrypt a file or folder from Windows Explorer, follow these steps:

1. Right-click the file or folder and select Properties.
2. Click the Advanced button in the Compress Or Encrypt Attributes section of the General tab of the folder's Properties sheet.
3. Click the Encrypt Contents To Secure Data checkbox in the Advanced Attributes dialog box.
4. Click OK.

5. Click OK in the Properties sheet. An empty folder will then become encrypted, and any files and folders that are placed within it are encrypted. If subfolders or files exist within the folder, the Confirm Attribute Changes dialog box, shown in Figure 2.23, appears.
6. Click either Apply Changes To This Folder Only or Apply Changes To This Folder, Subfolders And Files for the object(s) that you want encryption to affect.
7. Click OK; the encryption attribute is applied to the appropriate objects.

Accessing Encrypted Files and Data Recovery Agents (DRAs)

Encryption is just an extended (or advanced) attribute of a file or folder. If you set NTFS permissions to deny the Write Extended Attributes permission on a file or folder, the users to whom you have assigned this Deny permission cannot use encryption. Once a file has the encryption attribute, only the user who encrypted it or the DRA can access it. DRAs are users who are designated as recovery agents for encrypted files. Only these users have the ability to decrypt *any* encrypted file, no matter who has encrypted it. Other users who attempt to access an encrypted file receive an Access Is Denied message. The default DRAs are:

- Local Administrator account for Windows 2000 Professional non-domain member computers
- Local Administrator account for Windows 2000 Server non-domain member computers
- Domain Administrator account for Windows 2000 Server domain controllers, Windows 2000 domain member servers, and Windows 2000 Professional domain member computers

DRAs can log on to a system and decrypt files and folders so that they are once again accessible to other users. In fact, if you remove the DRA from a standalone Windows 2000 computer or from a Windows 2000 Server domain, no Data Recovery policy is in place and EFS *prohibits* users from encrypting files and folders.

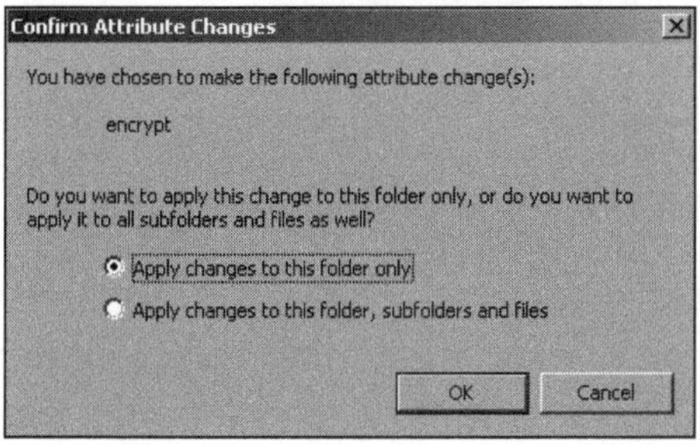

Figure 2.23 The Confirm Attribute Changes dialog box.

Moving and Copying Encrypted Files

Encrypted files that are moved or copied to another NTFS folder remain encrypted. Encrypted files that are moved or copied to a FAT or FAT32 drive volume become decrypted because EFS is supported only on NTFS 5 volumes. Files also become decrypted if they are moved or copied to a floppy disk. Users who did not originally encrypt a file or folder receive an Access Is Denied message if they try to copy an encrypted file or folder. If users other than the one who encrypted the file attempt to move it to a different NTFS volume, or to a FAT or FAT32 drive volume, they receive an Access Is Denied error message. If users other than the one who encrypted the file attempt to move the encrypted file to a different folder located on the *same* NTFS volume, the file is moved.

Managing and Troubleshooting Web Server Resources

Unlike its big brother, Windows 2000 Server, Windows 2000 Professional does not install Internet Information Services (IIS) by default. You must manually install IIS by going to the Control Panel, double-clicking the Add/Remove Programs icon, and clicking the Add/Remove Windows Components button. Mark the checkbox for Internet Information Services (IIS) and click Next to have the Windows Components Wizard install the Web server resources for you. If you *upgrade* your computer from Windows NT 4 Workstation to Windows 2000 Professional, IIS 5 is installed automatically only if you installed Peer Web Services on your previous version of Windows.

Before you can install IIS, your computer must already have the Transmission Control Protocol/Internet Protocol (TCP/IP) network protocol and its related connectivity utilities installed. In addition, Microsoft recommends that you have a Domain Name System (DNS) server available on your network for host name to IP address resolution. For very small networks, you may use a HOSTS file or an LMHOSTS file in lieu of a DNS server. A HOSTS file maps DNS host computer names to IP addresses. An LMHOSTS file maps NetBIOS computer names to IP addresses. Windows 2000 Professional looks for these two text files in the SystemRoot\system32\drivers\etc folder. Sample HOSTS and LMHOSTS files are also installed by default into this folder.

Once you have installed IIS, you manage the services from the Internet Information Services snap-in of the MMC. You can launch the IIS console by clicking on Start|Programs|Administrative Tools|Internet Service Manager. From the IIS console, you can administer the default FTP site, default Web site, and the default Simple Mail Transfer Protocol (SMTP) virtual server for the Windows 2000 Professional computer, as shown in Figure 2.24.

Additional, Web-based documentation on IIS administration is available by pointing to **http://localhost/iisHelp/iis/misc/default.asp** in your Web browser, as shown in Figure 2.25.

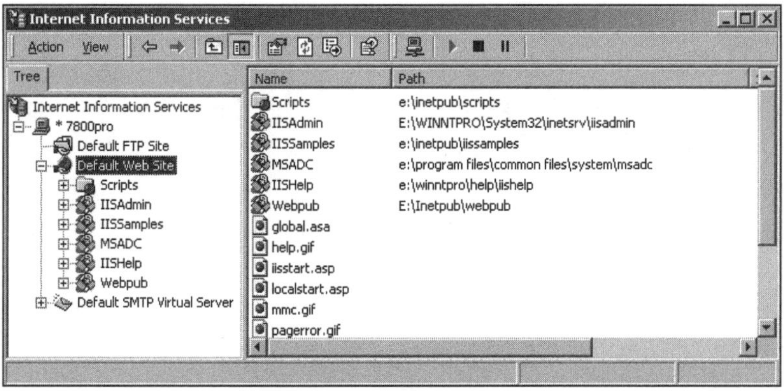

Figure 2.24 The Internet Information Services console.

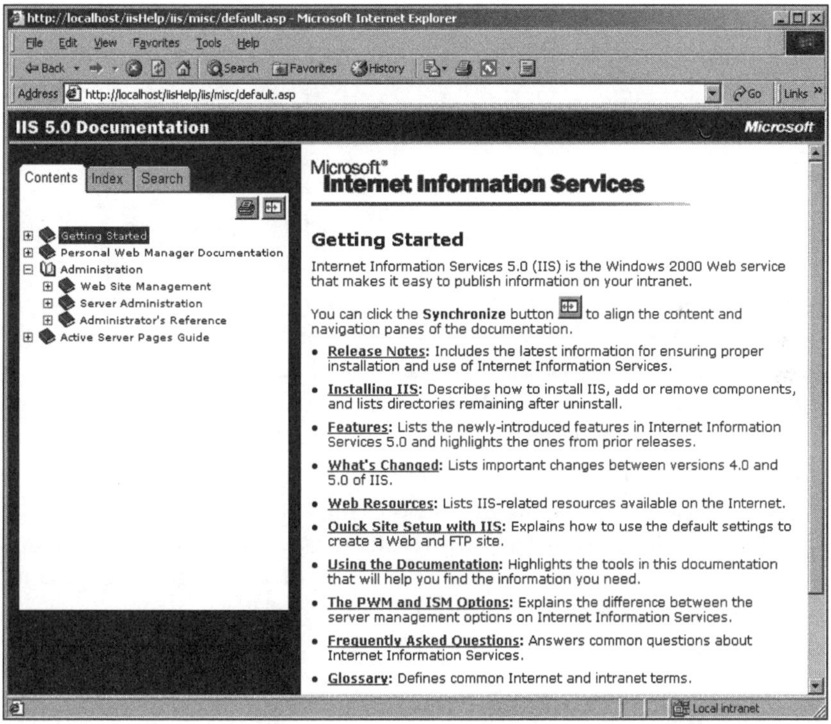

Figure 2.25 The Getting Started Web page for IIS HTML-based help documentation.

SystemRoot Console Administering the Default Web and FTP Sites

You can view and modify the settings for IIS through the IIS console by right-clicking on the computer name container in the left-hand pane of the console window and selecting Properties. From the computer name Properties sheet, you can view the system's overall Master Properties for both the World Wide Web (WWW) Service and the File Transfer Protocol (FTP) Service for all sites created on the computer. The WWW Service Master Properties that you can modify include the following:

- Web site identification, connections, and logging settings
- Performance tuning settings
- Internet Server API (ISAPI) filters
- Home directory settings
- Default document names
- Directory security
- Hypertext Transfer Protocol (HTTP) header information
- Custom HTTP error messages
- IIS 3 administration options

You can work with the properties for the default FTP site by right-clicking on the Default FTP Site folder and selecting Properties. Similarly, you can right-click the Default Web Site folder and choose Properties to configure many of the same settings that apply to the WWW Master Service Properties at the individual Web site level. You can create a new virtual directory for the default Web site by right-clicking on Default Web Site and selecting New|Virtual Directory. When the Virtual Directory Creation Wizard launches, you assign a name to the new virtual directory. You must also designate the path for the physical folder where the Web files are stored for the new virtual directory. After you have entered this information, you can complete the wizard and you will have set up a new virtual directory that users can access via the **http://computer_name/virtual_directory_name** Uniform Resource Locator (URL), also known simply as a Web address.

Troubleshooting IIS

If users are experiencing problems connecting to the default Web site, to the default FTP site, or to a new virtual directory that you have created, you can follow the steps listed in the next few sections to rectify the problem(s).

Internet Web Site

To isolate problems that may be preventing users from connecting to the Internet Web site:

- Check that the Web server contains HTML files in the drive_letter:\inetpub\wwwroot folder.
- Attempt to connect to the Web server's home directory using a browser on a computer that has a live connection to the Internet. Your Web site must have a public IP address that is registered with the InterNIC, and that public IP address must be registered with the Internet's DNS servers. For example, if your registered domain name is **ExamCram.com** and you want to view a virtual directory on that Web site named "aboutus", type in **www.ExamCram.com/aboutus** in the Address line of your Web browser. The Web page that you requested should appear within your Web browser's window.

Intranet Web Site

To isolate problems that may be preventing users from connecting to an intranet Web site:

- Check that the Web server and the client computers have active network connections.
- Verify that a Windows Internet Naming Service (WINS) and/or DNS server is available and functioning on your network for computer name to IP address name resolution.
- Go to a client computer, launch a Web browser, and type in a valid URL for the Web server computer. Intranet URLs take the **http://computer_name/home_page_name.htm** or **http://computer_name/virtual_directory_alias_name** form. Examples of this syntax are **http://computer1/myhomepage.htm** and **http://computer1/myvirtualdirectory**.

Managing Local and Network Print Devices

You manage print devices in Windows 2000 Professional from the Printers folder, which is accessible from the Control Panel or by clicking Start|Settings|Printers. When working with printing in Windows 2000, you need to fully understand the following printing terminology as defined by Microsoft:

- *Printer*—A *software* interface between the operating system and a print device. It defines ports through which print jobs get routed. Printer names direct print jobs to one or more print devices.

- *Print device*—A piece of equipment (hardware) that physically produces printed documents. A print device may be attached to a local computer or connected via a network interface.
- *Printer port*—A software interface through which print jobs get directed to either a locally attached print device or a network-connected print device. Windows 2000 supports local line printer terminal (LPT), COM (serial), and Universal Serial Bus (USB) ports. It also supports network-connected printer port devices such as the Intel NetPort and the Hewlett-Packard (HP) JetDirect.
- *Print server*—A computer that serves as the host for printers that are associated with print devices.
- *Printer driver*—Software specific to each print device (designed to run in Windows 2000) that translates printing commands into printer language codes for each print device. PCL5 and PostScript are examples of two types of printer languages.
- *Print job*—The actual document to be printed along with the necessary print processing command.
- *Print resolution*—What determines the quality and smoothness of the text or images that the print device will render. This specification is expressed in dots per inch (DPI). Higher DPI numbers generally result in better print quality.
- *Print spooler*—The process (service) that runs in the background of Windows 2000 that initiates, processes, and distributes print jobs. The spooler saves print jobs into a temporary physical file on disk. Print jobs are then de-spooled and transferred to the appropriate print device.
- *Print queue*—A logical "waiting area" where print jobs are temporarily stored until the print device is available and ready to process each job according to the job's priority level and according to its order within the queue.

Connecting to Local and Network Printers

Once you add a local printer to a Windows 2000 Professional computer, you have the option of sharing it with other users on the network. To add a local printer to your system, follow these steps:

1. Log on as an administrator.
2. Click Start|Settings|Printers.
3. Double-click the Add Printer icon from the Printers folder. The Add Printer Wizard appears. Click Next to continue.

4. Click the Local printer button. If the printer that you are adding is not Plug and Play compatible, you may clear the Automatically Detect And Install My Plug And Play Printer checkbox. If the printer is Plug and Play compliant, Windows 2000 Professional automatically installs and properly configures it for you.

5. If the printer is not Plug and Play, the Select Printer Port dialog box appear. Click the port you want to use, or click the Create New Port button and choose the type of port to create from the drop-down list.

6. Click Next.

7. Select the printer Manufacturer and Model. Click the Have Disk button if you have a CD-ROM or diskette with the proper printer drivers from the manufacturer.

8. Click Next.

9. Enter a name for the printer. The name should not exceed 31 characters, and best practice dictates that the printer name should not contain any spaces. Specify whether this printer will be designated as the system's default printer.

10. Click Next.

11. In the Printer Sharing dialog box, click the Share As button if you want to share this printer with the network. Enter a share name for the printer; it's good to limit the share name to 14 characters or fewer and to place no spaces within the share name.

12. Click Next.

13. Enter an optional Location and Comment.

14. Click Next.

15. Click Next when prompted to print a test page; it's always a good idea to make sure that the printer has been set up and is working properly.

16. Click Finish to exit the Add Printer Wizard.

To connect to a network printer, you also use the Add Printer Wizard from the Printers folder. Simply follow these steps:

1. Log on as an administrator.

2. Click Start|Settings|Printers.

3. Double-click the Add Printer icon from the Printers folder. The Add Printer Wizard appears. Click Next to continue.

4. Click the Network printer button.
5. Click Next.
6. Type in the network Printer Name, or leave the Name box blank and click Next to browse for the printer on the network.
7. Locate the network printer at the Browse For Printer dialog box, shown in Figure 2.26.
8. Click Next.
9. If the print server for the printer that you are connecting to does not have the correct printer driver installed, you are prompted to install the correct version on the local Windows 2000 computer, as shown in Figure 2.27.
10. Click Yes or No about whether this printer should be the default printer for this computer.
11. Click Next.
12. Click Finish to exit the Add Printer Wizard.

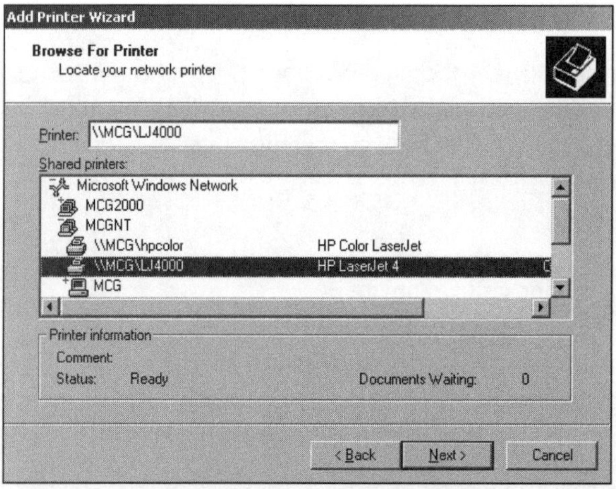

Figure 2.26 The Browse For Printer dialog box helps you locate a network printer.

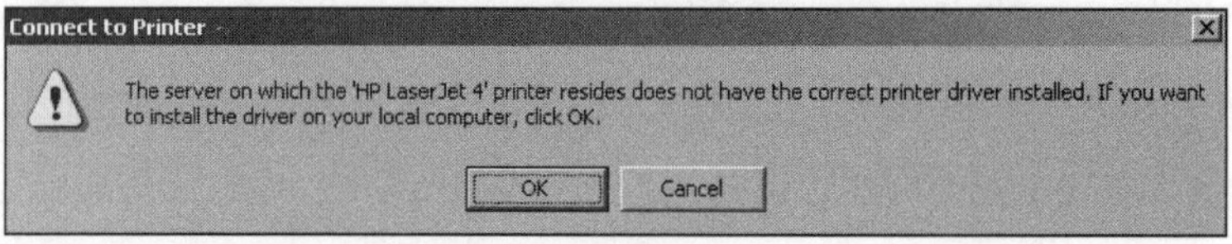

Figure 2.27 The Connect To Printer message box.

Connecting to Network Printers via the Command Line

As mentioned earlier in this chapter, you can use the **net use** command to connect to network drive shares. You can also use this command to connect to remote printers from a command prompt window. The syntax is as follows:

```
net use lptx: \\print_server_name\printer_share_name
```

Printer ports lpt1, lpt2, or lpt3 are represented by **lptx**. The **net use** command is the only way to connect client computers that are running MS-DOS to network printers.

Configuring Printer Properties

You can easily configure many of the properties of your Windows 2000 Professional system as a print server by clicking on the File menu from the Printers window and selecting Properties. You can configure many print server settings—such as changing the location of the Spool Folder—from the Print Server Properties dialog box, shown in Figure 2.28. Using this dialog box means that you don't have to edit the Registry directly.

By right-clicking on one of the available printer icons in the Printers folder and choosing Properties, you can configure that printer's settings and options. The printer Properties sheet contains six tabs: General, Sharing, Ports, Advanced, Security, and Device Settings.

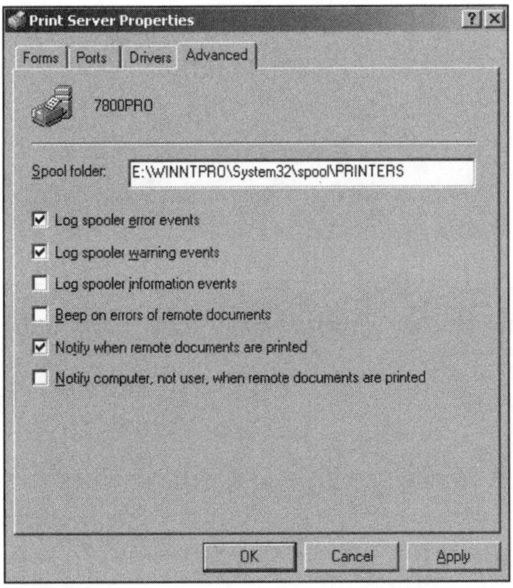

Figure 2.28 The Print Server Properties dialog box.

The General Tab

From the General tab, you can work with the following settings:

- Add or modify printer location and comment information
- Set printing preferences such as portrait or landscape orientation
- Select paper source and quality
- Print a test page

The Sharing Tab

The Sharing tab displays the following options:

- Share the printer, change the network share name, or stop sharing the printer
- Set printing preferences such as portrait or landscape orientation
- Install additional printer drivers for client computers that use different operating systems or different Windows NT CPU platforms

TIP: Windows 2000 print server computers automatically download the correct printer drivers for client computers running Windows 95, Windows 98, Windows NT, and Windows 2000 that connect to the print server, as long as the correct drivers have been installed on the print server.

The Ports Tab

On the Ports tab, you have these configuration options:

- Select a port to print to
- Add, configure, and delete ports
- Enable bidirectional printing support
- Enable printer pooling, which allows you to select two or more identical print devices that are configured as one logical printer; print jobs are directed to the first available print device

The Advanced Tab

On the Advanced tab, you work with scheduling and spooling settings, like these:

- Set time availability limits
- Set print job priority
- Change the printer driver or add a new driver

- Spool print jobs and start printing immediately, or start printing after the last page has spooled
- Print directly to the printer; do not spool print jobs
- Hold mismatched documents
- Print spooled documents first
- Retain documents after they have been printed
- Enable advanced printing features (such as metafile spooling) and enable advanced options (such as Page Order, Booklet Printing, and Pages Per Sheet); advanced options vary depending upon printer capabilities
- Set printing defaults
- Select a different print processor: RAW, EMF, or Text
- Specify a separator page

The Security Tab

You can configure the following security settings with the Security tab:

- Set permissions for users and groups (similar to NTFS file and folder permissions): Allow Print or Deny Print, Manage Printers, and Manage Documents.
- Set up printer auditing (similar to NTFS file and folder access auditing) via the Auditing tab by clicking on the Advanced button.
- Take ownership of the printer (similar to taking ownership of NTFS files and folders) via the Owner tab by clicking on the Advanced button.

The Device Settings Tab

The Device Settings tab allows you to configure printer-specific settings. The available settings on this tab vary depending on the manufacturer and the model of the printer that you are working with.

Managing Printers and Print Jobs

Members of the Printer Owners, Print Operators, and Print Job Owners groups have permissions to manage print jobs that are listed in the print queue. From the Printers folder, you manage print jobs by double-clicking on the printer icon that you want to work with. Once you have opened the printer's print queue window, you can pause printing or cancel all documents from the Printer menu. You can also take the printer offline from the Printer menu. If you select an individual print job that is listed, you can Pause, Resume, Start, or Cancel that job by selecting one of these options off the Documents menu. The print queue window itself displays the Document Name, the Status, the Document Owner, the number of Pages for each print job, the size of the job, the time and date that the job was Submitted, and the Port used.

Users may manage only their own print jobs unless they are members of the Administrators group, the Power Users group, or the Print Operators group (if the print server is a member of a domain). Users can also manage other users' print jobs if they have been granted the Allow Manage Documents permission.

Using Internet Printing Protocol (IPP)

Windows 2000 Professional computers can connect to printers that are attached to Windows 2000 print servers through a Web browser. IPP works over a corporate intranet or through an Internet connection. IPP gives users the ability to print over an Internet connection. You can enter one of two URLs into your Web browser:

- *http://print_server_name/printers*—This address connects you to the Web page for the Printers folder on the Windows 2000 print server computer.
- *http://print_server_name/printer_share_name*—This address connects you to the Web page for the print queue folder for the printer that you specify, as shown in Figure 2.29.

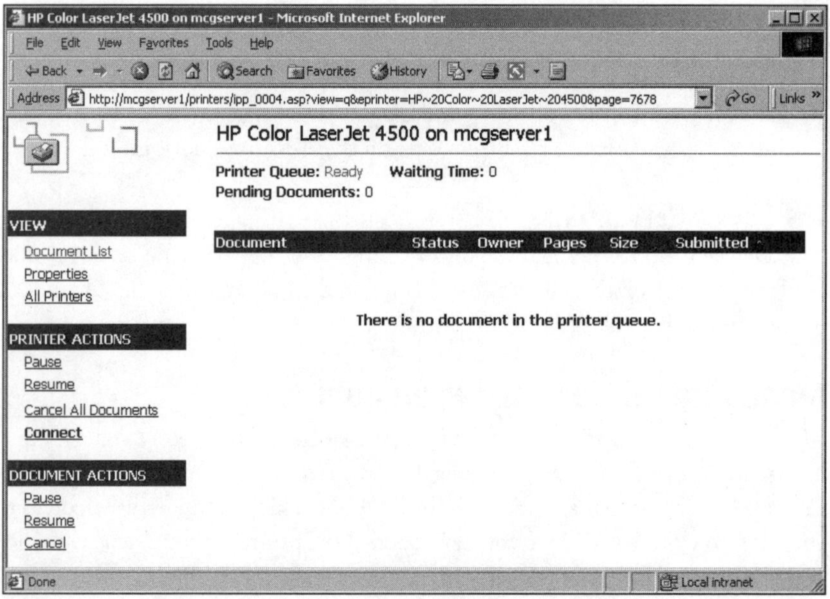

Figure 2.29 The Web browser interface for a network printer that uses IPP.

Practice Questions

Question 1

John Smith of XYZ Corporation has used EFS to encrypt all of the files stored within the \\Server1\Projects\JohnS folder. John subsequently leaves XYZ Corporation. John's boss has permissions to fully access the \\Server1\Projects\JohnS folder; however, he cannot work with any of the files because he receives an Access Is Denied message whenever he attempts to open any of the encrypted files. What does the company's IT department need to do so that John's files can become accessible to other users?

❍ a. Log on to the domain as a member of the Backup Operators group and decrypt the files.

❍ b. Log on to the domain as the DRA and decrypt the files.

❍ c. Restore the files from a recent backup.

❍ d. Have John's boss take ownership of the files.

Answer b is correct. Only a DRA can unencrypt files that someone else encrypted.

Question 2

Stuart Scott of ABC Company encrypts a folder named Spreadsheets and applies the encryption attribute to the folder, subfolders, and files. Two days later, Stuart's co-worker, Lisa, attempts to copy one of the encrypted files to a different NTFS folder located on the same drive volume on the same server. Neither Stuart nor Lisa is a member of the Administrators group, and neither user is a DRA. What will happen when Lisa attempts to copy the encrypted file?

❍ a. The encrypted file is copied successfully.

❍ b. The encrypted file is not copied successfully.

❍ c. Lisa is prompted for the password for the DRA before the copy process can be completed.

❍ d. The encrypted file is copied successfully, but an entry is logged into the Event Viewer about the encrypted file being copied.

Answer b is correct. Only the person who encrypted the files or the DRA can copy encrypted files.

Question 3

Where can Administrators view all of the shared folders for a Windows 2000 Professional computer?

- ❍ a. In the Shared Folders folder within the My Computer window.
- ❍ b. From the Control Panel Folder Options icon.
- ❍ c. From the System Tools folder of the Computer Management console.
- ❍ d. In the **usrmgr.exe** utility.

Answer c is correct. The Computer Management console is an MMC snap-in. Shared folders for the local computer are listed for Administrators within the System Tools|Shared Folders|Shares folder.

Question 4

Jeff is an Administrator who creates a network share named Docs on Server7. He sets the Share permissions on the shared folder by leaving the default Everyone group, but he clears the Allow checkboxes for Full Control, Change, and Read. Jeff sets NTFS permissions on the folder as well. He sets NTFS permissions to Allow Read for the Everyone group. What will happen when users attempt to connect to the Docs share over the network?

- ❍ a. Users will inherit the Allow Read permission for the folder.
- ❍ b. Users will inherit Allow Full Control permissions for the folder.
- ❍ c. Members of the Administrators group will be allowed access to the folder over the network.
- ❍ d. Users will be denied access to the shared folder over the network.

Answer d is correct. Whenever share permissions and NTFS permissions conflict, the most restrictive permissions take precedence. Clearing all the Allow checkboxes establishes an implicit Deny for those permissions.

Question 5

Amy moves a file from a FAT32 drive volume over to an NTFS drive volume folder named Compressed. The Compressed folder has been marked for NTFS compression for the folder, subfolders, and files. What happens when the file is moved into the Compressed folder?

❍ a. The file remains uncompressed within the "Compressed" folder.

❍ b. The file becomes compressed by inheriting the compression attribute from the destination folder.

❍ c. Amy receives an error message informing her that encrypted files cannot be compressed.

❍ d. Amy receives an error message informing her that files from FAT32 volumes do not support compression.

Answer b is correct. Files that are moved to an NTFS compressed folder from a non-NTFS drive volume inherit the compression attribute from the destination folder.

Question 6

Robert is using the network to print to \\wkstn4\printer11. All of a sudden, the print device for printer11 stops functioning. Fortunately, a similar print device is available on \\wkstn5\printer22. How can you, as an administrator, allow users to continue to print to the same network printer name without having to reconfigure any of the users' computers?

❍ a. Add a new port for \\wkstn4\printer11. Have the new port point to \\wkstn5\printer22.

❍ b. Modify the share name for printer11 to printer22.

❍ c. Change the print server properties for printer11 so that the Print Spool folder points to \\wkstn5\admin$\system32\spool\printers.

❍ d. Enable printer pooling on \\wkstn5\printer22.

Answer a is correct. By adding a new port with a UNC path for a similar printer on another computer, you are effectively redirecting the print jobs to another functioning printer.

Question 7

Greggory is member of the Administrators group. Some executives in his company feel that he may be reading or even altering confidential company documents. What can you do as the head of IT for the company to track which users are accessing sensitive files? [Check all correct answers]

- ❑ a. Enable auditing for success and failure of process tracking in the Local Security Settings console.
- ❑ b. Enable auditing for failure of object access in the Local Security Settings console.
- ❑ c. Enable auditing for success of object access in the Local Security Settings console.
- ❑ d. Enable auditing for the folder that contains the confidential files. Audit activities such as successful List Contents/Read Data and successful Create Files/Write Data.
- ❑ e. Turn on auditing for privilege use.

Answers c and d are correct. Enable auditing for success, failure, or both for object access from the Local Security Settings console. Then you can audit the success of object access events.

Question 8

As the network Administrator, you are concerned about several encrypted folders that contain very important data on Server A. You want to back up those folders while maintaining all security permission settings and having all the files retain their encryption. What is the best way to accomplish this?

- ❍ a. Copy the files and folders onto a network share on Server B that resides on a FAT32 drive volume using the **scopy.exe** utility from the *Windows 2000 Resource Kit*.
- ❍ b. Copy the files and folders onto a Novell NetWare server.
- ❍ c. Copy the files and folders onto a network share on Server B that is formatted as NTFS.
- ❍ d. Copy the files and folders onto CD-recordable media.

Answer c is correct. Only NTFS-formatted drive volumes in Windows 2000 support NTFS security permissions and EFS.

Question 9

The office administrative personnel are members of a group called Staff. The members of the Staff group are responsible for managing print jobs in the office. The Staff group has been assigned the Allow Manage Documents permission for all the printers in the office. Kimberly joins the company as a new Staff group member, and she is going to be responsible for managing the printers and the print jobs. What is the best way to assign permissions to Kimberly so that she can manage printers and print jobs?

❍ a. Create a new group named Printer Admins and add Kimberly to that group. Assign the Allow Manage Printers permission to the Printer Admins group for each printer in the office.

❍ b. Place Kimberly into the Print Operators group. Remove her from the Staff group.

❍ c. Keep her as a member of the Staff group and add her to the Administrators group.

❍ d. Modify the printer permissions for all the printers in the office to Allow Manage Printers for the Staff group. Assign the Deny Manage Printers permission individually for all members of the Staff group, except for Kimberly. Assign the Allow Manage Documents permission to the Everyone group for all the printers in the office.

Answer a is correct. It is best to assign permissions only to groups. The Print Operators group is a domain group. Membership in this group would give Kimberly authority to manage printers within the entire domain, and such a wide scope of authority is unnecessary. Therefore, answer b is incorrect.

Question 10

IIS is installed and running on your Windows 2000 Professional computer. Your users want to utilize IPP to print from their Web browsers over the corporate intranet. When users type in the URL **http://server1/printers**, they receive a Cannot Find Server message. However, you notice that you can type **http://192.168.1.103/printers** and you get connected to the printer's Web page for that server. What's the most probable cause of this problem?

❍ a. Dynamic Host Configuration Protocol (DHCP) is not functioning.

❍ b. DNS and/or WINS are/is not set up properly on the network.

❍ c. The default gateway IP address information is missing on the computer.

❍ d. Automatic Private IP Addressing is turned on by default. You need to make a change in the Registry to turn this feature off.

Answer b is correct. If you can access a TCP/IP network resource by its IP address but not by its computer name (host name), it is most likely a name resolution problem. You can solve it by installing either a DNS or WINS server, or by manually adding HOSTS or LMHOSTS files on each computer on the network.

Need to Know More?

Microsoft Corporation. *Microsoft Windows 2000 Professional Resource Kit*. Redmond, Washington: Microsoft Press, 2000. ISBN: 1-57231-808-2. The book provides invaluable information on administering resources and setting NTFS security permissions.

Stinson, Craig, and Carl Siechert. *Running Microsoft Windows 2000 Professional*. Redmond, Washington: Microsoft Press, 2000. ISBN: 1-57231-838-4. This guidebook to Windows 2000 Professional is a good source for information on administering resources.

Wood, Adam. *Windows 2000 Active Directory Black Book*. Scottsdale, Arizona: The Coriolis Group, 2000. ISBN: 1-57610-256-4. This book provides comprehensive coverage of Active Directory.

Search the TechNet CD-ROM (or its online version through **www.microsoft.com**) and/or the *Windows 2000 Professional Resource Kit* CD-ROM using the keywords "NTFS", "offline files", "EFS", "compression", "auditing", "shared folders", and "Internet Printing Protocol".

3

Implementing, Monitoring, and Troubleshooting Security Accounts and Policies

Terms you'll need to understand:

✓ Local users and groups

✓ Workgroup

✓ Domain

✓ Domain users and groups

✓ Active Directory

✓ Organizational Unit (OU)

✓ Policy

✓ Privilege, or user right

Techniques you'll need to master:

✓ Creating local users and groups

✓ Creating domain users and groups

✓ Managing user and group properties

✓ Dealing with changes in your user population: renaming and copying accounts

✓ Securing a system

✓ Creating a local and group policy

Networks' *raison d'être*—their life's purpose—is to allow users to access resources such as files, printers, and applications on computers other than the ones at which they are sitting. In an ideal world, we would trust every user with every file we create, and all we'd have to do is connect our computer to a network and share it all. Unfortunately, we don't. In the real world, certain users need access to resources that others should be restricted from accessing. Therefore, we need user accounts to identify and authenticate users when they attempt to access a resource. But imagine trying to define who can access a resource and at what level if you had to worry about each individual user! Using groups significantly eases the process of defining resource access—you can assign permissions and privileges to groups and thereby define access for their members, which may contain one, dozens, hundreds, or thousands of users.

This chapter highlights critical skills and concepts related to user, group, and computer accounts, and the process of creating security configurations and policies for a Windows 2000 Professional system.

User and Group Accounts

Now we'll discuss user and group accounts.

Local and Domain Accounts

User and group accounts are stored in one of two locations: the *local security database* or the domain's *Active Directory* database. When an account is created in the local security database, that account is called a *local user* or *local group*.

Each Windows 2000 Professional system has two default local user accounts, Administrator and Guest (which is disabled by default), and several built-in group accounts, which are discussed shortly. Local user and group accounts provide privileges and permissions to resources of the system on which they are defined. For example, the Users group has the privilege to log on locally. As you create local user accounts, they are members of the Users group by default; those users are then given the privilege to log on to that system.

Local user and group accounts cannot be given privileges or permissions to resources on any other system because the security database of the system where they are created is truly local—no other system can "see" it. If a user has logged on to a computer with a local account, the only way that user can be given access to resources of a remote system is to create an account for that user on the remote system. That account must be given privileges and permissions or must be placed into appropriate groups on that system. When a duplicate or redundant account is created with the same username and password, the user "seamlessly" accesses resources on the remote system—it is invisible to such users that the remote system is authenticating them. However, if the username or password on the remote system is different, users are prompted with an authentication dialog box when they first attempt to connect to the system.

When two or more systems that use only their own local accounts are on a network, this creates what is called a *workgroup*, a kind of peer-to-peer network. You can imagine how difficult managing redundant accounts for a single user on two different systems might become. If users change their passwords on one machine, they must remember to change it on the other; otherwise, they are prompted for authentication at each connection. Such challenges would become multiplied many times over in a larger workgroup with multiple users and multiple machines.

Thus, networks of any size turn to a *domain* model, in which one or more servers, called *domain controllers*, maintain a centralized database of users and groups. Security accounts in a domain are stored in the domain's Active Directory. When a user is created in a domain, that single user account can be given privileges and permissions to resources and systems throughout the domain, and in other domains within the enterprise's Active Directory. Active Directory is covered in more detail in the "Understanding Active Directory" section later in this chapter.

TIP

In a domain, it is unusual (and not a best practice) to create or use local user accounts. Most computers that are members of a domain have only the local Administrator and Guest user accounts in their security databases.

Managing Local User and Group Accounts

The Local Users And Groups snap-in allows you to manage—surprise—local users and groups. You can get to the snap-in by choosing Start|Settings|Control Panel|Administrative Tools|Computer Management and then by expanding the tree pane of the Computer Management console until you see snap-in. In this Snap-in, you can create, modify, duplicate, and delete users (in the Users folder) and groups (in the Groups folder).

Built-in User and Group Accounts

There are two built-in user accounts: Administrator and Guest. The Administrator account:

- Cannot be disabled, locked out, or deleted.
- Cannot be removed from the Administrators group.
- Has, through its membership in the Administrators group, all privileges required to perform system administration duties.
- Can be renamed.

The Guest account:

- Is disabled by default. Only an Administrator can enable the account. If it is enabled, it should be given a password, and User Cannot Change Password should be set if multiple users will log on with the account.
- Cannot be deleted.
- Can be locked out.
- Can be renamed.
- Does not save user preferences or settings.

Built-in local groups have assigned to them specific privileges (also called user rights) that allow them to perform specific sets of tasks on a system. The default local group accounts on a Windows 2000 Professional system are the following:

- *Administrators*—Have all built-in system privileges assigned. They can create and modify user and group accounts, manage security policies, create printers, and manage permissions to resources on the system. The local Administrator account is the default member and cannot be removed. Other accounts can be added and removed. When a system joins a domain, the Domain Admins group is added, but it can be removed.
- *Backup Operators*—Can back up and restore files and folders regardless of security permissions assigned to those resources. They can log on and shut down a system but cannot change security settings.
- *Power Users*—Can share resources and create user and group accounts. They cannot modify user accounts they did not create, nor can they modify the Administrators or Backup Operators Groups. Power Users cannot take ownership of files, back up or restore directories, load or unload device drivers, or manage the security and auditing logs. Power Users can run all Windows 2000-compatible applications as well as legacy applications, some of which members of the Users group cannot execute.

TIP: If you want certain users to have broad system administration capabilities but do not want them to be able to access all system resources, consider putting them in Backup Operators and Power Users rather than Administrators.

- *Users*—Can log on, shut down a system, use local and network printers, create local groups, and manage the groups they create. They cannot create a local printer or share a folder. Some down-level applications do not run for members of the Users group because security settings are tighter for the Users group in Windows 2000 than in Windows NT 4. By default, all local user accounts you create are added to the Users group. In addition, when a system joins a domain, the Domain Users group is made a member of that system's local Users group.

- *Guests*—Have limited privileges but can log on to a system and shut it down. Members cannot make permanent changes to their desktop or profile. By default, the built-in local Guest account is a member. When a system joins a domain, the Domain Guests group is added to the local Guests group.
- *Replicator*—Is used to support file replication services in a domain.

There are also built-in *system* groups, which you do not see in the user interface while managing other group accounts. Membership of system groups changes based on how the computer is accessed, not on who accesses the computer. Built-in system groups include the following:

- *Everyone*—Includes all users who access the computer, including the Guest account.
- *Authenticated Users*—Includes all users with a valid user account in the local security database or (in the case of domain members) in Active Directory's directory services. You use the Authenticated Users group rather than the Everyone group to assign privileges and group permissions because doing so prevents anonymous access to resources.
- *Creator Owner*—Contains the user account that created or took ownership of a resource. If the user is a member of the Administrators group, the group is the owner of the resource.
- *Network*—Contains any user with a connection from a remote system.
- *Interactive*—Contains the user account for the user logged on locally at the system.
- *Anonymous Logon*—Includes any user account that Windows 2000 did not authenticate.
- *Dial-up*—Contains all users that currently use a dial-up connection.

Creating Local User and Group Accounts

To create a local user or group account, right-click the appropriate folder (Users or Groups) and choose New User (or New Group), enter the appropriate attributes, and then click Create.

User account names:

- Must be unique.

- Are recognized only up to their 20th character, although the name itself can be longer.
- Cannot contain the following characters: " / \ [ ] ; : | = + * ? < >.
- Are not case sensitive, although the user account's name property displays the case as entered.

You should determine a policy for accommodating users with the same name, perhaps by adding a number after the username (JohnD1, JohnD2). Some organizations also identify certain types of users by their username (e.g., JohnDoe-Temp for a temporary employee).

User account passwords:

- Are recommended.
- Are case sensitive.
- Can be up to 127 characters, although down-level operating systems like Windows NT 4 and Windows 9x support only 14-character passwords.
- Should be a minimum of seven to eight characters.
- Should be difficult to guess and, preferably, should mix uppercase and lowercase letters, numerals, and nonalphanumeric characters (other than those listed above as prohibited).
- Can be set by the Administrator (who can then determine whether users must, can, or cannot change their password) or the user (if the Administrator has not specified otherwise).

Select User Must Change Password At Next Logon to ensure that the user is the only one who knows the account's password. Select User Cannot Change Password when more than one person (such as Guest) uses the account.

Note: *The User Cannot Change Password option is not available when User Must Change Password At Next Logon is selected.*

The Password Never Expires option is helpful when a program or a service uses an account. To avoid having to reconfigure the service with a new password, you can simply set the service's account to retain its password indefinitely.

Configuring Account Properties

The information you can specify when creating an account is limited in Windows 2000. Therefore, after creating an account, you often need to go to the account's properties sheet, which you can access by right-clicking on the account and choosing Properties. Figure 3.1 shows the Properties sheets of two accounts.

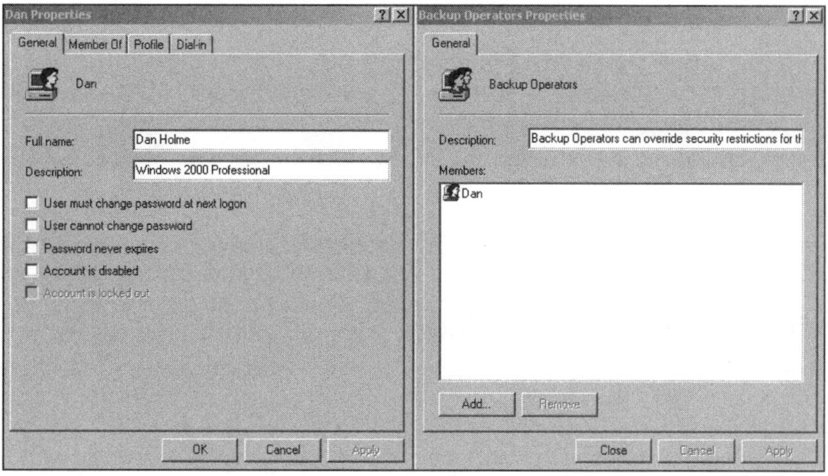

Figure 3.1 The properties sheets of Dan and Backup Operators.

Managing Local Group Membership

To manage the membership of a local group, right-click the group and choose Properties. To remove a member, select the account and click Remove. To add a member, click Add and select or enter the name of the account.

In a workgroup, local groups can contain only accounts defined in the same machine's local security database. When a system belongs to a domain, its local groups can also include domain accounts, including user accounts, universal groups, and global groups from the enterprise's Active Directory, as well as domain Local Groups from within the system's domain.

***Note:** Universal groups and domain local groups are available to add as members only when the domain is in native mode, meaning that it contains only Windows 2000 domain controllers and no legacy backup domain controllers.*

Renaming Accounts

To rename an account, right-click the account and choose Rename. Type the new name and press Enter. Each user and group account is represented in the local security database by a long, unique string called a *security identifier (SID)*, which is generated when the account is created. The SID is what is actually assigned permissions and privileges. The user or group name is just a user-friendly "face" on that process. Therefore, when you rename an account, the account's SID remains the same, so the account retains all of its group memberships, permissions, and privileges.

There are two situations that mandate renaming an account: The first occurs when one user stops using a system and a new user requires the same access as the first.

Rather than creating a new local user account for the new user, simply rename the old user account. The account's SID remains the same, so its group memberships, privileges, and permissions are retained. You should also specify a new password in the account's properties sheet and select the User Must Change Password At Next Logon option.

TIP: The easiest way to "replace" a user is to rename the account. Therefore, when one user leaves and another requires the same group memberships, rights, and resource access permissions, simply rename the former user's account. Don't forget to set an initial password because the new user won't otherwise know the old user's password.

The second situation that warrants renaming a user account is the security practice of renaming the built-in Administrator and Guest accounts. You cannot delete these accounts, nor can you disable or remove the Administrator account from the Local Administrators group, so renaming the accounts is a recommended practice for hindering malicious access to a system.

Disabling or Enabling User Accounts

To disable or enable a user account, open its Properties sheet and select or clear the Account Is Disabled checkbox. If an account is disabled, a user cannot log on to the system using that account. The Administrator account cannot be disabled, and only Administrators can enable the Guest account.

Deleting Accounts

You can delete a local user or group account (but not built-in accounts like Administrator, Guest, or Backup Operators) by right-clicking the account and choosing Delete. When you delete a group, you delete the group account only, not the accounts of its members. A group is a membership list, not a container.

Note: *When you delete an account, you are deleting its SID. Therefore, if you delete an account by accident and re-create the account, even with the same name, it will not have the same permissions, privileges, or group memberships—you will have to regenerate them. For that reason, and to facilitate auditing, it is recommended that you disable, not delete, any user that leaves an organization.*

Using The Users and Passwords Applet

Another tool for administering local user accounts is the Users And Passwords applet in Control Panel. This applet allows you to create and remove user accounts as well as specify group membership for those users. It is wizard driven and is useful for novice administrators and home users. To launch the Local

Users And Groups snap-in, click the Advanced tab and the Advanced button (in the Advanced User Management section).

Note: *The Users And Passwords applet provides an opportunity to override the logon requirement for a system. This feature will be discussed below in the "Authentication" section later in this chapter.*

Managing Domain User Accounts

Domain user accounts are managed with the Active Directory Users And Computers snap-in. To access it, choose Start|Settings|Control Panel|Administrative Tools|Active Directory Users And Computers. Note that, unlike in Windows NT 4, all domain controllers in Windows 2000 can make changes to the Active Directory database. When you open the tool, you connect to an available domain controller. If you want to specify which domain controller, or which domain you wish to connect to, right-click the Active Directory Users And Computers node and choose Connect To Domain or Connect To Domain Controller.

Unlike the local security database, which is a flat list of users and groups, Active Directory has containers like domains and Organizational Units (OUs), which collect database objects such as users that are administered similarly. Therefore, when you manage domain user accounts in Windows 2000, you need to start in the container or OU that you want to modify.

Creating Domain User Accounts

You create domain user accounts by right-clicking the OU or container in which you want the user account and then choosing New User. A wizard prompts you for basic account properties, including the following:

- First name
- Initials
- Last name
- Full name (by default, the combination of the first name and last name)
- User logon name and User Principal Name (UPN) suffix
- User logon name (pre-Windows 2000)
- Password and confirmed password

Windows 2000 user accounts have two logon names. The UPN is used for logon to a Windows 2000 system and consists of a logon name followed by the @ symbol and a suffix, by default the Domain Name System (DNS) name of the domain. Each user must have a unique UPN in the domain. The down-level logon name is used for logging on to pre-Windows 2000 systems such as Windows NT 4, and Windows 95, 98, and ME. Each user's pre-Windows 2000 logon name must be unique in the domain and by default is the same as the logon name portion of the UPN.

Modifying User Account Properties

Once an account is created, Active Directory provides dozens of attributes to further define that user. Right-click a user and choose Properties to open up a multi-tabbed dialog box full of attributes that can be defined for that user. The only properties you can specify when creating the user are those on the Account tab. You must set the remainder of the properties after the account has been instantiated.

Copying User Accounts

A user object in Active Directory may have numerous attributes defined, including work location, group membership, and organizational superiors. Often, a new user object shares many of its attributes with one or more other user objects. In that case, it is faster to copy an existing user object than to create a new object and define each and every property. To copy a user, right-click the object and choose Copy. You are asked to enter some of the basic account properties, such as name and password. You can copy a user only with domain user accounts, not with local user accounts.

Creating Template User Accounts

When you expect to create multiple user objects with highly similar properties, you can create a "template" account that, when copied, initiates the new accounts with its defined attributes. The only trick to working with templates is to *disable the template account*. Then, when copying the account to create a new user with predefined attributes, make sure to enable the new account.

TIP

When you copy a user account—whether a "real" user account or a template—the new copy belongs to all the same groups as the original and therefore has the same resource access that was assigned to the groups of the original account. However, the new copy does *not* have access to resources for which permissions were assigned directly to the original user account.

Disabling and Deleting User Accounts

The process for disabling and deleting domain user accounts is the same as for local user accounts, except that you use the Active Directory Users And Computers snap-in to perform the tasks. The checkbox for disabling an account is on the user's Account property sheet.

Adding Domain User Accounts to Local Groups

In Windows 2000, you can add a user to a group with either the group's Members property sheet or the user's Member Of property sheet, except when adding *domain* user accounts to *local* groups, in which case you must use the group's Members property sheet. A domain user's Member Of property sheet displays only memberships in global, domain, local, and universal groups.

Authentication

When a user wants to access resources on a machine, that user's identity must first be verified through a process called *authentication*. For example, when a user logs on, the security subsystem evaluates the user's username and password. If there is a match, the user is authenticated. The process of logging on to a machine where you are physically sitting is called *interactive logon*. Authentication also happens when you access resources on a remote system. For example, when you open a shared folder on a server, you are being authenticated as well, only this time, the process is called *remote* or *network logon* because you are not *physically* at the server.

The Security Dialog

The *security dialog* allows for interactive logon to a Windows 2000 system. You can access the Security dialog shortly after a system has started, and at any time after logon, by pressing Ctrl+Alt+Delete. If you are not currently logged on, you can enter a username and password. If the system belongs to a domain, you need to be certain that the domain in which your account exists is authenticating you. You can either select the domain from the drop-down list or enter your UPN. The UPN is an attribute of an Active Directory user object and, by default, is of the form **username@dnsdomain.name**. The suffix, following the @ symbol, indicates the domain against which to authenticate the user.

If you are currently logged on to a system, pressing Ctrl+Alt+Delete takes you to the Windows 2000 Security dialog, at which point you can:

- Log off the system, which closes all programs and ends the instance of the shell.
- Lock the system, which allows programs to continue running but prevents access to the system. When a system is locked, you may unlock it by pressing Ctrl+Alt+Delete and entering the username and password of the user who locked the system, or an administrator's username and password.

TIP

To lock a workstation automatically after a period of idle time, use a screensaver password.

- Shut down the system.
- Change your password.
- Open Task Manager.

Automating Logon

You can configure Windows 2000 Professional systems so that you are not required to enter a username and password but rather that the system automatically logs on as a specified user account. From the Users And Passwords applet in the Control Panel, click the Advanced tab and clear the Require Users To Press Ctrl+Alt+Delete Before Logging On checkbox. The same setting is available through Policy, which is discussed later in this chapter.

Understanding Active Directory

Windows 2000's Active Directory goes far beyond what the Security Accounts Manager (SAM) database did for Windows NT 4. Although SAM and Active Directory store security account information for users, groups, computers, and user rights, that's where the similarity ends. Active Directory's database stores *objects* that represent an enterprise resource, including users, groups, computers, printers, folders, applications, connections, security and configuration settings, and network topology. For each of these types, or *classes*, of objects, Active Directory can store numerous properties, or *attributes*. So a user account is far more than a username and password—it is now information about the user's mailbox, the user's address and phone number, the organizational role of the user (including the user's manager and location), and far, far more.

As a central store of information related to the enterprise network, Active Directory allows administrators to create a virtual representation or model of the enterprise—linking various objects together, grouping objects based on how they are administered, and structuring the enterprise information technology (IT) to best support the organization's goals. In addition, Active Directory's database is *extensible*, which means that you can customize and append it with additional attributes and object classes. So, if an organization wants to keep track of salary information for each employee, it can simply extend the information that Active Directory stores about employees to include salary or, better yet, purchase a payroll application that is Active Directory aware and would automatically extend the directory appropriately.

Now, a database is of no use if it simply stores information. One must be able to access and manipulate that information somehow, and Active Directory includes numerous services, most based on Internet standard, that allow you to do just that. To provide the functionality required to search or query the database for a particular enterprise resource, locate that resource out on the network, manage that resource's record in Active Directory, and ensure that the record is consistent throughout the network.

Active Directory's database and services reside on servers that have been designated domain controllers. Unlike with Windows NT 4, Windows 2000 domain controllers are not created while the operating system is installed. Rather, a functioning server is *promoted* to act as a domain controller, at which time it obtains a copy of Active Directory and launches the required services. Also unlike with NT 4, there is no "primary" domain controller. All domain controllers can write to the directory. So, a change to the domain is replicated to all domain controllers, making Active Directory a *multi-master* replication model.

On the Windows 2000 Professional exam, it is important to have a basic understanding of Active Directory's structure, which, like that of Windows NT 4, begins with a domain. The *domain* is the fundamental administrative, security, and replication unit of Active Directory. The domain is specified by two names: its down-level NetBIOS name—such as CONOSCO, which was also used in NT 4—and its DNS name, such as **conosco.com**. DNS is the primary name resolution methodology in Windows 2000.

When an enterprise decides to implement a multidomain model within its Active Directory, it creates what are called domain *trees* or *forests*. Multidomain models, however, fall outside the scope of the Windows 2000 Professional exam, so we will focus on what you need to know in a single-domain environment.

In a single domain, Active Directory can contain millions of objects. To make those objects more manageable, you can place those objects in containers called OUs. OUs can contain other OUs, allowing a nested, hierarchical structure to be created within a domain (see Figure 3.2).

An enterprise uses its OU structure to control the administration and configuration of objects in the enterprise. For example, the organization depicted in Figure 3.2 might give an IT Admins group full control over the OUs, which would allow that group to create, delete, and fully manage all of the objects in those OUs. A Help Desk group might be given permission to reset passwords for user objects in the Finance and Marketing OUs, and to put users in those OUs into groups based on the resource access they require. Workstations in the Finance OU could be configured to limit which users are allowed to log on locally. And users in the Payroll OU might have the payroll application installed on their machines, all through properties of the OU.

The OUs' virtual model of administration and configuration offers enormous flexibility and simplifies the effort it takes to manage large and small networks. As objects are moved between OUs, they are administered and configured differently.

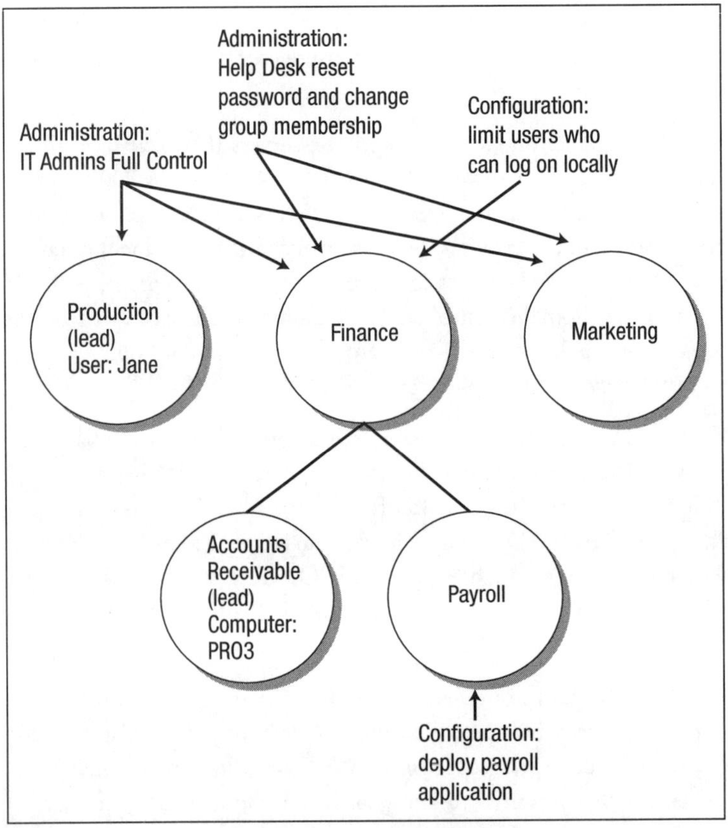

Figure 3.2 A sample Windows 2000 domain that contains several OUs.

For example, referring again to Figure 3.2, if a user named Jane is moved from the Production OU to the Payroll OU, the payroll application is deployed, automatically. In addition, the Help Desk can reset her password because, by default, properties of OUs (including delegated administrative permissions) are *inherited* from their parent OU. If a computer, PRO3, is moved from the Accounts Receivable OU to the Marketing OU, the limitation on which users can log on locally (which it was inheriting from the Finance OU) is removed.

The complexities and mechanics of designing and implementing Active Directory are not among the objectives of the Windows 2000 Professional exam. However, it is important to realize that within a domain, you can use OUs to control administration and configuration of all objects, including users and computers, and that OUs by default inherit the administrative and configuration properties of OUs higher up in the OU structure. We will see these concepts in action in the discussion of Group Policy later in this chapter.

Understanding and Implementing Policy

Configuring a particular system and the environment for a particular user begins with its defaults—the settings determined by Microsoft during the development of Windows 2000. Of course, there are always numerous settings for which Microsoft's defaults are not appropriate for one or more computers or users. Therefore, users and administrators alike often find themselves modifying the defaults.

In the past, if several settings needed to be changed, you often had to use several tools, including User Manager, Server Manager, System Policy Editor, and even the Registry Editor. If those settings needed to be changed on multiple computers, it was often necessary to make those changes on each system, individually. And if a setting you specified was later changed inappropriately, there was often no way to set it back to the desired setting except for manually making the change again.

Managing changes and configuration has been significantly improved in Windows 2000 thanks to the introduction into the Windows environment of *policy-based administration*. Policies provide administrators with a single list of configuration settings in one tool, rather than many tools, and allow administrators to apply those configuration settings to one machine, many machines, or every machine.

Local Policy

On a Windows 2000 Professional system, you can configure security-related settings using the Local Security console, which contains the Security Settings Microsoft Management Console (MMC) snap-in. Simply choose Start|Settings|Control Panel|Administrative Tools|Local Security Settings. Each of the nodes in the Local Security Settings console is a security area or scope, within which you will find dozens of security related settings, or attributes.

The Local Policy column of the details pane displays the settings specified by local policy. The Effective Policy column shows what is currently in effect. The two columns may differ if the local policy has not been implemented—changes to security settings take effect when the system is restarted, or following a refresh interval, which is by default 90 minutes. The columns may also differ as local policy is overridden by group policy, which is discussed later in this chapter.

Account Policies

Account policies control the password requirements and how the system responds to invalid logon attempts. The policies you can specify include the following:

- *Maximum password age*—This is the period of time after which a password must be changed.

- *Minimum password length*—This is the number of characters in a password. Passwords can contain up to 127 characters; however, most passwords should not exceed 14.
- *Passwords must meet complexity requirements*—This policy, if in effect, does not allow a password change unless the new password contains at least three of four character types: uppercase (A through Z), lowercase (a through z), numeric (0 through 9), and nonalphanumeric (such as !).
- *Enforce password history*—The system can remember a specified number of previous passwords. When a user attempts to change his or her password, the new password is compared against the history; if the new password is unique, the change is allowed.
- *Minimum password age*—This specifies the number of days that a new password must be used before it can be changed again.
- *Account lockout threshold*—This is the number of denied logon attempts after which an account is locked out. For example, if this is set to three, a lockout occurs if a user enters the wrong password three times; any further logon attempt will be denied. If this is set to zero, there is no lockout threshold.
- *Reset account lockout counter after*—This is the number of minutes after which the counter, which applies to the lockout threshold, is reset. For example, if the counter is reset after five minutes and the account lockout threshold is three, a user can log on twice with the incorrect password. After five minutes, the counter is reset, so the user can log on twice more. A third invalid logon during a five-minute period locks out the account.
- *Account lockout duration*—This specifies how long logon attempts are denied after a lockout. During this period, a logon with the locked out username is not authenticated.

Audit Policies

Audit policies specify what types of events are entered into the Security Log. The most important policies to understand are the following:

- *Logon events*—Authentication of users logging on or off locally and making connections to the computer from remote systems.
- *Account management*—Any change to account properties, including password changes and adding, deleting, or modifying users or groups.
- *Object access*—Access to objects on which auditing has been specified. Auditing object access, for example, enables auditing of files and folders on an NT File System (NTFS) volume, but you must also configure auditing on those files and folders. See Chapter 2 for a detailed discussion of auditing.

- *Privilege use*—Use of any user right, now called a *privilege*. For example, this policy audits a user who changes the system time because changing system time is a privilege.

For each policy, you can specify to audit successes, failures, or both. As events are logged, they appear in the Security Log, which can be viewed, by default, only by administrators. Other logs can be viewed by anyone.

User Rights Assignment

User rights, also called privileges, allow a user or group to perform system functions such as changing the system time, backing up or restoring files, and formatting a disk volume. Some rights are assigned to built-in groups. For example, the Administrators group can format a disk volume. You cannot deny that right to Administrators, nor can you assign that right to a user or group you create. Other rights are assignable. For example, the right to back up files and folders is given by default to Administrators and Backup Operators, but you can remove the right for those groups or assign the right to other users or groups. You can modify the rights that are visible in the Local Security Policy console. You do not see the "hard wired" rights in this interface.

User rights, because they are system-oriented, override object permissions when the two are in conflict with each other. For example, a user may be denied permission to read a folder on a disk volume. However, if the user has been given the privilege to back up files and folders, a backup of the folder succeeds, even though the user cannot actually read the folder.

Security Options

In the *Security Options* node are a number of useful security settings. This node highlights one of the advantages of policy, because while many of these settings are accessible elsewhere in the user interface (for example, you can specify driver signing in the System applet), policy allows you to compile all those settings, from all those tools and applets, into a unified configuration tool.

Some particularly useful options to be familiar with are the following:

- *Disable Ctrl+Alt+Delete requirement for logon*—If this policy is enabled, the logon dialog box does not appear at startup and the system boots directly to the desktop. This policy is enabled by default on standalone systems and disabled by default when a machine joins a domain, due to the obvious security implications of bypassing a secure logon.

- *Clear the Virtual Memory Pagefile when the system shuts down*—By default, the pagefile is not cleared and could allow unauthorized access to sensitive information that remains in the pagefile.

- *Do not display last username in logon screen*—This option forces users to enter both username and password at logon. By default, the policy is disabled and the name of the previously logged-on user is displayed.

Managing Local Policies

The local policy and the Local Security Policy tool are most helpful on standalone systems. The local policy drives configuration of the computer, and if a setting is changed through tools other than policy, the change is reverted to the policy-specified setting when the system is restarted, or following the policy refresh interval.

It is possible, however, to transfer security policies between systems. Right-click the Security Settings node and you can export and import policies. This allows you to copy a policy you have created on one machine to other machines. However, you can imagine the complexity of trying to maintain consistent local policies across multiple systems. That complexity is addressed by group policy.

EXAM ALERT

The Security Configuration And Analysis snap-in allows you to capture the security configuration of a system as a database, and to use that database as a baseline against which you can gauge changes to security settings. When modifications are made that deviate from the database setting, you can reapply the original setting. You can also save the database as a template, which you can then apply to other systems to duplicate security settings. There are also preconfigured security templates that you can apply to Windows 2000 systems to implement a variety of security environments.

Group Policy

Group policy takes the concept of policy-enforced configuration and applies it to one or more computers with one or more users. Like local policy, group policy provides a centralized enumeration of configuration settings, some of which are also available through other tools in the user interface, some of which are available only through Policy. However, you can apply, or *link*, a group policy to the following:

- *A domain*—This causes the configuration specified by the policy to be applied to every user or computer in the domain.

- *An OU*—This applies policy to users or computers in the OU.

- *A site*—This is an Active Directory object that represents a portion of your network topology with good connectivity—a local area network (LAN), for example.

To access group policy, you must go to the properties of a site, domain, or OU (SDOU), and click the Group Policy tab. Therefore, to work with group policy for a site, you use the Active Directory Sites And Services console, right-click on a site, and choose Properties. To work with group policy for a domain or OU, use Active Directory Users And Computers, right-click on a domain or OU, and choose Properties.

Whereas an individual machine can have only one local policy, a SDOU can have multiple policies. On the Group Policy Properties sheet, you can create a new Group Policy Object (GPO) by clicking New, or link an existing group policy to the SDOU by clicking on Add. If you select a group policy and click on Edit, you expose the GPO in the Group Policy Editor.

Application of Group Policy

GPOs are divided into the Computer Settings and User Settings nodes. The computer settings apply to every computer in the SDOU to which the policy is linked, and, by default, to all child OUs. Computer settings take effect at startup and every refresh interval, by default 90 minutes. User settings affect every user in the SDOU and its children at logon, and after each refresh interval.

When a computer starts up, its current settings are modified first by any configuration specified by the local policy. Then, the configuration in group policies is applied: first, the policies linked to the computer's site, then the policies for its domain, and finally the policies for each OU in the branch that leads to the computer's OU. If there is ever a conflict in a particular configuration setting, the last setting applied takes effect. Therefore, the policies that are "closest" to the computer—the policies linked to its OU, for example—take precedence if a conflict arises. The same application of policies applies to a user at logon: local policy, site policy, domain policy, and OU policy.

TIP

You can remember the order of policy application as LSDOU, or "el-stew." Policies are applied in the order local, site, domain, and OU.

It is a quite intuitive process, at first. But policy application can get extremely complex when multiple policies are applied to a single container (SDOU), when inheritance is blocked or No Override is specified, and when policies are modified by access control lists (ACLs). Luckily, the enterprise scale application of group policy is not an objective of the Windows 2000 Professional exam. Simply understand the basic order of policy application—LSDOU.

Group Policy and OU Design

Group policy is a major factor in determining an enterprise's OU structure. If an OU contains users or computers that require different configurations and settings, the best practice is to subdivide the OU into one or more OUs, each of which contains objects that are configured similarly. By doing so, you can then manage the configuration by applying an appropriate group policy to each OU.

For example, you might remember the organization depicted in Figure 3.2. If within the Marketing OU a group of salespeople needed a sales application, and that sales application was not appropriate for all users in the Marketing OU, the best practice would be to create an OU, perhaps called Sales, within the Marketing OU (see Figure 3.3). By placing the Sales OU within the Marketing OU, it inherits all of the existing administration and configuration of the Marketing OU. But now, you can create a policy linked only to the Sales OU, and you can use that policy to deploy the sales application. As users are moved into the Sales OU, the sales application is deployed to them. See Chapter 4 for more information about deploying applications through group policy.

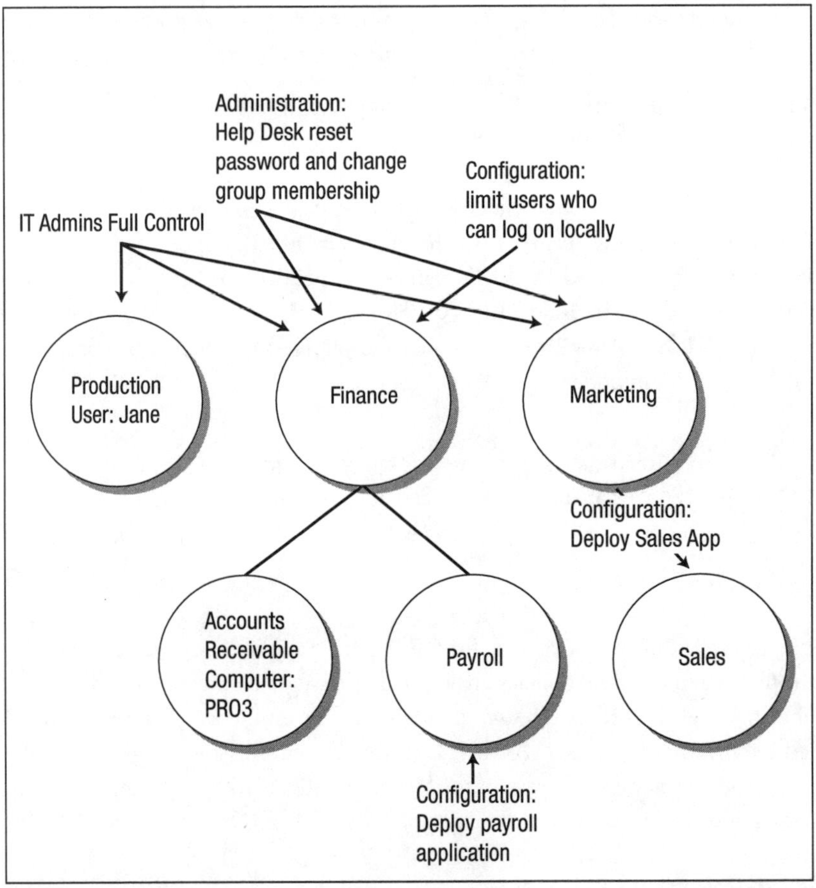

Figure 3.3 The OU Sales within the Marketing OU.

Practice Questions

Question 1

Computer1 is a member of the SAFTA domain. A local user account, John, is in the Administrators group. When John logs on to the domain, he is unable to perform all administrative functions on his system. What should you do to enable John to have full administrative control over his computer?

- ❍ a. Delete the local user account John.
- ❍ b. Add John's domain user account to the Administrators group.
- ❍ c. Add John's domain user account to the Administrators group on the domain.
- ❍ d. Give John Full Control permission to the C:\WINNT directory.

Answer b is correct. John is logging onto the domain, and even if his domain username is John, it is still a different account than the local user account. Therefore, he is not actually a member of the Administrators group when he is logging on to the domain.

Question 2

Susan is an administrator of Computer5. Other users who log on to Computer5 complain that Susan occasionally formats the D: drive to get rid of old files and folders, and that she is destroying their data in the process. You want Susan to be able to manage basic user and group accounts as well as restore files, but you want to prevent her from unnecessarily harming the system. What should you do? [Check all correct answers]

- ❑ a. Add Susan to the Backup Operators group.
- ❑ b. Add Susan to the Power Users group.
- ❑ c. Deny Susan Full Control permission to the System32 folder.
- ❑ d. Remove Susan from the Administrators group.

Answers a, b, and d are correct. The Backup Operators group can restore files and folders, and the Power Users group can manage basic user and group accounts. By removing Susan from the Administrators group, you are denying her many privileges that are built into that group, including the privilege to format disk volumes.

Question 3

You want to enable a colleague to access files on your Windows 2000 Professional system from her system, which is part of a Novell network. You have shared the folder in which the files are stored, and both share and NTFS permissions indicate that Everyone has Full Control. However, she calls you and indicates she still cannot access the files. What can you do to grant her access? [Check all correct answers]

- ❑ a. Give the Authenticated Users group Full Control of the folder.
- ❑ b. Create a user account for her and tell her the password.
- ❑ c. Enable the Guest account and tell her the password.
- ❑ d. Stop the WINLOGON service.

Answers b and c are correct. In order to access a resource, one must first have a valid user account. The system is part of a Novell network, implying that it is not in a domain and is a standalone or workgroup system. Therefore, all accounts must be created locally. You can either create an account for her or enable the Guest account.

Question 4

You have just installed Windows 2000 Professional and when it starts up it goes directly to the desktop, without asking for a username and password. You want to improve the security of the system by enforcing logon. What tools could you use? [Check all correct answers]

- ❑ a. Local Security Policy
- ❑ b. Domain Security Policy
- ❑ c. Group Policy
- ❑ d. Users And Passwords applet
- ❑ e. System applet
- ❑ f. Computer Management console

Answers a, c, and d are correct. All three tools expose the security setting to automate logon, or require logon. The System applet and Computer Management consoles do not expose the setting to require logon. Therefore, answers e and f are incorrect.

Question 5

You are deploying a mobile computer called Laptop3 for Maria. Laptop3 is in the Sales OU. Maria is in the Outside Sales OU, which is contained within the Sales OU. You want to ensure that the sales application is deployed to Maria and all others who take Laptop3 on the road. Which of the following is the best-practice solution for deploying the sales application?

- ❍ a. Use group policy's User Settings to deploy the application's MSI file to the Outside Sales OU.
- ❍ b. Use local policy to deploy the application's MSI file to Laptop3.
- ❍ c. Use group policy's User Settings to deploy the application's MSI file to the Sales OU.
- ❍ d. Use group policy's Computer Settings to deploy the application's MSI file to the Outside Sales OU.
- ❍ e. Use group policy's Computer Settings to deploy the application's MSI file to the Sales OU.

Answer e is correct. You want all users to have the application as long as they are on Laptop 3, so you want to use the Computer Settings node of group policy. Laptop3 belongs to the Sales OU. Applying the policy to the Outside Sales OU would not affect Laptop3, which is "above" the Outside Sales OU in the OU structure.

Question 6

Lou has an account in the domain that is a member of the Sales, Trainers, and Managers groups. You are hiring Beth, who will also be a member of the same groups. You want to create Beth's account with the least administrative effort. What should you do?

- ❍ a. Create an account for Beth and add the account to the Sales, Trainers, and Managers groups.
- ❍ b. Rename Lou's account as Beth.
- ❍ c. Copy Lou's account and call the new account Beth.
- ❍ d. Rename the Guest account Beth.

Answer c is correct. If you copy Lou's account, the new account will be a member of the same groups as Lou.

Question 7

Lou has a local user account that is a member of the Sales, Trainers, and Managers groups. You are hiring Beth, who will also be a member of the same groups. You want to create Beth's account with the least administrative effort. What should you do?

- ❍ a. Create an account for Beth and add the account to the Sales, Trainers, and Managers groups.
- ❍ b. Rename Lou's account as Beth.
- ❍ c. Copy Lou's account and call the new account Beth.
- ❍ d. Rename the Guest account Beth.

Answer a is correct. You cannot copy a local user account.

Question 8

Lou has an account in the domain that is a member of the Sales, Trainers, and Managers groups. The Sales group has access to the Sales Reports folder, the Trainers group can read the Curricula folder, and the Managers can read the Financials folder. Lou can also modify the Curricula folder. You hire Beth, who will be performing the same job function as Lou. You copy Lou's account and name the new account Beth. Which of the following statements are true? [Check all correct answers]

- ❑ a. Beth is a member of the Sales, Trainers, and Managers groups.
- ❑ b. Beth can read the Curricula folder.
- ❑ c. Beth can modify the Curricula folder.
- ❑ d. Beth's password is the same as Lou's.

Answers a and b are correct. The access Beth enjoys is because her account is a member of the same groups as Lou's, but access permissions assigned to a user account are not changed when you copy the account. Similarly, user passwords are not copied when an account is copied. Beth cannot modify the Curricula folder because that permission was assigned directly to Lou. Therefore, answer c is incorrect.

Question 9

You bring your system from your home network into the office and connect it to the enterprise network. When you log on, the settings and applications that normally affect you at the office do not apply. What can you do to correct the situation?

- ❍ a. Renew your system's DHCP=address.
- ❍ b. Log on as Administrator.
- ❍ c. Join your system to the domain and log on with your domain account.
- ❍ d. Log on as Guest.

Answer c is correct. The system is not part of the domain, so it does not apply policies that are part of your domain's Active Directory.

Question 10

You have configured the local policy of your domain workstation, a Windows 2000 Professional machine, to disable the requirement to press Ctrl+Alt+Delete and log on. However, when you start the computer, it still requires you to press Ctrl+Alt+Delete. What tool should you use to locate the source of the problem?

- ❍ a. Computer Management
- ❍ b. System Information
- ❍ c. Event Viewer
- ❍ d. Local Security Policy
- ❍ e. Group Policy

Answer e is correct. Your system's local policy is being overridden by a site, domain or OU group policy. Group Policy allows you to examine the policies applied to your system's SDOUs. Although Local Security Policy shows you that there is a discrepancy between the local policy and the effective policy, it does not help you locate the source of the discrepancy. Therefore, answer d is incorrect.

Need to Know More?

Microsoft Corporation. *Microsoft Windows 2000 Professional Resource Kit.* Redmond, Washington: Microsoft Press, 2000. ISBN: 1-57231-808-2. This book has invaluable information on implementing security accounts and policy.

Stinson, Craig, and Carl Siechert. *Running Microsoft Windows 2000 Professional.* Redmond, Washington: Microsoft Press, 2000. ISBN: 1-57231-838-4. This guidebook to Windows 2000 Professional is a good source for information on user and group account management.

Wood, Adam. *Windows 2000 Active Directory Black Book.* Scottsdale, Arizona: The Coriolis Group, 2000. ISBN: 1-57610-256-4. This book provides comprehensive coverage of Active Directory.

Search the TechNet CD (or its online version through **www.microsoft.com**) and/or the Windows 2000 Professional Resource Kit CD using the keywords "account", "policy", "SAM", "authentication", "group", "user rights", and "group policy."

4

Configuring and Troubleshooting the User Experience

Terms you'll need to understand:

- ✓ User profiles
- ✓ Offline Files and Folders
- ✓ Windows Installer Service
- ✓ MSI files
- ✓ ZAP files

Techniques you'll need to master:

- ✓ Configuring Offline File and Folder options
- ✓ Implementing Windows Installer Packages
- ✓ Understanding the functionality of various Control Panel applets
- ✓ Implementing software Group Policies

With Windows 2000 Professional, Microsoft has answered various complaints that many users had with Windows NT Workstation. Mobile users of Windows NT Workstation had a difficult job of keeping files on a network file server synchronized with copies they kept on their laptop. Windows 2000 Professional goes a long way toward fixing this age-old problem and other problems such as Dynamic Link Library (DLL) conflicts, application repair, and software updates. This chapter discusses how Windows 2000 Professional addresses these problems. Also, the user environment has been configured and enhanced in Windows 2000 Professional by using various control applets.

Configuring and Managing User Profiles

A *user profile* is the look and feel of the user's desktop environment. A profile is a combination of folders, data, shortcuts, application settings, and personal data. For example, users can configure their computer with the screen saver they like and their favorite desktop wallpaper. These settings are independent of other users' settings. When users log on to their computer for the very first time, a new profile is created for those users from a default user profile. So, when Joe logs on, a profile is created just for Joe. This type of profile is known as a *local profile* and is stored on the computer on which it was created. If Joe logged onto a different computer, his profile would not follow him to the computer he just logged onto. However, you can have a user's profile follow a user around the network if you so choose. This type of profile is called a *roaming user profile*. These profiles are stored on a network server. A local copy of the roaming profile is also found on the client computer.

User Profiles

User profiles in Windows 2000 contain a new folder structure compared to Windows NT. A new folder in a profile called Local Settings is local to the machine it resides on and won't roam. Also, a new folder called My Documents is contained in a profile. This folder is the default location where files are saved to. This folder does roam.

Local Profiles

Windows 2000 Professional local profiles are found in a different location than those in Windows NT 4 Workstation—maybe. If you perform a clean install of Windows 2000 Professional, a user profile is stored in a system partition called root\Documents and Settings\user_logon_name. If, however, you upgrade a Windows NT 4 Workstation to Windows 2000 Professional, the local profile is stored in the same location as it always was: %SystemRoot%\Profiles\user_logon_name.

Logon Scripts, Home Folders

When a user logs on, a *logon script* might execute and a *home folder* might be assigned to the user. Logon scripts are often used to map network drives or to execute some type of batch file. To configure a logon script for a user, perform the following steps:

1. Place the logon script in %SystemRoot%\sysvol\domain\scripts (this is a new location in Windows 2000 for logon scripts).
2. Next, open Active Directory Users And Computers and select the User Object Properties. Go to the Profile tab and simply type the name of the logon script in the Logon Script field.

A *home folder* is a central location on a network server where users can store their files. All users have their own home folder to store data. This way, if their computer fails, they don't lose all their data. Home folders also provide one central location in which users can back up all their data. To create a home folder, perform the following steps:

1. Create a share on a network server to enable home folders.
2. Next, open Active Directory Users And Computers and select the User Object Properties. Go to the Profile tab and select the Connect radio button.
3. Select the drop-down arrow and choose an available drive letter.
4. Type in the Uniform Naming Convention (UNC) path to the user's home folder (e.g., "\\server1\homedir\todd").

> **TIP:** Microsoft suggests that users store their data in My Documents instead of home directories. You can then enable a Group Policy to redirect My Documents from the local computer to a network file server. The Group Policy also activates offline caching of My Documents to the user's local computer. Group Policy as well as offline files and folders are covered later in this chapter.

Roaming User Profiles

If you have users who move from computer to computer, you can configure their profiles to move with them. A roaming profile is stored on a network server so that the profile is accessible regardless of which computer a user logs on to in the domain. You can put the profile on the server in two ways. You can copy a profile that is stored locally on a client computer to the profile server the next time the user logs on to the computer. Or, you can create on a client computer a profile that you will use as a company standard and then manually copy it to the profile server.

> **TIP** Roaming user profiles behave differently in Windows 2000 than in Windows NT 4 Workstation. When a user logs on to a computer for the first time, the roaming profile is copied to the client computer. From that point forward, whenever a user logs on to a computer, the locally cached copy of the profile is compared to the roaming user profile. If the local profile and the roaming profile are the same, the local copy is used. Windows 2000 copies only files that have changed, not the entire profile, as was the case in Windows NT.

Use the following steps to configure a roaming profile:

1. Create a shared folder on a server for the profiles.
2. Open the Control Panel and then open the System Control Panel.
3. Select the User Profile tab.
4. Select the user's profile you wish to roam and select Copy To. Then, type in the UNC path to the shared folder that was created (e.g., "\\server1\profiles\Todd").
5. In Active Directory Users And Computers, select the account properties for the user. Then select the Profile tab and enter the UNC path to the profile server in the Profile Path field.

> **TIP** In Windows 2000, new permissions are assigned to the Roaming Profile directory. If you create a roaming profile on an NT File System (NTFS) volume by using the **%username%** variable, the user and the built-in local Administrators group are assigned Full Control permission of that directory.

Note: Local or roaming profiles are protected from permanent change by renaming NTUSER.DAT to NTUSER.MAN. By renaming the file, you have effectively made the profile read only, meaning that Windows 2000 does not save any changes made to the profile when the user logs off. NTUSER.DAT is found in the root of a profile and is hidden by default. This file is responsible for the user portion of the Registry and contains all the user settings.

Using Offline Files and Folders

Windows 2000 offers a new feature called *Offline Files*. This feature addresses several file access problems that plagued Windows NT such as the file server is down now and users need to access files on the file server, or users are not connected to the network and cannot get access to the files they may need. By using Offline Files and Folders, users can select files on a network file server and mark them for offline usage. This means that users now have a cached copy of the file on their local computer and can work on the file just as if they were connected to the network. Any offline files that have been changed on a local computer are synchronized with the network file server when the users connect to the network.

Setting Up Offline Files and Folders

There are two steps involved in configuring offline files. The first is to configure the share point for offline usage. The second is to cache the files to the client computer.

Configuring Share Points

Use the following steps to configure the share point:

1. Share the files that you want to make available offline.
2. From the Sharing tab, select the Caching button.
3. Select the Allow Caching Of Files In This Shared Folder option (this option is selected by default).
4. Select one of the following three options from the Settings drop-down list and then click on OK:
    - *Manual Caching For Documents*—This option is the default setting. With this option selected, users must select the files they want available for offline usage.
    - *Automatic Caching For Documents*—This option caches all files that users have opened to their local disk for offline usage. Any older files that are out of synchronization are automatically deleted and replaced by a newer version of the same file.
    - *Automatic Caching For Programs*—This option provides the same capabilities as Automatic Caching For Documents but also caches applications that are run from the network.
5. Click on OK to close the Share Point dialog box and to accept the options that you selected.

> By default, Windows 2000 does not allow you to cache files with the .slm, .ldb, .mdw, .mdb, .pst, and .db extensions. However, you can override this setting through a Group Policy. Create a computer policy for Administrative templates\Network\Offline Files\Files not cached.

The policy excludes files with specific file extensions from being cached. However, if the policy is enabled and no file extensions are added, all file types can be made available offline. This setting overrides the default configuration; it does not allow files with the .slm, .ldb, .mdw, .mdb, .pst, and .db extensions to be cached.

Making Files and Folders Available Offline

By default, a Windows 2000 Professional computer is configured for offline file and folder usage. Use the following steps to make a file or folder available offline:

1. Connect to a share point on a domain or workgroup file server. Select and right-click on a file that you want.
2. Select Make Available Offline from the flyout menu.
3. A wizard appears if you are using this feature for the first time.
4. The wizard asks if offline files should be synchronized during logon and logoff. Click on the Next button to accept the default. (Additional options are available after the wizard is finished.)
5. If you want the operating system to remind you that you are not connected to the network, click on the Finish button to accept the default option, Enable Reminders. If you accept this option, a computer icon appears in the system tray. Whenever you are disconnected from the network, a balloon appears; it notifies you that offline files are available.

Once you have completed these steps, a little double arrow icon, shown in Figure 4.1, appears on the file or folder that you have selected for offline usage. This is simply a graphic indicator to inform users that the file is located on the network and that a local cached copy of the file is located on their computer.

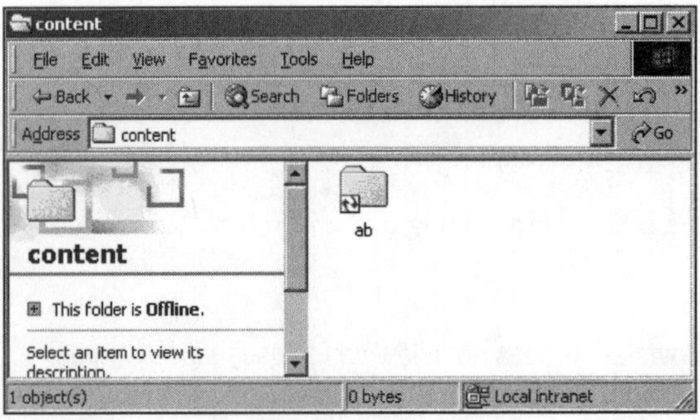

Figure 4.1 The offline file indicator.

Note: A Windows NT 4 client cannot use the offline feature of Windows 2000 servers. However, a Windows 2000 Professional client can make files available for offline usage from a Windows NT 4 server share.

To view offline files once you are disconnected from the network, open My Network Places. Yes, that is correct. Offline files maintain their original location even though the computer is offline. Go to My Network Places and select the file server that contains the files. You can see only the files that you made available while offline. Users don't see the "network" while they are offline.

Synchronizing Offline Files and Folders

Locate the file that you need and continue working. Once you have established a connection and have logged on to the network, any changes you made to the file while you were offline are then synchronized with the original file on the network. However, if you have logged on to the network from a slow dial-up connection, it could take a long time to synchronize offline files while you are logging on.

Several options are available to customize the synchronization process to deal with this type of problem. To customize the process when offline files are synchronized, open a Windows Explorer window, select the Tools menu item, and then choose Synchronize. The first dialog box displays the files and folders that are available offline. To configure synchronization, click on the Setup button. This brings up the Synchronization Settings dialog box, shown in Figure 4.2.

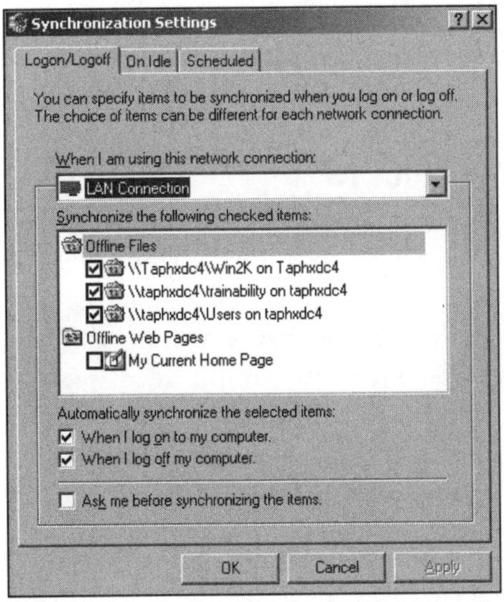

Figure 4.2 The Synchronization Settings dialog box.

This dialog box offers three tabs that help you determine when you should synchronize offline files: Logon/Logoff, On Idle, and Scheduled. However, you can also select over what network connection synchronization takes place. For example, to have synchronization occur only when you are connected to the network (versus when you have a slow dial-up connection), select LAN Connection in the When I Am Using This Network Connection drop-down list.

Synchronization Details

Now that you have configured synchronization, you are probably wondering what actually happens during this process. Well, that depends. Below are several synchronization scenarios:

- *An offline file has been deleted and the original network version of the file has not changed*—If this happens, Windows 2000 Professional removes the file from the network file server during synchronization.
- *A network file has been deleted and the offline version of the file has not changed*—If this happens, Windows 2000 Professional presents a dialog box of this state and gives you the option to either remove the file from the local computer during synchronization or keep the local version.
- *The offline file has changed and the network version has changed*—If this happens, you are presented with a dialog box during the synchronization; it asks you what should be done. The options are: keep the network version, keep the local version, and keep both and rename the local version.
- *Only files that have changed are synchronized*—If no changes have occurred, the locally cached copied is used before the network version of the offline file.

Accessing Offline Files and Folders

To access offline files, use My Network Places; however, that is not where the files are actually kept. Offline files are kept in %SystemRoot%\CSC. (CSC is hidden by default.) This directory contains a database of the offline files. You cannot view or edit individual files from this location. However, if the CSC directory gets quite large and if you use offline files frequently, it is advisable to move this directory from the system partition to a different partition or drive. However, you can't move this directory using the Explorer. To move the CSC directory from one partition to another, use the Windows 2000 Resource Kit utility named **Cachemov.exe**.

Managing Offline Files and Folders

To manage offline files, open a Windows Explorer window and select the Tools menu item. Select Folder Options and then select the Offline Files tab. The key options for managing offline folders are: turn off the Offline Files feature, delete

Offline Files, and view all the Offline Files in one window. You can also use a sliding bar to control the amount of disk space made available for files that have been automatically cached to the local drive. The default disk space made available for automatically cached files is 10 percent.

Configuring and Troubleshooting Desktop Settings

The Windows 2000 desktop is a combination of Windows NT options, Windows 98 options, and some new ones. In general, a regular local or domain user account can configure very few changes on a Windows 2000 Professional computer. The options that users can configure to customize their desktop are the following Control Panel applets and customization options:

- Keyboard applet
- Display applet
- Mouse applet
- Sound applet
- Personalized Start menu
- Quick Launch Pad
- Toolbars

Keyboard Applet

The Keyboard applet adjusts the cursor blink rate, the speed at which a character repeats when you hold down a key, the time lapse before a character repeats, and the input locale for different language groups of keyboard hardware. For example, you can use several language locales with a U.S. keyboard layout so that you can add foreign accent marks to documents that are written in French, Spanish, Italian, and so on. The Regional applet can also be used to configure Input Locales. Chapter 5 contains more information on this topic.

Display Applet

The Display applet has changed a little in Windows 2000 from Windows NT. You can now choose from six tabs to affect various aspects of the display:

- *Background*—Selects and adds a desktop wallpaper or pattern.
- *Screen Saver*—Selects a screen saver but is also a shortcut to the Power Options applet. The Power button on the Screen Saver tab allows you to adjust power schemes and configure Standby and Hibernate modes.

- *Appearance*—Adjusts the color and font schemes that are displayed in all dialog boxes and windows.
- *Web*—Is a new tab. It displays an HTML page on the desktop.
- *Effects*—Adjusts how menus fly out, changes the default icons, and makes other visual enhancements.
- *Settings*—Is probably the most important of the bunch. If Windows 2000 doesn't detect a Plug and Play monitor, it assigns default color depths and resolutions.

Often, these parameters need to be changed to suit the users' needs.

Mouse Applet

The Mouse applet adjusts for left-handed or right-handed use. It also adjusts the double-click speed and the rate at which the cursor moves across the screen.

Sound Applet

The Sound applet controls the startup and logoff sounds. It also controls what WAV files are used for critical error alerts and general alerts.

Personalized Start Menu

Windows 2000 makes it much easier to arrange and customize the Start menu items than Windows NT did. You can very easily sort menu items by dragging and dropping them. You can drag a menu item from one submenu to another. Also, you can open pop-up menus by right-clicking on them. Windows 2000 automatically adjusts menu items as well. Windows 2000 attempts to clean up the Start menu by displaying only those items that are used most frequently. Items that are not used often are hidden. Windows 2000 Professional displays a Screen Tip to click on a double down arrow so that you can access the infrequently used or hidden items on the Start menu. You can turn off this feature quite easily: Right-click on the taskbar and select the Properties command. Doing so displays the General tab of the Taskbar And Start Menu Properties dialog box. Deselect the option for Use Personalized Menus.

You can find even more options on the Advanced tab of the Taskbar And Start Menu Properties dialog box, as shown in Figure 4.3. You can add flyout menus for typical Start menu items such as the Control Panel. Some Start menu items such as Administrative Tools are hidden by default.

The following is a list of the items that you can configure from the Advanced tab:

- Display Administrative Tools
- Display Favorites

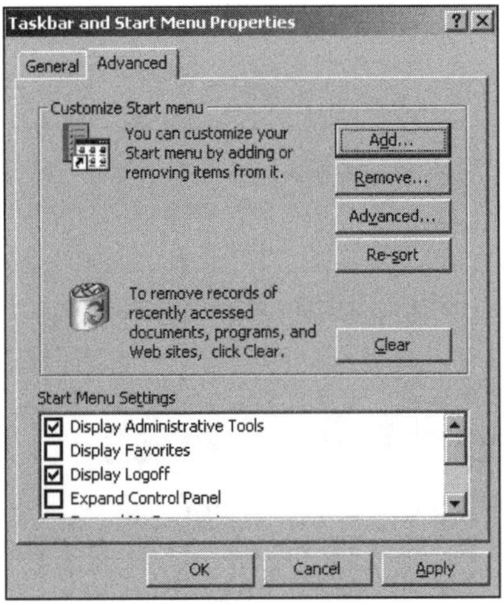

Figure 4.3 Customizing Start menu settings.

- Display Logoff
- Expand Control Panel
- Expand My Documents
- Expand Network And Dial-up Connections
- Expand Printers
- Scroll The Programs Menu

Quick Launch Pad

The taskbar can serve as a multipurpose tool to help make navigating the interface more efficient. The taskbar in Windows 2000, similar to that in Windows 98, contains a Quick Launch Pad, which is a location that contains shortcuts to programs that you use most frequently. By default, Windows 2000 places the Show Desktop (minimizes all windows), Internet Explorer, and Outlook Express shortcuts on the Quick Launch Pad. You can add or remove shortcuts simply by dragging and dropping them on or off the Quick Launch Pad.

Toolbars

The taskbar can also display *toolbars* that allow you to access frequently used files and folders. A default toolbar called the Address toolbar, for example, provides space on the taskbar to allow you to go directly to a Web site or a file path by simply typing the Uniform Resource Locator (URL) or the path to the file that you want to go to. For example, instead of opening a Web browser and then typing the URL, simply type the URL (such as **www.microsoft.com**) in the Address toolbar and press Enter on the keyboard. The Web browser starts automatically and goes to **www.microsoft.com**.

Use the following steps to configure an Address toolbar:

1. Right-click the taskbar and select the Toolbars submenu.
2. Select Address from the submenu. A field called Address is added to the taskbar.

Windows Installer Service Packages

Microsoft has created a new method for installing applications in Windows 2000 called *Windows Installer Service Packages*. The Windows Installer Service actually installs packages on a computer.

The Windows Installer Service has two essential functions:

- It is an operating system service that is responsible for installing, removing, and updating software by asking the Windows Installer Service Package for instructions on how the application should be installed, removed, or modified.
- To create a standard for installing, removing, or modifying applications, you use an application programming interface (API) to communicate with the Windows Installer Service about how a package should be modified after an application is installed.

Once an application has been installed, the Windows Installer Service checks the state of the application while it is being launched. This service provides "self-healing" capabilities to applications if they were installed as a Windows Installer Service Package. The service is always checking to see if the application needs to be repaired.

The service also helps to resolve DLL conflicts. Windows 2000 has devised a way to allow an application to alter the location from which DLLs are loaded, instead of having all DLLs located in the system32 directory. This helps to protect DLLs from being overwritten and from other conflicts.

Key parts of an application have a protected tag on them. A Windows Installer Service Package lists critical files that you would need to replace if they were deleted or missing. For example, executables are listed as critical files. If, for example, Todd.exe were deleted, the Windows Installer Service would locate Todd.exe from a network server or ask the user to insert the CD-ROM that contains Todd.exe. Once Todd.exe was located, it would be installed and the application would launch.

The Windows Installer Service does a much better job of removing applications compared to previous versions of Windows. During the installation of an application, the Windows Installer Service sits in the background looking at everything that is installed, where everything is installed, and what has been changed during the installation. When it comes time to uninstall an application, the Windows Installer Service knows exactly where every last component of the application is, thereby successfully uninstalling the application.

If during the installation of an application something happens and the install fails, the Windows Installer Service can restart the installation from the point of failure. That may not always be the best solution, though. The Windows Installer Service can also roll back everything that was installed up to the point of failure, allowing the user to start the install from scratch.

Installing Packages

A Windows Installer Package (.msi file) contains all the information necessary to tell the Windows Installer Service how the application should be installed. To take advantage of the features that Windows Installer Service offers, you must install an application as an .msi file. Applications such as Office 2000 have their own .msi files. Software developers must design their applications to use this new service. However, existing applications can still gain some of the functionality that .msi files have to offer.

An application can repackage existing applications using third-party tools such as WinInstall LE. WinInstall is available on the Windows 2000 Professional CD-ROM. This application tracks the installation process and note all the files that were installed, their locations, and modifications they made to the Registry. You can then customize this information and turn it into an .msi file.

You may be wondering what to do if you don't have an .msi file or if you can't repackage the file. Non-Windows Installer-based applications such as setup.exe must use a ZAP file to publish a package. A *ZAP file* is just a text file with a .zap extension. The file provides information about how to install a program and the application properties. The following is a basic example of how to create a ZAP file:

```
[application]
FriendlyName= "WinZip Version 7.0"
SetupCommand= \\server1\apps\winzip\WinZip70.EXE
DisplayVersion = 7.0
[ext]
ZIP =
```

Publishing MSI Packages

You typically install .msi files over the network or locally on the client computer. A common method for installing .msi files in a Windows 2000 domain environment is to publish or assign applications to users through the Active Directory. Users in the Active Directory can be grouped into containers called Organizational Units (OUs). You can create a Group Policy Object (GPO) for an OU that either publishes or assigns Windows Installer Packages (.msi files). Any users in the OU would then receive the software when they log on to their Windows 2000 Professional computer. The software they receive when they log on can be either published to them or assigned to them.

Using Group Policy to Publish or Assign Windows Installer Packages

Windows Installer Packages are published or assigned to users through an Active Directory-based Group Policy. Perform the following steps to create a software Group Policy:

1. Open Active Directory Users And Computers.
2. Select the domain to deploy the software to all users in the domain, or select a specific OU to deploy software to users just in that OU.
3. Right-click the domain or OU and choose Properties from the Context menu.
4. Select the Group Policy tab.
5. Click the New button to create a new Group Policy. Type in a name for the Group Policy and press Enter.
6. Select the policy and then press Edit.
7. Under User Configuration, expand Software Settings. Next, right-click Software Installation and then select New|Package from the Context menu.
8. Type the UNC path to the .MSI package on the network (e.g., "\\server1\office2000\data1..msi").
9. Select either Published or Assigned from the Deploy Software dialog box and then press the OK button.

Note: If you are using a transform, you must select Advanced Published Or Assigned. (You can create a transform to install only specific applications from a Software suite of applications.)

10. Close the Group Policy console and press the Close button for the OU properties.

The software Group Policy will take effect when the users of the domain or OU log on to the network. The users can then install the software.

Publishing Applications

A software package is typically published to users when it is not mandatory that they have a particular application installed on their computer. This is a means to make the applications available for users if they decide they want to use them. Once you have created a Group Policy Object to publish a software package, you can log on to your computer and find any applications that were published from Add/Remove Programs, shown in Figure 4.4.

Select the Add New Programs button to see which applications have been published. Users can install a published application with user credentials. The Windows Installer Service installs the published application with elevated credentials on behalf of users. This method provides a central location for users to install applications. This saves users from having to search for network share points that contain applications they want to install.

Assigning Applications

Assigning an application is very similar to publishing one. When an application has been assigned, you can install it from Add/Remove Programs. Additionally, a shortcut for the application that has been assigned is placed on the Start|Programs menu when users log on to their computer. The software does not get installed until users select the shortcut for the first time.

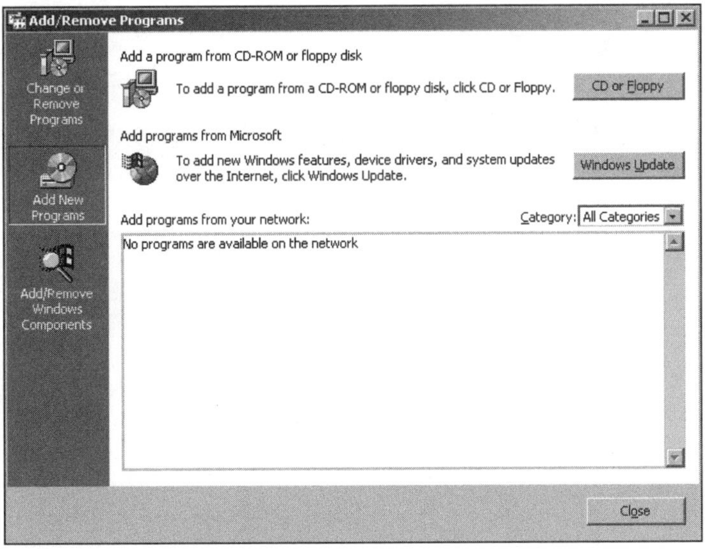

Figure 4.4 Add/Remove Programs.

TIP

Software that has been published or assigned is also installed if users double-click on a file with the extension supported by the published or assigned application.

Practice Questions

Question 1

A salesperson for your company has selected files from the network file server to be made available offline to her laptop computer. She needs access to the files for a sales presentation in another city. When she connects to the corporate office from her hotel room over a dial-up connection, the synchronization process is unacceptably long. What can be done to resolve this problem without disabling offline files?

- ❍ a. Verify that the share point on the network file server is set to Automatic Caching For Documents.
- ❍ b. Use the Synchronization Manager to synchronize files only during a scheduled interval.
- ❍ c. Use the Synchronization Manager to synchronize files only while the computer is connected to the local area network (LAN) connection.
- ❍ d. Select the Never Allow My Computer To Go Offline option from the Offline Files tab in the Folder Options dialog box.

Answer c is correct. When the Synchronization Manager is set to synchronize only while the computer is connected to the LAN, the offline files aren't synchronized via the dial-up connection. Therefore, answer a is incorrect. Automatic Caching has nothing to do with controlling when synchronizing of offline files will occur, but rather to make files available while offline. Scheduling an interval for synchronization while the computer is connected via a dial-up connection may simply delay the process of synchronization but won't prevent synchronizing of files while connected to a modem. Therefore, answer b is incorrect. If the Never Allow My Computer To Go Offline option is selected, the salesperson will not have access to the files she made available offline. Therefore, answer d is incorrect.

Question 2

A user that works for a global organization needs to add foreign accent characters to memos that are sent to its employees in France. How can this be accomplished? [Check all correct answers]

- ❑ a. Use the Regional Control Panel and select the language the user needs to communicate in.
- ❑ b. Install the Multilanguage edition of Windows 2000.
- ❑ c. Use the Keyboard applet and select Input Locales Properties For United States–International.
- ❑ d. Use the Regional Control Panel and select Input Locales Properties For United States–International.

Answers c and d are correct. Both the Keyboard applet and Regional Control Panel allow users to select a keyboard layout that they can use to add foreign accents to documents. It is not necessary to use the Regional Control Panel to select a separate language, nor is it necessary to install the separate Multilanguage edition of Windows 2000. Therefore, answers a and b are incorrect.

Question 3

While at work, you add data to an Access database that is located on a Windows 2000 network file server. You want to finish adding the data to the database from home. You select the database and make it available offline to your laptop computer. When you log off the network, the synchronization process begins but stops due to an error stating that files with an .mdb extension cannot be made available for offline usage. How do you resolve this problem?

- ❍ a. Verify that Access is installed on the laptop and manually synchronize the database.
- ❍ b. Ensure that the .mdb file extension is associated with the correct application.
- ❍ c. Enable a Group Policy to allow for files with the .mdb extension to be cached offline.
- ❍ d. View the Synchronization Manager options to ensure that the database is selected for offline usage.

Answer c is correct. By default, files with the .mdb extension cannot be cached for offline usage. To override this default, you must configure the Files Not Cached policy by not listing .mdb files for Access databases to be made available for offline usage. The error you received is not related to whether or not Access is installed. Therefore, answer a is incorrect. Synchronization proceeds normally whether or not a file extension is registered correctly to an application. Therefore, answer b is incorrect. An error is not displayed if the file isn't selected to be synchronized via the Synchronization Manager. Therefore, answer d is incorrect.

Question 4

A public library has consulted you to create a common desktop for all Windows 2000 Professional machines that the library patrons use. You need to ensure that if a library patron makes a change to the desktop, the change cannot be saved. Currently the library has a mixed environment of Windows 95, 98, and 2000 computers. The following is a list of user account configurations. Create a list of required settings and configurations to implement a common desktop for all Windows 2000 Professional machines. Place the items in the list in the correct order:

User Account Configurations

Logon Scripts for all clients

Home directories for all clients

Ntuser.man

User.man

UNC path to profile

Common Windows 2000 Profile

Common Windows 95 and 98 Profile

Required Settings

Common Windows 2000 Profile

Ntuser.man

UNC path to profile user Ntuser

User.dat is the profile settings file that Windows 95 and Window 98, not Windows 2000, uses. To lock down the patron's desktop, a mandatory profile is being implemented. You create a mandatory profile for Windows 2000 by renaming ntuser.dat to ntuser.dat and then pointing users to the profile via the UNC path. User.dat is the wrong file.

Question 5

A user at a Windows NT 4 workstation is logged on to a Windows 2000 domain and is accessing a Windows 2000 file server. The user reports that he cannot make files available for offline usage. What is the problem?

- ❍ a. The file server is not configured to allow caching of files in the shared folder.
- ❍ b. The user has not enabled offline files from the Offline tab in the Folder Options dialog box.
- ❍ c. The Offline Files and Folders is not available on the Windows NT 4 operating system.
- ❍ d. The Active Directory client needs to be installed on the Windows NT 4 workstation.

Answer c is correct. Windows NT 4 (Server and Workstation) cannot cache files for offline use therefore answer b is incorrect. Also, a Windows NT server lacks the capability for configuring caching options. Therefore, a is incorrect. However, a Windows 2000 computer can make files available for offline use from a Windows NT 4 server or workstation. Adding the Active Directory client will not enable is functionality on a Windows NT 4 workstation, therefore answer d is incorrect.

Question 6

You create a Group Policy for users at the domain level to publish a Windows Installer Package. When users log on to their computers, they report that the software has not been installed. What needs to be done to install the software?

- ❍ a. Users should select the shortcut for the application from the Programs menu. This will install the application.
- ❍ b. Users should use Add/Remove Programs to install the software.
- ❍ c. Users should configure a logon script to execute the Windows Installer Package when they log on.
- ❍ d. Users should configure the Group Policy to publish the software for computers.

Answer b is correct. When an application has been published to users, you can install the application in two ways. Users can use Add/Remove Programs or they can double-click on a file that is associated with the application that needs to be installed. Answer a is incorrect because the application was published, which does not create a shortcut from the Programs menu. Answers c and d are not related to the problem. The application has been published and is ready to install via the Add/Remove applet.

Question 7

Nurses need to log on to nursing stations equipped with Windows 2000 Professional in a Windows 2000 domain. A nurse may log on to three or four different stations. You need to ensure that each nurse's desktop environment is available no matter which station each nurse logs on to. What do you need to do to implement this?

- ❍ a. Configure the nurses' account profile on each workstation with the UNC path to the nurses' profiles.
- ❍ b. Configure the nurses' domain account with the UNC path to the nurses' home directory.
- ❍ c. Configure the nurses' domain account with the UNC path to the Profile directory.
- ❍ d. Configure a logon script to map the Profile directory.

Answer c is correct. To have the nurses' desktop be available on any workstation, you must create a roaming user profile. The workstations are in a domain environment, so the domain user account must have the UNC path for the Profile configured. Answer a is incorrect because the question states the nurses' are in a domain. Configuring each workstation would be correct for a workgroup environment. Answer b is incorrect because the home directory is not used for roaming profiles. Answer d won't make a user profile roam.

Question 8

You have implemented roaming user profiles and home directories for all users. However, users report that their files are being saved to their local hard disk instead of to the network server. What must be done to ensure that users' files are being saved to the network server? [Check all correct answers]

- ❑ a. Redirect the My Documents folder to a network file server using a Group Policy.
- ❑ b. Redirect the My Documents folder to a network file server by providing the UNC path to the user's home directory on the Target tab of the My Documents property sheet.
- ❑ c. Verify that the UNC path to the home directory is correct.
- ❑ d. Verify that the UNC path to the Profile directory is correct.

Answers a and b are correct. The default location that applications save their files to is the My Documents directory. The default location for the My Documents directory is in the user's profile. However, this portion of the profile is not included in the roaming user profile. The My Documents directory needs to be redirected via a Group Policy or through the My Documents property sheet. Therefore, answers c and d are incorrect.

Question 9

You create a Group Policy for users at the domain level to assign a Windows Installer Package. When users log on to their computers, they select the shortcut for the assigned application. The installation of the application fails. What needs to be done to ensure the assigned application will install?

- ❍ a. The users must install the application from Add/Remove Programs.
- ❍ b. The users must verify that the correct UNC path to the software distribution point was configured for the Group Policy.
- ❍ c. The users must double-click on a file with a file extension that is supported by the assigned application to trigger the installation process.
- ❍ d. The users must create a logon script that maps the software distribution point for the domain user accounts.

Answer b is correct. You must use a UNC path to point to the location of the Windows Installer Package to assign or publish a Windows Installer Package via a Group Policy. If the UNC path is incorrect or if a local path is used, the Group Policy points to the wrong location for the software distribution point and so the install will fail.

Question 10

You want to deploy a legacy application to all Windows 2000 Professional clients in the Windows 2000 domain via Group Policy. The legacy application is not a Windows Installer Package. What do you need to do to deploy this application by using a Group Policy?

- ❍ a. Non-Windows Installer applications cannot be deployed with a Group Policy.
- ❍ b. Create a .ZAP file for the legacy application.
- ❍ c. Add a transform to the package that executes a batch file to install the legacy application.
- ❍ d. Choose Advanced Published Or Assigned when creating the software package to select the Allow Legacy Application Environment variable.

Answer b is correct. Applications that install using a setup.exe command require a .ZAP file or a third-party utility to use a Group Policy to deploy the application. If a .ZAP file is used, non-Windows applications can be deployed with a Group Policy. Therefore, answer a is incorrect. You cannot use a transform with a setup.exe command to install the application. Therefore, answer c is incorrect. The Advanced Published Or Assigned option doesn't include any options to install legacy applications. Therefore, answer d is incorrect.

Need to Know More?

Finnel, Lynn. *MCSE Training Kit Microsoft Windows 2000 Server.* Redmond, Washington: Microsoft Press, 2000. ISBN: 1-57231-903-8. Chapter 7 discusses roaming user profiles. Chapter 15 provides information on deploying applications through Group Policy.

Wallace, Rick. *MCSE Training Kit Microsoft Windows 2000 Professional.* Redmond, Washington: Microsoft Press, 2000. ISBN: 1-57231-901-1. Chapter 4 discusses user account properties. Chapter 15 provides information on Offline Files and Folders.

www.microsoft.com/WINDOWS2000/library/planning/management/swinstall.asp. This Web site contains additional information regarding ZAP.

5

Configuring and Troubleshooting System Services and Desktop Environment

Terms you'll need to understand:

- ✓ User locales
- ✓ Input locales
- ✓ StickyKeys
- ✓ FilterKeys
- ✓ ToggleKeys
- ✓ MouseKeys
- ✓ Narrator
- ✓ Utility Manager
- ✓ Fax Service Management console
- ✓ Scheduled Task Wizard

Techniques you'll need to master:

- ✓ Configuring support for multiple languages
- ✓ Configuring accessibility options
- ✓ Implementing and configuring the Fax service
- ✓ Configuring and managing tasks with Task Scheduler

Windows 2000 offers many new services and options that can accommodate people's special needs. You can configure this new operating system very easily to adjust for different locales and languages. Also, you can customize Windows 2000 Accessibility options to adjust the interface and keyboard responses for people with disabilities. We will also learn how to configure and troubleshoot the Fax service and the Scheduled Task Wizard in this chapter.

Multiple Location and Language Support

The Windows 2000 operating system jumps ahead of previous versions of Windows support of multiple languages. It allows you to support people and companies that need to communicate in different languages by using locales. In addition, a Multilanguage version of Windows 2000 allows users to easily switch between different language user interfaces to suit their needs.

Language Options

There are essentially two key areas of language configuration options within Windows 2000 Locale and Language Group options.

Locales

A *locale* is a collection of information that Windows 2000 maintains about a user's language. A locale contains information such as the following:

- Currency symbol
- Format of date, time, and numbers
- Localized calendar settings
- Character encoding
- Country abbreviation

Applications use the locale information to input the correct symbols and characters. There are two types of locales:

- *User locale*—A separate locale is maintained for each user. This locale controls the settings for date, time, and numbers on a per-user basis. When a locale is changed, Windows 2000 adjusts all the regional settings (such as the currency symbol) to reflect the selected locale.
- *Input locale*—A language is associated with an input method. For example, you could add the Spanish input locale to combine the Spanish keyboard with the English and French languages. This configuration would allow a user to use the Spanish keyboard layout to input data in both English and French. Input locales allow users who need to converse in multiple languages

to use one keyboard layout that can be switched on the fly and that maps to other languages as needed.

Configuring User Locales

You configure all locales and language settings through the Regional Options applet in the Control Panel folder. Perform the following steps to select a different user locale:

1. Open the Regional Options applet.
2. Select the General tab.
3. Select the locale required in the Your Locale (Location) drop-down list.
4. Click OK.

No reboot is required. The change of locale takes effect immediately. In addition, applications that depend on these settings reflect the new locale immediately. When you change the locale, the Numbers, Currency, Time, and Date tabs reflect the new configurations that are related to the new locale. Another way to configure these settings is to type a new entry for the desired option. For example, a user could select the Currency tab and type in a new currency symbol to be used.

Configuring Input Locales

If a keyboard layout needs multiple layouts, you must add input locales. Doing so allows a user to switch between locales when working in different languages. Perform the following steps to add an input locale:

1. Open the Regional Options applet.
2. Select the Input Locales tab.
3. Click Add and choose an input locale from the drop-down list.
4. Click OK.
5. Select a method to switch between input locales:
   - Cycle through input locales by pressing left Alt+Shift.
   - Assign a hot key sequence to specific input locales.
6. Click OK to close the Regional Options applet.

When you have completed these steps, an icon appears in the system tray; it indicates the input locale that is currently being used. Another way to select input locales (besides assigning hot keys) is to click the Input Locale icon and then select the specific input locale that you need.

Note: Additional input locales are available for each new language that is installed. For example, if a user needs an input locale for Estonian, install the Baltic language setting.

Multilanguage Support

Locales are used to adjust keyboard layouts for entering text. However, what if a user needs to read text that is in a different language? In this situation, you can install additional language groups in Windows 2000. For example, if the English-language version of Windows 2000 is installed and a user needs to read documents written in French, you can add the French-language group to Windows 2000. In this instance the application that is being used to read the French text must also support the ability to use Windows 2000 language groups.

Installing Multiple Language Settings

Perform the following steps to install additional language settings:

1. Log on as an administrator (users can't install language settings).
2. Open the Regional Options applet.
3. Select the General tab.
4. Click the checkbox for the language settings to be installed.
5. Insert the Windows 2000 Professional CD-ROM to copy the files. After the files have been copied, reboot the computer for the changes to take effect.

Once the computer has been rebooted, the additional language settings and additional locales are available.

Multilanguage Version of Windows 2000

Companies that have a global presence often need different language versions of an operating system. Previous versions of Windows require that you install a separate version of the operating system for each language that you are using. This goes a step further than input locales and language settings. The separate language edition of Windows 95, 98, or NT displays the user interface of the language edition that was installed. For instance, if the French edition of Windows 98 were installed, the user interface would be displayed in French characters and symbols. This, however, adds a tremendous amount of administrative overhead. These operating systems are distinctly different from the English versions, so they require separate Service Packs (SPs) and hot fixes. In this environment, an administrator might have to support three or four different versions of Windows 98.

Windows 2000 changes all of this. You can install a separate Multilanguage version of Windows 2000, which allows you to install additional languages to the existing English version of the operating system. After you have completed the basic installation of Windows 2000, you can install additional user interfaces that support other languages. The end result is a single version of Windows 2000 that supports multiple languages. The same SPs, hot fixes, and upgrades that you apply to the standard English version of Windows 2000 also apply to the Multilanguage edition of Windows 2000.

After you have installed a language user interface, a user can easily switch between interfaces via the Regional Options applet. A new tab that selects the desired interface is added to the applet. After the interface has been selected, the user must log off and log back on for the change to take effect. The user interface selection is established on a per-user basis. Several people can use the same computer but have completely different interfaces. Each user's profile contains the settings for which user interface should be used. The user interface provides the local language characters and symbols for the operating system and for the installed applications.

Accessibility Options

Windows 2000 provides several options to make navigating and using the operating system easier. You can enhance the interface and keyboard settings for users who have limited vision, hearing, and manual dexterity.

Accessibility Options Applet

The Accessibility Options applet contains several useful tabs: Keyboard, Sound, Display, and Mouse.

Keyboard Tab

Several options are available on the Keyboard tab to control repeat rate and key combinations:

- *StickyKeys*—This option allows a user to press multiple keystrokes such as Ctrl+Alt+Delete, by using one key at a time. To enable this feature, select the StickyKeys option in the Accessibility Options applet. You can also enable it by pressing the Shift key five times. At that point, a dialog box appears; it asks the user if this feature should be turned on. Click OK to enable and close the dialog box. In addition, a StickyKeys icon appears in the system tray. Double-clicking this icon opens the Accessibility Options applet.

- *FilterKeys*—This option lets you control the keyboard repeat rate, ignore repeated keystrokes, and control the rate at which a key repeats the keystroke if a user holds it down. You can apply granular settings to configure the repeat delay in number of seconds. If, for example, a user presses the L key and holds the key down, the letter L will repeat every x seconds (x represents the number of seconds for the repeat key delay). When you have enabled FilterKeys, an icon in the shape of a stopwatch appears in the system tray. You can also enable FilterKeys by holding down the right Shift key for eight seconds.

> EXAM ALERT: If a user has enabled FilterKeys but finds that the keystrokes repeat with no delay, either someone has selected the No keyboard repeat settings or the repeat time delay has been configured to its lowest setting.

- *ToggleKeys*—When enabled, this option causes a high-pitched sound to be played when the Num Lock, Caps Lock, or Scroll Lock key is pressed. This feature is enabled via the Accessibility Options applet or by holding down the Num Lock key for 5 seconds.

Sound Tab

On the Sound tab, you can enable the following two sound features to help notify users of warnings and other events:

- *SoundSentry*—When enabled, this option displays visual warnings when Windows 2000 generates audible alerts. This feature is helpful for users with hearing impairments. A user can specify which part of the screen actually flashes when a sound is generated. The options are Flash Active Window, Flash Active Caption Bar, and Flash Desktop. To enable this feature, simply select the SoundSentry checkbox. No shortcut is available for this feature.

- *ShowSounds*—If applications use sounds to convey messages and information, this feature displays text captions that represent those sounds. Selecting the ShowSounds checkbox enables this feature. No shortcut is available for ShowSounds.

Display Tab

The Display tab allows you to set color schemes:

- *High Contrast*—When enabled it informs applications to change the color scheme to a High Contrast scheme to allow for easier reading. For example, you can enable a white on black scheme, a black on white scheme, or a custom color scheme. Doing so allows users to adjust colors and font sizes for Windows 2000 and all applications. To enable this feature, select the Use High Contrast checkbox; or, press left Alt+left Shift+Print Screen keys as a shortcut. When you press these three keys at the same time, a dialog box that asks if the feature should be turned on appears.

Mouse Tab

The Mouse tab allows you to use the keyboard as a mouse using these two features:

- *MouseKeys*—When enabled, this feature allows a user to use the numeric keypad to move the mouse pointer. The keypad can also perform single-click, double-click, and drag-mouse actions. In addition, you can assign settings that control the pointer speed. To enable this feature, select the MouseKeys checkbox or press left Alt+left Shift+Num Lock. A dialog box will appear asking if the MouseKeys feature should be enabled. If you click the OK button an icon will appear in the system tray to graphically indicate the feature has been enabled.

> You can turn off StickyKeys, FilterKeys, ToggleKeys, SoundSentry, High Contrast, and MouseKeys after a specified idle period has passed. For example, you could assign a five-minute idle period. These six features would then all be turned off if the computer were idle for five or more minutes. To assign an idle period, select the General tab in the Accessibility Options applet and then click the Turn Off Accessibility Features After Idle For option.

- *SerialKey*—Enable this option for users who cannot use a standard keyboard and must install an alternative input device into a serial port. This option is located on the General tab.

Accessibility Wizard

You can configure most of the accessibility options quite easily through the Accessibility Wizard. The wizard asks a series of questions to determine if you need to configure keyboard, sound, display, and mouse accessibility features. For example, the wizard displays a sentence in varying font sizes. The user then selects a sentence with the font size that is easy to read. After the user has answered all the questions, the interface immediately changes to reflect large fonts and any other options that were configured.

Note: *The Accessibility Wizard allows users to save the settings they have selected. These settings are saved in a file with the .acw file extension. These settings can be used on another computer or can serve as a backup. If many users require the same accessibility configurations, an administrator can save some time by saving the settings and using them on other computers that need the same configuration. However, there is a gotcha here. The default permissions assigned to the .acw file are for the user who is logged on and for the administrator. Before you can share the settings, make sure that you have added to the access control list (ACL) any global groups or individual user accounts that need access to this file.*

Additional Accessibility Features

Windows 2000 provides three additional accessibility tools that are not available in the Accessibility Options applet. These tools, which you can locate by navigating to Start|Programs|Accessories|Accessibility, are the following:

- *Narrator*—This tool is for people who have low vision or are blind. When enabled, the Narrator uses a synthesized voice to read what is displayed (such as menu options, text, dialog boxes, and alerts).
- *Magnifier*—This tool splits the screen into two portions, magnified and nonmagnified. The magnified portion of the screen magnifies the size of anything that the mouse pointer is hovering over. The nonmagnified area selects what needs to be magnified. You can increase or decrease the magnification level and the size of the magnification.
- *On-Screen Keyboard*—This tool displays a virtual keyboard on the Windows 2000 desktop. Users use the mouse pointer to press the virtual keys. They can also use a joystick with the on-screen keyboard to select keys.

Utility Manager

Utility Manager allows users to access these three tools from one interface. You can also use Utility Manager to check the status, and start or stop the tools. Also, an administrator can configure these tools to start when Windows 2000 starts.

Fax Features

Windows 2000 provides support for sending and receiving faxes via an internal or external modem. The Fax applet appears in the Control Panel folder once a modem has been installed. You use this applet to configure the Fax service and to access the Fax Service Management console. By default, the Fax service is configured to allow users to only send faxes, not receive them.

To fax a document, follow these steps:

1. Select the Print command within the application.
2. Select the fax printer and then click the Print option to submit a fax. The Send Fax Wizard opens. The wizard allows you to enter the recipient's name and fax number, cover page information, and other configurations. Figure 5.1 shows the Send Fax Wizard.

Configuring the Fax Service

The Send Fax Wizard gathers some information such as the sender's name and fax number. This information is gathered from settings contained in the Fax applet.

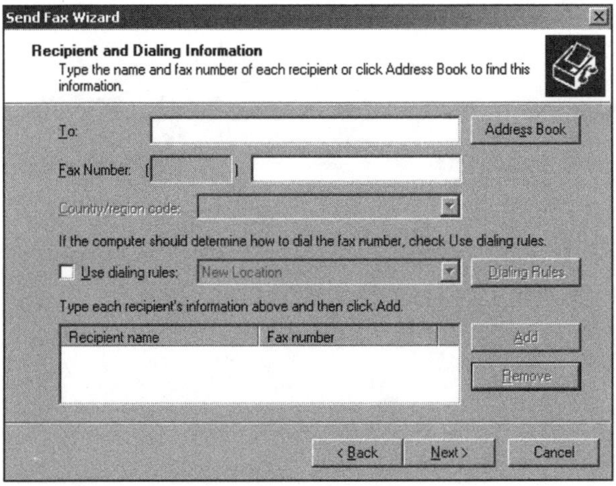

Figure 5.1 Send Fax Wizard.

You can also use this applet to troubleshoot and monitor fax transmissions. Here are the Fax applet tabs:

- *User Information*—This tab contains information such as fax number, email address, name, mailing address, and phone numbers. The Send Fax Wizard and the Fax Cover Page Editor use this information.
- *Cover Pages*—This tab contains options to add existing cover pages or to create new ones using the Fax Cover Page Editor.
- *Status Monitor*—This tab contains options to display the send/receive status monitor, stop fax transmissions, display a status icon on the taskbar, and manually answer incoming fax calls.
- *Advanced Options*—Important! This tab is visible only if the user logs on as an administrator. This is a key area of fax administration. You can configure the Fax service and add fax printers via this tab. Of particular importance is the Fax Service Management option. When this option is selected, the Fax Service Management console opens.

Managing the Fax Service Management Console

You can do the following with the Fax Service Management console:

- Configure the modem(s) to send or receive faxes. If more than one modem is installed, the first modem is used by default to send or receive faxes.
- Change or apply fax-related security permissions for users or groups. By default, the Everyone group can submit faxes and view fax jobs. However, only Administrators and Power Users can manage fax jobs, service, and devices.

- Configure the number of rings before a fax device answers a fax call. The default number is two.
- Configure the number of retries that are allowed before the fax device aborts sending the fax job.
- Choose where to store faxes that have been sent or received. The default location for both options is All User Profile\My Faxes.
- Adjust the priority for sending faxes.
- Change the detail of the fax logs.
- Print faxes upon reception.
- Prevent the use of personal cover pages.
- Configure the Transmitting Station Identifier (TSID), which is typically the sender's fax number.
- Configure the Called Station Identifier (CSID), which is typically the recipient's fax number.

Another way to open the Fax Service Management console (besides checking the Fax Service Management option, described earlier) is to select Start|Programs|Accessories|Communications|Fax|Fax Service Management. Any user can open it using this method. However, a user is denied access to making any configurations in the console. Only Administrators and Power Users can actually configure this service.

EXAM ALERT: One of the main reasons for having a computer network is to share resources. Unfortunately, the Windows 2000 fax printer cannot be shared.

If faxes aren't being sent or received, verify that a user has permission to use the fax device and make sure the fax device is configured to send and receive faxes. If those settings are correct and faxes are still not being sent or received, stop and restart the Fax service.

Task Scheduler

In Windows NT 4 Workstation the **at** command is used to schedule when batch files, scripts, or backups should run. Windows 2000 has a graphical user interface (GUI) utility called Task Scheduler to run these same tasks. This utility is almost a carbon copy of the Windows 98 Task Scheduler.

You can open Task Scheduler from the Scheduled Tasks folder (located in the Control Panel folder) or Start|Programs|Accessories|System Tools|Scheduled Tasks. The Scheduled Tasks folder is shared by default. You can create a task on a computer and then copy it to another one. This is helpful if a similar task needs to run on many computers. By copying the task from one computer to another, you don't have to recreate it multiple times.

Creating a Task

To create a new task, open the Scheduled Tasks folder and double-click the Add Scheduled Task icon to launch the Scheduled Task Wizard. This wizard steps users through the process of selecting a program, batch file, or a script to run automatically at a scheduled time. Perform the following steps to create a task:

1. Select the program to be scheduled and then click Next.
2. Choose how often the task should run and then click Next. The options are as follows:
   - Daily
   - Weekly
   - Monthly
   - One Time Only
   - When My Computer Starts
   - When I Log On
3. Depending on what you chose in Step 2, users may have to set up what time of the day, what days of the week, or what months of the year the task should run. Choose the appropriate options and then click Next.
4. The next step requires you to enter a username and password. The username must have the right to run the selected application. Click Next.
5. The last dialog box of the wizard asks users whether or not to open the Advanced Properties sheet after the task has been created. The Properties sheet allows the user to edit the schedule, delete the task if it is not scheduled to run again, stop the task, start the task during idle periods, and not start the task if the computer is running on batteries. Also, you can assign Security permissions to the task to control which users can modify the task options. Click Finish.

Once you have closed the Scheduled Task Wizard and the Advanced Properties sheet, an icon that represents the task is created. Users can double-click a task to view and configure its advanced properties after they have created the task.

Troubleshooting Tasks

The Scheduled Task Wizard makes it very easy to create tasks. However, sometimes, tasks do fail to run. The most common reason for this is that the wrong username or password was entered for the task. If a task failed, verify that you entered the correct username and password on the task.

Another area where an incorrect account can cause problems is if a task has been created for old 16-bit applications. It may fail to run if the system account is used on the task service. If an error relating to the task service is generated, change the account used to run the service. Open the Task Service, which is located in Start|Programs|Administrative Tools|Services, and select the Log On tab to change the account. Figure 5.2 shows the Task Service Properties sheet. If the task still won't run, stop and restart the Task Service. You can configure it to restart automatically if it fails. To do so, go to the Recovery tab of the Task Service Properties sheet.

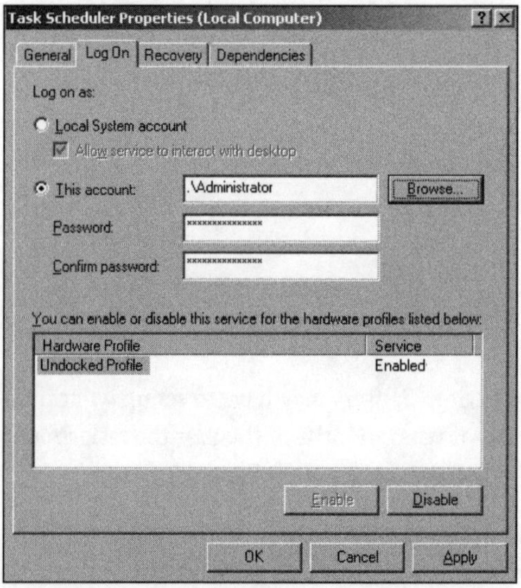

Figure 5.2 Task Service Properties sheet.

Practice Questions

Question 1

A user has the Fax service configured to send faxes, but when a fax is sent to this user, the computer cannot receive any faxes. What must be configured to allow the client computer to receive faxes?

- ❍ a. Install a new fax printer and select receive faxes when installing the printer.
- ❍ b. Reinstall the fax service and select receive faxes during the installation.
- ❍ c. Use the Fax Service Management console to redirect faxes to the My Faxes folder.
- ❍ d. Use the Fax Service Management console to configure the fax modem to receive faxes.

Answer d is correct. You can configure the fax modem to receive faxes after installation. It is not required to reinstall any fax-related services to configure the modem to receive faxes. Therefore, answer b is incorrect. You can configure the fax modem to receive faxes via the Fax Service Management console by selecting Devices, selecting the properties of the device, and choosing Receive.

Question 2

A user has completed a document that needs to be faxed. The user wants to fax the document using the Windows 2000 Fax service but there is no fax printer to print the document to. What needs to be installed or configured so the user can fax the document?

- ❍ a. Restart the Fax service so the user can print to the fax printer.
- ❍ b. Install a modem device.
- ❍ c. Select the Advanced Options tab in the Fax applet to Add A Fax Printer.
- ❍ d. Use the Add Printer Wizard to add a fax printer.

Answer b is correct. The Fax service won't install unless a modem has been detected which is why answer b is correct. Once Windows 2000 detects a modem, the Fax applet is present in the Control Panel folder and a fax printer driver is installed so a client can send and receive faxes. Answers a, c, and d are not viable options until a fax modem has been installed.

Question 3

A user has limited dexterity. You want to configure his Windows 2000 Professional computer to ignore brief or repeated keystrokes. What must be enabled to configure the computer for this user?

❍ a. FilterKeys

❍ b. StickyKeys

❍ c. ToggleKeys

❍ d. MouseKeys

Answer a is correct. Enable FilterKeys if you want Windows 2000 to ignore repeated keystrokes. StickyKeys allows keystrokes such as Ctrl+Alt+Delete to be selected individually therefore answer b is incorrect. ToggleKeys plays a high-pitched sound when the Num Lock, Caps Lock, or Scroll Lock key is pressed; therefore answer c is incorrect. The MouseKeys Accessibility option is used to control the mouse pointer with the numeric keypad. The other options do not allow for this functionality, therefore answer d is incorrect.

Question 4

You are the Administrator of a small network of 50 Windows 2000 Professional clients and 4 Windows 2000 servers. You want to use one of the Windows 2000 Professional clients as a fax server. How do you configure this client to function as a fax server?

❍ a. Enable sharing of the fax printer driver.

❍ b. Use the Fax Service Management console to select the properties of the modem and enable sharing.

❍ c. The Windows 2000 fax print driver cannot be shared.

❍ d. Open the Fax applet in Control Panel and enable sharing from the Advanced tab.

Answer c is correct. The current release of Windows 2000 Professional does not support the sharing of the fax printer therefore answer c is correct. Since Windows 2000 doesn't support fax sharing natively, answers a, b, and d are incorrect. Third-party fax software is required to configure Windows 2000 as a fax server.

Question 5

You require users to log on to your Windows 2000 domain to gain access to their computer and network resources. Several users in your organization have limited dexterity. You need to configure computers for these users to allow the Ctrl+Alt+Delete sequence to be pressed one key at a time. What must be enabled to allow for this functionality?

❍ a. FilterKeys

❍ b. StickyKeys

❍ c. ToggleKeys

❍ d. MouseKeys

Answer b is correct. Enable StickyKeys to allow multiple keystroke combinations such as Ctrl+Alt+Delete to be pressed one key at a time. Enable FilterKeys if you want Windows 2000 to ignore repeated keystrokes, therefore answer a is incorrect. ToggleKeys plays a high-pitched sound when the Num Lock, Caps Lock, or Scroll Lock key is pressed, therefore answer c is incorrect. The MouseKeys Accessibility option is used to control the mouse pointer with the numeric keypad. The other options do not allow for this functionality, therefore answer d is incorrect.

Question 6

You need to enable Windows 2000 Professional to read text from all dialog boxes and all applications to visually impaired users. What must you configure to allow for this functionality?

❍ a. SoundSentry

❍ b. ShowSounds

❍ c. Narrator

❍ d. Windows Media Player Close Caption

Answer c is correct. The Narrator accessibility option is used to read aloud onscreen text, dialog boxes, menus, and buttons that are selected in Windows 2000 Professional. SoundSentry generates visual warnings when the computer generates sound alerts, while ShowSounds tells applications to display captions for sounds the application may make, therefore answers a and b are incorrect. Windows Media Player cannot speak aloud written text, but can display text in Close Caption, therefore answer d is incorrect.

Question 7

You have been asked to help plan the deployment of Windows 2000 Professional for a company that has offices in New York, France, and Germany. The offices in Europe frequently send documents in their native language to the office in New York. The office in New York sends documents in English to the offices in Europe. Users in all offices need to quickly switch between their native language and the language they need to correspond in. Also, it is required that ongoing administration of this environment be kept to a minimum. How can you deploy Windows 2000 to facilitate this?

- ❍ a. Deploy the Multilanguage edition of Windows 2000 Professional to the offices in New York, France, and Germany.
- ❍ b. Include the input locales for each language and create and deploy them using a Remote Installation Service (RIS) image.
- ❍ c. Deploy the English-language edition and manually add input locales for each language as needed.
- ❍ d. Add the Keyboard layout/IME for each language.

Answer a is correct. To allow users to regularly work in multiple languages and to reduce the administration of a computer with different language requirements, you should deploy the Multilanguage edition of Windows 2000 Professional as it uses the same Service Packs and hot fixes as the English language edition of Windows 2000. To install a separate edition of Windows 2000 Professional for each language that is used would add to the ongoing administration of the environment as separate Service Packs and hot fixes would be required for these systems. Answers b, c, and d would add to the administrative overhead to maintain the required environment and would not achieve all the goals. Answers b, c, and d don't allow a user to change user interfaces on the fly. Only the Multilanguage edition of Windows 2000 provides this functionality.

Question 8

You have used Task Scheduler to configure a 16-bit application to run every night at 11 P.M. However, when you log on the next day, you see an error that states the application could not run due to a service error. How do you resolve this problem?

- ❍ a. Enter the correct password for the domain account on the scheduled task.
- ❍ b. Configure the Task Scheduler service to log on with a domain username and password.
- ❍ c. Verify that the task is set to run daily.
- ❍ d. Verify that the local administrator username and password were used to run the task.

Answer b is correct. By default, the Task Scheduler service runs under the context of the local system account. Some older applications may try to start the service with a different account; thus, a service-related error is displayed. Enter a domain username and password for the service to resolve this problem. The error that was displayed was not related to the user account that was entered for the task to run. Two accounts are used: one for the task and the other for the service. The problem here was the account on the service. Therefore answers a and d are incorrect. These answers are concerned with the account being used to run the task. The problem is with the account used to run the service and not the task. Answer c has nothing to do with the problem. Because the service won't run then the task won't run. Verifying if the task is set to run daily doesn't affect the underlying problem with the service account.

Question 9

You have configured Task Scheduler to run a disk defragmentation tool at 11 P.M. each evening. You want five other Windows 2000 Professional computers to use this same task. How can you configure the five computers to use the same task without recreating the task?

❍ a. Configure a Group Policy for the five computers to run a logon script that executes the task.

❍ b. Go to each computer and copy the task that was created from its shared Scheduled Tasks folder to each of the five clients' Scheduled Tasks folder.

❍ c. Import the scheduled task using the **at** command.

❍ d. Import the scheduled task using the Task Scheduler service properties sheet.

Answer b is correct. Tasks are placed in the Scheduled Tasks folder. This folder is shared to everyone by default. Users can access any Scheduled Tasks folder on the network and either move or copy a task that has already been created to their Scheduled Tasks folder. Group Policy is not used to take tasks that were create on one computer and then copy them to another computer, therefore answer a is incorrect. The **at** command is a command line scheduler that does not allow for the importation of tasks that were created using the Scheduled Task Wizard, therefore answer c is incorrect. The Task Scheduler property pages do not provide any options for importing a task; therefore answer d is incorrect.

Question 10

You need to configure a Windows 2000 Professional computer to use Danish configurations (such as Danish usage of numbers and Danish currency) for an employee visiting the head office of your company in the United States. You want to allow the user to quickly switch from one locale to another using a key sequence or the system tray. Currently, the computer is using only the Western Europe and United States settings. How do you configure the computer to also use Danish settings?

- ❍ a. Open the Regional Options applet and select the General tab. Add the Danish locale.
- ❍ b. Open the Regional Options applet and select the General tab. Add the Danish language group for the system.
- ❍ c. Open the Regional Options applet and select the Input Locales tab. Add Danish as a new locale and assign a hot key to this locale.
- ❍ d. Open the Regional Options applet and manually enter the Danish configurations on the Numbers, Currency, Time, and Date tabs.

Answer c is correct. The Input Locales tab allows you to assign which input languages are loaded into memory every time the computer is started. It also allows you to assign hot keys that let you switch between input locales, and it places a small icon in the system tray to also allow a user to switch between input locales on the fly. Answer a would change the user locale to Danish and would then be used as the default locale. The goal is to allow users using a English keyboard to switch on-the-fly to Danish when needed which is not achieved by making Danish the default locale, therefore answer a is incorrect. Adding Danish group simply makes the keyboard layout available as an input locale, which it is as a default. This option doesn't add the Danish keyboard layout to the system tray, only input locales provide that functionality, therefore answer b is incorrect. Answer d does simply hard codes these options as default configurations. It does not allow a user to select the Danish keyboard layout from the system tray or via a keystroke; therefore answer d is incorrect.

Need to Know More?

Microsoft Corporation. *Microsoft Windows 2000 Professional Resource Kit.* Microsoft Press: Redmond, WA, 2000. ISBN: 1-57231-808-2. The book provides invaluable information on Windows 2000 Professional.

Stinson, Craig, and Carl Siechert. *Running Microsoft Windows 2000 Professional.* Microsoft Press: Redmond, WA, 2000. ISBN: 1-57231-838-4. This guidebook to Windows 2000 Professional is a good source for information on administering and configuring Windows 2000 Professional.

Search the TechNet CD-ROM (or its online version through **www.microsoft.com**) and/or the *Windows 2000 Professional Resource Kit* CD-ROM using the keywords "Fax", "Accessibility", "Regional Options".

6

Installing Windows 2000 Professional

Terms you'll need to understand:

- ✓ winnt32.exe
- ✓ winnt.exe
- ✓ unattend.txt
- ✓ sysprep folder
- ✓ Remote Installation Service (RIS)
- ✓ winnt32.exe/checkupgradeonly
- ✓ Migration Dynamic Link Libraries (DLLs)
- ✓ Slipstreaming

Techniques you'll need to master:

- ✓ Understanding the different options available for installing Windows Professional
- ✓ Performing upgrades
- ✓ Applying service packs (SPs)
- ✓ Understanding RIS configurations

Microsoft has made available several ways to install Windows 2000 Professional. This chapter looks at the key areas involved in deploying a manual or automated installation of Windows 2000 Professional. In addition, you need to understand how to use all the utilities that are required for installing, upgrading, and verifying compatibility with Windows 2000.

Performing Attended Installations of Windows 2000 Professional

An attended installation of Windows 2000 Professional requires someone to sit in front of the target computer and answer all the installation prompts such as the End User License Agreement (EULA). Before you start the installation process, you need to ensure that the computer meets the minimum hardware requirements of Windows 2000 Professional. Unlike Windows NT, Windows 2000 supports only Intel-based computers. The following are the minimum hardware requirements for installing Windows 2000 Professional:

- 133MHz Pentium, or higher, Central Processing Unit (CPU)
- 32MB of memory (Microsoft recommends 64MB)
- A 2GB hard drive with a minimum of 650MB of free space
- VGA, or higher-resolution, monitor
- Keyboard
- Mouse
- 10X CD-ROM for CD-ROM installations

Once you've verified that the computer meets these minimum hardware requirements, you should check to see if devices such as the video adapter and the network adapter are compatible. To do this, check the Hardware Compatibility List (HCL), which every Windows 2000 CD-ROM contains. However, that file is out of date. To view the most current HCL, visit **www.microsoft.com/hcl**.

Installation Methods

You can perform an attended install of Windows 2000 in three ways: using a CD-ROM, the setup disks, or the network.

CD-ROM

One of the easiest methods for installing Windows 2000 Professional is simply to put the Windows 2000 Professional CD-ROM in the computer and boot the computer. The computer boots from the CD-ROM, starts the first phase of the installation, and copies the installation files to the local hard drive. Then, the computer reboots (remember to remove the CD-ROM) and starts the graphical user interface (GUI) phase of the installation. You can install Windows 2000 Professional in this fashion if your computer's BIOS supports the option to boot from a CD-ROM drive and the CD-ROM is El-Torito compatible.

Setup Disks

If you can't configure your computer to boot from a CD-ROM, you can install Windows 2000 Professional by using the four floppy setup disks that came with your Windows 2000 Professional CD-ROM. Simply place setup disk number one in the computer to start the installation.

Note: *If the four setup disks are lost or become corrupted, you can create them using the Windows 2000 Professional CD-ROM. Open the Bootdisk folder on the CD-ROM and execute either makeboot.exe or makebt32.exe. A command prompt window that asks you to insert a floppy disk into drive A opens. Continue the process until you have created all four disks. Use makeboot.exe if you are running in a DOS environment or Windows for Workgroup. Use makebt32.exe if you are running in Windows 95, 98, NT, or 2000. This method of creating a boot disk replaces the Windows NT 4 method of executing the* ***winnt32.exe /ox*** *switch, which does not create Windows 2000 setup disks.*

Network

Another installation method is to place the contents of the Windows 2000 Professional CD-ROM in a folder on a network server and then share the folder. This network server is referred to as a *distribution server*. Establish a network connection to the distribution server to start the installation. If Windows 95, 98, or NT is on the target computer, connect to the share point and execute winnt32.exe to start the installation process. If no operating system is on the target computer, use a network boot disk to connect to the source files and use winnt.exe to start the installation. You use winnt32.exe in a 32-bit environment, whereas you use winnt.exe in a 16-bit/DOS environment.

Automating the Installation of Windows 2000 Professional

When you use the three attended installation options, someone must be in front of the computer to answer all the installation prompts. This is a very inefficient means of installing Windows 2000 Professional when you need to install the operating system on many computers. This section discusses how to use Setup Manager, the System Preparation Tool, and Remote Installation Service (RIS) for automating the installation process.

Using Setup Manager to Create an Unattended Installation

The Setup Manager utility answers the installation prompts and saves the answer results in an answer file called unattend.txt. Windows 2000 can then use unattend.txt during the installation to configure the screen resolution and other typical hardware and operating system settings. This tool is much improved in Windows 2000 and adds more options and greater flexibility than its predecessor. Setup Manager can now:

- Agree to the EULA
- Create a distribution share point
- Create a listing of unique computer names for a Uniqueness Database File (UDF)
- Add third-party Plug and Play drivers and other resources
- Add printers, scripts, batch files, and other commands to the distribution share

You must extract Setup Manager from a cab file on the Windows 2000 Professional CD-ROM to create unattend.txt. To extract Setup Manager, perform the following steps:

1. Insert the Windows 2000 Professional CD-ROM into the computer and select the deploy.cab file, located in the Support\Tools folder.
2. Double-click on the deploy.cab file to view the contents.
3. Right-click on setupmgr.exe and select Extract. Choose a location from the Explorer menu to extract the file. Right-click setupmgx.dll and extract this file to the same location of setupmgr.exe.

You can now create the answer file. Double-click on the setupmgr.exe icon to launch the wizard. The setupmgr.exe utility is a multipurpose tool because you can use it to create answer files for several types of unattended installations. We will concentrate on a Windows 2000 unattended installation. Perform the following steps to create an answer file:

1. Double-click on the setupmgr.exe icon to start the utility.
2. Click on Next to pass the welcome page.
3. Select the Create A New Answer File radio button (it will be selected by default) and click Next.
4. The next page displays which product the answer file installs. There are three choices: Windows 2000 Unattended Installation, Sysprep Install, or RIS. Select the Windows 2000 Unattended Installation radio button and click Next.

5. Choose the Windows 2000 Professional radio button and click Next.
6. The next page displays several options regarding user interaction. Typically, no user interaction is required. If, however, you want the installation to stop so you can enter the computer name, select Hide Pages. This option hides all pages in which answers were provided but stops at any areas that you have left blank. Select the Fully Automated radio button and click Next.
7. Select the checkbox to agree to the EULA and click Next.
8. Type in a name and an organization and click Next.
9. Type in the computer names or import a comma-delimited file that contains all computer names that should be used for the installation of new computers. Optionally, you can select the Automatically Generate Computer Names Based On Organization Name checkbox. Checking this results in a combination of the organization name that you typed in the dialog box and a unique alphanumeric combination (e.g., coriol-1AD2RT). Use either method and click on the Next button.
10. Enter a password that the local administrator of the computer will use.

Note: *The password can be up to 127 characters long.*

Enter a password and click Next.

11. Select display settings such as Color, Screen area, and Refresh frequency. Unless all computers have identical video cards with identical monitors, you should set these fields to Use Windows Default. Click on Next to continue.
12. This page provides two options for Network Settings—Typical and Custom. If you select Typical, Microsoft Client, File and Print Sharing as well as the Transmission Control Protocol/Internet Protocol (TCP/IP) protocol are installed. Additionally, the client will be configured as a Dynamic Host Configuration Protocol (DHCP) client. If you need to enter a static IP address or add or subtract network services, use the Custom option. Select Typical or Custom and click Next.
13. The Workgroup or a Domain page appears next. If the computer is to join a domain during the installation, you must type in the name of the domain as well as enter a user name and password of a user who has the right to add workstations to a domain. Fill in the appropriate fields and click Next.
14. The Time Zone page appears next. Simply choose the correct time zone the computer is located in and click Next.
15. You've reached the end of creating a basic answer file. If you need to add other drivers or scripts, select the Yes, Edit The Additional Settings radio

button. For the purposes of our discussion, select No, Do Not Edit The Additional Settings and click Next.

16. You can use the next page to create a distribution share for the Windows 2000 Professional files or to simply create an answer file that you will use in conjunction with the CD-ROM distribution.

Note: *If you choose to create a distribution share, you must name the answer file winnt.sif and you must place it on a floppy disk. A CD-ROM-based install looks for the presence of this file on a floppy disk and uses it to provide an unattended install via the CD-ROM distribution.*

For demonstration purposes, select Yes, Create Or Modify A Distribution Folder and click Next to continue.

17. The next page offers suggested locations and folder names for the distribution share point. If you have already created the distribution share, select Modify An Existing Distribution Folder. If you select this option, just the answer file is created. Accept the default by clicking the Next button.

18. If you need drivers for a hardware Redundant Array of Independent Disks (RAID) controller card, add them here. Click Next to continue.

19. If you need a third-party Hardware Abstraction Layer (HAL) for multiple processor support or other configurations, add that now and click Next.

20. If you need to run a batch file after the installation is done, add those files in the Additional Commands page and click Next.

21. The OEM Branding page appears next. It allows you to replace the default bitmaps that are displayed during the installation process with custom bitmaps and logos. Click Next to continue.

22. The Additional Files Or Folders page appears. Here, you can place files on the computer and install any third-party Plug and Play drivers that don't come with Windows 2000. Click Next.

23. We're almost finished. Enter a name for the answer file and the location of the distribution share. The default name for the answer file is unattend.txt. In a working environment, you should change this name because setupmgr.exe takes a basic answer file from the Windows 2000 CD-ROM that overwrites the one you just created. Click Next.

24. You now have to copy the distribution files from the Windows 2000 Professional CD-ROM to the distribution share. Put the CD-ROM in the computer and click Next.

25. The files are copied to the distribution share; the last page displayed is a summary page of the files that you created. Click Finish.

Putting It All Together

Now that you have created the answer file and the distribution share, let's put it all together to see how to launch an unattended install of Windows 2000 Professional. To master this task, you must understand a few switches that are involved. winnt.exe has multiple switches to control its functionality. Below is a list of switches that relate to unattended installs:

- */u:answer file*—This switch is used for an unattended installation. The file contains answers to the installation prompts.
- */s:sourcepath*—This switch points to the location of the Windows 2000 installation files.
- */udf:id*—This switch is used in conjunction with a UDF file, which overrides the values of the answer file. You typically use this file to provide unique configuration parameters during the installation process. ID designates which settings contained in the UDF file should be used.
- */unattend*—This switch is used with winnt32.exe to create an unattended upgrade to Windows 2000.

You use these switches in combination to launch an unattended installation of Windows 2000 Professional using Setup Manager. To launch an unattended install, follow these steps:

1. Use a network boot disk to connect the target computer to the network.
2. Next, use the **net use** command to map to the distribution share point using an available drive letter.
3. Then, switch the command prompt to the mapped drive letter (such as I) and use the following as an example to launch an unattended install for a computer called machine1:

```
I:\WINNT.EXE /s:I:\i386 /u:unattend.txt /
udf:machine1,unattend.udf
```

Practice using the Setup Manager several times while choosing different options each time to see how the results vary. Remember that you can use this Setup Manager utility to also create answer files for System Preparation Tool installs, which is our next topic, and RIS installs, which are discussed a bit later.

Using the System Preparation Tool

The *System Preparation Tool* prepares a master image of a computer that contains Windows 2000 Professional and any software applications that users might need. You can use this tool in conjunction with third-party disk imaging software. Disk imaging software makes an exact mirror image of whatever is on the computer, including all the unique parameters of Windows 2000. Each Windows 2000 computer has its own unique Security Identifier (SID) and its own unique computer name. Other computers can't use these settings. If you applied an image that contained these unique settings to several computers, they would all have the same computer name and the same SID. The System Preparation Tool removes all the unique parameters from a Windows 2000 computer before the computer is imaged. It is a very easy tool to use, but you must follow several specific steps to use it. The first step is to create a folder called sysprep in %SystemRoot% (e.g., c:\sysprep).

To use the System Preparation Tool, you must extract it from the deploy.cab file and place it in the sysprep folder. Perform the following steps to extract sysprep.exe and a helper file called setupcl.exe:

1. Insert the Windows 2000 Professional CD-ROM into the computer and select the deploy.cab file, located in the Support\Tools folder.
2. Double-click the deploy.cab file to view the contents.
3. Right-click on sysprep.exe and select Extract. Use the Explorer menu to extract the file to the sysprep folder that you created. Right-click setupcl.exe and extract it to the sysprep folder.

The next step is to install and configure all applications that must be in the disk image. Once you have accomplished this, run sysprep.exe in the sysprep folder. Sysprep.exe removes all unique parameters from the computer and then shuts down the computer. Reboot the computer with a disk image boot disk and create an image of the computer.

After you have applied an image to a computer, a Mini-Setup Wizard runs. It prompts you to put back the unique parameters that you took out. The SID is generated automatically at this point. However, you'll have to input the following settings:

- Computer Name
- User Name
- Product ID
- Regional Settings
- Company Name
- Network Settings
- Time Zone
- Place Computer In A Workgroup Or Join A Domain

As you can see, you need to enter a fair amount of information for every computer you apply the image to. You can use Setup Manager, discussed earlier in this chapter, to create an answer file called sysprep.inf. This file provides the above settings to the Mini-Setup Wizard to answer all the installation prompts. The end result is an unattended install of the image.

Note: *You must place sysprep.inf in the sysprep folder or on a floppy disk, which are the default locations where the Mini-Setup Wizard looks for the answer file (it checks the sysprep folder first) after you have applied the image. Another point: You should apply the image to computers with similar hardware. When you apply the image, sysprep.exe triggers Plug and Play into action. Plug and Play can resolve some differences in hardware. However, if the hard disk controller and the HAL on the image are different than those on the computer to which you are applying the image, the image installation will fail (e.g., if you create the image on a computer that contains an HAL for a computer with multiple processors but you are applying the image to a uniprocessor computer.)*

Using Remote Installation Services (RIS)

You can use RIS to deploy Windows 2000 Professional over a network from a remote installation server. RIS integrates a few of the installation methods we have discussed into one tight bundle. You can use it to install Windows 2000 Professional to a computer with a blank hard drive or to reinstall Windows 2000 Professional to repair a corrupted installation.

The main goal of RIS is to reduce total cost of ownership (TCO) by having one central location for either the end users or administrators to install Windows 2000 Professional. To install Windows 2000 Professional using RIS, a user presses the F12 key during the boot process to find RIS server and start the installation. Three steps are involved in making RIS work: configure the client, configure network servers for RIS, and create a Windows 2000 Professional image. The next few sections uncover the details of these areas.

Configuring Clients

The client computer can connect to an RIS server in two ways. The first method is to install a peripheral connection interface (PCI) network adapter that contains a Preboot Execution boot ROM (PXE). You then have to configure the computer's BIOS to boot from the PXE network adapter. When the computer boots from the PXE network adapter, it attempts to get an IP address from a DHCP server. Once the network adapter has an IP address, the user is prompted to press the F12 key to locate an RIS server.

In the second method if the network adapter is not PXE compliant, you can use an RIS boot disk with some network adapter manufacturers such as 3Com and Intel. Use the rbfg.exe utility to create an RIS boot disk. Once you have installed RIS, you can find the utility in RemoteInstall\Admin\i386\rbfg.exe.

Configuring Network Services and Hard Drive Space Requirements

Before you can install and configure the RIS service, several prerequisites must be in place on the network. The following is a list of the RIS requirements you must meet before you install it:

- *DHCP server*—The client needs to obtain an IP address from a DHCP server during the boot process. You cannot configure RIS until a DHCP server is available. A Windows 2000 DHCP server cannot give IP addresses to clients unless it is authorized to do so. Perform the following steps to authorize the DHCP server:

    1. Open the DHCP Manager Microsoft Management Console (MMC) by going to Start|Programs|Administrative Tools|DHCP.
    2. Select the DHCP node and choose Action from the menu bar.
    3. Choose Manage Authorized Servers from the menu.
    4. Click on the Authorize button and type the host name or IP address of the DHCP server. Click on OK and close the dialog box.

- *Active Directory and Domain Name Service (DNS)*—Once the network adapter has an IP address, it needs to find an RIS server. The client finds RIS by querying a DNS server to find where an Active Directory server (domain controller—DC) is. The Active Directory then tells the client where an RIS server can be found.
- *Its own partition*—RIS demands its own partition. You cannot install RIS on a system or boot partition, usually the C partition.

Once you have met the three conditions for an RIS installation, make sure a separate partition is available (or will be created) for RIS. It is recommended to reserve at least 2GB for an RIS partition.

Installing and Configuring the RIS Service

You can install the RIS service on a Windows 2000 DC or on a Windows 2000 member server if you have met all the prerequisites. After you have installed the service, you must configure it. Perform the following steps to install the RIS service:

1. Log on to the server as an Administrator.

2. Open the Control Panel (Start|Settings|Control Panel) and double-click Add/Remove Programs.

3. Click on the Add/Remove Windows Components button and select the Remote Installation Services checkbox.

4. Insert the Windows 2000 Server CD-ROM. The service is copied to the server and you are prompted to reboot the server once the service has been installed.

Now that you have installed the RIS service, you must run risetup.exe to respond to clients' requests for an RIS server and to put the initial image of Windows 2000 Professional on the RIS server. The initial image is simply a copy of the I386 folder found on the Windows 2000 Professional CD-ROM. Perform the following steps to configure the RIS service:

1. Type "risetup.exe" from Start|Run and click the OK button.

2. The Remote Installation Services Setup Wizard presents a welcome page that reminds you of some of the RIS prerequisites. Click the Next button.

3. By default, the Wizard offers to create the RIS folder structure and files on the C partition (even though the wizard itself reminds us that this can't be done). Choose a drive letter for a nonsystem partition to place the files into and click the Next button.

4. The next dialog box asks if the RIS server should respond immediately to client requests before you have even finished the configuration. Leave the checkbox deselected. You can select it after you have configured Active Directory Users And Computers.

5. The next dialog box asks where the system should look for the Windows 2000 Professional installation files. Type the drive letter for the CD-ROM drive and the path to the installation files (e.g., D:\I386). Click Next.

6. The next dialog box suggests a folder name for the initial image. Each image that is created has its own folder. Use the default name provided or type in a different name, and then click Next.

7. The next dialog box asks you to provide a descriptive name for this image. Use the default or type in a different name. Click the Next button to get to the finish line.

8. You're at the end. The final dialog box summarizes the parameters that you selected. Click on the Finish button. Risetup.exe now copies the contents of the I386 folder to the folder structure that you just created and completes the installation process.

When the installation is finished, you need to configure the RIS server to respond to RIS clients. You have to log on as a domain administrator to complete this final step. Launch the Active Directory Users And Computers console by clicking on Start|Programs|Administrative Tools|Active Directory Users And Computers. Next, double-click on the Domain Controllers container if RIS was installed on a DC; otherwise, double-click on the Computers container. Next, right-click on the RIS Server Computer object and select Properties from the Context menu. Click on the Remote Install tab from the Properties page. On this tab, select the Respond To Client Computers Requesting Service option, shown in Figure 6.1.

Creating Additional Images

The risetup.exe Wizard created the first image of Windows 2000 Professional for us. However, that image provides only an attended installation of the operating system. You can create additional images that contain the operating system as well as any necessary applications and configuration. RIS installs a utility called riprep.exe that you can use to create images of the operating system and any installed applications. The functionality of riprep.exe is similar to that of a third-party disk imaging application. However, riprep.exe has some limitations. It can only make an image of the C partition of a computer. If a computer contains a C and D partition, only the C partition will be part of the image. Also, when you apply the image to a computer via RIS, any existing partitions are deleted. The entire hard drive is repartitioned as a single partition and then is

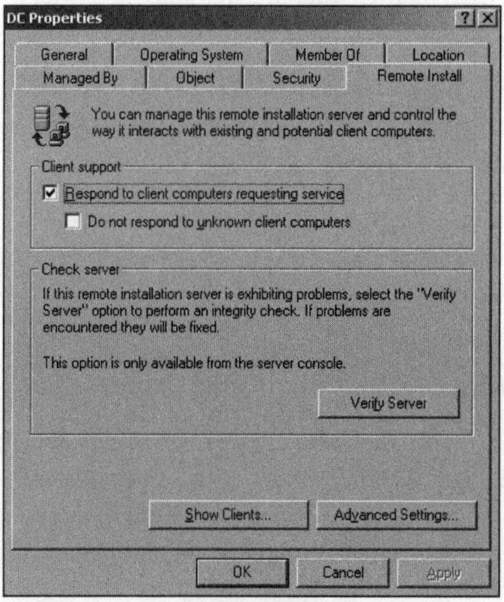

Figure 6.1 The Remote Install tab.

formatted with the NTFS file system. If you can work within those limits, you can easily configure and deploy riprep.exe images. Perform the following steps to create a riprep.exe image:

1. Connect the computer that you are imaging to the network.
2. Install Windows 2000 Professional and any applications that users may need. Connect to the REMINST share point on the RIS server. Run riprep.exe from \RIS Server\REMINST\Admin\I386\riprep.exe.
3. The Remote Installation Preparation Wizard is launched. It asks you on which RIS server the image should be placed and the name of the folder to which the image should be copied.
4. The last task is to provide a user-friendly name for the image (such as the Marketing or the Sales image).

After you complete these steps, riprep.exe copies the image to the designated RIS server. However, riprep.exe acts a lot like sysprep.exe. In addition to creating an image, riprep.exe removes the unique attributes, such as the SIDs and the computer name. When the RIS client downloads the image, a Mini-Setup wizard that asks you to put back what was taken out.

Note: *You can use Setup Manager to create answer files for RIS images.*

Downloading an Image

After you have configured an RIS server with several images, users can boot their computers from the network adapter and press F12 to find an RIS server. The server then displays a welcome screen; simply press Enter to bypass this screen. Next, users must log on to the domain. Once they are logged on, they see a list of images to choose from. The users select an image from the list, and RIS reformats the entire drive as well as downloads the image to the target computer. After about 30 to 40 minutes, users have a clean install of the operating system and applications.

Upgrading to Windows 2000 Professional

Windows NT 4 supports only upgrades from previous Windows NT operating systems. Windows 2000, on the other hand, allows for many upgrade paths. The following is a list of Windows operating systems that you can directly upgrade to Windows 2000 Professional:

- Windows NT 4 and 3.51
- Windows 95 (all editions)
- Windows 98 (all editions)

Note: You can directly upgrade Windows NT 4 or 3.51 with or without service packs (SPs). Installing a specific SP before installation is not required when you are upgrading. SPs are discussed later in this chapter.

The easiest operating system to upgrade from is Windows NT. This operating system shares a lot of features with Windows 2000, including its Registry. You can upgrade Windows 95 and 98 quite smoothly as well, but you need to take some precautions, which are detailed in the next section.

Pre-Upgrade Checklist

Before you upgrade to Windows 2000 Professional, you need to check the current operating system configuration for any of the following areas that could cause conflicts during and after the upgrade process:

- *Hardware and software compatibility*—The Windows 2000 Professional CD-ROM contains a utility called chkupgrd.exe, which scans the current operating system and hardware to see if there are any known items incompatible with Windows 2000 Professional. You can run the utility using various methods. One of the most common methods is to place the Windows 2000 CD-ROM in the computer and click on the Upgrade option. The utility runs before the upgrade to alert you about any incompatibilities. However, if you are not prepared to perform an upgrade on the computer, you can run the utility by placing the Windows 2000 Professional CD-ROM in the computer, selecting Start|Run, and then typing "D:\I386\winnt32.exe /checkupgradeonly" (where D: is the drive letter your CD-ROM drive uses). The utility scans the system and creates a text file of the results, which you can save to the computer or print. Chkupgrd.exe tool is also referred to as the Readiness Analyzer.
- *Update packs*—Due to the major differences between the Windows 2000 Registry and those of Windows 95 and 98, some applications may not work after the upgrade. Software vendors may supply an update pack (also called *migration Dynamic Link Libraries—DLLs*) that you can use during the upgrade process. Obtain an upgrade pack and place it on the local hard drive. During the upgrade process, the installer asks if any upgrade packs should be used. Select Yes and then type in the file path to the upgrade pack to continue the installation process.
- *Disk utilities*—Windows 2000 Professional uses a new version of NT File System (NTFS) that causes conflicts with antivirus software and disk defragmenting software. You should remove such applications before you upgrade.
- *Drive compression*—Before upgrading, you should uncompress any drives that you have compressed with DriveSpace or DoubleSpace. These Windows 95 and 98 drive compression utilities are incompatible with Windows 2000.

Deploying Service Packs (SPs)

Installing SPs in Windows NT is a very time-consuming process. First, you have to install the operating system, and then you must apply the SP. Windows 2000 allows you to incorporate an SP with the installation files. Combining the latest SP with the Windows 2000 installation files allows you to install them as one. In Windows NT, however, if you installed a new service after applying an SP, you had to reapply the SP for the new service to gain any benefits the SP might have to offer. Additionally, you had to reinstall some services after you applied an SP. Thankfully, you don't have to contend with these situations in Windows 2000.

Slipstreaming SPs

The process of combining the Windows 2000 installation files with an SP is called *slipstreaming*. You apply an SP to a distribution share of the installation files by executing **update.exe /s**.

Note: *As of this writing, the switch that is used for slipstreaming is the* ***/s*** *switch. Some older references state that the slipstreaming switch is* ***/slip****. That is no longer the case. However, if you encounter the* ***/slip*** *switch on an exam, you should probably select that option (if the* ***/s*** *switch is not an available choice).*

If you install Windows 2000 using the slipstreamed distribution, the installations contain the SP. Using this method can save you a ton of time and helps you avoid having to apply an SP after each installation.

Applying SPs after Installing Windows 2000

If you didn't have the opportunity or ability to create a slipstreamed distribution share, you can apply an SP simply by running update.exe on the local machine. If you install any new services after applying the SP, Windows 2000 gets any files it needs for those services from the installation files or the SP. This process updates a service or an application without requiring you to continually reapply the SP whenever you add something new.

Troubleshooting Failed Installations

Windows 2000 Professional should install on most new computers without too much difficulty. However, there are some common reasons why it may not install properly. The following is a list of typical installation problems:

- *Media errors*—These are problems you encounter with the distribution CD-ROM. Make sure the problem exists with the media itself, not access to the media. If you place the Windows 2000 Professional CD-ROM in a shared drive for installation, too many people could be using the drive at one time.

This may generate some errors. However, if only one person is connected to the shared drive and errors persist, get a replacement for the distribution CD-ROM. In addition, always restart failed installations due to media errors.

- *Noncompatible CD-ROM drive*—There are many specifications for CD-ROM drives. You can install Windows 2000 from most drives, but there are always exceptions. If the CD-ROM drive is not compliant, replace it or place the distribution files on the network. Also, as mentioned earlier in this chapter, the Windows 2000 CD-ROM is bootable and can be installed from El-Torito-compatible drives. If the CD-ROM can't boot, ensure that the drive is compliant and that the boot order in the BIOS has been set to the CD-ROM drive. Also, the controller card for the CD-ROM drive could be failing, or the drive itself could be failing.

- *Installation halts or errors*—If a STOP error occurs during the installation, it is typically the result of incorrect or incompatible drivers. Obtain the correct and current drivers and restart the installation process. Also, the installation may stop just after the copy or text phase due to a warning that the master boot record has a virus. This warning typically results when the BIOS has enabled the virus warning option. Turn this option off and restart the installation. As a final measure, ensure that all devices are on the HCL.

- *Lack of drive space*—Windows 2000 needs much more free space compared to its predecessors. Ensure that at least 650MB of free space is available.

- *Dependency failures*—For the installation to be completed successfully, all services must be able to start when needed. Some services depend upon others to complete a task. For example, if the drivers for the network adapter could not load, that will affect all services that depend on the network adapter's successful installation. As a result, the computer won't be able to join the domain.

- *Problems joining the domain*—If the network adapter has initialized but the computer still can't join the domain, verify that the DNS server is online and that you are using the correct IP address of the DNS. Also, verify that you typed the domain name correctly. If problems persist, install the computer to a workgroup to complete the installation.

Practice Questions

Question 1

You want to use an RIS server to install Windows 2000 Professional on 200 client computers. To use RIS, what other network services must you install and configure? Create a list of network services that must be installed in order to implement an RIS server. The list can be in any order.

Active Directory

Remote Access Services (RAS) server

DHCP server

Windows Internet Naming Service (WINS) server

Proxy server

DNS server

Answer

Active Directory

DHCP server

DNS server

Active Directory contains information about the RIS servers, DHCP gives IP addresses to the RIS clients during the boot process, and DNS locates the RIS server. You cannot configure RIS for use until Active Directory, DHCP, and DNS are installed. RAS, WINS, and Proxy are not used by RIS nor are they used for the installation and configuration of RIS. These servers can be in place, but they do not provide any roles for an RIS Server.

Question 2

You want to install Windows 2000 Professional on 500 client workstations using an RIS server. The workstations do not have a PXE-compliant network card. How can these clients boot to the network to locate an RIS server?

- ❍ a. You can't use RIS without a PXE-compliant network card.
- ❍ b. Boot the client workstation with an rbfg.exe boot floppy.
- ❍ c. Use Network Client Administrator to create a network boot floppy.
- ❍ d. Configure the BIOS to boot from the PC Card.

Answer b is correct. If the computer doesn't have a PXE-compliant network card, use rbfg.exe to create an RIS boot disk. Answer a is false, a remote boot disk can be used. The Network Client Administrator does not create remote boot disk floppies, just network boot disks. Answer d is incorrect because the computers don't have a PXE-compliant network card.

Question 3

You want to use an unattend.txt file to automate the installation of Windows 2000 Professional from a CD-ROM. You place unattend.txt on a floppy disk and boot from the Windows 2000 Professional CD-ROM. However, the installation proceeds without using the unattend.txt file. What do you need to do to automate the installation?

- ❍ a. You can't automate a CD-ROM-based install.
- ❍ b. Rename unattend.txt to winnt.sif.
- ❍ c. During the text phase of the installation, press F3 to locate unattend.txt on a network server.
- ❍ d. During the text phase of the installation, press F3 to locate unattend.txt on the floppy disk.

Answer b is correct. You can automate a CD-ROM-based install if an answer file called winnt.sif is located on a floppy disk during the installation. The default unattended.txt answer file can be renamed to winnt.sif and used for a CD-ROM based installation. Answer a is false. A CD-ROM-based install can be automated with winnt.sif. Answers c and d are incorrect as pressing F3 won't allow a user to locate these files from a network server or from a floppy disk.

Question 4

You used sysprep.exe to prepare a model computer to be imaged using a third-party imaging software. You created the sysprep folder at the root of c:\, and you placed sysprep.exe and setupcl.exe in this directory. You used Setup Manager to create an answer file for the sysprep image. However, once you applied the image to a workstation, the Mini-Setup Wizard prompted you for every installation parameter. Why did this happen?

- ❍ a. You did not place sysprep.sif in the sysprep folder.
- ❍ b. You did not place unattend.txt in the sysprep folder.
- ❍ c. You did not place winnt.inf in the sysprep folder.
- ❍ d. You did not place sysprep.inf in the sysprep folder.

Answer d is correct. For the Mini-Setup Wizard to use the sysprep answer file, sysprep.inf must be located in the sysprep folder. Answer a is incorrect because the wrong file extension was used. Answers b and c are incorrect because the wrong file was used. The correct file is sysprep.inf.

Question 5

You want to upgrade a Windows 95 computer to Windows 2000 Professional. You need to ensure that applications on the Windows 95 computer will run after the upgrade has completed. What do you do?

- ❍ a. You can't upgrade and run applications that run on Windows 95 under Windows 2000.
- ❍ b. Use upgrade packs for the required applications during the upgrade process.
- ❍ c. Use the apcompat.exe utility and select Windows 95 so that applications will run in Windows 2000.
- ❍ d. Import the comptwa.inf security template to allow the applications to run in Windows 2000.

Answer b is correct. You can obtain upgrade packs (migration DLLs) from third-party vendors to ensure that the Windows 95 applications will run in Windows 2000 Professional after the upgrade. Answer a is false, a Windows 95 computer can be upgraded but some applications that run under Windows 95 may not be compatible with Windows 2000. Answer c is incorrect as apcompat.exe doesn't ensure that applications will be compatible. Only upgrade packs can ensure this.

Apcompat.exe can be used as a last resort to try to run a noncompliant application in Windows 2000. Answer d is incorrect, as the security settings found in comptwa.inf do not relate to application compatibility. They relate to security compatibility.

Question 6

Before you upgrade 100 Windows 98 computers to Windows 2000 Professional, you want to see if there are any hardware or software incompatibility issues. What should you run before the upgrade to search for incompatibilities?

- ❍ a. winnt.exe /checkupgradeonly
- ❍ b. apcompat.exe
- ❍ c. winnt32.exe /cmdcons
- ❍ d. winnt32.exe /checkupgradeonly

Answer d is correct. You use winnt32.exe /checkupgradeonly to run the Readiness Analyzer, which searches for any hardware or software incompatibilities with Windows 2000. The Readiness Analyzer is a GUI tool, and you run it only within an operating system. Winnt.exe /checkupgradeonly will not work. Therefore, answer a is incorrect. Answer b is incorrect because this tool is not used to test hardware and software compatibility. Answer c is incorrect as it would install the Recovery Console, which is used after Windows 2000 has been installed.

Question 7

You want to upgrade a Windows 98 computer that has 16MB of memory, a 1GB hard drive with 200MB of free space, and a Pentium 200MHz CPU. The installation of Windows 2000 fails due to insufficient hardware. What hardware do you have to upgrade before the installation can proceed?

- ❍ a. Install an additional 16MB of memory.
- ❍ b. Install an additional 16MB of memory and a 2GB hard drive.
- ❍ c. Install a Pentium II 400MHz CPU.
- ❍ d. Install an additional 32MB of memory.

Answer b is correct. The minimum requirements for Windows 2000 Professional are 32MB of memory, a 2GB drive with 650MB of free space, and a Pentium 133MHz or higher CPU.

Question 8

You've downloaded the most current SP and need to incorporate it into the distribution share. How do you accomplish this?

❍ a. Run setup.exe /s.

❍ b. Run update.msi /sl.

❍ c. Run update.exe.

❍ d. Run update.exe /s.

Answer d is correct. Slipstreaming, via running update.exe /slip, is a new method to upgrade Windows 2000 to incorporate SPs into the operating system. This method replaces the current files with the files that are contained in the SP. Answer a is incorrect as setup.exe is used to install Windows 2000, not to update it. Answer b is incorrect because service packs don't have a .msi file extension. Answer c will apply the service pack but it won't slipstream the service pack because the slip switch was not used.

Question 9

After the text phase of the installation of Windows 2000 Professional has finished, an error states that the master boot record is corrupted. How do you fix this problem?

❍ a. Boot with the Windows 2000 CD-ROM, install the Recovery Console, and run the **fixmbr** command.

❍ b. Turn off virus checking in the BIOS.

❍ c. Run winnt32.exe /checkupgradeonly.

❍ d. Run the fixmbr.exe utility from the Windows 2000 CD-ROM.

Answer b is correct. The error occurred because virus checking was enabled in the BIOS, so you need to turn it off. Answer a is incorrect as the Recovery Console is only used after Windows 2000 has been installed. It cannot be used to troubleshoot a failed installation. Winnt32.exe /checkupgradeonly is only just to verify the compatibility of hardware and software with Windows 2000. It cannot be used to troubleshoot failed installations. Therefore answer c is incorrect. Fixmbr.exe is a command that runs inside the Recovery Console. Therefore answer d is incorrect for the same reason answer a was incorrect.

Question 10

How do you apply an SP after you have installed Windows 2000 Professional?

- ❍ a. Run setup.exe /s.
- ❍ b. Run update.msi /s.
- ❍ c. Run update.exe.
- ❍ d. Run update.exe /s.

Answer c is correct. You use update.exe to install SPs after you install Windows 2000. You apply update.exe /slip to distribution files. Therefore, answer d is incorrect. Answer a is incorrect as setup.exe is used to install Windows 2000, not to apply a service pack. Answer b is incorrect because service packs don't have a .msi file extension. Answer c will apply the service pack but it won't slipstream the service pack because the slip switch was not used.

Need to Know More?

Read unattend.doc for more information regarding the unattended installation process. This document is located on every Windows 2000 CD-ROM in Support\Tools\deploy.cab\unattend.doc.

For more information regarding the installation and configuration of Remote Installation Service download Microsoft's white paper on this topic at: **www.microsoft.com/windows2000/library/planning/management/remoteos.asp.**

7

Implementing, Managing, and Troubleshooting Hardware Devices and Drivers

Terms you'll need to understand:

- ✓ Universal Serial Bus (USB)
- ✓ Plug and Play versus non Plug and Play
- ✓ Advanced Power Management (APM)
- ✓ Advanced Configuration and Power Interface (ACPI)
- ✓ Add/Remove Hardware Wizard
- ✓ Device Manager
- ✓ Driver signing
- ✓ FireWire, or IEEE (Institute of Electrical and Electronics Engineers) 1394
- ✓ Internet Printing Protocol (IPP)
- ✓ Spooler Service
- ✓ Smart cards and smart card readers
- ✓ Multilink support
- ✓ Infrared Data Association (IrDA) devices
- ✓ Network adapter, or network interface card (NIC)
- ✓ Multiple-display support
- ✓ Video adapter
- ✓ Mobile computer power modes
- ✓ Hardware profiles
- ✓ Multiple-processor support

Techniques you'll need to master:

- ✓ Installing, configuring, and troubleshooting hardware devices and drivers
- ✓ Updating drivers and system files
- ✓ Managing and troubleshooting driver signing
- ✓ Managing and troubleshooting various types of input/output (I/O) devices
- ✓ Configuring and troubleshooting Multilink support for a Dial-up Connection
- ✓ Configuring and troubleshooting multiple-display support, hardware profiles, and multiple-processor support

Implementing, Managing, and Troubleshooting Hardware

Hardware includes any physical device that is connected to your computer and that your computer's processor controls. This includes equipment that was connected to your computer when it was manufactured, as well as equipment that you added later. Modems; disk drives; CD-ROM drives; printers, network cards, keyboards, and display adapter cards and USB cameras, are all examples of devices. Windows 2000 contains full support for Plug and Play devices and partial support for nonPlug and Play devices. "Partial" support means only one thing: Some work; some do not. Sometimes, testing a device may be the only sure way to determine if it will work with Windows 2000. Always consult the latest Windows 2000 Hardware Compatibility List (HCL) before installing a new device.

For a device to work properly with Windows 2000, software (a device driver) must be installed on the computer. Each device has its own unique device driver(s), which the device manufacturer typically supplies. However, many device drivers are included with Windows 2000 and work even *better* with Windows 2000 than the manufacturer's own driver. Look for Microsoft to recommend using its own drivers for a given device rather than those of the manufacturer. Big surprise there.

Because Windows 2000 controls your computer's resources and configuration, you can install Plug and Play hardware devices and many other devices *without* restarting your computer. Windows 2000 automatically identifies the new hardware and installs the drivers it needs. If you are using an older computer that does not support Advanced Power Management (APM) or the "newer APM" called Advanced Configuration and Power Interface (ACPI), you must set up the device manually and restart your computer when installing new hardware devices. For now, you need ACPI-compliant hardware to make your Windows 2000 hardware setup experience smoother. We will discuss APM and ACPI in greater detail later in this chapter.

Installing, Configuring, and Managing Hardware

You configure devices on Windows 2000 machines using the Add/Remove Hardware Wizard in the Control Panel, or the Device Manager. Keep in mind that in most cases, you need to be logged on to the local machine as a member of the Administrators group to add, configure, and remove devices.

EXAM ALERT

You can use the System Information snap-in to view (yes, view *only*!) configuration information about your computer.

Installing Plug and Play Devices

Connect the device to the appropriate port or slot on your computer according to the device manufacturer's instructions. You may need to start or restart your computer, but this happens *much less often* than it did with previous versions of Windows NT and 9x. If you are prompted to restart your computer, do so. Windows 2000 should detect the device and then immediately start the Found New Hardware Wizard.

Installing Non Plug and Play Devices

To install a device that is not Plug and Play, follow these steps:

1. Open Add/Remove Hardware in the Control Panel.
2. Click Next, click Add/Troubleshoot A Device, and then click Next. Windows 2000 attempts to detect new Plug and Play devices.
3. If your device is not in the device list, click Add A New Device.
4. Click Next, and then do one of the following:
    - *Click Yes, Search For New Hardware*—Do this if you want Windows 2000 to try and detect the new non Plug and Play device you want to install.
    - *Click No, I Want To Select The Hardware From A List*—Do this if you know the type and model of the device you are installing and if you want to select it from a list of devices.
5. Click Next, and then follow the instructions on your screen.
6. You may be prompted to restart your computer, depending on the type of non Plug and Play device you just installed.

Tips on Installing Devices

Using a Plug and Play driver to install a *non* Plug and Play device may provide *some* Plug and Play support. (Don't get your hopes up.) Although the system cannot recognize the hardware and load the appropriate drivers on its own, Plug and Play can oversee the installation by allocating resources, interacting with Power Options in the Control Panel, and recording any issues in the Event Log.

If your computer is connected to a network, network policy (Group Policy) settings may prevent you from installing any devices on your computer. To add and set up a *non* Plug and Play device connected directly to your computer, you *must* be logged on as an administrator or a member of the Administrators group.

EXAM ALERT: If an administrator has already loaded the drivers for the device, you can install the device *without* having administrator privileges.

Driver Updates

Keeping drivers and system files updated ensures that your operating system performs at peak level. Microsoft recommends using *Microsoft* digitally signed drivers whenever possible. The driver.cab cabinet file on the Windows 2000 CD-ROM contains all of the drivers that Windows 2000 ships with. This cabinet file is copied to the %SystemRoot% folder when Windows 2000 is installed. Whenever a driver is updated, Windows 2000 looks in the driver.cab file first. The location of driver.cab is stored in a registry key and can be changed via HKLM\Software\Windows\CurrentVersion\Setup\DriverCachePath.

Updating Individual Drivers

To update individual drivers, follow these steps:

1. You update Drivers using the Device Manager. Right-click the device and choose Properties. A Properties dialog box appears.

2. Choose the Drivers tab and then the Update Driver button.

You use Driver Verifier to troubleshoot and isolate driver problems. It is not enabled by default. To use it, you must enable it by changing a registry setting. The Driver Verifier Manager, verifier.exe, provides a command-line interface for working with Driver Verifier.

Just know that the Driver Verifier tool does exist—it is not a figment of anyone's imagination. You do not need to learn the various parameters and switches that work with it.

Updating Your System Files Using Windows Update

Windows Update is a Microsoft database of items such as drivers, patches, help files, and Internet products that you can download to keep your Windows 2000 installation up to date. Using the Product Updates section of Windows Update, you can scan your computer for outdated system files, drivers, and help files, and automatically replace them with the most recent versions.

To update your system files using Windows Update, follow these steps:

1. Go to Windows Update at **www.windowsupdate.microsoft.com**. (This Uniform Resource Locator—URL—can change at any time, because Microsoft is prone to shuffling Web page locations frequently.) You can also open Windows Update by clicking on Start|Windows Update.

2. On the Windows Update home page, click Product Updates.

- You must be logged on as an administrator or a member of the Administrators group to complete this procedure. If your computer is connected to a network, network policy settings may prevent you from updating any system files or drivers.
- The first time you go to the Product Updates page, click Yes when prompted to install any required software or controls.

Managing and Troubleshooting Device Conflicts

You configure devices using the Add/Remove Hardware Wizard in the Control Panel, or the Device Manager. Each resource—e.g., a memory address range, Interrupt Request (IRQ), input/output (I/O) port, Direct Memory Access (DMA) channel, and so on—that is assigned to your device must be unique or the device does not function properly. For Plug and Play devices, Windows 2000 attempts to ensure automatically that these resources are configured properly. For devices where there is a resource conflict, or where the device is not working properly, you see next to the device name a yellow circle with an exclamation point inside it.

Occasionally, two devices require the same resources, but keep in mind that this does not always result in a device conflict—especially if the devices are Plug and Play compliant. If a conflict arises, you can manually change the resource settings to be sure that each setting is unique. Sometimes, two or more devices can share resources, such as interrupts on peripheral connection interface (PCI) devices, depending on the drivers and the computer. For example, get accustomed to seeing Windows 2000 share IRQ 9 among multiple devices on many laptops.

When you install a nonPlug and Play device, the resource settings for the device are not automatically configured. Depending on the type of device you are installing, you may have to manually configure these settings, which should be supplied in the instruction manual that came with your device.

EXAM ALERT

Generally, you should *not* change resource settings manually, because when you do so, the settings become fixed, and Windows 2000 then has less flexibility when allocating resources to other devices. If too many resources become fixed, Windows 2000 may not be able to install new Plug and Play devices.

Managing and Troubleshooting Driver Signing

Microsoft is promoting driver signing for devices as a method to advance the quality of drivers and to reduce support costs for vendors and total cost of ownership (TCO) for customers. Windows 2000 uses a driver signing process to make sure drivers have been certified to work correctly with the Windows Driver Model (WDM) in Windows 2000. If you are having problems, it may be because you are using a driver not correctly written for Windows 2000. To identify such drivers, use the Signature Verification tool. This utility, sigverif.exe, helps you quickly identify unsigned drivers if a device is not working or if you want to ensure that all drivers in use are signed.

Using the Signature Verification Tool

To use the Signature Verification tool, perform the following steps:

1. Start sigverif.exe (Start|Run|sigverif.exe).
2. Click Advanced.
3. Select Look For Other Files That Are Not Digitally Signed.
4. For the folder, select %SystemRoot%\system32\drivers.

Controlling the Use of Signed and Unsigned Drivers Using Group Policy

Windows 2000 can provide a good degree of control over whether or not users can install signed or unsigned drivers, or both, for a chosen device. The selection in the Group Policy Object (GPO) or Local Computer Policy is an object called Driver Signing. The three choices for the Driver Signing piece of policy are:

- *Ignore*—Selecting this does just what the name indicates: ignores whether a driver is signed or not, allowing the user to proceed with the driver installation.
- *Warn*—This issues a dialog box warning if an unsigned driver is encountered during a device installation, and gives the user the option of continuing with the installation or terminating the device's setup.
- *Block*—This is the most important of the three selections. To prevent the installation of any unsigned device drivers, this is the option you should select in Group Policy or the Local Computer Policy.

Managing and Troubleshooting I/O Devices

Windows 2000 supports a wide variety of I/O devices, including printers, scanners, and multimedia devices (such as cameras, keyboards, mice, smart card readers, modems, infrared devices, and network adapters). This is just the beginning of the list! This section covers the specifics you need to know about supporting I/O devices on Windows 2000 Professional for the exam. Think "big picture" when you are studying these hardware sections, and remember you do *not* need to know specifics about certain brands or models of hardware.

Using Printers

Windows 2000 Professional supports the following printer ports: line printer terminal (LPT), Component Object Model (COM), USB, FireWire, or Institute of Electrical and Electronics Engineers (IEEE) 1394, and network attached devices with a Universal Naming Convention (UNC) path. Print services can be provided only for Windows and Unix clients on Windows 2000 Professional. Windows 2000 Professional automatically downloads the printer drivers for clients that are running Windows 2000, NT 4, NT 3.51, and 9x.

EXAM ALERT: Windows 2000 Server is required to support Apple and Novell clients.

Internet Printing Protocol (IPP)

Internet printing using IPP is a feature in Windows 2000 that is also supported in Windows 98. Clients have the option of entering a URL to connect to network printers and manage their network print jobs. This is proving to be much easier for users than browsing aimlessly within My Network Places or Network Neighborhood to locate network printers. IPP's other advantage is that it can significantly contribute to efforts to cut down browse traffic on your network.

The print server must be either a Windows 2000 Server running Internet Information Server (IIS) 5, or a Windows 2000 Professional system running Personal Web Server (PWS), which is the "junior" version of IIS. You can view all shared IPP printers at **http://servername/printers**, for example **http://Server2/printers**.

Printer Property Settings

The following are some useful printer property settings:

- *Print Pooling*—This allows you to install two or more identical printers as one logical printer.
- *Print Priority*—You set this by creating multiple logical printers for one physical printer and assigning different priorities to each. Priority ranges from 1, the lowest (the default), through 99, the highest.
- *Availability*—Enabling this option allows Administrators to specify the hours the printer is available. This option is good for large print jobs that you want to print in the middle of the night or early morning so they do not interfere with routine business.
- *Separator Pages*—These are available to separate print jobs at a shared printer. You can create and save a template for the design and appearance of the separator page in the %SystemRoot%\system32 directory with a .sep file extension.

- *Restart*—You can select this in the printer's menu to reprint a document. It is useful when a document is printing and the printer jams. You can select Resume to start printing where you left off.

Advanced Server Properties allows you to change the directory that contains the print spooler for the printer. This feature is new to the Windows operating system with the release of Windows 2000.

Restarting the Spooler Service

You must restart your spooler service if purging a print queue does not resolve your printing problem. To remedy a "stalled spooler," you must stop and restart the Spooler Service in the Services applet in Administrative Tools in the Control Panel. You *do* need to be logged on as an administrator or member of the Administrators local group to successfully restart the Spooler Service.

Using Keyboards and Mice

You install keyboards under Keyboards in the Device Manager. On the other hand, you install mice, graphics tablets, and other pointing devices under Mice And Other Pointing Devices in the Device Manager. See the "USB" section later in this chapter for more information on USB graphics tablets and pointing devices. You troubleshoot I/O resource conflicts using the System Information snap-in. Take a look under Hardware Resources, I/O for a list of memory ranges in use.

Using Smart Cards and Smart Card Readers

Smart cards and smart card readers, which interpret the data on the cards, are fully supported in Windows 2000. Smart cards enable portability of user credentials and other private information among computers in many locations—such as at work, at home, or on the road. Smart card technology eliminates the need for you to transmit sensitive information, such as user authentication tickets and private keys, over networks. Smart cards also support certificate-based authentication. See the "Mobile User" section later in this chapter for more information on certificate-based authentication.

Installing Smart Card Readers

To install a smart card reader on a computer, perform the following steps:

1. Shut down and turn off the computer.
2. Depending on the type of card reader you have purchased, attach your reader to an available serial port or insert the PC card reader into an available PCMCIA Type II slot.

3. Restart your computer and log on as an administrator.

4. One of the following happens next:

   - If the device driver software for the smart card reader is available in the driver.cab file (installed on the hard drive as part of the Windows 2000 installation), the driver is installed without any prompting. This could take a few minutes.

   - If the device driver software for the smart card reader is not available in the driver.cab file, the Add/Remove Hardware Wizard starts. Follow the directions for installing the device driver software.

You can confirm that installation has successfully taken place by the appearance of the Unplug Or Eject Hardware icon in the toolbar (if it was not previously present) and by the appearance of the just-installed reader in the list of hardware devices in the Unplug Or Eject Hardware dialog box.

If the smart card reader is not installed automatically or the Add/Remove Hardware Wizard does not start automatically, your smart card reader is probably not Plug and Play compliant. You should contact the smart card reader manufacturer for the device driver and instructions on how to install and configure the device for Windows 2000.

Logging on to a Computer with a Smart Card

To log on to a computer with a smart card, perform the following steps:

1. At the Windows logon screen, insert your smart card in the smart card reader.

2. Type the personal identification number (PIN) for the smart card when your computer prompts you.

If the PIN you enter is recognized as legitimate, you are logged on to the computer and to the Windows domain, based on the permissions that the domain administrator has assigned to your user account. If you enter the incorrect PIN for a smart card several times in a row, you cannot log on to the computer using that smart card. The number of allowable invalid logon attempts before you are locked out varies according to the smart card manufacturer.

Mobile User

If you are a *mobile user*, you need to enable the use of certificates on your computer. Unless your system administrator preconfigures your computer with machine and user certificates before you receive it, you must connect to your corporate network using conventional, password-based authentication methods to get your machine and user certificates. When you connect, you join your computer to the corporate domain, obtain certificates, and set certificates policy. The next time you connect to the corporate network, you can use certificate-based authentication methods such as Extensible Authentication Protocol (EAP), an extension to Point-to-Point Protocol (PPP).

EAP was developed in response to the increasing demand for remote access user authentication that uses other security devices, such as smart cards. EAP provides a standard mechanism for supporting additional authentication methods within PPP. By using EAP, you can add support for a number of authentication schemes, including token cards, one-time passwords, public key authentication using smart cards, certificates, and others. EAP, in conjunction with strong EAP authentication methods, is a critical technology component for secure Virtual Private Network (VPN) connections because it offers more security against brute-force or dictionary attacks and password guessing than other authentication methods, such as Challenge Handshake Authentication Protocol (CHAP).

A Windows 2000 Professional computer that needs to authenticate to a Remote Access Services (RAS) server using a smart card and a certificate must have EAP, and Microsoft Challenge Handshake Authentication Protocol (MSCHAP) and/or MSCHAP version 2 enabled in the dial-up connection's properties settings.

Enabling the Use of Certificates

To enable the use of a certificate on a computer, perform the following steps:

1. Connect to a network by using a dial-up or Point-to-Point Tunneling Protocol (PPTP) network connection, and authentication protocols such as MSCHAP or MSCHAP version 2. When you connect, your Windows 2000 computer joins the corporate domain and receives machine certificates.

2. Request a user certificate from one of the possible Certificate Authorities.

3. Create another connection that uses *certificate-based authentication*, and then connect again by using certificate-based authentication methods such as EAP or IPSec.

Using Cameras and Other Multimedia Hardware

Cameras and scanners appear in the Control Panel when you install your first digital camera or scanner. If you have a Plug and Play camera or scanner, Windows 2000 detects it and installs it automatically. Then you can use the Scanners And Cameras applet in the Control Panel to install other scanners, digital still cameras, digital video cameras, and image-capturing devices.

After a device is installed, Scanners And Cameras can link it to a program on your computer. For example, when you push Scan on your scanner, you can have the scanned picture automatically open in the program you want.

Installing Scanners or Digital Cameras

To install a scanner or digital camera, perform the following steps:

1. Open Scanners And Cameras in the Control Panel.
2. Click Add, and then follow the instructions on the screen.

Remember that you must be logged on as an administrator or a member of the Administrators group to complete this procedure. If your computer is connected to a network, network policy settings may prevent you from installing devices.

Testing Scanners or Digital Cameras

To test a scanner or digital camera, perform the following steps:

1. Open Scanners And Cameras in the Control Panel.
2. Click the scanner or camera you want to test, and then click Properties.
3. On the General tab, click Test Scanner Or Camera.

An onscreen message tells you if the camera or scanner completed the test successfully. You can also check your Event Log to see if the test was successful.

Using Modems

At one time or another, if you've used a computer, you have probably used a modem to connect to your office or an Internet Service Provider (ISP) using a dial-up connection. This section details what you need to know about modem support and troubleshooting in Windows 2000 Professional.

Installing Modems

If Windows 2000 starts the Install New Modem Wizard as soon as your new modem is physically in your machine, you are in luck! You have nothing more to do than follow the prompts the wizard provides, if any, to complete the setup of your new modem.

If the Install New Modem Wizard does not detect your modem or you cannot find it listed, you are faced with installing an unsupported modem. Good luck on your mission. Windows 2000 *cannot* automatically detect certain internal modems. You must install the modem manually through the Add/Remove Hardware Wizard in the Control Panel, or by following these instructions:

1. Open Phone And Modem Options in the Control Panel.
2. (Optional) If you are prompted for location information, enter dialing information for your location and click OK.
3. On the Modems tab, click Add.
4. Follow the instructions in the Install New Modem Wizard.

Using Multilink Support

Multilinking, or multiple-device dialing, allows you to combine two or more modems or integrated services digital network (ISDN) adapters into one logical link with increased bandwidth. The Network And Dial-up Connections feature performs PPP Multilink dialing over multiple ISDN, X.25, or modem lines. The feature combines multiple physical links into a logical bundle, and the resulting aggregate link increases your connection bandwidth. For example, you could use Multilink to combine the power of two 33.6Kbps modems to achieve approximately a 67.2Kbps dial-up connection. Although you will not see this frequently in the real world, Multilinking is definitely a term to understand for the 70-210 exam.

Configuring Multilink

To configure Multilink, perform the following steps:

1. Select Start|Settings|Network And Dial-up Connections.
2. Right-click the connection where you want Multilink enabled, and then select Properties.
3. On the Options tab, in Multiple Devices, do one of the following:
   - If you want Windows 2000 to dial only the first available device, click Dial Only First Available Device.
   - If you want Windows 2000 to use all of your devices, click Dial All Devices.
   - If you want Windows 2000 to dynamically dial and hang up devices as needed, click Dial Devices Only As Needed, and then click Configure.
4. In Automatic Dialing, click the Activity At Least percentage and Duration At Least time you want to set. Another line is dialed when connection activity reaches this level for the amount of time that you specify.
5. In Automatic Hangup, click the Activity No More Than percentage and Duration At Least time you want to set. A device is hung up when connection activity decreases to this level for at least the amount of time that you specify.

Multilink Tips

If you use multiple devices to dial a server that requires callback, only one of your Multilinked devices is called back. This is because only one phone number is stored in a user account. Therefore, only one device connects, all other devices fail to complete the connection, and your connection loses Multilink functionality. You can avoid this problem if the Multilinked phonebook entry is to an ISDN line or modem with two channels that have the same phone number.

If you select Dial All Devices, links that get dropped in the Multilinked bundle are not automatically reinitialized. You can force links to reinitialize by selecting Dial Devices Only As Needed and then Configure, and then by setting easily achieved Automatic Dialing conditions, which cause another line to be dialed. For example, set Activity At Least to 1 percent and Duration At Least to 3 seconds.

To dial multiple devices, both your connection and your remote access server must have Multilink enabled.

Troubleshooting Modems

You can verify that your modem is working properly by using the diagnostic tool that is available through the Phone And Modem Options icon in the Control Panel, or the Device Manager. Another choice for troubleshooting a modem problem is use the Hardware Troubleshooter, available in the Add/Remove Hardware Wizard in the Control Panel, but use this as a last resort because it is similar to Windows Help.

Supporting Faxes

If a fax device or fax modem is installed, the Fax applet appears in the Control Panel. It does not appear if no fax device is installed. You use the Fax applet to set up rules for how your device receives faxes, the number of retries when it is sending, where to store retrieved and sent faxes, user security permissions, and so on. If the Advanced Options tab is not available in the Fax applet, you must log off and then log back on as an administrator.

You *cannot* share the Fax printer in your Printers folder.

Using Infrared Data Association (IrDA) Devices and Wireless Devices

Windows 2000 supports IrDA protocols that enable data transfer over infrared connections. This provides an infrastructure that allows other devices and programs to communicate with Windows 2000 through the IrDA interface. Windows 2000 installs with the Wireless Link program, which transfers files to or from another computer that runs Windows 2000 or 98.

Windows 2000's Plug and Play architecture automatically detects and installs the infrared component for computers with built-in IrDA hardware. For computers without built-in IrDA hardware, a user can attach a serial port IrDA transceiver to a serial COM port and use the Add/Remove Hardware Wizard to install the device in Windows 2000.

After an infrared device is installed, the Wireless Link icon appears in the Control Panel. When another IrDA transceiver comes in range, the Wireless Link icon appears on the desktop and on the taskbar. You can then send a file over the infrared connection with any of the following actions:

- Specify a location and one or more files using the Wireless Link dialog box
- Use drag-and-drop operations to move files onto the Wireless Link icon on the desktop
- Right-click any selection of files on the desktop, in Windows Explorer, or in My Computer, and then click Send To Infrared Recipient
- Print to a printer configured to use an infrared port

In addition to sending or printing files, you can create a network connection that connects two computers using the infrared port. You can use this capability to map shared drives on a host computer and work with files and folders in Windows Explorer or My Computer. You can also use an infrared network connection to connect directly to another computer without modems, cables, or network hardware.

Enabling or Preventing Receiving Files

To enable or prevent receiving files, perform the following steps:

1. Open the Wireless Link applet in the Control Panel.
2. On the File Transfer tab, do *one* of the following:
    - *To enable your computer to receive files from others*—Select the Allow Others To Send Files To Your Computer Using Infrared Communications checkbox.
    - Or select the Send Files To Your Computer Using Infrared Communications checkbox.

Viewing Power Allocations for USB Hubs

To view power allocations for USB hubs, perform the following steps:

1. Open the Device Manager.
2. Double-click Universal Serial Bus Controller.

3. Right-click USB Root Hub, and then click Properties.
4. On the Power tab, view the power consumed by each device in the Devices On This Hub list.

Hubs for USB devices are self-powered or bus-powered. Self-powered, or plugging a hub into an electrical outlet, provides maximum power to the device, whereas bus-powered, plugging a device into another USB port, provides minimum power. Devices that require a lot of power, such as cameras, should be plugged into self-powered hubs. Universal Serial Bus Controller appears only if you have a USB port on your computer. The Power tab appears only for USB hubs.

Viewing Bandwidth Allocations for USB Host Controllers

To view bandwidth allocation for a USB host controller, perform the following steps:

1. Open the Device Manager.
2. Double-click Universal Serial Bus Controllers.
3. Right-click Intel PCI To USB Universal Host Controller, and then click Properties.
4. On the Advanced tab, view the bandwidth consumed by each device in the Bandwidth Consuming Devices list.

You can view bandwidth only for a USB controller.

Certain ports are not listed in the Ports tab unless a printer that requires one of them is installed. USB and FireWire printers support Plug and Play, so when you plug a printer into the correct physical port (USB or IEEE 1394), the correct port monitor is installed automatically. Windows 2000 detects the device and displays its settings on the screen, prompting you to approve.

Dealing with USB Controllers That Do Not Install Properly

In the Device Manager, USB controllers are listed under Human Interface Devices (when you are viewing Devices By Type, which is the default view). If the controller does not appear in the Device Manager, USB may not be enabled in the system's BIOS. When prompted during system startup, enter the BIOS setup and enable USB.

If USB is enabled in the BIOS, but the USB host controller does not appear in the Device Manager (under Universal Serial Bus Controllers), or a yellow warning icon appears next to the host controller name, the version of BIOS may be outdated. Contact your computer's maker or vendor and obtain the current version of BIOS.

If the controller appears in the Device Manager, right-click the controller name and select Properties. In Device Status, a message describes any problems and suggests what action to take. USB ports have a separate entry in the Device Manager. To check the device status, select Universal Serial Bus Controllers, right-click USB Root Hub, and then select Properties.

Using Network Adapters

You install network adapters using the Add/Remove Hardware applet in the Control Panel. You can make changes to the binding order of protocols and the network provider order using Advanced Settings under the Advanced menu of the Network And Dial-up Connections window (accessed by right-clicking on the My Network Places icon, or via the Control Panel). Each network adapter has its own separate icon in the Network And Dial-up Connections folder. Right-click a network adapter icon to set its properties, install protocols, change addresses, or perform any other configuration changes for the connection.

Internet Connection Sharing (ICS)

With the ICS feature of Network And Dial-up Connections, you can use Windows 2000 to connect your home or small-office network to the Internet. For example, you might have a home network that connects to the Internet using a dial-up connection. By enabling ICS on the computer that uses the dial-up connection, you are providing network address translation (NAT), addressing, and name resolution services for all computers on your home network. The ICS feature is intended for use in a small office or home office where network configuration and the computer running Windows 2000 where the shared connection resides manages the Internet connection. It is assumed that on your small network, this computer is the *only* Internet connection—the only gateway to the Internet—and that it sets up all internal network addresses.

After you enable ICS and users verify their networking and Internet options, home or small-office network users can use applications such as Internet Explorer and Outlook Express as if they were already connected to the ISP. The ICS computer then dials the ISP and creates the connection so that the user can reach the specified Web address or resource. To use the ICS feature, users on your home-office or small-office network must configure Transmission Control Protocol/Internet Protocol (TCP/IP) on their local area connection to obtain an IP address automatically. Also, home-office or small-office network users must configure Internet options for ICS.

You might need to configure applications and services on the ICS computer to work properly across the Internet. For example, if users on your home network want to play a game such as Doom with other users on the Internet, you must configure Doom on the connection where ICS is enabled. Conversely, you must configure services that you provide so Internet users can access them. For example, if you are hosting a Web server on your home network and want Internet users to be able to connect to it, you must configure the Web server service on the ICS computer. Here are some guidelines for using ICS:

- To configure ICS, you must be a member of the Administrators group on the computer where you want to set this up.
- You should not use this feature in an existing network with other Windows 2000 Server domain controllers, DNS servers, gateways, Dynamic Host Configuration Protocol (DHCP) servers, or systems configured for static IP addresses. If you are running Windows 2000 Server, and one or more of these components exist, you must use NAT to achieve the same result.
- A computer with ICS needs two connections. One connection, typically a local area network (LAN) adapter, connects to the computers on the home network. The other connection connects the home network to the Internet. You need to ensure that ICS is enabled on the connection that connects your home network to the Internet. If you do so, the home network connection appropriately allocates TCP/IP addresses to its own users, the shared connection can connect your home network to the Internet, and users outside your home network are not at risk of receiving inappropriate addresses from your home network. If you enable ICS on a connection, the ICS computer becomes a DHCP allocator for the home network. DHCP distributes TCP/IP addresses to users as they start up.

EXAM ALERT: **If ICS is enabled on the wrong network adapter, the home network DHCP allocator might grant TCP/IP addresses to users outside your own home network, causing problems on their own networks.**

- When you enable ICS, the adapter connected to the home-office or small-office network is given a new static IP address configuration. Consequently, TCP/IP connections established between any small-office or home-office computer and the ICS computer when ICS is enabled are lost and need to be reestablished.
- You cannot modify the default configuration of ICS. This includes items such as disabling the DHCP allocator or modifying the range of private IP addresses that are distributed, disabling the DNS proxy, configuring a range of public IP addresses, or configuring inbound mappings. If you want to modify any of these items, you must use NAT.

- If your home-office users need to access a corporate network that is connected to the Internet by a tunnel server from an ICS network, they need to create a VPN connection to tunnel from the computer on the ICS network to the corporate tunnel server on the Internet. The VPN connection is authenticated and secure; creating the tunneled connection allocates proper IP addresses, DNS server addresses, and Windows Internet Naming Service (WINS) server addresses for the corporate network.

Managing and Troubleshooting Display Devices

You manage desktop display properties (software settings) through the Display applet in the Control Panel. You install, remove, and update the drivers of display adapters through Display Adapters under the Device Manager. To do the same for monitors, use Monitors under the Device Manager.

Display Settings

Much of your display settings deal with aesthetics such as wallpaper, screen fonts, and screensavers. The exam will test your knowledge of the technical aspects of display settings, not aesthetics. For example, if you receive an error about an unavailable overlay surface, reduce the display resolution or number of colors. You may also get the—Unable To Create Video Window. Please Try Altering Your Display Settings—error. Troubleshooting these display errors is covered in this section.

Modifying Your Display Settings

To modify your display settings, perform the following steps:

1. Right-click your desktop and select Properties, or open the Display applet in the Control Panel.

2. Select the Settings tab and make the appropriate changes.

Configuring Multiple-Display Support

Windows 2000 has a new multiple-monitor functionality that increases your work productivity by expanding the size of your desktop. Multiple displays do have to use PCI or Accelerated Graphics Port (AGP) port devices to work properly with Windows 2000.

EXAM ALERT: You can connect up to 10 individual monitors to create a desktop large enough to hold numerous programs or windows.

You can easily work on more than one task at a time by moving items from one monitor to another or by stretching them across numerous monitors. Edit images or text on one monitor while viewing Web activity on another. Or you can open multiple pages of a single, long document and drag them across several monitors to easily view the layout of text and graphics. You could also stretch a spreadsheet across two monitors so you can view numerous columns without scrolling.

One monitor serves as the primary display; you see the Logon dialog box when you start your computer. In addition, most programs display windows on the primary monitor when you initially open them. You can set different resolutions and different color depths for each monitor. You can also connect multiple monitors to individual graphics adapters or to a single adapter that supports multiple outputs.

Arranging Multiple Monitors

To arrange multiple monitors, perform the following steps:

1. Open the Display applet in the Control Panel.
2. On the Settings tab, click Identify to display a large number on each of your monitors, showing which monitor corresponds with each icon.
3. Click the monitor icons and drag them to positions that represent how you want to move items from one monitor to another, and then click OK or Apply to view the changes.

The icon positions determine how you move items from one monitor to another. For example, if you are using two monitors and you want to move items from one monitor to the other by dragging left and right, place the icons side by side. To move items between monitors by dragging up and down, place the icons one above the other. The icon positions do not have to correspond to the physical positions of the monitors. You can place the icons one above the other even though your monitors are side by side.

Changing the Primary Monitor

To change the primary monitor, perform the following steps:

1. Open the Display applet in the Control Panel.
2. On the Settings tab, click the monitor icon that represents the monitor you want to designate as the primary one.
3. Select the Use This Device As The Primary Monitor checkbox. This checkbox is unavailable when you select the monitor icon that is currently set as your primary monitor.

The monitor that is designated as the primary monitor displays the Logon dialog box when you start your computer. Most programs display their window on the primary monitor when you first open them.

Moving Items between Monitors or Viewing the Same Desktop on Multiple Monitors

To move items between monitors, or to view the same desktop on multiple monitors, perform the following steps:

1. Open the Display applet in the Control Panel.
2. On the Settings tab, click the monitor icon that represents the monitor you want to use in addition to your primary monitor.
3. Select the Extend My Windows Desktop Onto This Monitor checkbox. Selecting this checkbox allows you to drag items across your screen onto alternate monitors. You can also resize a window to stretch it across more than one monitor.

Troubleshooting Multiple Displays

The default refresh frequency setting is typically 60Hz, although your monitors may support a higher setting. A higher refresh frequency might reduce flicker on your screens, but choosing a setting that is too high for your monitor can make your display unusable, not to mention damage your hardware.

> If your refresh frequency is set to anything higher than 60Hz and your monitor display(s) go(es) black when you start Windows 2000, restart the system in Safe Mode. Change your refresh frequency for all monitors to 60Hz. You may need to double-check this setting in your Unattended Installation script file, commonly called unattend.txt. Again, set it to 60Hz.
>
> Multiple-display support in Windows 2000 presents some challenges when you are dealing with some older applications and DOS applications. If you start a DOS application on your multidisplay Windows 2000 machine, and then both of your screens flicker and completely go dark, you can fix the problem without much difficulty. Multiple-display support allows you to adjust the display settings so that your application runs and is viewable on both monitors. First, you may need to restart your system; then, you select Safe Mode at the F8 startup menu. Then, once you can see the contents of your desktop, you configure the DOS application to run in a window and change your Display settings from Default to Optimal.

Installing, Configuring, and Supporting a Video Adapter

When Windows 2000 is being installed, your system's BIOS selects the primary video/display adapter based on PCI slot order. You can install and configure any additional video adapters you want to use with your system using the Display applet or the Add/Remove Hardware applet in the Control Panel.

Mobile Computer Hardware

PCMCIA (PC Card) adapters, USB ports, IEEE 1394 (FireWire), and infrared devices are now supported in Windows 2000. You manage these through the Device Manager. Support is provided in Windows 2000 Professional for APM and ACPI, which we discuss shortly.

Hot (computer is fully powered) and warm (computer is in suspend mode) docking and undocking are now fully supported for computers with a Plug and Play BIOS. Hibernation (complete power down while maintaining the state of open programs and connected hardware) and Suspend (deep sleep with some power) modes are also now supported, extending battery life.

When you install a PC Card, USB, or infrared device, Windows 2000 automatically recognizes and configures it (if it meets Plug and Play specifications). If Windows does not have an entry in its driver.cab file for the new hardware, you are prompted to supply one.

Equipping mobile computers with smart cards and NTFS using Encrypting File System decreases the likelihood of confidential data being compromised if the computer is stolen, lost, or simply placed into the wrong hands.

Managing Hardware Profiles

A *hardware profile* stores configuration settings for a collection of devices and services. Windows 2000 can store different hardware profiles so that users' needs can be met even though their computer may frequently require different device and service settings depending on the circumstances. The best example is that of a laptop or portable computer that is used in an office while in a docking station that is then undocked so the user can travel with the laptop. The two situations do require different power management settings, possibly different network settings, and various other configuration changes.

You can enable and disable devices in particular profiles through their properties in the Device Manager snap-in. You manage services using the Services applet in the Control Panel. You create and manage hardware profiles using the System applet in the Control Panel, or by right-clicking on the My Computer icon on the desktop and choosing Properties. Once inside the System applet, go to the Hardware tab and select Hardware Profiles.

At installation, Windows 2000 creates a single hardware profile called Profile 1 (Current). You are prompted to select a hardware profile at system startup only when two or more hardware profiles are stored on your machine. You can create and store as many hardware profiles on your machine as you like. You select the desired hardware profile at Windows 2000 startup to select which device and service configuration settings you need for the current session. If Windows 2000 detects that your computer is a portable (laptop), it tries to determine whether your system is docked or undocked; then it selects the appropriate hardware profile for the current conditions. Do not confuse hardware profiles with *user profiles*—the two are *unrelated*!

APM

Windows 2000 supports the APM 1.2 specification. APM helps to greatly reduce your computer's power consumption, which is particularly helpful for laptop users. You use the Power Options applet in the Control Panel to configure your computer to use APM. Once you are in the Power Options applet, look for a tab labeled APM. On the APM tab, select the Enable Advanced Power Management checkbox to enable APM. You do not need to restart your system.

If your computer does not have an APM-compliant BIOS, Windows 2000 cannot install APM. This means no APM support for your machine, plus no APM tab in the Power Options applet in the Control Panel. Keep in mind, though, that your machine can still function as an ACPI computer if your BIOS is ACPI-compliant. The ACPI-based BIOS will take over your system configuration and power management from the Plug and Play BIOS.

APM is available only in Windows 2000 Professional. It is not available in any of the Windows 2000 Server versions.

ACPI

Many people call ACPI the next-generation replacement for the APM specification. ACPI is an open industry specification that defines a flexible and extensible hardware interface for your system board. Windows 2000 is a fully ACPI-compliant operating system. Software developers and designers use the ACPI specification to integrate power management features throughout a computer system, including hardware, the operating system, and application software. This integration enables Windows 2000 to determine which applications are active and to handle all of the power management resources for computer subsystems and peripherals.

ACPI enables the operating system to direct power management on a wide range of mobile, desktop, and server computers and peripherals. ACPI is the foundation for the OnNow industry initiative, which allows manufacturers to deliver computers that will start at the touch of a key on a keyboard.

ACPI design is *essential* when you want to take full advantage of power management and Plug and Play in Windows 2000. If you are not sure if your computer is ACPI-compliant, check your manufacturer's documentation. To change power settings that take advantage of ACPI, use the Power Options applet in the Control Panel.

Power Options Overview

By using Power Options in the Control Panel, you can reduce the power consumption of any number of your computer devices or of your entire system. You do this by choosing a *power scheme*, which is a collection of settings that manages your computer's power usage. You can create your own power schemes or use the ones provided with Windows 2000.

You can also adjust the individual settings in a power scheme. For example, depending on your hardware, you can:

- Turn off your monitor and hard disks automatically to save power.
- Put your computer on standby, which puts your entire system in a low-power state, if you plan to be away from your computer for a while. While on standby, your entire computer switches to a low-power state, where devices such as the monitor and hard disks turn off and your computer uses less power. When you want to use the computer again, it comes out of standby quickly, and your desktop is restored exactly as you left it. Standby is useful for conserving battery power in portable computers.

> **EXAM ALERT:** Standby does not save your desktop state to disk, so if there is a power failure while the computer is on standby, you can lose unsaved information. If there is an interruption in power, information in memory is lost. If this concerns you, hibernation or a complete power down might be better choices to consider.

- Put your computer in hibernation mode. When you restart your computer, your desktop is restored exactly as you left it. It takes longer to bring your computer out of hibernation than out of standby. Put your computer in hibernation when you will be away from the computer for an extended time or overnight.

The hibernation feature saves everything in memory on disk, turns off your monitor and hard disk, and then turns off your computer.

Managing Battery Power on a Portable Computer

Using the Power Options applet in the Control Panel, you can reduce consumption of battery power on your portable computer and still keep the computer available for immediate use. You can view multiple batteries separately or as a whole, and set alarms to warn you of low battery conditions.

Using a Portable Computer on an Airplane

Most airlines request that you turn off portable computers during certain portions of the flight such as takeoff and landing. To comply with this request, you must turn off your computer *completely*. Do not get cute, here, folks. Turn it off.

When you board an airplane, your mobile computer must be completely powered down or turned off. *None* of the power modes (hibernation, suspend, standby, and so on) are acceptable substitutes. You want to avoid interfering with the aircraft's instrumentation, and completely powering down is the only way to guarantee that.

Your computer may *appear* to be turned off while in either standby or hibernation mode. However, the operating system might automatically reactivate itself to run certain preprogrammed tasks or to conserve battery power. To prevent this from occurring during air travel, be certain to shut down your computer completely when it's not in use. In addition, if your computer is equipped with a cellular modem, you must ensure that this modem is completely turned off during air travel, as required by FCC and FAA regulations.

Managing Power When Installing a Plug and Play Device

Plug and Play works with Power Options in the Control Panel to be sure that your system runs efficiently while you are installing or removing hardware devices. Power Options controls the power supply to the devices attached to your computer, supplying power to those that you are using and conserving power for those you are not. Windows 2000 automatically manages the power for devices. However, some devices may have options you can set in the Device Manager.

To take full advantage of Plug and Play, you need to use Windows 2000 on an ACPI-compliant computer that is running in ACPI mode, and the hardware devices must be Plug and Play and/or ACPI compliant. In an ACPI computer, the operating system, not the hardware, configures and monitors the computer's devices.

Monitoring and Configuring Multiple Processors

Adding an additional processor to your Windows 2000 system to improve performance is called *scaling*. Windows 2000 Professional can support up to two processors. You add a second processor usually due to the demands of Central Processing Unit (CPU)-intensive applications, such as Computer Aided Design (CAD) and graphics rendering. Windows 2000 supports Symmetric Multiprocessing (SMP) as well as processor affinity. Asymmetric Multiprocessing (ASMP) is not supported.

Windows 2000 provides support for single or multiple CPUs. However, if you originally installed Windows 2000 on a computer with a single CPU, you must update the Hardware Abstraction Layer (HAL) on your computer for it to be able to recognize and use multiple CPUs.

Windows 2000 Professional supports a maximum of two CPUs, without Original Equipment Manufacturer (OEM) modifications. If you need more than 2 CPUs, consider using Windows 2000 Server (up to 4 CPUs), Advanced Server (up to 8 CPUs), or Data Center Server (maximum of 32 CPUs).

Keep monitoring performance after you add an additional processor because upgrading to multiple CPUs might increase the load on other system resources.

In NT 4, the uptomp.exe tool added support for multiple CPUs. However, this tool is no longer used in Windows 2000. Instead, you use the Device Manager to make these changes. Before changing the computer type, contact your computer manufacturer to determine if there is a vendor-specific HAL you should use instead of the standard ones included in Windows 2000.

Installing Support for Multiple CPUs

To install support for multiple CPUs, perform the following steps:

1. Click Start|Settings|Control Panel, and then click System.
2. Click the Hardware tab, and then click the Device Manager.
3. Double-click the Computer branch to expand it. Note the type of support you currently have.
4. Double-click the computer type listed under the Computer branch, click the Drivers tab, click Update Driver, and then click Next.
5. Click Display A List Of Known Drivers For This Device, and then click Show All Hardware Of This Device Class.

6. Click the appropriate computer type (one that matches your current type, except for multiple CPUs), click Next, and then click Finish.

Note: *You can use this procedure only to upgrade from a single-processor HAL to a multiple-processor HAL. If you use this procedure to change from a standard HAL to an ACPI HAL (for example, after a BIOS upgrade) or vice versa, unexpected results may occur, including an inability to boot the computer.*

Practice Questions

Question 1

You have several MPS-compliant machines that you have upgraded from NT 4 Workstation to Windows 2000 Professional. Each machine has dual Pentium III 400MHz processors because the machines are used for high-end AutoCAD and CAD drawing applications. After the upgrade, users tell you that these machines are running their drawing applications much slower than they did in NT 4. What should you do?

❍ a. Use the Device Manager to install ACPI-compliant drivers for the second processor in each machine.

❍ b. During startup, press F8. Then install the MPS-compliant drivers for the second processor in each machine.

❍ c. Use the Device Manager to install the MPS-compliant drivers for the second processor in each machine.

❍ d. Double the amount of memory in each machine.

❍ e. Use the Device Manager to enable the AGP bridge controller in each of the machines.

Answer c is correct. The MPS-compliant drivers for the second processor in each machine have not been installed. Drivers for a second processor will be MPS-compliant, not necessarily ACPI-compliant, therefore answer a is incorrect. You do not need the F8 startup menu for this scenario, nor does this question have anything to do with adding memory or enabling AGP bridge controllers. Therefore, answers b, d, and e are incorrect.

Question 2

You have eight Windows 2000 Professional computers in your company's Art department. They all have built-in USB controllers. You install a USB tablet-pointing device on each machine. You also install the manufacturer's 32-bit tablet software on each machine. A tablet icon shows up in the Control Panel, but none of the tablets work. You examine the Device Manager and notice no device conflicts. What do you need to do to get the USB tablets to work?

- ❍ a. Enable the USB ports in the system BIOS, and then reinstall the USB tablet device drivers.
- ❍ b. Enable the USB root hub controller, and then reinstall the USB tablet device drivers.
- ❍ c. Disable USB error detection for the USB root hub controller, and then enable the USB tablet device in each machine's hardware profile.
- ❍ d. Reinstall the USB tablet device drivers, and then disable the USB error detection.

The correct answer is a. You do not need a USB root hub controller for these devices to work properly. Disabling error detection for a USB root hub controller is also irrelevant to this question. Reinstalling the device drivers and then disabling USB error detection makes no sense because you would always attempt to disable error detection prior to reinstalling the drivers.

Question 3

You buy a USB-based ISDN terminal adapter for your Windows 2000 Professional laptop. You plug it into the USB port and are surprised when Plug and Play fails to detect the device. You test the adapter on a Windows 2000 desktop machine at your office, and Plug and Play detects the adapter with no difficulty. You have examined the Device Manager on your laptop, and there are no device conflicts. You need this adapter to work with your laptop because you travel frequently. What should you do?

- ❍ a. Turn off your laptop. Plug in the adapter and restart the machine.
- ❍ b. Contact the hardware manufacturer to get an upgrade for the Plug and Play BIOS on your laptop.
- ❍ c. Use the Device Manager to enable the USB root hub in the current hardware profile.
- ❍ d. Use the Device Manager to enable the USB host controller in the current hardware profile.

Answer b is correct. Answer a is not a good choice because essentially you have already tried this, and it did not work. Answers c and d deal with a USB root hub and USB host controller, neither of which are needed to get this ISDN adapter to work properly. All that is really needed is a BIOS upgrade so that your USB support is current and can accommodate the new ISDN adapter.

Question 4

You have Windows 2000 Professional installed on six machines that are all equipped with network cards and static IP addresses. Setup detected and installed a 10/100Mbps Unshielded Twisted Pair (UTP)-only NIC on Workstation 3 and Workstation 5, and a 10Mbps BNC/UTP combination NIC on the other four machines. You accepted the default settings for the network cards on all six machines. All six machines are connected to a 10/100 switch that uses Category 5 UTP cable. Now, only Workstation 3 and Workstation 5 can talk to each other on your network, but you need all the machines to be able to communicate with each other. What should you do?

- ❍ a. Configure the 10/100 NICs to transmit at the 10Mbps rate.
- ❍ b. Configure the 10/100 switch to transmit at only the 100Mbps rate.
- ❍ c. Change the BNC/UTP combination NICs so that they use the BNC transceiver setting only.
- ❍ d. Change the BNC/UTP combination NICs so that they use the UTP transceiver setting only.

Answer d is correct. All devices were detected, and the switch allows for cards at different speeds to communicate. Therefore the issue is most likely a transceiver setting—the BNC cards are using BNC. Changing the transmission rates would not help if the cards were still using different transceiver settings. Therefore answers a, b, and c are incorrect.

Question 5

You install Windows 2000 Professional on your computer at home. You create a new Dial-up Connection to connect to your company's RAS server. You configure the connection to use both of your external modems and to use Multilink to bind the modems together. You start the Dial-up Connection and connect to the RAS server. You notice that only one of the modems is connected to the RAS server. What should you do to get both modems to connect successfully to the RAS server?

❍ a. Configure the Dial-up Connection to use a Serial Line Internet Protocol (SLIP) connection instead of a PPP connection.

❍ b. Replace your modems with new ones that support Multilink and ACPI.

❍ c. Configure the company's RAS server to accept Multilink connections.

❍ d. Grant your user account Multilink permission on the company's RAS server.

Answer c is correct. Remember that for Multilink to work, not only must the client have setup Multilink properly, but also the RAS server must allow Multilink connections. Until the RAS server is configured to accept Multilink connections, it allows only one of your modems to connect at a time.

Question 6

Your Windows 2000 Professional computer has a 33.6Kbps built-in modem. You've just installed a new 56Kbps Industry Standard Architecture (ISA) modem. You want your computer to use only the 56Kbps modem. When you start up the computer, you notice in the Device Manager that the two devices are in conflict. What change should you make? (This question could be multiple choice or drag and drop, so be prepared.)

❍ a. Disable the 33.6Kbps modem in the Device Manager and reinstall the 56Kbps modem.

❍ b. Remove the 33.6Kbps modem in the Device Manager and reinstall the 56Kbps modem.

❍ c. No "action" is required; just reboot the computer and Plug and Play will detect the device.

❍ d. Remove both modems in the Device Manager. Reboot into Safe Mode, and then reinstall the 56Kbps modem.

Answer a is correct. Disabling the built-in 33.6Kbps modem prevents it from being reenabled upon startup. Removing the 33.6Kbps modem in the Device Manager produces an undesirable result: redetection of the device at system startup. Therefore, answer b is incorrect. You know that some action is required to fix this problem. Therefore, answer c is incorrect. Booting into Safe Mode is not going to help further your cause. Therefore, answer d is incorrect.

Question 7

You attach an IrDA transceiver to a serial port on your Windows 2000 machine. What step should you take to correctly install the device?

- ❍ a. Use the Device Manager.
- ❍ b. Restart the computer and let Plug and Play detect the device.
- ❍ c. Use the Add/Remove Hardware Wizard.
- ❍ d. Use the Wireless Link icon in the Control Panel.

Answer c is correct. You must install an external IrDA device attached to a serial port with the Add/Remove Hardware Wizard. You can use the Device Manager to view Port settings, but you must use the Add/Remove Hardware Wizard to add new hardware. Therefore, answer a is incorrect. Only internal IrDA devices are detected during Windows 2000 Setup or at the next system reboot. Therefore, answer b is incorrect. The Wireless Link icon is of use to you only *after* the device is correctly installed. Therefore, answer d is incorrect.

Question 8

You have replaced the network card on a computer running Windows 2000 Professional. The new card uses a different driver than the original network card. What utility should you use to ensure that the device driver for the original card is removed from your system's hard disk?

- ❍ a. Device Manager
- ❍ b. Add/Remove Programs
- ❍ c. Network And Dial-up Connections
- ❍ d. Add/Remove Hardware Wizard
- ❍ e. Network icon in the Control Panel

Answer d is correct. You must use the Add/Remove Hardware Wizard to make certain that the network card drivers no longer in use are completely removed from your hard disk. The Device Manager would allow you to remove the device, but it would not remove the drivers from disk. Add/Remove Programs is not used to remove devices and their related drivers. Network and Dial-up Connections can be used to disable a network connection, but it has no functionality to allow you to remove a device and its drivers from disk. The Network icon in the Control Panel has the same limitation.

Question 9

You need to tell your Windows 2000 users how to connect to shared IPP printers on your network, as well as how to manage their own print jobs, using their Web browser. The printers are all shared from a single Windows 2000 server on your network named PrintBoss. What is the correct syntax for users to type in the URL bar within their browsers to make this type of connection?

- ❍ a. **ftp://PrintBoss/Printers**
- ❍ b. **ipp://PrintBoss/Printers**
- ❍ c. **http://PrintBoss/Printers**
- ❍ d. **http://PrintBoss/Printer_Share_Name**

Answer c is correct. The Windows 2000 Server machine that is your print server has IIS installed and a default virtual directory configured under the name "Printers". Your clients and the print server use the Web service to communicate using IPP, so the correct URL address to type in is **http://servername/Printers**. Your server name is PrintBoss, and the virtual directory name is Printers. This is the default virtual directory configured for shared printers on a Windows 2000 machine running IIS or PWS with the default Web site started.

Question 10

You are deciding on specifications for 50 new computers your company will purchase. These computers will run Windows 2000 Professional for the Engineering department. You want Windows 2000 to be able to use all the hardware that comes in the computers. What is the maximum amount of memory you *could* have in your new Windows 2000 computers?

❍ a. 2GB

❍ b. 4GB

❍ c. 8GB

❍ d. 16GB

Answer b is correct. Windows 2000 Professional can address up to a maximum of 4GB of RAM. This is a hard-coded limitation of Windows 2000 Professional, and knowing your RAM maximum is helpful when deciding on machine configurations. Original equipment manufacturers (OEMs) may modify this limitation in versions of Windows 2000 Professional that they ship preinstalled on their hardware.

Need to Know More?

Microsoft Corporation. *Microsoft Windows 2000 Professional Resource Kit*. Microsoft Press: Redmond, Washington, 2000. ISBN: 1-57231-808-2. This book has invaluable information on installing, managing, and troubleshooting hardware devices.

Nielsen, Morten Strunge. *Windows 2000 Professional Configuration and Implementation*. The Coriolis Group: Scottsdale, AZ, 2000. ISBN: 1-57610-528-8. This book is a good reference because it has a wealth of information on configuring and troubleshooting hardware on Windows 2000 Professional.

Stinson, Craig, and Carl Siechert. *Running Microsoft Windows 2000 Professional*. Microsoft Press: Redmond, Washington, 2000. ISBN: 1-57231-838-4. This guidebook to Windows 2000 Professional is a good source for information on configuring devices and managing hardware devices.

Search the TechNet CD (or its online version through **www.microsoft.com**) and/or the *Windows 2000 Professional Resource Kit* CD using the keywords "devices", "hardware", "driver updates", "driver signing", "APM", "ACPI", and "Device Manager".

8

Implementing, Managing, and Troubleshooting Disk Drives and Volumes

Terms you'll need to understand:

- ✓ Basic versus dynamic disks
- ✓ Partitions and logical drives
- ✓ Simple, spanned, and striped volumes
- ✓ **diskperf.exe**
- ✓ File allocation table (FAT), or FAT16
- ✓ FAT32
- ✓ NT File System (NTFS) version 5
- ✓ **convert.exe**
- ✓ Mounted drives, or mount points
- ✓ Disk quotas
- ✓ NTFS compression

Techniques you'll need to master:

- ✓ Using the Disk Management tool
- ✓ Monitoring and troubleshooting disks using the Performance tool
- ✓ Using the Disk Cleanup Wizard and Disk Defragmenter
- ✓ Selecting a file system for Windows 2000
- ✓ Using **convert.exe** to convert a FAT partition to NTFS version 5
- ✓ Establishing and managing disk quotas
- ✓ Managing NTFS compressed files and folders
- ✓ Using Device Manager to manage tape devices and DVD drives

Hard Disk Management

This chapter discusses how to manage and troubleshoot hard disks in Windows 2000 Professional. We will look at options for creating partitions, formatting partitions, and disk administration available in Windows 2000. In addition, we will uncover features of the new disk storage types. Windows 2000 now supports two new disk configuration types—basic storage and dynamic storage. We will compare the differences between basic and dynamic storage types and learn how to configure and manage disks that have been initialized with either type of storage.

Basic Disks

A Windows 2000 *basic disk*, which is similar to the disk configuration we're used to in NT, is a physical disk with primary and extended partitions. As long as you use the file allocation table (FAT) file system (discussed in detail later in this chapter), Windows 2000, Windows NT, Windows 9x, and DOS can access basic disks. You can create up to three primary partitions and one extended partition on a basic disk, or just four primary partitions. You can create a single extended partition with logical drives on a basic disk. You *cannot* extend a basic disk.

Basic disks store their configuration information in the master boot record (MBR), which is stored on the first sector of the disk. The configuration of a basic disk consists of the partition information on the disk. Basic fault tolerant sets inherited from Windows NT 4 are based on these simple partitions, but they extend the configuration with some extra partition relationship information, which is stored on the first track of the disk.

Basic disks may contain spanned volumes (volume sets), mirrored volumes (mirror sets), striped volumes (stripe sets), and Redundant Array of Independent Disks (RAID)-5 volumes (stripe sets with parity) created using Windows NT 4 or earlier. These kinds of volumes are covered later in this chapter.

Dynamic Disks

A Windows 2000 *dynamic disk* is a physical disk that does not use partitions or logical drives. Instead, a single partition is created that includes the entire disk, which can then be divided into separate volumes. Also, dynamic disks do not have the same constraints of basic disks. For example, a dynamic disk can be resized on-the-fly without requiring a reboot. Dynamic disks are associated with *disk groups*, which are disks managed as a collection, which helps to organize dynamic disks. All dynamic disks in a computer are members of the same disk group. Each disk in a disk group stores replicas of the same configuration data. This configuration data is stored in a 1MB region at the end of each dynamic disk.

Dynamic disks can contain any of the types of volumes discussed later in this chapter. You can extend a volume on a dynamic disk. Dynamic disks can contain an unlimited number of volumes, so you are not restricted to four volumes per disk, as you are with basic disks. Regardless of the type of file system, only Windows 2000 computers can *directly* access dynamic volumes. However, computers that are not running Windows 2000 can access the dynamic volumes remotely when they are connected to shared folders over the network.

Comparing Basic Disks to Dynamic Disks

When you install Windows 2000, the system automatically configures the existing hard disks as basic disks. Windows 2000 does *not* support dynamic disks on laptops, and, if you're using an older (nonlaptop) machine that is not Advanced Configuration and Power Interface (ACPI)-compliant, the Upgrade To Dynamic Disk option (discussed later in this chapter) is not available. Dynamic disks have some additional limitations. You can install Windows 2000 on a dynamic volume that you *converted* from a basic disk, but you can't extend either the system or the boot partition. Volumes and upgrading are covered later in this chapter. Any troubleshooting tools that cannot read the dynamic Disk Management database work only on a basic disk.

Basic and dynamic disks are Windows 2000's way of looking at hard disk configuration. If you're migrating to Windows 2000 from NT, the dynamic disk concept might seem odd in the beginning, but once you understand the differences, working with dynamic disks is not complicated. You can format partitions with FAT16, FAT32, or NT File System (NTFS) on a basic or a dynamic disk. FAT and NTFS are discussed later in this chapter. Table 8.1 compares the terms used with basic and dynamic disks.

Table 8.1 Terms used with basic and dynamic disks.

Basic Disks	Dynamic Disks
Active partition	Active volume
Extended partition	Volume and unallocated space
Logical drive	Simple volume
Mirror set	Mirrored volume (Server only)
Primary partition	Simple volume
Stripe set	Striped volume
Stripe set with parity	RAID-5 volume (Server only)
System and boot partitions	System and boot volumes
Volume set	Spanned volumes

Upgrading Disks

Upgrading Basic Disks to Dynamic Disks

You use Windows 2000's Disk Management tool to upgrade a basic disk to a dynamic disk. To access Disk Management, click Start|Programs|Administrative Tools|Computer Management; or simply right-click the My Computer icon on the desktop and select Manage. You'll find Disk Management under Storage.

For the upgrade to succeed, any disks to be upgraded must contain at least 1MB of unallocated space. Disk Management automatically reserves this space when creating partitions or volumes on a disk, but disks with partitions or volumes created by other operating systems may not have this space available. (This space can exist even if it is not visible in Disk Management.) Before you upgrade disks, close any programs that are running on those disks.

To change or convert a basic disk to a dynamic disk, perform the following steps:

1. Open the Disk Management tool.
2. Right-click the basic disk you want to change to a dynamic disk and then click Upgrade To Dynamic Disk.

When you upgrade a basic disk to a dynamic disk, you do not need to reboot. However, if you do upgrade your startup disk or upgrade a volume or partition, you must restart your computer for the change to take effect. The good news is that you do not need to select a special command like **Commit Changes Now** before restarting your computer or closing the Disk Management tool.

When you upgrade a basic disk to a dynamic disk, any existing partitions on the basic disk become simple volumes on the dynamic disk. Any existing mirrored volumes, striped volumes, RAID-5 volumes, or spanned volumes become dynamic mirrored volumes, dynamic striped volumes, dynamic RAID-5 volumes, or dynamic spanned volumes, respectively.

You *cannot* dual-boot to another operating system if you upgrade a basic disk to a dynamic disk, which typically isn't an issue for servers. However, it's something to consider for Windows 2000 Professional machines. After you upgrade a basic disk to a dynamic disk, you cannot change the dynamic volumes back to partitions. Instead, you must delete all dynamic volumes on the disk and then use the **Revert To Basic Disk** command.

Note: *Upgrading to a dynamic disk is a one-way process. Yes, you can convert a dynamic disk with volumes back to a basic disk, but you'll lose all your data. Major downside! If you find yourself needing to do this, though, first save your data, convert the disk to basic, and then restore your data.*

Because the upgrade from basic to dynamic is per physical disk, all volumes on a physical disk must be either basic or dynamic. Again, you do not need to restart your computer when you upgrade from a basic to a dynamic disk. The only times you must restart your computer are if you upgrade your startup disk or if you upgrade a volume or partition.

Convert Dynamic Disks to Basic Disks

You must remove all volumes from the dynamic disk before you can change it back to a basic disk. Once you change a dynamic disk back to a basic disk, you can create only partitions and logical drives on that disk. Once upgraded, a dynamic disk cannot contain partitions or logical drives, nor can Microsoft operating systems other than Windows 2000 access it.

To convert a dynamic disk to a basic disk, perform the following steps:

1. Open Disk Management.
2. Right-click the dynamic disk you want to change back to a basic disk and then click Revert To Basic Disk.

Moving Disks to Another Computer

To move disks to another computer, perform the following steps:

1. Before you disconnect the disks, look in Disk Management and make sure the status of the volumes on the disks is healthy. If the status is not healthy, repair the volumes *before* you move the disks.
2. Turn the computer off, remove the physical disks, and then install the physical disks on the other computer. Restart the computer that contains the disks you moved.
3. Open Disk Management.
4. Click Action and then on Rescan Disks.
5. Right-click any disk marked Foreign, click Import Foreign Disks, and then follow the instructions on your screen.

Guidelines for Relocating Disks

Every time you remove or import disks to a computer, you must click Action, click Rescan Disks, and then verify that the disk information is correct. Aside from following Steps 1 through 5 above, you can choose which disks from the group you want to add by clicking on Select Disk—you do not have to import all of the new disks.

Disk Management describes the condition of the volumes on the disks before you import them. Review this information carefully. If there are any problems, you will know what will happen to each volume on these disks once you have imported them. After you import a dynamic disk from another computer, you can see and use any existing volumes on that disk.

Reactivating a Missing or Offline Disk

A dynamic disk may become missing when it is corrupted, powered down, or disconnected. Only dynamic disks can be reactivated—not basic disks. Sorry!

To reactivate a missing or offline disk, perform the following steps:

1. Open Disk Management.
2. Right-click the disk marked Missing or Offline, and then click Reactivate Disk.
3. The disk should be marked Online after the disk is reactivated.

Basic Volumes

Basic volumes include partitions and logical drives, as well as volumes created using Windows NT 4 or earlier, such as volume sets, stripe sets, mirror sets, and stripe sets with parity. In Windows 2000, these volumes have been *renamed* to spanned volumes, striped volumes, mirrored volumes, and RAID-5 volumes, respectively. You can create basic volumes on basic disks only.

Spanned Volumes on Basic Disks

Disk Management offers limited support of spanned volumes on basic disks. You can delete spanned volumes, but you *cannot* create new spanned volumes or extend spanned volumes on basic disks. You can create new spanned volumes only on dynamic disks. Deleting a spanned volume deletes all the data contained in the volume as well as the partitions that make up the spanned volume. You can delete only entire spanned volumes. Disk Management renames all existing volume sets to Spanned Volumes. These spanned volumes reside only on basic disks. In Windows 2000, you can delete spanned volumes created using Windows NT 4 or earlier.

Striped Volumes on Basic Disks

Likewise, Disk Management offers limited support of striped volumes on basic disks. You can delete striped volumes, but you *cannot* create new striped volumes on basic disks. You can create new striped volumes on dynamic disks only. Deleting a striped volume deletes all the data contained in the volume as well as the partitions that make up the volume. You can delete only entire striped volumes. Disk Management renames all stripe sets to Striped Volumes. These striped volumes reside only on basic disks. In Windows 2000, you can delete striped volumes created using Windows NT 4 or earlier.

Partitions and Logical Drives on Basic Disks

You can create primary partitions, extended partitions, and logical drives only on basic disks. You should create partitions instead of dynamic volumes if your computer also runs a down-level Microsoft operating system.

Partitions and logical drives can reside only on basic disks. You can create up to four primary partitions on a basic disk, or up to three primary partitions and one extended partition. You can use the free space in an extended partition to create multiple logical drives.

EXAM ALERT: You should create basic volumes, such as partitions or logical drives, on basic disks if you want computers running Windows NT 4 or earlier, Windows 98 or earlier, or MS-DOS to access these volumes.

Creating or Deleting a Partition or Logical Drive

To create or delete a partition or logical drive, perform the following:

1. Open Disk Management.
2. Right-click an unallocated region of a basic disk and then click Create Partition; alternatively, right-click free space in an extended partition and then click Create Logical Drive. (Delete Partition would be your selection if that were your goal.)
3. Using the Create Partition Wizard, click Next; click Primary Partition, Extended Partition, Or Logical Drive; then follow the instructions on your screen.

If you choose to delete a partition, all data on the deleted partition or logical drive is lost. You cannot recover deleted partitions or logical drives. You cannot delete the system partition, boot partition, or any partition that contains the active paging file.

EXAM ALERT: Windows 2000 requires that all the logical drives or other volumes in an extended partition be deleted before you can delete the extended partition.

Dynamic Volumes

What are called *sets* (like mirrored sets and striped sets) in Windows NT 4, are called *volumes* (now mirrored volumes and striped volumes) in Windows 2000. Dynamic volumes are the only type of volume you can create on dynamic disks. With dynamic disks, you are no longer limited to four volumes per disk (as you were with basic disks). The only dynamic volumes that you can install Windows 2000 on are simple and mirrored volumes, and these volumes must contain the partition table (which means that these volumes must be either basic or upgraded from basic to dynamic). Only computers running Windows 2000 can access dynamic volumes. The five types of dynamic volumes are simple, spanned, mirrored, striped, and RAID-5.

Simple Volumes

A *simple volume* is made up of disk space on a single physical disk. It can consist of a single area on a disk or multiple areas on the same disk that are linked together.

To create a simple volume, perform the following steps:

1. Open Disk Management.
2. Right-click the unallocated space on the dynamic disk where you want to create the simple volume and then click Create Volume.
3. Using the Create Volume Wizard, click Next, click Simple Volume, and then follow the instructions on your screen.

Here are some guidelines about simple volumes:

- You can create simple volumes on dynamic disks only.
- Simple volumes are not fault tolerant.
- Simple volumes cannot contain partitions or logical drives.
- Neither MS-DOS nor Windows operating systems other than Windows 2000 can access simple volumes.

Spanned Volumes

A spanned volume is made up of disk space on more than one physical disk. You can add more space to a spanned volume by extending it at any time.

To create a spanned volume, perform the following steps:

1. Open Disk Management.

2. Right-click the unallocated space on one of the dynamic disks where you want to create the spanned volume and then click Create Volume.
3. Using the Create Volume Wizard, click Next, click Spanned Volume, and then follow the instructions on your screen.

Here are some guidelines about spanned volumes:

- You can create spanned volumes on dynamic disks only.
- You need at least two dynamic disks to create a spanned volume.
- You can extend a spanned volume onto a maximum of 32 dynamic disks.
- Spanned volumes cannot be mirrored or striped.
- Spanned volumes are not fault tolerant.

Extending a Simple or Spanned Volume

To extend a simple or spanned volume, perform the following steps:

1. Open Disk Management.
2. Right-click the simple or spanned volume you want to extend, click Extend Volume, and then follow the instructions on your screen.

Here are some guidelines about extending a simple or a spanned volume:

- You can extend a volume only if it contains *no* file system or if it is formatted using NTFS. You cannot extend volumes formatted using FAT or FAT32.
- You can extend a simple volume within its original disk or onto additional disks. If you extend a simple volume across multiple disks, it becomes a *spanned volume*.
- Once a volume is extended onto multiple disks (spanned), you cannot mirror or stripe it.
- Once a spanned volume is extended, no portion of it can be deleted without the entire spanned volume being deleted.
- You can extend a simple or extended volume only if the volume was created as a dynamic volume. You cannot extend a simple or extended volume that was upgraded from basic to dynamic.
- You can extend simple and spanned volumes on dynamic disks onto a maximum of 32 dynamic disks.

***Note:** You cannot extend a system volume or boot volume. You cannot extend striped, mirrored, and RAID-5 volumes.*

Striped Volumes

A *striped volume* stores data in stripes on two or more physical disks. Data in a striped volume is allocated alternately and evenly (in stripes) to the disks of the striped volume. Striped volumes can substantially improve the speed of access to your data on disk. In addition, you can create striped volumes on both Windows 2000 Professional and Server machines.

To create a striped volume, perform the following steps:

1. Open Disk Management.
2. Right-click unallocated space on one of the dynamic disks where you want to create the striped volume and then click Create Volume.
3. Using the Create Volume Wizard, click Next, click Striped Volume, and then follow the instructions on your screen.

Here are some guidelines about striped volumes:

- You need at least two physical, dynamic disks to create a striped volume.
- You can create a striped volume onto a maximum of 32 disks.
- Striped volumes are not fault tolerant and cannot be extended or mirrored.

RAID-5 Volumes

You can create RAID-5 volumes *only* on Windows 2000 Server machines.

Note: *Mirrored and RAID-5 volumes are available only on computers that are running Windows 2000 Server. Windows 2000 Professional computers can use basic and dynamic disks but cannot host software-based fault-tolerant disk configurations such as mirror sets and stripe sets with parity. You can, however, use a computer running Windows 2000 Professional to create mirrored and RAID-5 volumes on a remote computer running Windows 2000 Server.*

Limitations of Dynamic Disks and Dynamic Volumes

You can use dynamic disks and dynamic volumes in specific circumstances; you need to be familiar with when you can and cannot utilize them.

When You Are Installing Windows 2000

If you create a dynamic volume from unallocated space on a dynamic disk, you cannot install Windows 2000 on that volume. The setup limitation occurs because Windows 2000 Setup recognizes only dynamic volumes that contain partition tables. Partition tables appear in basic volumes and in dynamic volumes only when they have been upgraded from basic to dynamic. If you create a new dynamic volume on a dynamic disk, that new dynamic volume does not contain a partition table.

When You Are Extending a Volume

If you upgrade a basic volume to dynamic (by upgrading the basic disk to a dynamic one), you can install Windows 2000 on that volume, but you *cannot* extend the volume. The limitation on extending volumes occurs because the boot volume, which contains the Windows 2000 files, cannot be part of a spanned volume. If you extend a simple volume that contains a partition table (that is, a volume that was upgraded from basic to dynamic), Windows 2000 Setup recognizes the spanned volume but cannot install to it because the boot volume cannot be part of a spanned volume.

You can extend volumes that you created only after you convert the disk to a dynamic disk. You can extend volumes and make changes to disk configuration in most cases without rebooting your computer. If you want to take advantage of these features in Windows 2000, especially software fault-tolerant features, you must change or upgrade a disk from basic to dynamic status, covered earlier in this chapter. Use dynamic disks if your computer runs only Windows 2000. If you want to use more than four volumes per disk, create fault-tolerant volumes such as RAID-5 and mirrored volumes, or extend volumes onto one or more dynamic disks.

Troubleshooting Disks and Volumes

If a disk or volume fails, naturally you want to repair it as soon as possible to avoid losing data. The Disk Management snap-in makes it easy to locate problems quickly. In the Status column of the list view, you can view the status of a disk or volume. The status also appears in the graphical view of each disk or volume.

Diagnosing Problems

To diagnose disk and/or volume problems, perform the following steps:

1. Open Add/Remove Hardware in the Control Panel. Click Next.
2. Click Add/Troubleshoot A Device and then click Next. Windows 2000 tries to detect new Plug and Play devices.
3. Choose the device you want to diagnose and fix, and then click Next.
4. Follow the instructions on the screen.

Monitoring Disk Performance

The *Windows 2000 Performance tool* is composed of two parts: System Monitor and Performance Logs And Alerts. On the Start menu, the Performance tool is no longer labeled Performance Monitor; it's just Performance. With *System Monitor*, you can collect and view realtime data about disk performance and activity in graph, histogram, or report form. *Performance Logs And Alerts* allows you to configure logs to record performance data and to set system alerts to notify you when a specified counter's value is above or below a defined threshold.

To open Performance, perform the following steps:

1. Click Start|Settings|Control Panel.
2. In the Control Panel, double-click Administrative Tools, and then double-click Performance. You will use System Monitor within Performance to monitor disk performance.

Diskperf.exe

Diskperf.exe controls the types of counters that you can view using System Monitor. You must enable **diskperf.exe** *before* you can monitor logical disks. By default, the system is set to collect *physical* drive data. Logical drive data is *not* collected by default; you enable it specifically with **diskperf.exe**. Table 8.2 lists the available **diskperf.exe** parameters, or switches.

Detecting and Repairing Disk Errors

In pre-Windows 2000 operating systems, ScanDisk detected and fixed disk errors. In Windows 2000, you can use the Error-Checking tool to check for file system errors and bad sectors on your hard disk.

To run the Error-Checking tool, perform the following steps:

1. Open My Computer and right-click the local disk you want to check.
2. Select Properties.
3. Click the Tools tab.
4. Under Error-Checking, click Check Now.
5. Under Check Disk Options, select the Scan For And Attempt Recovery Of Bad Sectors checkbox.

All files must be closed for the Error-Checking process to run. Your volume is not available to run any other tasks while this process is running. If the volume is currently in use, a message asks if you want to reschedule the disk checking for the next time you restart your system. Then, the next time you restart your system, disk-checking runs. If your volume is formatted as NTFS, Windows 2000 automatically logs all file transactions, replaces bad clusters automatically, and stores copies of key information for all files on the NTFS volume.

Table 8.2 Diskperf.exe parameters.

Parameter	Description
-y	Sets the system to start both physical and logical disk performance counters when the system is restarted.
-yd	Enables disk performance counters that are used for measuring performance of physical drives when the system is restarted. This is the default setting.
-yv	Enables disk performance counters that are used for measuring performance of logical drives when the system is restarted.
-n	Sets the system to not use any disk performance counters when the system is restarted.
-nd	Disables disk performance counters for physical drives when the system is restarted.
-nv	Disables disk performance counters for logical drives when the system is restarted.
Computername	Specifies the computer on which you want to see or set disk performance counter use. If a computer name is not specified, the local computer is assumed.

Using Disk Defragmenter

Disk Defragmenter rearranges files, programs, and unused space on your computer's hard disk(s), allowing programs to run faster and files to open more quickly. Putting the pieces of files and programs in a more contiguous space on disk reduces the time the operating system needs to open a requested item.

To run Disk Defragmenter, perform the following steps:

1. Click Start|Programs|Accessories|System Tools and then click Disk Defragmenter tool.

2. Select which disk(s) you would like to defragment and any additional options you would like.

Understanding Why Files Are Not Moved to the Beginning of NTFS Volumes

On NTFS volumes, Windows 2000 reserves a portion of the free space for a system file called the *master file table (MFT)*. The MFT is where Windows stores all the information it needs to retrieve files from the volume. Windows stores part of the MFT at the beginning of the volume. Windows reserves the MFT for exclusive use, so Disk Defragmenter cannot and does not move files to the beginning of volumes.

Using the Disk Cleanup Wizard

Disk Cleanup helps free up space on your hard drive by searching your drive(s) and then showing you a list of temporary files, Internet cache files, and unnecessary program files that you can safely delete. You can instruct Disk Cleanup to delete none, some, or all of those files.

To use the Disk Cleanup Wizard, perform the following steps:

1. Click Start|Programs|Accessories|System Tools.
2. Click the Disk Cleanup icon.

File Systems Supported in Windows 2000

The *Compact Disc File System (CDFS)* does have full support for CD-based media in Windows 2000. Although Windows 2000 does not support *High Performance File System (HPFS)*, it fully supports the FAT, FAT32, and NTFS file systems.

FAT and FAT32

Windows 2000 has full FAT (also known as FAT16) and FAT32 file system support with the following conditions or specifications:

- Pre-existing FAT32 partitions up to 127GB mount and are supported in Windows 2000.
- Windows 2000 allows you to create only new FAT32 volumes of 32GB or less.
- You can install Windows 2000 onto a FAT, FAT32, or NTFS partition. Keep in mind that you have *no* local security for Windows 2000 unless you place the operating system on an NTFS partition.
- If you initially install Windows 2000 to a FAT or FAT32 partition and then later used the Convert.exe utility to convert the partition to NTFS, default security settings are not applied.

The New Flavor of NTFS: Windows 2000's NTFS 5 File System

Windows 2000 contains a new version of NTFS File System. NTFS 5 is Windows 2000's native file system. This newest version of NTFS includes capabilities such as much more granular file permissions than NTFS 4, such as, disk quotas, an Encrypting File System (EFS), and a number of other useful features. Disk quotas is covered later in this chapter.

When you install Windows 2000, existing NTFS volumes are automatically upgraded to NTFS 5. No options are presented to choose NTFS 5 during the installation. The existing volumes are simply converted to NTFS 5 whether you want it or not.

When you install Windows 2000 to an NTFS partition, part of the Setup process is to apply default security settings to the system files and folders located on the boot partition (essentially the \WINNT and \Program Files structures).

All local NTFS volumes, including removable media, are upgraded to the new version of NTFS. This occurs after you restart your computer the first time after the graphical portion of Setup. Any NTFS volumes that are removed or powered off during the installation or upgrade process are upgraded automatically when those drives are mounted. If, during the installation, the system detects a version of Windows NT earlier than NT 4 Service Pack 4 (SP4), you see a warning message indicating that an earlier version of Windows NT was found; which states that Windows NT will not be accessible if you continue. Windows NT *can* be upgraded without service packs. However, if you want to create a new installation of Windows 2000 and dual boot with Windows NT 4, then the warning will be seen.

If you want to configure your computer to run Windows NT 4 and Windows 2000, you need to upgrade your version of Windows NT to SP4 or later. There is an updated NTFS.SYS driver in NT 4 SP4 and later SPs that allows NT 4 to read from and write to NTFS 5 volumes in Windows 2000. If you expect to dual-boot Windows 98 and Windows 2000, remember that Windows 98 can read only FAT and FAT32 file systems.

Converting from One File System to Another

Windows 2000 supports converting from one file system to another, with some special caveats and limitations that you need to be well aware of.

Reality—Converting a FAT Partition to an NTFS Partition

Let's say that you want to convert drive D to NTFS, from either FAT or FAT32. No problem! From the command line (CMD.EXE), enter the command **convert d: /fs:ntfs**. This command is one way and is not reversible. If the FAT or FAT32 partition is the system partition, the conversion takes place when the machine reboots next.

After the conversion, NTFS file permissions are set to Full Control for the Everyone Group. However, if you install Windows 2000 directly to NTFS, the permissions for the \WINNT folder and \Program Files folder structures are best secured.

Myth—Converting an NTFS Partition to a FAT Partition

You *cannot* convert an NTFS partition to a FAT partition. A simple conversion using the **convert.exe** command is not possible. Your only course of action if you want to keep the data is to back up all the data on the drive. Then, use the Disk Management tool to reformat the disk to the flavor of FAT you prefer and restore your data backup to your newly formatted disk.

Reapplying Default NTFS Permissions

You may need or want to reapply the default NTFS permissions to the system boot partition if you changed them or if you never applied them to begin with (because you converted the boot partition to NTFS after installation). To reapply the default NTFS permissions, use the secedit.exe utility, which comes with Windows 2000, from the command prompt. The computer must still be bootable to Windows 2000 for this to work.

Assigning, Changing, or Removing a Drive Letter

To assign, change, or remove a drive letter, perform the following steps:

1. Open Disk Management.
2. Right-click a partition, logical drive, or volume, and then click Change Drive Letter And Path.
3. Do one of the following:
    - *To assign a drive letter*—Right-click target volume and select Add, click the drive letter you want to use, and then click OK.
    - *To change a drive letter*—Right-click target volume and select Edit, click the drive letter you want to use, and then click OK.
    - *To remove a drive letter*— Right-click target volume and then select Remove from the context menu.

An old "gotcha" still applies. Be careful when assigning drive letters because many MS-DOS and Windows applications refer to a specific drive letter, especially at installation. For example, the path environment variable shows specific drive letters in conjunction with program names.

You can use up to 24 drive letters, from C through Z. Drive letters A and B are reserved for floppy disk drives. However, if you do not have a floppy disk drive B, you can use the letter B for a network drive. You cannot change the drive letter of the system volume or boot volume.

An error message may appear when you attempt to assign a letter to a volume, CD-ROM drive, or other removable media device, possibly because a program in the system is using it. If this happens, close the program that is accessing the volume or drive, and then click the Change Drive Letter And Path command again.

Windows 2000 allows you to statically assign drive letters on volumes, partitions, and CD-ROM drives. This means that you permanently assign a drive letter to a specific partition, volume, or CD-ROM drive. When you add a new hard disk to an existing computer system, it does not affect statically assigned drive letters. You can also mount a local drive at an empty folder on an NTFS volume by using a drive path instead of a drive letter. Read on—we'll get to this shortly.

Mounted Drives

Mounted drives, also known as *mount points* or *mounted volumes*, are useful for increasing a drive's "size" without disturbing it. For example, you could create a mount point to drive E as C:\CompanyData, thus seeming to increase the size available on the C partition, which would specifically allow you to store more data in C:\CompanyData than you could otherwise. Drive paths are available only on empty folders on NTFS volumes. The NTFS volumes can be basic or dynamic.

Creating a Mounted Drive

To create a mounted drive, perform the following steps:

1. Open Disk Management.
2. Right-click the partition or volume you want to mount and then click Change Drive Letter And Path.
3. Do one of the following:
    - *To mount a volume*—Select Add. Click Mount In This NTFS Folder and type the path to an empty folder on an NTFS volume, or click Browse to locate it.
    - *To unmount a volume*—Select the volume and then click Remove.

When you mount a local drive at an empty folder on an NTFS volume, Windows 2000 assigns a drive path to the drive rather than a drive letter.

To modify a drive path, remove it and then create a new drive path using the new location. You cannot modify the drive path directly. If you are administering a local computer, you can browse NTFS folders on that computer. If you are administering a remote computer, browsing is disabled and you must type the path to an existing NTFS folder.

The Logical Drives Tool

Logical Drives is a tool within the Computer Management snap-in that lets you manage mapped drives and local drives on a remote computer or local computer. You can change drive properties only on computers for which you are an Administrator.

Viewing Drive Properties, Changing Drive Labels, and Changing Security Settings

To view drive properties, change drive labels, or change security settings, perform the following steps:

1. Open Computer Management (Local). You can view drive properties on a remote computer as well if you want. To access a remote computer, right-click Computer Management (Local), click Connect To Another Computer, and then select the computer you wish to manage.
2. In the console tree, click Logical Drives. Perform the following actions to view the Logical Drives:
   - Expand the Computer Management (Local) item.
   - Expand the Storage item.
   - Expand the Logical Drives item.
3. Right-click the drive for which you want to view the properties and then click Properties.

The General tab shows the drive label, its type, the file system for which the drive is formatted, its total capacity, how much space on the drive is used, and how much space is free (available). The Security tab shows the access permissions, audit entries, and ownership that have been set for the drive. The Security tab appears only on drives formatted to use NTFS.

Disk Quotas

Windows 2000 disk quotas track and control disk usage per user and per volume. You can apply disk quotas only to Windows 2000 NTFS volumes. Quotas are tracked for each volume, even if the volumes reside on the same physical disk. The per-user feature of quotas allows you to track every user's disk space usage regardless of which folder the user stores files in. Disk quotas do not use compression to measure disk space usage, so users cannot obtain or use more space simply by compressing their own data. To enable disk quotas, open the Properties dialog box for a disk, select the Quota tab, and configure the options.

When a user no longer stores data on a volume, you need to delete disk quota entries. The catch to this is that you can delete the user's quota entries only after you have removed from the volume all files that the user owns, or after another user has taken ownership of the files. By default, only members of the Administrators group can view and change quota entries and settings.

Set identical or individual disk quota limits for all user accounts that access a specific volume. Then, use per-user disk quota entries to allow more (a fairly common scenario) or less (for those disk space hogs!) disk space to individual users when necessary.

NTFS Compression

NTFS in Windows 2000 allows you to compress individual files and folders so that they occupy less space on the NTFS volume. Any Windows- or DOS-based program can read and write to compressed files *without* having to decompress them first. They decompress when opened and recompress when closed. NTFS handles this entire process. You can use Windows Explorer to have compressed items display in a different color than uncompressed items.

Setting the compression state (compressed or uncompressed) on a file or folder is as simple as setting a file or folder attribute. Simply right-click the object you'd like to compress/uncompress and select Properties. On the General tab, select the Advanced button. Check or clear the Compress Contents To Save Disk Space checkbox. Click OK twice to exit both dialog boxes.

Moving and Copying Compressed Files and Folders

There is a simple method to remembering whether the original compression attribute of an object is retained or inherited when you are moving and/or copying files and folders. When you move a compressed or uncompressed file or folder from one location to another within the same NTFS volume, the original compression attribute is retained. That's it. That is the only piece of this puzzle you need to remember because in *all* other scenarios, the compression attribute is inherited from the new, or target, location.

NTFS Compression Guidelines

NTFS allocates disk space based on the *uncompressed* size of a file. If you try to copy a compressed file to an NTFS volume with enough space for the compressed file, but not the uncompressed file, you get an error message telling you there is inadequate disk space to copy the file to the target. Plan ahead.

If you attempt to copy or move a compressed file to a floppy, be prepared for the Insufficient Disk Space error. If the uncompressed size of the file is larger than the capacity of the floppy, you cannot copy or move the file. Use a third-party compression tool, such as WinZip, for this operation.

Make it a practice to compress only static data rather than data that frequently changes, because applying or removing the compression attribute does incur system overhead. NTFS encryption and compression are mutually exclusive. You can encrypt or compress a file or folder but not both. Windows 2000 does not support NTFS compression for volumes with cluster sizes larger than 4KB because of the performance degradation it would cause.

Managing Tape Devices

Windows 2000 provides comprehensive control of tape devices. You can back up or restore from tape devices, enable or disable specific tapes in your library, insert and eject media, and mount and dismount media. Good news: Tape devices are no longer the exclusive media that the Windows Backup program utilizes. Backing up to tape is still very popular, though.

If the tape device is Plug and Play compliant, you can rely on Windows 2000 to detect the device and install the appropriate drivers, as well as allocate system resources for the device. If you are using a tape device that is not Plug and Play compliant, use the Add/Remove Hardware applet in the Control Panel to install the drivers and assign resources for the device. Use Device Manager to enable, disable, or edit settings for any tape device.

Configuring and Managing DVD Devices

Windows 2000 supports a variety of DVD drives and formats. Check with the most recent Hardware Compatibility List (HCL) or your hardware vendor to see if your DVD device will work with Windows 2000. For more details on managing hardware in Windows 2000, see Chapter 7.

If the DVD device is Plug and Play compliant, you can rely on Windows 2000 to detect the device and install the appropriate drivers, as well as allocate system resources for the device. If you are using a DVD drive that is not Plug and Play compliant, use the Add/Remove Hardware applet in the Control Panel to install the drivers and assign resources for the device.

> You can control whether or not unsigned drivers for DVD drives and other hardware are permitted. You can make this decision in two places. If you are performing unattended installations of Windows 2000, you can add an entry to the Unattend.txt file in the [Unattended] section called DriverSigningPolicy=Ignore. The other location where you can control whether drivers must be signed is within Policy—either a Group Policy Object applied to a site, domain, or OU (SDOU); or simply the Local Computer Policy. Within Policy, you have three choices for how unsigned drivers are handled when they are encountered: Ignore them; Warn about them, but allow their installation; and Block their installation completely.

Your DVD drive needs either a hardware or software decoder to play movies, as well as Windows 2000-compatible sound and video cards with their respective drivers. Your decoder must be Windows 2000 compliant to play movies after you install Windows 2000. Most hardware decoders are Windows 2000 compliant. Most software decoders, however, need an update. You do not need a decoder for reading data DVDs. If no update is available, buy a new decoder that is Windows 2000 compliant.

Practice Questions

Question 1

You upgrade a computer that is running Windows NT 4 Workstation to Windows 2000 Professional. The computer has a single disk drive with three primary partitions and one extended partition. The extended partition is configured with four logical drives. One of the primary partitions is configured as drive F and is formatted as NTFS. You convert the disk to a dynamic disk. You add a second hard disk, convert it to a dynamic disk, and then attempt to extend drive F to include 2GB of the unallocated space on the new disk. The bad news: You cannot extend drive F. What is the most likely reason for this?

- ❍ a. Drive F is formatted with a pre-Windows 2000 version of NTFS.
- ❍ b. You do not have enough free space (at least 1MB) on the original hard disk.
- ❍ c. A volume can be extended only on its original hard disk.
- ❍ d. You cannot extend a volume that was originally created on a basic disk.

Answer d is correct. When Windows 2000 is installed on a machine running Windows NT Workstation 4, any existing NTFS partitions and logical drives are updated to the Windows 2000 version of NTFS, also called NTFS 5. If a primary partition or a logical drive is created on a basic disk and the disk is then converted to a dynamic disk, the partitions and logical drives on the disk are converted to simple volumes. You cannot extend these simple volumes that were originally created on a basic disk. It is true that 1MB of free space must be available on a basic disk before it can be converted to a dynamic disk. It is also true that a volume can be extended to include available space on another fixed disk. Once this is done, the extended volume becomes, in Windows 2000 terms, a spanned volume instead of a simple volume.

Question 2

You want to run Windows 98 and Windows 2000 Professional on your computer. Your computer has three disks that are each configured as a single partition. Disk 0 is where you have Windows 98 installed. Disk 1 is where Windows 2000 is installed. You need file security for Windows 2000. Disk 2 is where you are storing Graphics department files and projects. You need to be able to access the data on Disk 2 regardless of which operating system you are using. Drag and drop the best file system choice for each drive next to the appropriate place.

Disk 0 ______________	FAT16
Disk 1 ______________	FAT32
Disk 2 ______________	NTFS

The correct answer should show Disk 0 as FAT32, Disk 1 as NTFS, and Disk 2 as FAT32. FAT32 is needed on Disk 2 so both operating systems can access files stored on this disk, plus it is the most efficient file system. NTFS is needed on Disk 1 as file security is needed.

Question 3

You create two primary partitions and one extended partition on a basic disk of a computer that is running Windows 2000 Professional. The disk has 8GB of unallocated space. You create three logical drives in the extended partition. You format one of the logical drives (let's call it drive G) as NTFS and use it for storing Engineering department data. You decide that you need more space allocated to this logical drive. You have 4GB of unallocated space available on a second disk drive on the same machine. What can you do to increase the amount of storage available in that logical drive?

❍ a. Convert both disk drives to dynamic disks. Extend the simple volume that was the original logical drive by using that volume and unallocated space from the second disk drive.

❍ b. Extend drive G by creating a volume set using the logical drive and unallocated space from the second disk drive.

❍ c. Create a new partition or volume on the second disk drive. Create a new folder on drive G. Mount the new partition or volume to that folder.

❍ d. Create a new partition or volume on the second disk drive and mount it to the folder in which the Engineering department data resides.

Answer c is correct. You need to create a new partition (basic disk) or volume (dynamic disk) and mount it to an empty folder on drive G. A partition or folder can be mounted only to an empty folder. Only a volume you initially create on a dynamic disk can be extended. Because the logical drive here was created on a basic disk, it cannot be extended, therefore answers a and b are incorrect. Answer d is incorrect as it makes the problem worse. Mounting the folder in the Engineering department partition is the partition in which we are trying to increase the amount of space. Mounting the folder to this partition would decrease the amount of space available.

Question 4

For a new DVD drive, you have decided to use a vendor-supplied hardware driver that is not digitally signed. You are preparing for the unattended installation of 150 Windows 2000 Professional machines that will have identical hardware, including the new DVD drive. How do you prepare for using non-signed drivers in an unattended installation to avoid interactive warnings?

- ❍ a. In the driver subdirectory of the distribution folder, change this vendor-supplied driver's .INF file where it references the driver catalog file.
- ❍ b. In the [Unattended] section of the answer file, add an entry with this syntax: "DriverSigningPolicy=Ignore".
- ❍ c. On the server where your distribution source resides, go to the System Properties Hardware tab. Select the Driver Signing button and then choose the Ignore radio button. After you complete the unattended installations, change this setting back to the default.
- ❍ d. Flag this specific driver in the Txtsetup.oem file specified in the [OEMBootFiles] section of the answer file.

Answer b is correct. You must use the answer file to indicate that there is a non-signed driver so that Setup will continue without requiring user intervention. Any manual settings in this case, other than within the answer file, are incorrect and will cause Setup to halt and require intervention. Therefore, answers a and c are incorrect. The [OEMBootFiles] section is the wrong place to make the setting change in the answer file. Therefore, answer d is incorrect. The txtsetup.oem file cannot be used for assigning an unsigned driver parameter, which makes answer d incorrect.

Question 5

You install Windows 2000 Professional on a computer in your office on which Windows NT 4 Workstation was installed. During the installation, you create a new 3.5GB partition and indicate the partition should be formatted as FAT. You want to be able to boot back to Windows NT 4, so you indicate that the Windows 2000 system files should be installed on this new 3.5GB partition. Once installation is finished and you boot the computer back to Windows NT 4, you discover that you cannot access the new partition from Windows NT 4. What's the most likely reason?

- ❍ a. Setup converted the partition to FAT32.
- ❍ b. Windows NT 4 cannot access a partition that is larger than 2.5GB.
- ❍ c. Setup converted the partition to Windows 2000 NTFS when you indicated that the partition should be used for the system files.
- ❍ d. The Windows NT logon account you are using does not have permission to access the new partition.

Answer a is correct. When you use Setup to create and format a partition, Setup formats a partition larger than 2GB as FAT32, even if you indicate that it is to be formatted as FAT. The FAT file system does not support partitions larger than 2GB. Windows 2000 system files do not have to be on an NTFS partition, so Setup does not convert the partition to NTFS 5. Therefore, answer c is incorrect. If you have at least SP4 for NT 4 installed, you can access NTFS 5 partitions from your Windows NT 4 installations. Windows NT can access partitions larger than 2GB—in fact, it can access partitions as large as 16EB! Therefore, answer b is false. Permissions for your NT account are a potential problem only if you formatted the new partition as NTFS. For both NT 4 and Windows 2000, the default NTFS permissions for a new partition give Full Control to the everyone group. Therefore, answer d is incorrect.

Question 6

You are teaching people in your office how to manage NTFS permissions and compression attributes because they are unfamiliar with NTFS. You want to give them a simple system to help them remember what happens to the original NTFS file and folder permissions and attributes when you move and/or copy data. Drag and drop the correct result on the right to the actions on the left. You may of course use each selection more than once if needed.

Files and folders moved among different NTFS volumes ___________	RETAINED INHERITED
Files and folders moved within the same NTFS volume ___________	
Files and folders copied to a different NTFS volume ___________	
Files and folders copied within the same NTFS volume ___________	

The correct answer should show INHERITED, RETAINED, INHERITED, INHERITED from top to bottom. There is only one instance when file permissions are retained and that is when a file has been moved to a new location on the same partition. In all other instances file permissions will be inherited.

Question 7

You want to delete a quota entry defined for a user's account on drive E of a computer that is running Windows 2000 Professional. What utility or command should you use to locate the files owned by the user and move the files to a shared folder on another Windows 2000 machine on your network?

❍ a. System applet in Control Panel

❍ b. Windows Explorer

❍ c. Disk Management

❍ d. Active Directory Users And Computers

Answer c is correct. You use the Disk Quota Management System within Disk Management. From the dialog box where Quota Entries for drive E are listed, delete the user's quota entry. Doing so yields the Disk Quota dialog box and allows you to move, delete, or take ownership of the files that the user owns on drive E. Therefore, answer a is incorrect as the System applet can be used to open the Disk Management console, but it cannot be used to edit quota entries. Windows Explorer does have a search feature, but a file's owner is not an available search criteria. Therefore, answer b is incorrect. Information about individual files that a user owns is not available in Active Directory Users And Computers, not to mention that Active Directory Users And Computers is not installed by default on Windows 2000 Professional. Therefore, answer d is incorrect.

Question 8

You install a new 10GB hard drive in your Windows 2000 Professional computer, and you want to divide it into five equal 2GB sections. How can you accomplish this? [Check all correct answers]

- ❑ a. Leave the disk as a basic disk. Create three primary partitions of 2GB each. Create one extended partition and make two logical drives of 2GB each within the extended partition.
- ❑ b. Leave the disk as a basic disk. Create four primary partitions of 2GB each. Create one extended partition of 2GB for the fifth partition.
- ❑ c. Upgrade the disk to a dynamic disk and create five 2GB simple volumes on it.
- ❑ d. Upgrade the disk to a dynamic disk. Create five primary partitions of 2GB each on the disk.

Answers a and c are correct. You cannot have more than four partitions on a basic disk, but you can overcome this limitation by converting a disk from basic to dynamic. Dynamic disks do not contain partitions or logical disks; they contain volumes. Answer d is incorrect as a dynamic disk cannot contain primary partitions. It just contains volumes. A basic disk can have the maximum of four primary partitions or three primary partitions, and one extended partition, therefore answer b is incorrect.

Question 9

You are trying to create a striped volume on your Windows 2000 Professional computer to improve performance. You confirm that you have plenty of unallocated free space on two disks in your computer. When you right-click an area of free space on a disk, your only option is to create a partition. Explain the problem and the best way to resolve it.

- ❍ a. You can create striped volumes only when you have at least one dynamic disk. Upgrade one of the disks from basic to dynamic, and then you can create the striped volume.
- ❍ b. You can create striped volumes only if the disks involved are dynamic, not basic. Upgrade the disks that will be participating in the striped volume from basic to dynamic. After the disks are dynamic, you can create the striped volume.
- ❍ c. In order to create a striped set, you need a second controller in the computer so that there is a single controller for each disk. Upgrading the disks from basic to dynamic is also required.
- ❍ d. Windows 2000 Professional does not support striped volumes. To create a striped volume, you need to first install Windows 2000 Server or Advanced Server on your computer.

Answer b is correct. You can create striped volumes only on dynamic disks, but you do not need multiple controllers. The option to create a partition rather than a (striped) volume indicates that the disk you are trying to use is a basic disk. If you upgrade all the disks to dynamic, they can be part of a striped volume. Answer a is incorrect as the minimum of two dynamic disks are required to create a striped volume, not one. Answer c is incorrect because a second controller is not needed. Windows 2000 Professional does support striped volumes but it does not support RAID-5 volumes, therefore answer d is incorrect.

Question 10

You add a new disk to your computer. Next, you try to extend an existing volume to include the unallocated space on the new disk, but the option to extend the volume is not available. What is the most likely cause of the problem?

- ❍ a. The existing volume is part of a striped volume on a dynamic disk.
- ❍ b. The existing volume is part of a spanned volume on a basic disk.
- ❍ c. You cannot extend the volume because the disk is basic instead of dynamic.
- ❍ d. The existing volume is not formatted with NTFS. Only NTFS volumes can be extended.

Answer d is correct. A volume can be extended regardless of whether it is on a basic or dynamic disk therefore answer c is incorrect. The option to extend the disk is only related to the fact the drive had not been formatted with NTFS yet, and therefore answers a and b are incorrect.

Need to Know More?

Microsoft Corporation. *Microsoft Windows 2000 Professional Resource Kit*. Redmond, Washington: Microsoft Press, 2000. ISBN: 1-57231-808-2. Chapter 1 of this book has invaluable information on file systems and disk concepts. Chapter 6 offers valuable details on file system considerations and multiple boot configurations.

Nielsen, Morten Strunge. *Windows 2000 Professional Configuration and Implementation*. Scottsdale, Arizona: The Coriolis Group, 2000. ISBN: 1-57610-528-8. This book provides useful information on NTFS 5 and working with Windows 2000 disks, volumes, and file systems.

Stinson, Craig and Carl Siechert. *Running Microsoft Windows 2000 Professional*. Redmond, Washington: Microsoft Press, 2000. ISBN: 1-57231-838-4. This guidebook to Windows 2000 Professional is a good source for information on NTFS 5 and disk management.

Search the TechNet CD (or its online version through **www.microsoft.com**) and/or the Windows 2000 Professional Resource Kit CD using the keywords "Disks," "Volumes," "Basic and dynamic," "NTFS 5," "File systems," "Disk quotas," and "Disk management."

9

Implementing, Managing, and Troubleshooting Network Protocols and Services

Terms you'll need to understand:

- ✓ Transmission Control Protocol/Internet Protocol (TCP/IP)
- ✓ Dynamic Host Configuration Protocol (DHCP)
- ✓ Domain Name System (DNS)
- ✓ Windows Internet Name Service (WINS)
- ✓ Automatic Private IP Addressing (APIPA)
- ✓ Serial Line Internet Protocol (SLIP)
- ✓ Point-to-Point Protocol (PPP)
- ✓ Point-to-Point Tunneling Protocol (PPTP)
- ✓ Layer 2 Tunneling Protocol (L2TP)
- ✓ World Wide Web (WWW)
- ✓ Hypertext Transfer Protocol (HTTP)
- ✓ Internet Information Services (IIS) 5
- ✓ File Transfer Protocol (FTP)
- ✓ Simple Mail Transfer Protocol (SMTP)
- ✓ Address Resolution Protocol (ARP)
- ✓ **hostname**
- ✓ **ipconfig**
- ✓ **ping**
- ✓ **route**
- ✓ **tracert**
- ✓ Dial-up Networking (DUN)
- ✓ Remote Access Services (RAS)
- ✓ Virtual Private Network (VPN)
- ✓ Internet Connection Sharing (ICS)

Techniques you'll need to master:

- ✓ Configuring and troubleshooting TCP/IP
- ✓ Setting up DUN connections
- ✓ Establishing VPN connections
- ✓ Configuring and troubleshooting ICS

You can think of computer networking protocols as languages. Just as two people must speak the same language in order to communicate well, two or more computers on a network must share the same protocol so that they can communicate. Imagine that we could build a bridge to China from the United States—think of the bridge as the physical cabling of a network that allows traffic to pass over it. But even though traffic can be physically transported over the bridge, if the people going across the bridge can't speak a common language (e.g., English or Chinese), very little communication will take place. The popularity of the Internet has made the TCP/IP protocol a *de facto* standard for networking today. Windows 2000 makes extensive use of TCP/IP.

Configuring and Troubleshooting Transmission Control Protocol/Internet Protocol (TCP/IP)

TCP/IP is a time-proven and robust set of computer networking tools and services. Born in the 1960s out of the ARPANET project for the U.S. Department of Defense (DoD), TCP/IP encompasses a vast array of utilities and network services. This suite of services has evolved to become a de facto standard for both the Internet and for local area networks (LANs) using personal computer network operating systems like Novell NetWare 5 and Windows 2000.

TCP/IP is the default protocol when you install Windows 2000 Professional. It provides a means for connecting dissimilar computer systems. TCP/IP scales well—it works well for small, medium-sized, or large organizations. TCP/IP and its name resolution partner, Domain Name System (DNS), are both required components for implementing Active Directory in the Windows 2000 Server family of products.

Deciphering the TCP/IP Protocol Suite for Windows 2000

TCP/IP is more than just a standardized specification for data transport over a network wire. It is a sophisticated toolbox of data transport services, name resolution services, and troubleshooting utilities. Microsoft's implementation of TCP/IP for Windows 2000 includes the following network services and components:

- *Dynamic Host Configuration Protocol (DHCP)*—This service is based on an industry-standard specification for automatically assigning (or leasing) IP addresses to computers connected to the network. The addresses are assigned from a pre-defined pool (or *scope*) of IP addresses that an administrator must specify. DHCP makes the chore of assigning and maintaining TCP/IP addresses on hundreds or thousands of computers much easier than having to maintain an exhaustive list of IP addresses and computer names by hand. However, administrators should manually assign static IP addresses for server computers. You can install the DHCP service only in the Windows 2000 Server product line, but DHCP can assign addresses to both servers and workstations. Any operating system that can make DHCP-compliant requests for IP addresses can utilize a DHCP server that is running Windows 2000. DHCP-compatible operating systems include Windows 3.x, 9x, ME, NT, and 2000.

- *DNS server*—Computers understand and work well with numbers, but unfortunately, we humans have more of an affinity for names. TCP/IP requires that each network device be assigned a numeric IP address. DNS, in conjunction with DNS servers, maps numeric IP addresses to computer (host) names and vice versa. DNS employs a hierarchical system of domains and subdomains that helps to make this name resolution service very scalable. DNS servers mitigate the need for a manually maintained HOSTS file to be stored on each computer. Windows 2000 DNS servers offer added functionality such as Active Directory Integrated Zones, Incremental Zone Transfers, and Dynamic Updates. DNS is a requirement for implementing Active Directory.

- *Windows Internet Name Service (WINS)*—This service is Microsoft's implementation of a name resolution mechanism to match IP addresses to NetBIOS computer names and vice versa. WINS servers can greatly reduce NetBIOS traffic on networks by decreasing the amount of broadcast traffic that occurs when computers attempt to resolve unknown IP addresses to NetBIOS computer names. For an Active Directory-based network in Windows 2000 native mode with no applications that require NetBIOS, WINS becomes unnecessary.

- *Auto Private IP Addressing (APIPA)*—Microsoft first introduced this feature in Windows 98. For computers that are configured to obtain an IP address automatically, APIPA kicks in if no DHCP server is available on the network to lease out an IP address. APIPA automatically queries the other computers on the network and then assigns a unique IP address to the local computer using the IP address scheme of 169.254.x.y with the subnet mask of 255.255.0.0. The Internet Assigned Numbers Authority (IANA) has reserved the IP address range of 169.254.0.0 through 169.254.255.255 for APIPA. This ensures that any IP address that APIPA generates does not conflict with any public, routable addresses. This feature is turned on by default in Windows 2000 Professional.

- *Serial Line Internet Protocol (SLIP)*—This specification is an older Unix standard for serial communications. Windows 2000 supports SLIP primarily for backward-compatibility purposes. You can use SLIP only for outbound connections on Windows 2000 Professional.

- *Point-to-Point Protocol (PPP)*—PPP has effectively replaced SLIP. PPP is a remote access/dial-up protocol that supports industry-standard network protocols such as TCP/IP, NWLink, NetBEUI, and AppleTalk. PPP is optimized for low-bandwidth connections, so it is the preferred remote access protocol for dial-up/modem connections.
- *Point-to-Point Tunneling Protocol (PPTP)*—The only Virtual Private Network (VPN) protocol that shipped with Windows NT 4, PPTP encapsulates TCP/IP, Internet Protocol Exchange (IPX), or NetBEUI data packets and encrypts the data being transmitted as it travels (tunnels) through the Internet. PPTP clients can connect to any Microsoft-compatible PPTP servers via the Internet with proper security credentials. This service, shipped with Windows 2000 Professional, allows users to connect to the Internet using local (non-long distance) connections and offers them a way to connect to PPTP computers in remote locations without incurring toll charges or requiring dedicated data lines.
- *Layer 2 Tunneling Protocol (L2TP)*—An alternative to PPTP, L2TP is new to Windows 2000 and offers similar functionality. However, L2TP is an industry-standard VPN protocol and is shipped with Windows 2000 Professional. L2TP also encapsulates TCP/IP, IPX, or NetBEUI data packets and encrypts the data being transmitted as it travels (tunnels) through the Internet. You can also use L2TP in conjunction with Microsoft IP Security (IPSec) for enhanced security. L2TP is covered in more detail later in this chapter.
- *IPSec*—This is a relatively new Internet security protocol, also referred to as Secure IP. It provides computer-level authentication in addition to data encryption for VPN connections that use the L2TP protocol. IPSec negotiates between the client computer and the remote tunnel server before an L2TP connection is established, which secures both passwords and data. L2TP uses standard PPP-based authentication protocols, such as Extensible Authentication Protocol (EAP), Microsoft Challenge Handshake Authentication Protocol (MSCHAP), CHAP, Shiva Password Authentication Protocol (SPAP), and Password Authentication Protocol (PAP) with IPSec. IPSec and EAP are covered in more detail later in this chapter.
- *World Wide Web (WWW) publishing service*—This is a major component of Internet Information Services (IIS) 5, that ships with Windows 2000 Professional. Although not installed by default in Windows 2000 Professional, IIS 5 and the WWW publishing service provide Web page hosting for HTML-based and Active Server Pages (ASP)-based documents.
- *File Transfer Protocol (FTP) service*—This is another major component of IIS 5. FTP is an industry standard protocol for transferring files between computers over TCP/IP-based networks, such as the Internet.

- *Simple Mail Transfer Protocol (SMTP)*—The Microsoft SMTP service implements the industry-standard SMTP to transport and deliver email messages. The SMTP service for Windows 2000 is also a component of IIS 5.

Understanding TCP/IP Computer Addresses: It's All about Numbers

TCP/IP assigns a unique set of numbers to each computer that is connected to a TCP/IP-based network or internetwork. This set of numbers consists of four separate numbers, each delimited by a period or a dot (.). For example, an IP address of 192.168.1.20 illustrates this concept, known as *dotted decimal notation*. Each device on a TCP/IP-based network must be assigned a *unique* IP address so that it can send and receive data with the other devices on the network. A network device can be a computer, a printer, a router, a firewall, and so on.

We write IP addresses in a dotted decimal format for ease and convenience. However, TCP/IP addresses are actually 32-bit *binary* numbers! By converting these binary numbers into decimal, most of us can work with these addresses much more easily than if we had to work with them in their native binary format. The real binary address of 192.168.1.20, mentioned above, translates into 11000000.10101000.1.10100.

> **TIP** If you're not sure how to convert decimal numbers into binary or vice versa, just use the Windows Calculator by clicking Start|Run, typing **calc**, and clicking OK. Click View|Scientific from the menu bar and you can easily perform these conversions.

Certain IP addresses are reserved for specific functions:

- The address 255.255.255.255 (11111111.11111111.11111111.11111111 in binary) is reserved for network broadcasts.
- The IP address 127.0.0.1 (1111111.0.0.1 in binary) is reserved as a loopback address for testing proper configuration of the IP address(es) for the local host computer.
- The address schemes 192.168.x.y and 10.0.x.y have been reserved as nonroutable by the bodies that govern the Internet.

Therefore, IP addresses such as 192.168.1.20 and 10.0.0.7 are restricted to being used only for the internal addressing of LANs. By definition, you cannot route these addressing schemes onto the Internet. Routers (devices that route network data packets) do not forward any data packets that originate with a nonroutable addressing scheme.

Configuring TCP/IP

TCP/IP is installed by default when you install Windows 2000 Professional, unless you override this default setting. In addition, the protocol's default configuration is to *obtain an IP address automatically*. This means that the computer automatically requests a unique TCP/IP address for your network from a DHCP server. If no DHCP server is available, the operating system invokes APIPA to query the other computers that are currently powered on and connected to the network so that it can assign itself a unique IP address.

If you work with TCP/IP, you need to become familiar with the following terms:

- *Subnet mask*—This is essentially an IP address filter that gets applied to each unique IP address. The subnet mask (or filter) determines which part of the IP address for a computer specifies the network segment where the computer is located versus which part of the IP address specifies the unique node (or host) address for that individual computer. As an example, an IP address of 192.168.1.20 with a subnet mask of 255.255.255.0 is determined to have the network segment address of 192.168.1. The node or host address for the computer, therefore, is 20. This is analogous to the street name of a postal address versus the actual house number of the address. There may be many houses on the same street, but only one house has a house number of 20.
- *Default gateway*—This IP address specifies the router for the local network segment (or subnet). If this address is absent, the computer cannot communicate with other computers that are located outside of the local network segment (also known as a *subnet* or *subnetwork*). Default gateway information is often obtained through DHCP if the computer is configured to obtain an IP address automatically.
- *Preferred and alternate DNS servers*—Having more than one DNS server on a network helps provide load balancing and fault tolerance for client computers that need to perform IP address to hostname lookups as well as hostname to IP address lookups. Name resolution is a critical issue in TCP/IP. DNS server information is often obtained through DHCP if the computer is configured to obtain an IP address automatically.
- *WINS addresses*—WINS provides name resolution between IP addresses and NetBIOS computer names. WINS server addresses are often obtained through DHCP if the computer is configured to obtain an IP address automatically.

To manually set up a Windows 2000 Professional computer with a static IP address for the TCP/IP network protocol, click Start|Settings|Network And Dial-up Connections. Right-click the Local Area Network (LAN) Connection icon that you want to configure and select Properties. If TCP/IP is not currently installed, follow these steps:

1. Click Install from the LAN connection's Properties sheet.
2. Click Protocol and then click Add.
3. Click Internet Protocol (TCP/IP) and then click OK.
4. Restart the computer.

To configure the necessary settings so that TCP/IP can communicate with other computers and devices over the network, follow these steps:

1. Click Internet Protocol (TCP/IP) and then click Properties.
2. Click Use The Following IP Address.
3. Type the IP Address, Subnet Mask, and Default Gateway.
4. Type the proper IP address for a Preferred DNS Server and an Alternate DNS Server (if any).
5. Click the Advanced button to add additional IP addresses and default gateways. You can also add, edit, or remove DNS server address information, and you can change other DNS settings. You can specify IP addresses for any WINS servers on the network, you can enable NetBIOS name resolution using an LMHOSTS file, and you can enable or disable NetBIOS over TCP/IP. You can also set up IPSec and TCP/IP filtering as optional settings from the Advanced TCP/IP Settings Properties sheet.
6. Click OK to close the Advanced TCP/IP Settings Properties dialog box.
7. Click OK to close the Internet Protocol (TCP/IP) Properties dialog box.
8. Click OK to close the Local Area Connection Properties dialog box.

Troubleshooting TCP/IP

Windows 2000 Professional comes with several software tools and utilities to help you isolate and resolve TCP/IP-related issues. You must run all of these utilities from the command line. Connectivity tools include the following:

- *Finger*—Displays information about a user for a particular computer. The target computer must be running the Finger service.
- *FTP*—Copies files to and from FTP servers over a TCP/IP connection.
- *LPR*—Sends one or more files to be printed via a line printer daemon (LPD) printer.
- *RCP*—Copies files between a Windows 2000 Professional computer and a computer system running the remote shell daemon (RSHD).

- *REXEC*—Executes commands on remote computer systems that are running the REXEC service.
- *RSH*—Executes commands on remote computer systems that are running the RSH service.
- *Telnet*—Establishes a terminal emulation session for working on remote systems, including environments such as Unix, Mainframe, and Mini computers.
- *TFTP (Trivial File Transfer Protocol)*—Copies files to and from remote computers that are running the TFTP service.

Diagnostic tools include the following:

- *ARP (Address Resolution Protocol)*—Lists and edits the IP-to-Ethernet (or Token Ring) physical translation tables that ARP uses.
- *HOSTNAME*—Lists the name of the local host (computer).
- *IPCONFIG*—Shows all of the current TCP/IP configuration settings for the local computer such as its IP address, subnet mask, and any WINS servers and DNS servers assigned to the computer.
- *LPQ*—Shows the current status of the print queue on a computer that is running the LPD service.
- *NBTSTAT*—Delineates network protocol statistics and lists the current connections that are using NetBIOS over TCP/IP.
- *NETSTAT*—Delineates network protocol statistics and lists the current TCP/IP connections.
- *PING*—Is used to test TCP/IP-related connectivity to remote computers. This command also verifies the proper TCP/IP configuration of the local host computer by attempting to **ping** the loopback address for the local host (computer). For example: **ping 127.0.0.1**.
- *ROUTE*—Edits the local computer's routing tables.
- *TRACERT*—Displays the route (path) that data packets follow as they travel from the local computer to a remote destination computer.

Troubleshooting TCP/IP Configuration and Connectivity

Whenever you initially set up TCP/IP, you should always test and verify that the protocol is working properly. Here are the steps you can take to check the computer's TCP/IP configuration and to test its connectivity:

1. Open a command prompt window; **ipconfig** and **ping** are strictly command-line utilities.

2. Run **ipconfig** to display the computer's current IP configuration. Use **ipconfig /all** to display more detailed information (see Figure 9.1).
3. Use the **ping** command to ping the computer's loopback address: **ping 127.0.0.1**. This tests whether TCP/IP is correctly installed and bound to the network adapter card (see Figure 9.2).
4. Ping the IP address of the local computer to verify the uniqueness of the IP address on the network.
5. Ping the IP address of the default gateway for the local subnet to check that the default gateway is up and running. This step also demonstrates whether the computer can successfully communicate over the local network segment.
6. Ping the IP address of a computer that is located on a different network segment (subnet). This step indicates whether the computer can send and receive network data packets through a router.

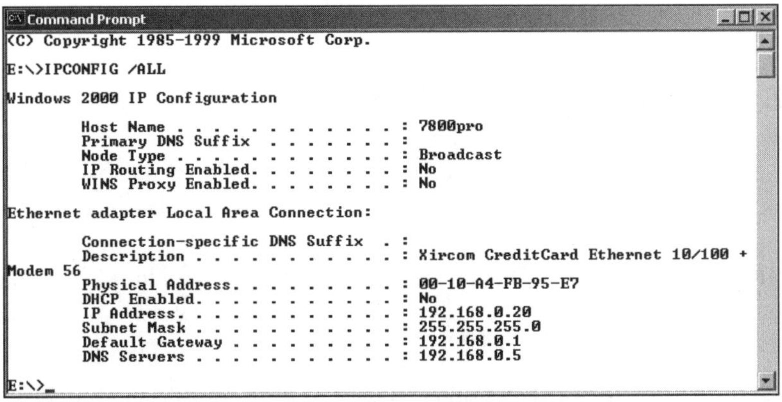

```
Command Prompt
(C) Copyright 1985-1999 Microsoft Corp.

E:\>IPCONFIG /ALL

Windows 2000 IP Configuration

        Host Name . . . . . . . . . . . . : 7800pro
        Primary DNS Suffix  . . . . . . . :
        Node Type . . . . . . . . . . . . : Broadcast
        IP Routing Enabled. . . . . . . . : No
        WINS Proxy Enabled. . . . . . . . : No

Ethernet adapter Local Area Connection:

        Connection-specific DNS Suffix  . :
        Description . . . . . . . . . . . : Xircom CreditCard Ethernet 10/100 +
Modem 56
        Physical Address. . . . . . . . . : 00-10-A4-FB-95-E7
        DHCP Enabled. . . . . . . . . . . : No
        IP Address. . . . . . . . . . . . : 192.168.0.20
        Subnet Mask . . . . . . . . . . . : 255.255.255.0
        Default Gateway . . . . . . . . . : 192.168.0.1
        DNS Servers . . . . . . . . . . . : 192.168.0.5

E:\>_
```

Figure 9.1 An example of running the **ipconfig** command.

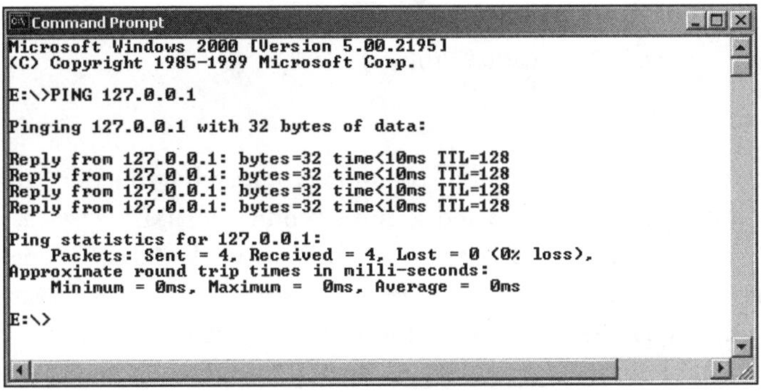

```
Command Prompt
Microsoft Windows 2000 [Version 5.00.2195]
(C) Copyright 1985-1999 Microsoft Corp.

E:\>PING 127.0.0.1

Pinging 127.0.0.1 with 32 bytes of data:

Reply from 127.0.0.1: bytes=32 time<10ms TTL=128
Reply from 127.0.0.1: bytes=32 time<10ms TTL=128
Reply from 127.0.0.1: bytes=32 time<10ms TTL=128
Reply from 127.0.0.1: bytes=32 time<10ms TTL=128

Ping statistics for 127.0.0.1:
    Packets: Sent = 4, Received = 4, Lost = 0 (0% loss),
Approximate round trip times in milli-seconds:
    Minimum = 0ms, Maximum =  0ms, Average =  0ms

E:\>
```

Figure 9.2 An example of pinging a computer's loopback IP address.

Using APIPA

If a computer is set up to obtain an IP address automatically from a DHCP server but no DHCP servers are available, APIPA temporarily assigns an IP address to the local computer while it searches the network to make sure that no other network devices have been assigned the same IP address. By running **ipconfig**, you can view the current TCP/IP information for the local computer. An address such as 169.254.x.y generally indicates that APIPA is currently in effect.

Connecting to Remote Computers Using Dial-up Connections

Dial-up connectivity still maintains an important role for connecting remote computers. In Microsoft terms, *Dial-up Connections* generally refers to client computers dialing out to server computers. Remote Access Services (RAS) generally refers to server computers that accept inbound remote connections from dial-up clients. Dial-up Connections usually involve regular phones using analog modems and/or dial up integrated services digital network (ISDN) lines.

New Authentication Protocols

Windows 2000 Professional provides advanced support for remote access authentication protocols, which offer enhanced security and dynamic bandwidth allocation for remote access. These authentication protocols, some of which have already been mentioned in this chapter, validate the logon credentials for all users who attempt to connect to a Windows 2000-based network. Windows 2000 Professional supports all the authentication protocols that Windows NT 4 offered, including PAP, CHAP, MSCHAP, SPAP, and PPTP (used for VPN support).

Windows 2000 Professional also supports several new authentication protocols that greatly enhance its dial-up and remote access capabilities for data encryption, user authentication, and bandwidth allocation. These newly supported standards include IPSec, L2TP, EAP, Remote Authentication Dial-in User Service (RADIUS), and Bandwidth Allocation Protocol (BAP).

IPSec

IPSec is a suite of security-related protocols and cryptographic functions for establishing and maintaining private and secure IP connections. IPSec is easy to implement and offers vigilant security for potential network attacks. IPSec-enabled clients establish a Security Association (SA) that serves as a private key for encrypting data. IPSec uses policies for configuring its security services. IPSec policies support different gradations of security levels for different types of network traffic. Administrators can set IPSec policies at the User, Group, Application, Domain, Site, or Global Enterprise level. You configure IPSec policies with the IP Security Policy Management snap-in of the Microsoft Management Console (MMC).

L2TP

You can compare L2TP to PPTP in that it provides an encrypted "tunnel" for data to pass through an untrusted (public) network such as the Internet. However, although *L2TP* does provide a tunnel for data to pass through, it does *not* provide encryption for the data. L2TP works in conjunction with other encryption services and security protocols, such as IPSec, to provide a secure VPN connection. Both L2TP and PPTP use PPP to establish initial communications. Some of the major differences between L2TP and PPTP are:

- L2TP requires IPSec for encryption services; PPTP uses the encryption functions of PPP.
- L2TP provides header compression support. When you enable header compression, L2TP uses only 4 bytes for its overhead. PPTP requires 6 bytes for its overhead and does not support header compression.
- L2TP offers support for tunnel authentication; PPTP does not support tunnel authentication. If you implement IPSec with L2TP or PPTP, IPSec provides its own tunnel authentication, rendering L2TP's tunnel authentication unnecessary.
- Unlike PPTP, L2TP does not have to run over an IP-based network transport. L2TP needs only a packet-oriented, point-to-point connection. L2TP can function using User Datagram Protocol (UDP), Frame Relay Permanent Virtual Circuits (PVCs), X.25 Virtual Circuits (VCs), or Asynchronous Transfer Mode (ATM) VCs over TCP/IP.

EAP

EAP is an extension of PPP for DUN, L2TP, and PPTP clients. EAP supports a negotiated authentication model where the actual authentication mechanism is determined between the dial-up connection client and the remote access server. EAP provides support for several authentication protocols, including the following:

- *Message Digest 5 Challenge Handshake Authentication Protocol (MD5-CHAP)*—This encrypts usernames and passwords using its own MD5 algorithm.
- *Generic token cards*—These cards provide passwords for users and can support multiple authentication methods.
- *Transport Level Security (TLS)*—The TLS protocol works with smart cards and other types of security certificates. A smart card stores a user's security certificate and private key electronically inside the card. Smart card technology requires physical cards and card readers.

Note: By using EAP application programming interfaces (APIs), software developers can design and implement new authentication methods for smart cards, generic token cards, and even biometric devices like fingerprint identification scanners. In this way, EAP can support authentication technologies that will be developed in the future. To add EAP authentication methods, go to the Security tab of the remote access server's Properties sheet.

RADIUS

RADIUS offers accounting services and authentication functions for distributed dial-up connections. Windows 2000 Professional can take on the role of a RADIUS server or a RADIUS client, or it can assume the roles of both. A RADIUS client is often used as a remote access server for an Internet Service Provider (ISP). The RADIUS client forwards authentication requests to a RADIUS server. A Windows 2000 RADIUS client can also forward remote access accounting information to a RADIUS server. You configure RADIUS client settings from the Security tab of the remote access server's Properties sheet.

RADIUS servers validate requests from RADIUS clients. For authentication, Windows 2000 provides Internet Authentication Services (IAS) as an optional Windows component that you can add during installation or through the Add/Remove Programs icon in the Control Panel. RADIUS servers maintain RADIUS accounting data from RADIUS clients in associated log files.

BAP

BAP works in conjunction with the Bandwidth Allocation Control Protocol (BACP) as an enhancement to the Multilink feature found in Windows NT 4. Multilink enables you to bind together two or more modem or ISDN lines, allowing you to achieve higher throughput (more bandwidth) than you would if you used the lines individually. BAP and BACP work together to dynamically add or drop lines for Multilinked devices on an on-demand basis. Both protocols serve as PPP control protocols. These protocols provide a means for optimizing bandwidth while holding down connection costs by responding to network bandwidth needs on demand. For organizations that incur line-usage charges based on bandwidth use (such as ISDN lines), BAP and BACP can significantly cut costs.

Administrators can turn on the Multilink feature as well as BAP and BACP from the PPP tab of each remote access server's Properties sheet. You configure BAP settings using remote access policies. By implementing a remote access policy using BAP, you can specify that an extra line should be dropped if the connection for that line falls below 65 percent usage, for example, for a particular group. You can additionally specify that an extra line should be dropped only if usage falls below 35 percent for a different group of users.

Connecting to Remote Access Servers

You create new connections to remote access servers from the Network And Dial-Up Connections window. You can make new connections as well as modify or delete existing dial-up connections from this window. To create a new DUN connection for connecting to remote access servers, follow these steps:

1. Click Start|Settings|Network And Dial-up Connections.
2. Click Make New Connection to display the Network Connection Wizard.
3. Click Next.
4. At the Network Connection Type dialog box, you can accept the default choice—Dial-up To Private Network, as shown in Figure 9.3.
5. Click Next.
6. Mark the checkbox for the device(s) that you want to use for this connection.
7. Click Next.
8. Specify the phone number for the remote access server to which you want to connect. Mark the Use Dialing Rules checkbox if you want your system's dialing rules to automatically determine how to dial from different locations.
9. Click Next.
10. Specify the Connection Availability For This Dial-up entry. Click For All Users or Only For Myself.
11. Click Next.

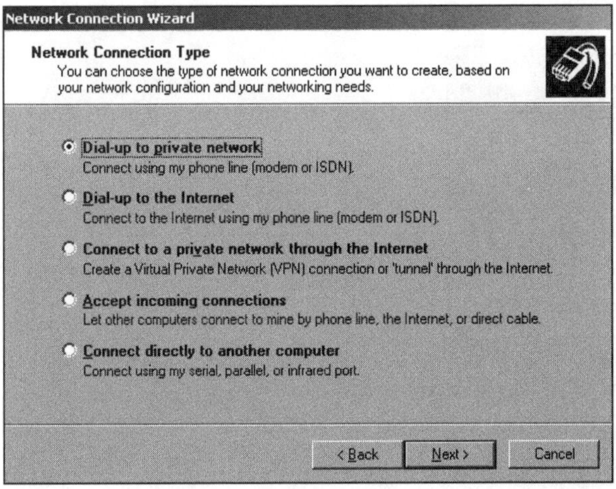

Figure 9.3 The Network Connection Type dialog box of the Network Connection Wizard.

12. Complete the Network Connection Wizard by typing the name that you want to assign to this connection. Mark the Add A Shortcut To My Desktop checkbox if you would like a shortcut added.
13. Click Finish.

As soon as you complete the Network Connection Wizard, a Connect dialog box appears. It prompts you for a User Name and a Password and offers a Dial drop-down list for the phone number to be dialed (see Figure 9.4). You can type the proper User Name and Password as well as verify the phone number to be dialed for connecting to the remote access server. Click the Dial button to initiate the connection. Click the Properties button to modify some of the dial-up connection's properties.

You can modify the properties of any Dial-up Connection or network connection listed in the Network And Dial-up Connections window by right-clicking on the connection's icon and selecting Properties, as shown in Figure 9. 5. From the Dial-up Connection's Properties sheet, you can configure connection devices (modems and so on), list alternate phone numbers, and configure dialing options and redialing options. You can specify security options, configure dial-up server settings, and modify network connection components. You can also set up Internet Connection Sharing (ICS) from the Sharing tab, if this connection connects to the Internet. ICS is covered in more detail later in this chapter.

The Networking tab of a Dial-up Connection's Properties sheet allows you to configure several essential components for successful connections (see Figure 9.6). Be sure to specify the proper dial-up server type to which you will be connecting (either PPP or SLIP). You can change PPP settings by clicking on the Settings button (as shown in Figure 9.7). Be sure that your connection has at least one

Figure 9.4 The Connect dialog box for connecting to remote access servers.

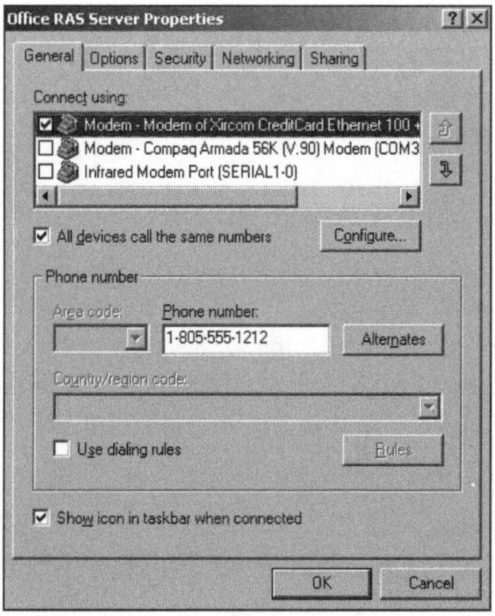

Figure 9.5 The Properties sheet for a Dial-up Connection.

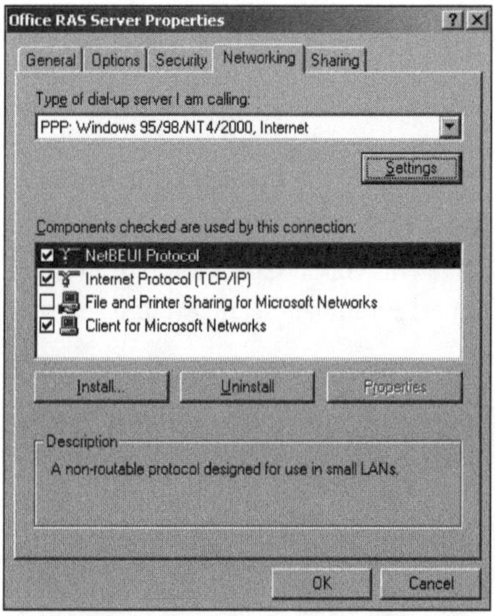

Figure 9.6 The Networking tab of a Dial-up Connection's Properties sheet.

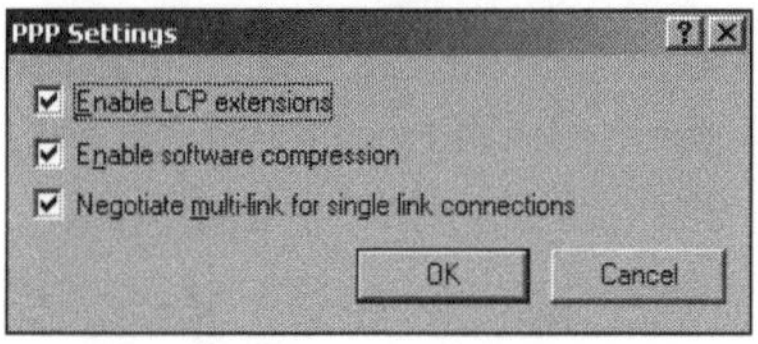

Figure 9.7 The PPP Settings dialog box.

dial-up network protocol in common with the remote access server to which it will be attempting to connect. You can install and uninstall networking components, such as protocols, from the Networking tab. You can also enable or disable any listed component by marking or clearing its checkbox.

Setting up and Configuring VPN Connections

Setting up and configuring VPN connections is similar to establishing dial-up connections. VPN connections allow you to connect to remote computers anywhere in the world by tunneling through the Internet using a VPN protocol such as PPTP or L2TP. VPN protocols encapsulate TCP/IP, NetBEUI, or NWLink data packets for transport over TCP/IP via the Internet. PPTP and L2TP utilize encryption to secure all the data that they encapsulate as it travels to the destination VPN server. To create a new VPN connection, follow these steps:

1. Click Start|Settings|Network And Dial-up Connections.
2. Click Make New Connection to display the Network Connection Wizard.
3. Click Next.
4. At the Network Connection Type dialog box, click Connect To A Private Network Through The Internet.
5. Click Next.
6. At the Public Network dialog box, select Do Not Dial The Initial Connection If This Computer Does Not Need To Dial Up To Connect With The Internet. Click the Automatically Dial This Initial Connection drop-down list to select an existing Dial-up Connection for connecting to the Internet.
7. Click Next.
8. Type the host name or IP address of the computer or network to which you will be connecting.
9. Click Next.
10. Specify the Connection Availability for this dial-up entry. Click For All Users or Only For Myself.
11. Click Next.
12. Complete the Network Connection Wizard by typing the name that you want to assign to this connection. Mark the Add A Shortcut To My Desktop checkbox if you would like a shortcut added.
13. Click Finish.

When you double-click the Virtual Private Connection icon to access a VPN server, you are prompted to connect to the Internet using the Dial-up Connection you specified. Once you have established a connection to the Internet, Windows 2000 Professional attempts to connect to the remote VPN server.

Connecting to the Internet Using Dial-up Connections

Creating dial-up connections to the Internet is similar to adding a connection for a remote access server. To set up a new Dial-up Connection to connect to an ISP, perform the following:

1. Click Start|Settings|Network And Dial-up Connections.
2. Click Make New Connection to display the Network Connection Wizard.
3. Click Next.
4. At the Network Connection Type dialog box, click Dial-up To The Internet.
5. Click Next. The Internet Connection Wizard appears.
6. Select the type of Internet connection that you want to use. Unless you want to establish a new Internet access account with an ISP through the Microsoft Internet Referral Service, you can select the one of the other two options: I Want To Set Up My Internet Connection Manually or I Want To Connect Through A Local Area Network .
7. Click Next.
8. Specify how this computer will connect to the Internet: I Connect Through A Phone Line And A Modem or I Connect Through A Local Area Network. To use a Dial-up Connection, choose the first option.
9. Click Next.
10. Specify the communications device (modem) to use for this dial-up connection to the Internet from the drop-down list.
11. Click Next.
12. Type the area code and telephone number for the ISP connection that you will be using. Clear the Use Area Code And Dialing Rules checkbox if you do not wish to use those features.
13. Click the Advanced button to specify settings for your ISP's connection. You can modify the Connection Type and Logon Procedure settings from the Connection tab, if necessary.
14. Click the Addresses tab for the Advanced Connection Properties dialog box. From this page, you can click Always Use The Following and type An

IP Address Required By The ISP if the ISP requires that you use a static IP address.

15. In the DNS Server Address section, click Always Use The Following and type a Primary IP Address and Alternate IP Address for the ISP's DNS servers (unless the ISP provides this information automatically).
16. Click OK to close the Advanced Connection Properties dialog box.
17. Click Next.
18. Type the User Name and Password for the ISP account to which you will be connecting.
19. Click Next.
20. Type a Connection Name for this dial-up Internet connection.
21. Click Next.
22. Click No when you are prompted to set up an Internet mail account. You can always set up Internet email accounts later.
23. Click Next.
24. Complete the Network Connection Wizard by clearing the To Connect To The Internet Immediately, Select This Box checkbox.
25. Click Finish.
26. Right-click the Internet connection you just created and select Properties. Click the Security tab. Verify that Typical is selected and that The Validate My Identity As Follows drop-down list has Allow Unsecured Password selected.
27. Click OK.

After completing the preceding steps, you should be able to connect to the Internet via a dial-up connection. By double-clicking the icon for the Internet connection that you just configured, you will see a Connect dialog box that displays the username and password that you specified. Clear the Save Password checkbox if you do not want the password saved for future connection attempts. Click the Dial button to have the connection established.

Configuring and Troubleshooting ICS

Windows 2000 Professional allows you to have one IP address from an ISP and share that connection (through the Windows 2000 Professional computer) with other computers on the network. This feature is known as Internet Connection Sharing (ICS). Microsoft accomplishes this feat by enabling a new feature of Windows 2000, network address translation (NAT). NAT translates (or maps) a set of nonroutable IP addresses (such as 192.168.x.y) to an external (public) IP address that exists on the Internet. Computers on the LAN can then access external resources on the Internet, like Web sites and FTP sites, but they are somewhat sheltered from outside intrusions because the LAN computers are using nonroutable IP addresses.

TIP

Although turning on NAT can be a good idea, you should never use it as a substitute for a quality firewall product that can provide a much higher level of security between the LAN and the public Internet. Generally speaking, you should always place a firewall product between your internal local network and the external public network. With more and more people gaining access to the Internet, you need to keep security concerns at the forefront to ensure the integrity of all your internal systems and your users' valuable, private, and confidential data.

Configuring ICS

To set up ICS, follow these steps:

1. Click Start|Settings|Network And Dial-up Connections.
2. Right-click a connection icon for an Internet connection and select Properties.
3. Click the Sharing tab.
4. Click the Enable Internet Connection Sharing For This Connection checkbox. Once you have marked this checkbox, the other settings for ICS become available.
5. Select the Enable On-Demand Dialing checkbox if you want this Internet connection to automatically dial and establish a connection to the Internet when another computer on the LAN attempts to access Internet resources through this computer.
6. Click the Settings button. From the Applications tab, you can specify individual application programs that you want to enable for other computers that will be sharing this connection over the LAN.
7. Click the Services tab. Mark the checkboxes for each Internet-related service you want to enable for this shared connection. You can also add services that are not currently listed by clicking on the Add button.
8. Click OK to close the Internet Connection Sharing Settings dialog box.
9. Click OK to close the Properties sheet for the Internet connection. As soon as you close the Properties sheet, you see a message box, as shown in Figure 9.8.

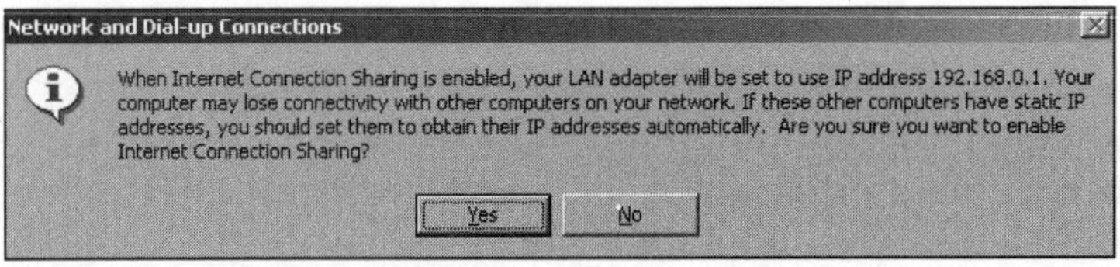

Figure 9.8 Internet Connection Sharing message box.

10. Click Yes in this message box if you are sure that you want to enable this feature.

After you have set up ICS, you should verify that the computer's IP address is now set to 192.168.0.1 with a subnet mask of 255.255.255.0. Test the local Internet connection to verify that the computer can connect to the Internet successfully. For each computer on the LAN that wants to take advantage of the shared Internet connection, perform the following steps:

1. Click Start|Settings|Network And Dial-up Connections.
2. Right-click the LAN connection and select Properties.
3. Click Internet Protocol and then click Properties.
4. Configure TCP/IP to obtain an IP address automatically. This is the preferred method to use with ICS (as opposed to obtaining the address manually, covered shortly). When you enable ICS, the Windows 2000 Professional DHCP Allocator uses the default IP addressing range of 192.168.0.1 through 192.168.0.254 and the DNS Proxy service becomes enabled so that clients on the network can connect to the shared Internet resource.

As an alternative, you can manually set up workstations to work with ICS; however, this is not the recommended method according to Microsoft. To do this, follow these steps:

1. Click Start|Settings|Network And Dial-up Connections.
2. Right-click the LAN connection and select Properties.
3. Click Internet Protocol and click on Properties.
4. Click Use The Following IP Address and type a unique IP address in the range from 192.168.0.2 through 192.168.0.254.
5. Type **255.255.255.0** for the Subnet Mask.
6. Type **192.168.0.1** for the Default Gateway (the IP address for the Windows 2000 Professional computer that is hosting the shared Internet connection).
7. Type the Preferred DNS Server according to your ISP's documentation (if your ISP does not provide this information automatically).

8. Type the Alternate DNS Server according to your ISP's documentation (if your ISP does not provide this information automatically).
9. Click OK in the Internet Protocol (TCP/IP) Properties sheet.
10. Click OK in the LAN connection Properties window.

Troubleshooting ICS

Here are some tips for troubleshooting ICS:

- If you encounter problems with computers on the network not being able to connect to Web sites through the shared Internet connection, verify the DNS server IP addresses with your ISP.
- To verify that the new IP settings have taken effect, type **ipconfig** at a command prompt; sometimes you may need to restart the computer for all the settings to become active.
- Check the subnet mask; it must read 255.255.255.0 or else the computer that is attempting to connect to the ICS computer cannot connect.
- Make sure that each IP address that you assign to the other computers on the network falls within the range of 192.168.0.2 through 192.168.0.254, with no duplicate addresses on any computer.
- If computers on the network can connect to the Internet only after you manually initiate the Internet connection from the ICS host computer, check that Enable On-Demand Dialing is checked on the Sharing tab of the Internet connection's Properties sheet.

Practice Questions

Question 1

A computer named Station01 is configured with TCP/IP and is set up to obtain an IP address automatically. There is a DHCP server on the network. When Mary turns on the workstation, she cannot access any network resources. As the administrator, you run **ipconfig** on the workstation and discover that the computer has an IP address of 169.254.0.2. What is the most likely cause of this problem?

❍ a. Someone has entered a static IP address for the workstation for a different subnet.

❍ b. The DHCP server is currently down, or the network cable for the workstation has become disconnected.

❍ c. DHCP has been configured with an incorrect scope.

❍ d. The WINS server is currently unavailable.

Answer b is correct. If a computer that is configured with TCP/IP to obtain an IP address automatically cannot contact a DHCP server, Windows 2000 Professional invokes APIPA to assign a unique, nonroutable IP address in the range of 169.254.0.1 through 169.254.255.254. The computer's IP address of 169.254.0.2 would indicate that it obtained its IP address from APIPA.

Question 2

As the Administrator, you need to set up a Dial-up Connection using TCP/IP on a Windows 2000 remote access server computer. Which settings do you need to configure for the Windows 2000 Professional dial-up client to create the dial-up connection and enable it to connect to the remote access server?

❍ a. The type of connection, the server's phone number, and which EAP the server is using.

❍ b. The DNS IP addresses for the server and whether DHCP is enabled.

❍ c. The phone number for the server, how IP addresses are allocated to dial-up clients, and which authentication options have been enabled on the server.

❍ d. The phone number for the server, whether to use PPTP or L2TP, and the scope of IP addresses for the subnet.

Answer c is correct. A Dial-up Connection must know the server's phone number. In addition, the connection must either have a static IP address that is compatible with the remote access server's addressing scheme or it must obtain a dynamic IP address from the remote access server when it connects. The dial-up client must also be compatible with at least one of authentication methods for which the server is configured.

Question 3

What additional settings must you configure to enable smart card support with custom settings for Dial-up Connections?

- ❍ a. From the Dial-up Connection's Properties sheet, go to the Advanced Security Settings dialog box, select Use Extensible Authentication Protocol (EAP), and choose Smart Card Or Other Certificate (encryption enabled) from the drop-down list.
- ❍ b. From the Dial-up Connection's Properties sheet, go to the Advanced Security Settings dialog box, select Use Extensible Authentication Protocol (EAP), and choose MD5-Challenge from the drop-down list.
- ❍ c. From the Dial-up Connection's Properties sheet, go to the Advanced Security Settings dialog box, select Allow These Protocols, and choose Shiva Password Authentication Protocol (SPAP) from the drop-down list.
- ❍ d. From the Dial-up Connection's Properties sheet, go to the Advanced Security Settings dialog box, select Allow These Protocols, and choose Challenge Handshake Authentication Protocol (CHAP) from the drop-down list.

Answer a is correct. EAP provides smart card support. The Advanced Security Settings dialog box allows you to specify custom settings for smart card support.

Question 4

You are the Administrator for a LAN with four different subnets. TCP/IP is the only network protocol used. The network has 110 Windows 2000 Professional workstations, 4 Windows 2000 servers, and 3 Windows NT 4 servers. Currently, the network uses NetBIOS computer names for name resolution on the network. The workstations are all set up using static IP addresses. What do you need to configure on a new Windows 2000 Professional computer to get it up and running on the network?

- ❍ a. A unique IP address, the subnet mask, and DNS server address.
- ❍ b. A unique IP address, the subnet mask, the DHCP server address, and the default gateway address.
- ❍ c. A unique IP address, the subnet mask, the default gateway address, and a properly configured HOSTS file.
- ❍ d. A unique IP address, the subnet mask, the default gateway address, and a WINS server address.

Answer d is correct. WINS resolves NetBIOS computer names to IP addresses and vice versa.

Question 5

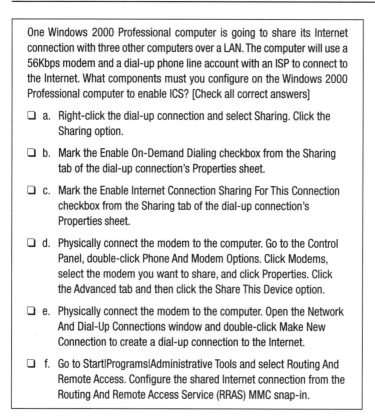

One Windows 2000 Professional computer is going to share its Internet connection with three other computers over a LAN. The computer will use a 56Kbps modem and a dial-up phone line account with an ISP to connect to the Internet. What components must you configure on the Windows 2000 Professional computer to enable ICS? [Check all correct answers]

- ❑ a. Right-click the dial-up connection and select Sharing. Click the Sharing option.
- ❑ b. Mark the Enable On-Demand Dialing checkbox from the Sharing tab of the dial-up connection's Properties sheet.
- ❑ c. Mark the Enable Internet Connection Sharing For This Connection checkbox from the Sharing tab of the dial-up connection's Properties sheet.
- ❑ d. Physically connect the modem to the computer. Go to the Control Panel, double-click Phone And Modem Options. Click Modems, select the modem you want to share, and click Properties. Click the Advanced tab and then click the Share This Device option.
- ❑ e. Physically connect the modem to the computer. Open the Network And Dial-Up Connections window and double-click Make New Connection to create a dial-up connection to the Internet.
- ❑ f. Go to Start|Programs|Administrative Tools and select Routing And Remote Access. Configure the shared Internet connection from the Routing And Remote Access Service (RRAS) MMC snap-in.

Answers b, c, and e are correct. To enable ICS, you need a LAN connection or a dial-up connection to the Internet. You also need to mark Enable Internet Connection Sharing checkbox for this connection. For a dial-up Internet connection, you should mark the Enable On-Demand Dialing checkbox.

Question 6

Robert wants to be able to use a VPN connection via dial-up to connect to his company's headquarters in New York. He already uses a dial-up connection to access the Internet from his notebook PC. At times, he wants to have the option of logging onto the corporate Windows 2000 network domain from the Log On To Windows dialog box by selecting the Log On Using Dial-Up Connection checkbox. He wants to use the corporate VPN connection for this purpose. What must Robert configure to accomplish this?

- ❍ a. When creating the VPN connection, he must select For All Users in the Connection Availability dialog box of the Network Connection Wizard.
- ❍ b. He must mark the Include Windows Logon Domain checkbox from the Options tab of the VPN connection's Properties sheet.
- ❍ c. He must make sure that the Net Logon service Startup Type is set to Automatic. Use the Services console in the MMC.
- ❍ d. No special settings are necessary after the VPN connection has been created.

Answer a is correct. To display the VPN option for logging on to a Windows 2000 Professional computer, you cannot select the Only For Myself option in the Connection Availability dialog box of the Network Connection Wizard.

Question 7

Heidi uses a Windows 2000 Professional computer at her company's branch office in San Mateo, California. Her computer is connected to the LAN for the branch office. Heidi's computer uses a public IP address for Internet access over the LAN. What is the best method for her to connect to a remote access server computer in Toronto, Canada (the company's headquarters), which has a public Internet IP address of 197.41.146.12?

❍ a. Heidi can use a dial-up connection to the Internet to use a VPN connection to the remote access server.

❍ b. Heidi can use a dial-up connection to connect directly to the remote access server using a modem and a phone line.

❍ c. Heidi can use her computer's public IP address for Internet access to establish a VPN connection to the remote access server over the existing LAN.

❍ d. Heidi can take advantage of an infrared connection to the remote access server.

❍ e. Heidi can connect directly to the remote access server by using SLIP and the remote access server's IP address of 197.41.146.12.

Answer c is correct. A VPN connection works well over a LAN connection to the Internet. VPN connections via LANs are always preferable to VPN connections over dial-up links.

Question 8

Alexis is the Administrator for a LAN with 2 Windows 2000 servers and 17 Windows 2000 Professional computers. TCP/IP is the only network protocol that is used on the LAN. One of the server computers is also a DHCP server for the network, and all 17 workstations are configured to obtain their IP addresses automatically. Alexis decides to give her users access to the Internet by connecting a 56Kbps modem with a phone line to one of the Windows 2000 Professional computers and enabling ICS. After Alexis sets up the computer to dial up to the Internet successfully, she turns on ICS. However, none of the other computers on the LAN can access the shared connection. What is the most likely cause of this problem?

- ❍ a. Alexis needs to add the ISP's DNS server addresses as DHCP options.
- ❍ b. Alexis must remove the DHCP server service from the network.
- ❍ c. Alexis must assign all the computers on the LAN static IP addresses.
- ❍ d. Alexis needs to configure ICS for the LAN connection instead of the dial-up connection to the Internet.

Answer b is correct. When ICS is enabled, it becomes the DHCP Allocator as long as no active DHCP server is on the network. A DHCP server on the same network inhibits ICS from operating as the DHCP allocator. DNS server settings are by proxy in ICS as long as the ISP is acting as the external DNS host.

Question 9

What is APIPA?

- ❍ a. It's DHCP for Windows 2000 Professional.
- ❍ b. It's used only in conjunction with ICS to assign IP addresses to other computers on the network so that they can share the Internet connection.
- ❍ c. It's a scope of IP addresses assigned to Windows 2000 Professional computers by default.
- ❍ d. It's a feature of Windows 2000 Professional for computers using the TCP/IP protocol that are configured to obtain an IP address automatically. APIPA becomes active only if no DHCP server is available on the network. APIPA assigns nonroutable IP addresses to computers on a LAN.

Answer d is correct. APIPA becomes active only if the Windows 2000 Professional computers connected to the LAN cannot contact any DHCP servers. APIPA uses a reserved IP address range of 169.254.0.0 through 169.254.255.254, which is nonroutable, with a subnet mask of 255.255.0.0.

Question 10

You are the Administrator for a Windows 2000 Server network, complete with DNS servers, WINS servers, and DHCP servers, that is installed as well as up and running. You will be installing 30 new Windows 2000 Professional computers with all the default installation settings. You want to ensure that all these new workstations will obtain their IP addresses automatically. What do you need to do?

❍ a. Open the Network And Dial-Up Connections window. Right-click the LAN and select Properties. Click Client For Microsoft Networks and then click Properties to configure automatic IP addressing.

❍ b. Open a command prompt window and run the command **ipconfig /configure** to allow the computer to obtain an IP address automatically.

❍ c. Open the Network And Dial-Up Connections window. Right-click the LAN and select Properties. Select Internet Protocol (TCP/IP) and click Properties. Click the Advanced button and enable automatic IP addressing from the IP Settings tab.

❍ d. Nothing. Life is good.

Answer d is correct. The TCP/IP network protocol is the default protocol when you install Windows 2000 Professional. Obtaining an IP address automatically is the default selection for TCP/IP. Therefore, the Administrator does not need to make any adjustments for the new computers to be automatically assigned IP addresses from the DHCP server(s) on the existing LAN.

Need to Know More?

Microsoft Corporation. *Microsoft Windows 2000 Professional Resource Kit.* Redmond, Washington: Microsoft Press, 2000. ISBN: 1-57610-808-2. This book has invaluable information on setting up LANs, working with dial-up connections, and troubleshooting TCP/IP issues.

Stinson, Craig, and Carl Siechert. *Running Microsoft Windows 2000 Professional.* Redmond, Washington: Microsoft Press, 2000. ISBN: 1-57231-838-4. This guidebook to Windows 2000 Professional contains good information on administering and troubleshooting LAN configurations and dial-up connections.

Wood, Adam. *Windows 2000 Active Directory Black Book.* Scottsdale, Arizona: The Coriolis Group, 2000. ISBN: 1-57610-256-4. This book provides comprehensive coverage of Active Directory.

Search the TechNet CD-ROM (or its online version through **www.microsoft.com**) and/or the *Windows 2000 Professional Resource Kit* CD-ROM using the keywords "APIPA", "Dial-Up Connection", "TCP/IP", "PPTP", "L2TP", "DNS", and "ICS."

10

Monitoring and Optimizing Performance Reliability

Terms you'll need to understand:

✓ Windows 2000 Backup

✓ Normal backup

✓ Differential backup

✓ Incremental backup

✓ System state

✓ Safe Mode startup options

✓ Last Known Good Configuration

✓ Recovery Console

✓ Emergency Repair Disk (ERD)

✓ makeboot.exe and makebt32.exe

✓ Optimization

✓ Counters

✓ Objects

✓ Sample (or update) interval

✓ Baselining

✓ Paging file

Techniques you'll need to master:

✓ Backing up and restoring data

✓ Backing up and restoring the system state

✓ Starting a Windows 2000 system in the appropriate Safe Mode

✓ Using the Last Known Good Configuration

✓ Installing and using the Recovery Console

✓ Creating an ERD

✓ Using the emergency repair process

✓ Creating a set of Windows 2000 setup boot disks

✓ Using System Monitor

✓ Creating a log with Performance Logs And Alerts

✓ Setting performance alerts

✓ Establishing a baseline

✓ Configuring the paging file

✓ Changing process priorities

✓ Viewing performance with Task Manager

Once a Windows 2000 system has been installed, configured, and secured, an administrator's goal is to ensure reliable and optimal performance. This chapter will explore the skills required to prepare for, and recover from, system failures, and will provide a foundation for performance monitoring and optimization.

Backing Up and Restoring Data

In Windows 2000, Windows Backup helps you plan for and recover from data loss by allowing you to back up and restore files, folders, and system state data (which includes the registry) manually, or on a schedule. The new-and-improved backup tool supports all kinds of storage devices and media, including tape drives, logical drives, removable disks, and recordable CD-ROMs. The tool also has wizards to help administrators new to Windows 2000 to implement backup and recovery processes.

Using Windows Backup

To open Windows Backup, perform the following:

1. Click Start|Run and then enter "ntbackup". Click OK.
2. Open Backup from System Tools in the Programs folder on the Start menu.

You can also open Windows Backup from within Administrative Tools on the Start menu, or from within the Control Panel. Windows Backup provides a Backup Wizard that steps you through the choices and configurations related to the backup, or you can manually configure the backup by clicking on the Backup tab of the Windows Backup tool.

Permissions and Rights

To successfully back up or restore data on a Windows 2000 system, users must have appropriate *permissions* and *user rights*. Users can back up all of their own files and folders, plus files for which they have the Read permission. To restore files and folders, users must have the Write permission.

Each system has two user rights: Backup Files And Directories and Restore Files And Directories. Users with these rights can back up or restore all files, regardless of the permissions assigned to them. By default, administrators, backup operators, and (on a server) Server Operators groups have these two user rights. You can assign one or both of these rights to any other security principal (user, group, or computer), although the best practice is to assign rights to a domain local group in a Windows 2000 native mode domain.

Backup Types

There are several different kinds of backup jobs that allow you to create a backup procedure that maximizes efficiency, minimizes media utilized, and minimizes performance impact. Each file has an archive attribute, also called a *backup marker*. When a file is changed, the archive attribute or marker is set, indicating that the file has been modified since the last backup. This marker is the focus of the different backup types because some types look for the marker; others do not. Some types clear the marker; others do not. Table 10.1 clarifies the different backup types.

Table 10.1 The different backup types.

Backup Type	Looks for Marker	Clears Marker	Resulting Backup Set
Normal	No	Yes	Backup of all selected files and folders. The most complete backup and the most straight-forward to recover, but also the lengthiest to create.
Copy	No	No	Copies all selected files and folders.
Differential	Yes	No	Backup of selected files that have changed since the last normal backup. If you create a normal backup, then one week later a differential backup, and then another week later another differential backup, you could restore all data using the normal backup and the second differential backup, which contains all files that have changed since the normal backup. You could, in this example, discard the first differential backup.
Incremental	Yes	Yes	Backup of all data that has changed since the most recent (normal or incremental) backup. If you create a normal backup, then one week later an incremental backup, and then another week later a second incremental backup, you would need all three backups to recover data.
Daily	Yes	No	Backup of all files and folders that have changed during the day.

Backup Strategies

Backup strategies generally combine different backup types. Some backup types require more time to create the backup. A normal backup takes the most time to create because it is backing up all selected files; however, it creates a "baseline" or complete backup. The second backup could be incremental or differential—the result would be the same. The third and subsequent backups are where the difference starts to be significant. If the second and third backups are differential, the third backup includes all files changed since the normal backup. If the second and third backups are incremental, the third backup includes only files changed since the second, incremental, backup.

So why wouldn't you just do a normal backup and then do incremental backups until the end of time? Because incremental backups take longer than a differential backup to *recover*. Imagine recovering a machine that had a normal backup one year ago, and an incremental backup every week since. To recover that system after a catastrophe, you would have to restore the normal backup and then restore 51 incremental backups. If you had used differential backups, you would have to restore only the normal backup and the most recent differential backup.

Therefore, you should balance the "cost" of backup time against the "cost" of recovery time. Also factor in the media required to support your backup plan. You must save incremental backups until the next normal backup. You need keep only the most recent differential backup, along with the most recent normal backup.

Configuring File and Folder Backup

When you create a backup job using the Backup Wizard or the Backup tab of the Windows Backup utility, you can specify:

- Drives, files, or folders to back up. Select the checkmark next to a drive, file, or folder. Selected items are backed up according to the backup type. Cleared items are not backed up. A grayed-out checkmark indicates a container (disk or folder) in which some, but not all, contents are selected.
- A backup destination. You can back up to a file or to any other storage device configured on your system.
- A path and file name for the backup file, or a tape to use.
- Backup options such as backup type and log file type.
- A description of the job, to help you identify the job.
- Whether the backup medium already contains existing backup jobs.
- Advanced backup options, including compression and data verification.

Backing Up the System State

The Backup utility can back up what is called *system state* data, which includes critical files that you can use to rebuild the system. You can reinstall a failed system with the Windows 2000 CD-ROM. Then, you can restore the system state data, bringing the system back to its original condition as of the system state backup.

Be familiar with backing up the system state! Know that the backup program *can* provide you with a backup of the system's registry as a whole, but it cannot back up individual components of system state data.

System state data includes the following:

- The registry
- The component services class registration database—Component Object Model + (COM+) objects
- System startup files
- Certificate Services database—domain controllers (DCs) and member servers running Certificate Services only
- Active Directory—DCs only
- Sysvol folder—DCs only

Configuring System State Backup

To configure system state backup, perform the following steps:

1. In the Backup Wizard, on the What To Back Up page, select Only Back Up The System State Data.
2. In the Backup Wizard, on the Items To Back Up page, expand My Computer and select the System State Data checkbox.

Scheduling Backup Jobs

You can use the Backup utility in conjunction with Task Scheduler to schedule backups to occur at regular intervals or during periods of relative inactivity on a network.

Scheduling a Backup When Using the Backup Wizard

To schedule a backup when using the Backup Wizard, perform the following steps:

1. In the Backup Wizard, on the Completing The Backup Wizard page, click Advanced.

2. On the When To Back Up page, click Later.
3. Enter a Job Name.
4. Click Set Schedule.
5. In the Schedule Job dialog box, you can configure start time and frequency.
6. Click OK.

Configuring a Job Using the Scheduled Jobs Tab

To configure a job using the Scheduled Jobs tab, perform the following steps:

1. In the Backup utility, click the Scheduled Jobs tab.
2. Double-click the day you wish to start scheduled backups.
3. Complete the information in the Backup Wizard.

Restoring Files and Folders

You can restore files and folders by using the Backup utility, using the Restore Wizard, or manually restoring them (without the wizard). When you restore files and folders, you specify which ones to restore, a restore location (original location, alternate location, or a single folder), and options (such as replace existing files with backup files).

If you backed up data from an NT File System (NTFS) volume, you must restore data to an NTFS volume to avoid data loss and preserve permissions, Encrypting File System (EFS) settings (encryption), disk quota settings, mounted drive configuration, and remote storage information.

Troubleshooting and Repairing a Windows 2000 System

Windows 2000 has several features that allow you to repair a system that will not start or will not load Windows 2000: Safe Mode (and other advanced startup options), the Recovery Console, and the Emergency Repair Disk (ERD). These features are useful if some of your system files become corrupted or are accidentally erased, or if you have installed software or device drivers that cause your system to not work properly.

Safe Mode and Other Advanced Startup Options

Safe Mode lets you start your system with a minimal set of device drivers and services. For example, if newly installed device drivers or software are preventing your computer from starting, you may be able to start your computer in Safe Mode and then remove the software or device drivers from your system. Safe Mode does not work in all situations, especially if your system files are corrupted or missing, or if your hard disk is damaged or has failed. All Safe Modes start using standard VGA and create a boot log, which is useful when you are determining the exact cause of system startup problems.

In Safe Mode, Windows 2000 uses default settings, including the VGA monitor, Microsoft mouse driver, no network connections, and the minimum device drivers required to start Windows. If your computer does not start successfully using Safe Mode, you may need to use the Recovery Console feature or ERD, covered later in this chapter, to repair your system.

Windows 2000 also provides several startup modes to help you troubleshoot and repair Windows 2000 systems, as well as recover from various types of disaster. Understanding each mode allows you to make informed decisions about the best startup method to use in a particular crisis situation. To select an advanced startup option, press F8 during the operating system selection phase of the Windows 2000 startup process. These startup options definitely provide extra troubleshooting capabilities for your Windows 2000 machines.

Safe Mode with Networking

This starts Windows 2000 using only safe mode drivers and services and drivers required to enable network connections. If you are confident that network issues are not the cause of your problem, it can be useful to boot to a mode that allows you to connect to a remote system, access installation files and service packs, or back up data.

Safe Mode with the Command Prompt

This option uses the Safe Mode configuration but displays the command prompt instead of the Windows graphical user interface (GUI) after you log on successfully. This is useful if you believe a process spawned by the Explorer shell is causing your problem.

Advanced Startup Option: Enable Boot Logging

This starts Windows 2000 and logs all drivers and services that the system loads (or fails to load) to a log file called ntbtlog.txt, located in the %SystemRoot% directory. Safe Mode, Safe Mode with Networking, and Safe Mode with Command Prompt also create a boot log file. The boot log is useful when you are determining the exact cause of system startup problems.

Advanced Startup Option: Enable VGA Mode

This option employs the extremely stable and well-debugged standard VGA driver for Windows 2000. This mode is useful when you have installed a new video card or have configured the wrong or faulty driver. Video is a common troubleshooting issue in the Windows environment. This driver is used in the various Safe Modes.

Advanced Startup Option: Last Known Good Configuration

Windows 2000 starts using the registry configuration (ControlSet) that was saved at the last successful logon to Windows 2000. Last Known Good Configuration helps you recover from incorrect configuration of hardware device drivers and services. However, it does not solve problems caused by corrupted or missing drivers or files. Any changes made to the ControlSet key of the registry since the last successful startup and logon are lost when you select to start up with the Last Known Good Configuration. You should try this option before resorting to the emergency repair process, discussed later in this chapter.

Advanced Startup Option: Directory Services Restore Mode

This option applies only to Windows 2000 DCs and is used to restore Active Directory and the sysvol folder.

Advanced Startup Option: Debugging Mode

In this mode, Windows 2000 starts and sends debugging information through a serial cable to another computer.

Advanced Startup Option: Remote Installation Options

If you are using or have used Remote Installation Service (RIS) to install Windows 2000 on your computer, you may see additional options related to restoring or recovering your system using RIS. RIS is covered in detail in Chapter 4.

Specifying Windows 2000 Behavior if the System Stops Unexpectedly

To specify Windows 2000 behavior if the system stops unexpectedly, follow these steps:

1. Right-click My Computer and then select Properties.
2. On the Advanced tab, click Startup And Recovery, and under Recovery, select the actions that Windows 2000 should perform if a Stop error occurs.

Available Recovery Actions

The following are the available recovery actions:

- If you select Write An Event To The System Log or Send An Administrative Alert, you must have a paging file that is at least 2MB on the computer's boot volume.

- The Write An Event To The System Log option is available only on Windows 2000 Professional. On Windows 2000 Server, this action occurs by default every time a Stop error occurs.
- The Write Debugging Information To option requires a paging file on the boot volume large enough to hold all of the computer's physical RAM, plus 1MB. If you also select the Write Kernel Information Only checkbox, Windows 2000 writes only kernel information to the listed file instead of the entire contents of system memory.
- You can save some memory if you clear the Write Debugging Information To, Write An Event To The System Log, or Send An Administrative Alert options. The memory saved depends on the computer, but the drivers that enable these features typically require about 60KB through 70KB.
- If you contact Microsoft Product Support Services about a Stop error, it may ask for the system-memory dump file generated by the Write Debugging Information To option. For each dump file generated, Windows always writes to the same file name. To save successive dump files, change the file name after each Stop error.

Setting Up Recovery Actions to Take Place When a Service Fails

To set up recovery actions to take place when a service fails, perform the following steps:

1. Open Services.
2. Right-click the service for which you want to set recovery actions and then click Properties.
3. On the Recovery tab, click the actions you want in First Attempt, Second Attempt, and Subsequent Attempts.

If you select Run A File, do not specify programs or scripts that require user input. If you select Reboot The Computer, you can specify how long to wait before restarting the computer by clicking on Reboot Computer Information. You can also create a message to display to remote users before the computer restarts.

The Recovery Console

The *Recovery Console* is a startup option that provides you with a command-line interface that lets you repair system problems using a limited set of command-line commands. Using the Recovery Console, you can start and stop services, read and write data on a local drive (including drives formatted to use NTFS), format drives, repair a corrupted master boot record, and perform many other administrative tasks. This feature gives you maximum control over the repair process; only advanced users and administrators should use it.

The Recovery Console is particularly useful if you need to repair your system by copying a file from a floppy or CD-ROM to your hard drive. It can also help you when you need to reconfigure a service that is preventing your computer from starting properly. You should try this option before resorting to the emergency repair process, discussed later in this chapter.

Running the Recovery Console on a System that Will Not Start

To run the Recovery Console on a system that will not start, perform the following steps:

1. Insert the Windows 2000 Professional Setup Disk 1 (3.5-inch floppy) into your disk drive; or, if you have a bootable CD-ROM drive, insert the Windows 2000 Professional CD-ROM into your CD-ROM drive.
2. Restart your computer.
3. Follow the directions on the screen. If you are using the Setup Disks, you are prompted to insert the others into the disk drive. It may take several minutes to load files. Choose the options to repair your Windows 2000 installation and, finally, to start the Recovery Console.

> **TIP** Before a system fails, open a command prompt in Windows 2000, and, from the i386 folder on the Windows 2000 CD-ROM or an equivalent distribution, enter the command **winnt32/cmdcons**. Doing so installs the command console on the local hard drive (this requires 7MB of disk space) and configures it as a valid startup option. Then, if you wish to start the system to the Recovery Console, you do not require the Windows 2000 CD-ROM or Setup Disks. Simply boot the machine and press F8 for startup options.

Launching the Recovery Console

The Recovery Console is quite powerful, so only advanced users who have a thorough knowledge of Windows 2000 should use it. Also, it is recommended that you install the Recovery Console on each Windows 2000 machine so it is always an available startup option.

After you start the Recovery Console, you must choose which drive you want to log on to (if you have a dual-boot or multiboot system), and you must log on with a local administrator account and password. The design of Recovery Console grants the administrator access to the root of the hard drives, the **\cmdcons** directory if it exists, and the **\winnt directory** and all directories below it. You will have full access to the CD-ROM and to floppy drives. These limitations are in place for security concerns, and access to other devices or systems is functionally beyond the scope and purpose of the Recovery Console. You use the Recovery Console only to allow you to repair the existing installation and to successfully boot Windows 2000.

Recovery Console Commands

The easiest way to work in the Recovery Console—as in any unfamiliar environment—is to type "help" at the command prompt and then press the Enter key. The commands available in the Recovery Console are listed in Table 10.2.

Table 10.2 Recovery Console commands.

Command	Description
chdir (cd)	Displays the name of the current folder or changes the current folder.
chkdsk	Checks a disk and displays a status report.
cls	Clears the screen.
copy	Copies a single file to another location.
delete (del)	Deletes one or more files.
dir	Displays a list of files and subfolders in a folder.
disable	Disables a system service or a device driver.
enable	Starts or enables a system service or a device driver.
exit	Exits the Recovery Console and restarts your computer.
fdisk	Manages partitions on your hard disks.
fixboot	Writes a new partition boot sector onto the system partition.
fixmbr	Repairs the master boot record of the partition boot sector.
format	Formats a disk.
help	Displays a list of the commands that you use in the Recovery Console.
logon	Logs on to a Windows 2000 installation.
map	Displays the drive letter mappings.
mkdir (md)	Creates a folder.
more	Displays a text file.
rename (ren)	Renames a single file.
rmdir (rd)	Deletes a folder.
systemroot	Sets the current folder to the SystemRoot folder of the system that you are currently logged on to.
type	Displays a text file.

Emergency Repair Disks (ERDs) and the Emergency Repair Process

The *ERD* feature helps you repair problems with system files, your startup environment (if you have a dual-boot or multiboot system), and the partition boot sector on your boot volume. Before you use the emergency repair process feature to repair your system, you must create an ERD. Without a recent ERD, you may not be able to leverage the full functionality of the repair process.

The ERD is quite different in Windows 2000 than it was in Windows NT 4, and you create the ERD using a different method than in NT 4. It does not contain a complete, or even partial, copy of the registry—it simply contains system and disk configuration information. But the ERD remains a very important tool.

> The rdisk.exe tool, which in Windows NT allowed you to create the ERD, *does not exist* in Windows 2000.

To create an ERD, perform the following steps:

1. Open the Backup utility.
2. Click Emergency Repair Disk on the Welcome tab.
3. Insert a blank, 1.44MB floppy into the floppy disk drive and click OK.

You can also specify to back up the registry to the repair directory to help recover from a damaged registry. When the process is complete, click OK, and then remove and label the floppy.

> *No*, you cannot boot a Windows 2000 machine with the ERD. The ERD never has been, and *is not* a bootable disk. Read your exam questions and answers closely!

Using the Emergency Repair Process

The *emergency repair process* will enable you to restore corrupted system files and configuration. Even if you have not created an ERD, you can still try to use the emergency repair process; however, you may lose any changes you have made to your system, such as service packs and updates, and you may need to reinstall them.

You can also use the emergency repair process to reinstall Windows 2000 over a damaged Windows 2000 system. This may be time-consuming but is useful if the emergency repair process does not solve your problem. To have a chance at making the emergency repair process work properly, you must follow five steps closely.

Step 1: Starting with the Windows 2000 Setup Disks or CD-ROM

Boot the computer using the Windows 2000 CD-ROM (you may need to configure your system's BIOS to enable booting to the CD-ROM if your system supports bootable CDs). You can, alternatively, boot with the first of the four Windows 2000 Setup Disks (the process will prompt you for subsequent disks). If you don't have a bootable CD-ROM and don't have the boot disks handy, run the batch file in the CD-ROM's bootdisk folder.

makeboot.exe and **makebt32.exe** in Windows 2000 replace the **winnt /ox** or **winnt32 /ox** commands from NT. You can produce the boot disks on any system—it does not have to be a Windows 2000 system. Simply execute **makeboot.exe** on 16-bit operating systems and **makebt32.exe** on 32-bit platforms.

Step 2: Choosing the Repair Options during Setup

As the computer starts, Windows 2000 Setup launches. During Setup, you are prompted whether you wish to continue installing Windows 2000. Press Enter to confirm and start the process. You are then asked whether you want to install a new installation of Windows 2000 or repair an existing installation. To repair a damaged or corrupt system, press R. You are then prompted as to whether you wish to use the Recovery Console or the emergency repair process. To select the emergency repair process, press R again.

Step 3: Choosing the Type of Repair

There are only two types of repair to choose from. You are asked to select either of the following:

- *Fast Repair*—This requires no further interaction or choices. It checks your system and attempts to repair any problems related to the registry, system files, partition boot sector on the boot volume, and startup environment (in a multiboot environment). The Fast Repair option restores the registry from the repair directory, so it is important to have updated that directory recently. You can back up the registry to the repair directory as part of the ERD creation procedure. If your repair directory is quite outdated, Fast Repair is not the best choice because you may lose any recent changes to hardware, software, drivers, services, or other settings.

- *Manual Repair*—This requires user interaction and prompts you to select whether to repair system files, boot sector problems, or startup environment problems.

***Note:** Manual Repair does not allow you to repair the registry. To have that option, you must perform a Fast Repair.*

Step 4: Starting the Repair Process

To start the repair process, you should have the ERD for the system. It is *not* advised to repair a system with another system's repair disk because each system is unique; as such, each system's ERD is also unique. You should also have the Windows 2000 installation CD handy. If you do not have the ERD, the emergency repair process attempts to locate the Windows 2000 installation on the system and begin the repair process, but it may fail.

Step 5: Restarting the Computer

Assuming the repair was successful, you should be able to restart into a functional Windows 2000 system. If not, you should consider other recovery options or, perhaps, the option of recovering by re-installing the system and restoring data from backup sets.

Optimizing and Troubleshooting Performance

Although Windows 2000 Professional performs extremely well as a general workstation platform, with the right tools, techniques, and knowledge, you can further optimize the operating system for particular roles as well as troubleshoot performance challenges. This section looks at System Monitor, Performance Logs And Alerts, Task Manager, and other tools you can use to improve Windows 2000's performance.

System Monitor

The *System Monitor snap-in* is a node of the Performance console (Start|Settings|Control Panel|Administrative Tools|Performance) and available for inclusion in custom MMC consoles. This tool allows you to visually inspect the activity of system components such as the memory, processor, disk subsystem, network cards, paging file, and applications. The plethora of performance metrics, or *counters*, available for monitoring can make the task a daunting one, indeed. We will examine the most useful counters after a tour of the Performance console's snap-ins.

Using System Monitor

System Monitor, like all MMC snap-ins, is best controlled by right-clicking. If you right-click the main portion of the Details pane, you can select Add Counters. Counters are the granular statistics related to a specific aspect of system performance. The thousands of available counters are organized hierarchically:

- *Computer*—You can monitor performance on the local (default) or a remote system.

- *Object*—Is a system component, such as processor, memory, disk, or network protocol.
- *Counter*—This is a performance metric related to the object on the computer selected above. There can literally be thousands of counters available for monitoring, so take advantage of the Explain button in the Add Counters dialog box—clicking on it produces a description of the selected counter.
- *Instance*—When an object occurs more than once on a computer, you see instances. For example, a multiprocessor machine has instances for each processor when you select the processor object. When you select the logical disk object, you see instances for each drive volume on a system. Often, instances are numbered, with the first instance being 0, the second instance 1, and so on. Often, an additional instance provides the total for all instances. For example, a dual processor system has a _Total, which reflects the combination of processors 0 and 1.

After you select a computer, object, counter, and (if necessary) instance, click Add to add the counter to your System Monitor view. By right-clicking the view and choosing Properties, you can alter all properties of the monitor, including the display color of counters, the scale and sample rate, and the format of the monitor's display—which can be in graph (default), histogram (bar chart), or report (numeric display) format.

Performance Logs And Alerts

The *Performance Logs And Alerts snap-in*, also part of the Performance console, allows you to collect and save performance data as well as proactively configure a system to generate a notification based on a performance threshold.

Configuring Alerts

Alerts allow you to generate actions based on a counter reaching a particular threshold. For example, you might want to be notified when a disk's capacity reaches 90 percent so that you might work to increase the disk's capacity before it fills up. By specifying a counter (such as %Free Space for a logical disk) and a threshold (under 10 percent), you can cause an event to be logged, a program to be run, a log to be started, or a network message to be sent.

To configure alerts, select the Alerts node in the Performance Logs And Alerts snap-in. Then, right-click in the Details pane and choose New Alert Settings. Enter a name for your alert settings—the name is for your use only. Then in the Properties dialog box, add the counter(s) appropriate for the alert you are configuring. For each counter, you must specify a threshold (over or under a particular amount) on the General tab. You can then configure, on the Action tab, what will happen when those alerts are generated. On the Schedule tab, you can specify when the selected counters should be scanned. If you specify no schedule, scanning will begin as soon as you click OK. The alert settings you have specified will appear in the Alerts node of the snap-in. Right-click an alert setting to change its configuration, delete it, or stop or start scanning.

Configuring Logs

Logs collect and store performance counters. You can view them using System Monitor, retrieve them in a spreadsheet like Excel, or import them into a database. There are two types of logs:

- *Counter logs*—These record data captured over a span of time and are useful for detecting trends, setting baselines of performance, and spotting performance bottlenecks. Baselines are discussed later in this chapter.
- *Trace logs*—These collect performance data when an event such as a process creation, disk input/output (I/O), or page fault occurs. Trace logs are useful for debugging.

To create a counter log, select the Counter Logs node of the snap-in and then right-click the Details pane and choose New Log Settings. Give the log a name that will help you identify it in the future and then click OK. In the Log dialog box, add one or more counters to be recorded and then specify the sample rate—the interval at which counter data will be collected. Obviously, a shorter sample rate provides more data but also fills up the log more quickly.

Logs are stored, by default, in the %SystemDrive%\Perflogs folder. The default format is binary (.blg extension). You can stop and start logs as desired and view them in System Monitor. To view a log with System Monitor, right-click the Display and choose Properties. Then, on the Source tab, click Log File and enter or browse to the log file name.

To analyze a log with Excel, Access, or other database and reporting tools, save the log as a comma- or tab-delimited file (.csv or .tsv extensions). Once you stop these logs, you cannot restart or append them as you can with binary logs.

Managing Performance

Monitoring, troubleshooting, and optimizing performance are some of the most important tasks you will perform as an administrator of Windows 2000 Professional systems. Managing performance involves several steps:

1. Creating a baseline
2. Proactively monitoring
3. Evaluating performance

4. Identifying potential bottlenecks
5. Taking corrective action
6. Monitoring the effectiveness and stability of the change
7. Returning to Step 2

Creating a Baseline

One of the most important, and most often overlooked, steps of managing performance is creating a baseline. A *baseline* is a range of acceptable performance of a system component under normal working conditions. Baselining, or establishing a baseline, requires that you capture key counters while a system performs with normal loads and all services running. Then, you can compare future performance against the baseline to identify potential bottlenecks, troubleshoot sudden changes in performance, and justify system improvements.

TIP: A baseline should cover a relatively large timeframe so that it captures a range of data reflecting acceptable performance. The sample interval for the log should be somewhat large as well, so the baseline log does not become enormous. You should generate baselines regularly—perhaps even once a month—so that you can identify performance trends and evaluate bottlenecks to system and network performance. If you follow these guidelines, you will produce a baseline that gives an accurate overview of system performance.

The most useful objects to understand and monitor are the following:

- *Cache*—Physical memory used to store recently accessed disk data.
- *Memory*—RAM used to store code and data.
- *Paging file*—The file used to extend physical RAM and create virtual memory.
- *Physical disk*—The disk drive or Redundant Array of Independent Disks (RAID) device. A physical disk may contain multiple logical disks.
- *Logical disk*—The disk volume, including simple, logical, spanned, striped, mirrored, or RAID-5 volumes. A logical disk may span multiple physical disks.
- *Process*—Executable code that represents a running program.
- *Processor*—The Central Processing Unit (CPU).
- *Server*—The server service, which offers data and print services, even on a Windows 2000 Professional system.

- *System*—Counters that apply to all system hardware and software.
- *Thread*—Code that the processor is processing.

Baselines should include these critical objects as well as the other counters discussed in this chapter.

Managing Memory Performance

The counters in the Memory object represent the memory available through the system's physical RAM and virtual memory or paging file. The most important counters in the memory object are the Pages/sec counters and the Available Bytes counter:

- *Memory:Pages/sec, threshold over 20 pages/sec*—This counter, and all related counters (including Page Reads/sec, Page Writes/sec, Page Faults/sec, Page Inputs/sec, and Page Outputs/sec) reflect the transfer of data and code from physical RAM to the virtual paging file, and paging-related events. When any one of these counters is high, it indicates a potential memory shortage, because when a system does not have enough RAM to satisfy its needs, inactive data and code are moved from physical RAM to the virtual paging file to make room for active data and code.
- *Memory:Available Bytes, threshold under 4MB*—Available Bytes reflects the amount of physical RAM available after the working sets of applications and the cache have been served. Windows 2000 Professional trims working sets and page memory to the disk to maintain at least 4MB of available RAM. If this counter is consistently lower than 4MB, it generally indicates a memory shortage.

> **TIP** Memory is often the first performance bottleneck in the "real world." The counters related to processor and hard drive utilization might be well beyond their thresholds simply because inadequate memory is causing paging, which impacts those two components. So always check the memory counters to make sure that they are not the "root" performance bottleneck.

To correct a memory shortage, your first reaction might be to add more RAM, which is certainly one solution. However, it is often equally valid to optimize memory usage by stopping unnecessary services, drivers, and background applications, or moving services or applications to systems with excess capacity.

Managing the Paging File

When physical RAM is not sufficient to support active processes, the *Virtual Memory Manager (VMM)* moves less active data or code from physical RAM to virtual memory stored in the paging file. When a process later attempts to address data or code currently in the paging file, the VMM transfers that memory space into physical RAM. The paging file thus provides for efficient utilization of a system's physical RAM and allows a system to support more activity than its physical RAM alone would allow. Transfer of pages, 4KB blocks of memory, to and from the paging file is normal on any system, but excessive paging or *thrashing* indicates a memory shortage. In addition, the paging file itself can impede performance if it is not properly optimized.

You configure the paging file using the System applet in Control Panel. Click the Advanced tab, the Performance Options button, and then, in the Virtual Memory section, click Change. The paging file, called pagefile.sys, is created on the %SystemRoot% volume by default, and its default initial size is 1.5 times physical RAM. You can configure the paging file to be placed on other volumes or to be split across multiple volumes, in which case there will be a pagefile.sys on selected volumes, and the total size of the paging file is the sum of all paging files. You can also configure the Initial Size, the space created initially by the VMM and reserved for paging activity, and the Maximum Size, a setting that can permit the VMM to expand the paging file to a size greater than the Initial Size.

You can optimize paging by doing the following:

- *Remove the paging file from the system and boot partitions.* The system partition is technically the partition that is used to start the system—it contains NTLDR and the boot sector. To make things confusing, the boot partition contains the operating system and is indicated by the variable %SystemRoot%. Luckily, most computers are configured with Windows 2000 on the C: drive (the first partition), making the boot partition, the system partition, and %SystemRoot% all equal to C:. To remove the paging file from a partition, set its Initial Size and Maximum Size to 0 and click the Set button.

- *Configure the paging file to reside on multiple physical disks, and configure the Initial Size and Maximum Size identically on all drives.* The paging subsystem then spreads written pages evenly across all available pagefile.sys files.

- *Configure the paging file to reside on fast, less active drives.* If you have drives of various speeds, put the paging file on the fastest one. If you have drives that are less active, put the paging file on those so the paging system doesn't have to compete as often with other read or write requests.

- *Before moving the paging file, defragment the volumes on which you will put the paging file.* Doing so helps prevent a fragmented paging file.

- *Set the Initial Size to be sufficient for the system's paging requirements, and then set the Maximum Size to the same size.* When the Maximum Size is greater than the Initial Size, and the system must expand the paging file, the expansion puts an additional burden on both the processor and disk subsystems. In addition, the paging file is likely to become fragmented, further hitting the performance of paging.

TIP: The ideal paging file configuration is to split it evenly over multiple *physical* disks except for the disk with the system and boot partitions.

Managing Disk Performance

The PhysicalDisk and LogicalDisk performance objects collect metrics related to individual disk drives and logical disk volumes, respectively. PhysicalDisk counters focus on a storage device, so you should use them to analyze hardware performance. Use LogicalDisk counters, which focus on a specific volume, analyze read and write performance.

In Windows 2000, PhysicalDisk counters are available in System Monitor and Performance Logs And Alerts, but LogicalDisk counters are not gathered until you run the **diskperf –yv** (**v** for "volume") command. The switches for the **diskperf** command include **–yd** (enables PhysicalDisk counters, which is the default), **-y** (enables both PhysicalDisk and LogicalDisk counters), **-nv**, **-nd**, and **–n** (disable LogicalDisk, PhysicalDisk, and both sets of counters, respectively).

TIP: Until you enable the counters with the appropriate **diskperf** switch, the counters are not visible in System Monitor or Performance Logs And Alerts.

The following disk counters will help you to monitor and manage disk performance:

- *PhysicalDisk/LogicalDisk: %DiskTime, threshold close to 100%*—This reports the amount of time that a disk is busy servicing read or write requests.
- *PhysicalDisk/LogicalDisk: Disk Queue Length, threshold 2*—The Average and Current disk queue length counters reflect the read/write requests that are pending and being serviced. If the queue is long, processes are being delayed.

When disk performance is a bottleneck, you can add capacity; replace disks with faster hardware; move applications, services, or data to underutilized disks; or implement spanned, striped, or RAID-5 volumes.

Managing Network Performance

Although Windows 2000 Server can support Network Monitor for relatively sophisticated network traffic analysis, Windows 2000 Professional has limited network performance tools. Counters are available for the number of bytes and packets received and sent over a particular network interface. However, you cannot analyze the contents or properties of packets using Windows 2000 Professional tools alone.

To conduct detailed network analysis for a Windows 2000 Professional system, install the Network Monitor Driver. From the Network And Dialup Connections folder, right-click a connection, choose Properties, and then click Install|Protocol|Network Monitor Driver. Network Monitor Driver can collect packets that the Windows 2000 Professional's network interfaces send or receive. You can then analyze those packets using the version of Network Monitor that ships with Systems Management Server (SMS) 2, SP1, or later.

Managing Processor Performance

A system's processor is one of the more difficult components to optimize because every other component impacts it. Low memory leads to paging, which increases processor usage; fragmented disk drives increase processor usage; hardware interrupts keep the processor busy; and, of course, applications and services are placing demands on the processor. Therefore, to optimize a processor, you need to look at Processor counters, as well as counters for other objects. Some of the most useful Processor counters are the following:

- *Processor:%ProcessorTime, threshold near 100%*—A processor being fully used (100 percent) is not necessarily a sign of a performance bottleneck—in fact, one would hope that you would be utilizing this expensive system component at its full capacity. Therefore, although %ProcessorTime is a flag that indicates a potential bottleneck, it is not in itself enough to prescribe a solution. Check Memory:Pages/sec to examine paging and determine whether low memory is causing excessive paging.

- *Processor:Interrupts/sec, threshold varies*—A malfunctioning hardware device may send excessive interrupts to the processor. Compare this counter to a baseline; a significant rise in this counter without a corresponding increase in system activity may indicate a bad device. Network cards are particularly infamous for generating bogus interrupts.

- *System:Processor Queue Length, threshold 2*—A queue length that is regularly above 2 indicates that threads are backing up as they wait for processor attention.

- *Process:%ProcessorTime (Instance—each service or application)*—This counter enumerates the activity of individual applications and services, allowing you to identify processes that are placing demands on the processor.

If Processor Queue Length is low and %ProcessorTime is averaging above 85 percent for extended periods of time, these settings indicate that a single threaded application or service is keeping the processor busy. A faster processor may improve performance of such a system. However, if Processor Queue Length is high, a second processor would be a better solution, or you might consider moving processes to underutilized systems.

Task Manager

Task Manager enables you to view applications and processes and a number of other common performance counters. To open Task Manager, right-click the taskbar and choose Task Manager, or press Ctrl+Shift+Esc. The Applications tab enumerates active applications. The Performance tab displays useful performance metrics beginning when Task Manager is opened. The Processes tab can display a number of process-related counters. Click View|Select Columns to indicate which counters you wish to view.

Managing Application Performance

Windows 2000 preemptively multitasks active processes, ensuring that all threads gain access to the processor. Processes do run at different priorities, however. Priority levels of 0 to 31 are assigned to a process, and higher-level processes are executed before lower-level processes. As a user, you can specify process priority using Task Manager. Right-clicking a process on the Processes tab enables you to set a process' priority. Processes are assigned a priority of Normal by default. Choosing Above Normal or High will increase the priority of a process and thereby increase the frequency with which its threads are serviced. Choosing Below Normal or Low will diminish the servicing of a process.

TIP

Do not use the Realtime priority. This priority should be reserved for real-time data gathering applications and operating system functions. Setting an application to Realtime priority can cause instability and can be difficult to reverse without restarting the system.

Process priority can also be controlled when an application is launched, using the **start** command with the **/low, /belownormal, /normal, /abovenormal, /high,** and **/realtime** switches.

Practice Questions

Question 1

You have just installed a new tape drive in your Windows 2000 Professional computer. You want to create a reliable backup of your machine's entire registry, all system settings, and your COM+ objects. How would you accomplish this?

❍ a. Use Windows Backup to back up the system state to tape.

❍ b. Use Windows Backup to perform an incremental backup of the system to tape.

❍ c. Use Windows Backup to perform a full backup of the system to tape.

❍ d. Copy the contents of \WINNT\SYSTEM32\CONFIG to a secure network share on a server.

Answer a is correct. Remember that backing up the system state is how Windows 2000 provides a method for you to obtain a backup of the registry and system settings, as well as COM+ objects. Backing up data does not back up these settings, so answers b and c are incorrect. The **config** directory's files are locked during operation, so they cannot be copied therefore answer d is incorrect.

Question 2

You are attempting to install a Plug and Play modem in a Windows 2000 Professional computer. The modem appears to be working when you install it, but later it stops working entirely. You try several more times to reinstall the modem, but it keeps failing. What should you do?

- ❍ a. Use the Add/Remove Hardware Wizard to remove the modem driver. Power down the computer. Let Windows 2000 locate the device driver of its choice.
- ❍ b. Start the computer in Safe Mode. Remove the device driver for the modem. Restart the computer normally and let Windows 2000 find the device driver of its choice.
- ❍ c. Use the Add/Remove Hardware program to troubleshoot the device. Select the modem from the list that appears. The Hardware Troubleshooter starts.
- ❍ d. Install the modem in another computer to see if it fails there as well. If not, reinstall it in the first computer and use the manufacturer's most current driver when Windows 2000 prompts for the file location of the driver files.

Answer b is correct. To fix a device installation "gone wrong" (when reinstallation doesn't work), use Safe Mode to remove the device driver and then let Windows 2000 select a device driver. Remember that the manufacturer's driver may not work as well as a driver from Windows 2000, which is similar. Answers a, c, and d will not enable the modem to function.

Question 3

You have been editing the Windows 2000 registry with regedt32.exe to try to get a device to work. Now, as punishment for your attempted good deed, your Windows 2000 computer will not boot. What should you try first for a quick system restoration?

- ❍ a. Power on the computer and hit the F8 key to get into Safe Mode.
- ❍ b. Power on the computer and hit the F8 key to select Last Known Good Configuration.
- ❍ c. Use the Emergency Recovery Disk to boot and restore system files.
- ❍ d. In the Recovery Console, set the path to a floppy drive or a CD where you have a backup of the system files. Copy the files from the floppy or CD to the hard drive.

Answer b is correct. Powering on the computer and hitting the F8 key to select Last Known Good Configuration is your first choice because you know that the registry was just changed—by you! Safe Mode is better for situations where a new device or software was just added and now your system won't start up. Therefore, answer a is incorrect. You cannot boot using the ERD. Therefore, answer c is incorrect. The Recovery Console is an option, but you would resort to it if selecting Last Known Good Configuration did not work. Therefore, answer d is incorrect.

Question 4

You performed a normal backup of your Windows 2000 Professional computer on Sunday. For the remaining days of the week, you want to back up only the files and folders that have changed since the previous day. What is the best backup type for you to select?

- ❍ a. Daily
- ❍ b. Differential
- ❍ c. Incremental
- ❍ d. Normal

Answer c is correct. An incremental backup backs up the changes since the last markers were set and then clears the markers. So, for Monday through Saturday, you back up only the changes since the previous day. Differential, normal, and daily backups do not perform the same function, and therefore answers a, b, and d are incorrect.

Question 5

You install a new device driver for a SCSI adapter in your Windows 2000 machine. When your restart the computer, though, trouble is on the horizon. Windows 2000 stops responding after the kernel load phase. How can you get Windows 2000 to restart successfully?

- ❍ a. Boot your computer with the Emergency Repair Disk, and then remove the new device driver.
- ❍ b. Boot your computer with the Windows 2000 CD-ROM and then select Restore to restore the system state.
- ❍ c. Restore the system from the most recent backup.
- ❍ d. Select the Last Known Good Configuration option to start Windows 2000.

Answer d is correct. The Last Known Good Configuration option is the best, and quickest, choice because it does not contain any reference to the new (and possibly noncompliant) device driver for your SCSI adapter. The Emergency Repair Disk is not bootable, and there is no "Restore" startup option, therefore answers a and b are incorrect. Answer c may produce something like the desired result, but is not the *best* answer.

Question 6

You want to monitor PhysicalDisk performance counters of a logical drive. With a standard installation of Windows 2000 Professional, what additional operation must you perform to enable the monitoring of the PhysicalDisk counters?

- ❍ a. Install the Network Monitor Driver.
- ❍ b. Run the **diskperf** command with the **–y** switch.
- ❍ c. Install the Network Monitor Driver and run **diskperf –yv**.
- ❍ d. No additional operations are required. The PhysicalDisk counters are accessible by default.

Answer d is correct. PhysicalDisk counters are enabled in Windows 2000 Professional, unlike in Windows NT 4. Network Monitor Driver is used for collecting network traffic counters and for capturing packets. It is not used for any physical disk monitoring. Therefore, answers a and c are incorrect. The **diskperf –y** command *does* enable the PhysicalDisk counters if they have been disabled, as will **diskperf –yd** in answer c, but it is not *necessary* to run these commands because the counters are enabled by default. Therefore, answer b is incorrect.

Question 7

A user runs the CADDraw application several times a day to produce renderings of technical drawings. While CADDraw is running, the user catches up on email and writes memos and reports. You want to teach the user how to maximize the responsiveness of CADDraw so that the renderings don't take as long to complete. What do you teach the user?

- ❍ a. Configure Performance Options in the System applet to optimize for applications.
- ❍ b. Use Task Manager to change the priority of all applications to Above Normal.
- ❍ c. Use Task Manager to set the CADDraw process priority to Realtime.
- ❍ d. Use Task Manager to set the CADDraw process priority to High.

Answer d is correct. By setting the CADDraw process priority to High, CADDraw will be relatively higher than all other applications, including email and word processors, which launch at a default priority of Normal. Using Task Manager to set the CADDraw process priority to High increases the amount of attention CADDraw receives from the processor and improves its performance. Answer a is incorrect because Performance Options changes the performance for *all* applications, not just CADDraw—this does not maximize CADDraw. Answer b is incorrect because raising all applications to Above Normal does not maximize CADDraw—it will still be at the same priority level as the other applications. Answer c, although it might maximize CADDraw, would likely cause system instability and would not be the best choice. Therefore, answer c is incorrect.

Question 8

Your Windows 2000 Professional system is experiencing decreased performance, and you suspect excessive paging. Which counter provides you with the best measure with which to confirm your suspicion?

- ❍ a. Paging File:%Usage
- ❍ b. Paging File:%Usage Peak
- ❍ c. Memory: Pages/sec
- ❍ d. PhysicalDisk: Disk Writes/sec

Answer c is correct. The Pages/sec counters (and there are many of them) all relate to paging activity—the transfer of memory from physical RAM to the virtual memory of the paging file. The paging file counters are useful to determine if you need a larger paging file but do not really tell you what is excessive. For example, you might have a %Usage counter of 90 percent, but if your paging file is only 20MB, there might not be too much paging—you might just have too small a paging file. Therefore, answers a and b are incorrect. PhysicalDisk counters increase when there is paging, but they do not tell you specifically that paging is causing the disk activity. Therefore, answer d is incorrect.

Question 9

A Windows 2000 Professional system is not performing to specifications. You want to determine what course of action to take, and you examine a performance log, which reveals the following:

Processor: %ProcessorTime: 95

System: Processor Queue Length: 3

Memory: Pages/sec: 10

PhysicalDisk: Avg Disk Queue Length: 1

Paging File: %Usage: 25

What should you do to improve performance?

- ❍ a. Add a second processor.
- ❍ b. Add memory.
- ❍ c. Replace the hard disk with a faster disk drive.
- ❍ d. Enlarge the paging file.

Answer a is correct. The processor is overworked, and the processor queue indicates that threads are backed up and are not being serviced. Answer b would often be correct, because memory is often the primary bottleneck, but in this instance, paging is well within the acceptable range. Therefore, answer b is incorrect. The disk subsystem and paging file are not beyond thresholds either. Therefore, answers c and d are incorrect.

Question 10

Which of the following tools is best suited for creating a baseline of system performance?

❍ a. System Monitor

❍ b. Performance Logs And Alerts

❍ c. Task Manager

❍ d. System Information

❍ e. NTBackup

Answer b is correct. Performance Logs And Alerts captures counters during a representative period of normal activity to create the baseline. You can use System Monitor to *view* the baseline, but it is not appropriate for creating the baseline in the first place. Therefore, answer a is incorrect. Task Manager, System Information, and NTBackup are not suited for baselining either. Therefore, answers c, d, and e are incorrect.

Need to Know More?

Microsoft Corporation. *Microsoft Windows 2000 Professional Resource Kit.* Redmon, Washington: Microsoft Press, 2000. ISBN: 1-57231-808-2. This has invaluable information on backing up and recovering data, as well as on using the Recovery Console and the emergency repair process.

Nielsen, Morten Strunge. *Windows 2000 Professional Configuration and Implementation*. Scottsdale, Arizona: The Coriolis Group, 2000. ISBN: 1-57610-528-8. This book offers comprehensive coverage of configuration and implementation with Windows 2000 Professional.

Stinson, Craig and Carl Siechert. *Running Microsoft Windows 2000 Professional.* Redmon, Washington: Microsoft Press, 2000. ISBN: 1-57231-838-4. This guidebook to Windows 2000 Professional is a good source for information on optimizing and troubleshooting Windows 2000 systems, and on using the Recovery Console.

Search the TechNet CD (or its online version through **www.microsoft.com**) and/or the Windows 2000 Professional Resource Kit CD using the keywords "backup," "restore," "Recovery Console," "emergency repair," "system state," "taskman," "performance," "optimizing," "counters," and "last known good."

11

Sample Test

Question 1

You wish to secure a Windows 2000 Professional system beyond the default security level, with as little guesswork as possible. Which tool do you use?

- ❍ a. Local Policy
- ❍ b. Group Policy
- ❍ c. Security Configuration And Analysis
- ❍ d. Domain Security Policy

Question 2

You have a domain policy that clears the name of the last user who logged on from the logon dialog box. You want your Windows 2000 laptop to display your name each time you log on, to save time logging on. What must you do to achieve this?

- ❍ a. Change the DontDisplayLastUser registry entry.
- ❍ b. Configure a local security policy that disables the Do Not Display Last User Name In Logon Screen policy.
- ❍ c. Configure a security database with the Do Not Display Last User Name In Logon Screen option cleared.
- ❍ d. Configure a Group Policy for the OU of your laptop that disables the Do Not Display Last User Name In Logon Screen policy.

Question 3

What can you use to configure user rights in Windows 2000? [Check all correct answers]

- ❑ a. Local Security Policy
- ❑ b. Group Policy
- ❑ c. User Manager
- ❑ d. Users and Passwords applet

Question 4

You want Cory to be able to format partitions on the hard drive of her Windows 2000 Professional system. Which tool will you use to give her this privilege?

- ❍ a. The Users And Passwords applet
- ❍ b. Disk Management snap-in
- ❍ c. Local Security Policy
- ❍ d. Registry Editor

Question 5

You have a template account created for all new salespeople. It specifies group membership, logon script, profile location, dial-up permission, and other attributes common to sales users. Immediately after you create individual user accounts based on the template, users report that they cannot log on. Which setting is causing the problem?

- ❍ a. Account Is locked out.
- ❍ b. Account Is disabled.
- ❍ c. User Must Change Password At Next Logon.
- ❍ d. Enforce Password Complexity.

Question 6

You back up PRO1 each morning using the following backup strategy:

Monday: Incremental

Tuesday: Incremental

Wednesday: Incremental

Thursday: Incremental

Friday: Normal

On Wednesday afternoon, PRO1 crashes and you must recover the hard drive. Which backup sets must you restore, and in which order?

Monday

Tuesday

Wednesday

Thursday

Friday

Question 7

You want to back up service and software settings on a Windows 2000 Professional system. What must you do?

❍ a. Create an ERD.

❍ b. Back up the system state.

❍ c. Copy the WINNT folder to a server.

❍ d. Back up the user profile folder.

Question 8

You are monitoring performance of a Windows 2000 Professional system that seems to be performing below expectations. You note the following counters:

Memory: Pages/sec—80

Processor: % Utilization—90

Physical Disk: % Disk Time—85

System: Processor Queue Length—3

Which of the following would be most likely to overcome the performance bottleneck on this system?

❍ a. Additional memory

❍ b. A faster processor

❍ c. A second processor

❍ d. A faster hard drive

❍ e. A larger hard drive

Question 9

You are monitoring performance of a Windows 2000 Professional system that seems to be performing below expectations. You note the following counters:

Memory: Pages/sec—10

Processor: % Utilization—99

Physical Disk: % Disk Time—20

System: Processor Queue Length—2.5

Which of the following would be most likely to overcome the performance bottleneck on this system?

❍ a. Additional memory

❍ b. A faster processor

❍ c. A second processor

❍ d. A faster hard drive

❍ e. A larger hard drive

❍ f. A larger paging file

Question 10

You have noticed steadily decreasing performance of your system and suspect drive fragmentation. From what tool can you initiate a disk defragmentation?

❍ a. The Properties sheet of a drive volume

❍ b. The Disk Management snap-in

❍ c. The Add/Remove Hardware Wizard

❍ d. The System applet in Control Panel

Question 11

Which of the following tools allows you to monitor an application's priority?

❍ a. Computer Management

❍ b. System applet in Control Panel

❍ c. Task Manager

❍ d. Add/Remove Programs

Question 12

What folder contains local profiles on a clean installation of a Windows 2000 Professional computer?

❍ a. %SystemRoot%\Winnt\system32\profiles

❍ b. %SystemRoot%\Winnt\profiles

❍ c. %SystemRoot%\Winnt\documents and settings

❍ d. %SystemRoot%\documents and settings

Question 13

Your sales staff needs to keep a locally cached copied of the presentations share on server1, which is a Windows 2000 server. When the sales staff selects the presentations share on \\server1, they report there is no option to make files available offline. How do you resolve this problem?

❍ a Configure the caching properties to allow caching of files for the presentation share on the sales staff's computers.

❍ b. Configure the caching properties to allow caching of files for the presentation share on \\server1.

❍ c. Configure the caching properties to manual caching for documents for the presentation share on the sales staff's computers.

❍ d. Configure the caching properties to manual caching for documents for the presentation share on \\server1.

Question 14

As the administrator for your Windows 2000 domain called **corp.com**, you create a Group Policy to deploy a Windows Installer Package service release to update the clients' word processing application. The update applied successfully to all but one client computer. What should you do to apply the service pack to the remaining client?

❍ a. Redeploy the service package with a zap file.

❍ b. Redeploy the service package with a mst file.

❍ c. Restart the Windows Installer service on the domain controller.

❍ d. Restart the Windows Installer service on the failed client computer.

Question 15

A user, Jerry, has enabled files located on the network to be available for offline usage. Jerry has configured synchronization to occur every day at 4:30 P.M. and has disabled synchronization during logon or logoff. Today, Jerry needs to leave at 3:00 P.M. and must synchronize the changes that have been made before logging off. How can he synchronize the offline files before logging off from the network?

❍ a. Configure Synchronization Manager to synchronize during an idle period.

❍ b. Use Synchronization Manager to force synchronization before leaving.

❍ c. Configure Synchronization Manager to synchronize during logon.

❍ d. Copy the files that have been changed to the network file server share point.

Question 16

You need to enable Windows 2000 Professional to read text from all dialog boxes and all applications to visually impaired users. What must you configure to allow for this functionality?

❍ a. SoundSentry

❍ b. ShowSounds

❍ c. Narrator

❍ d. Windows Media Player captioning

Question 17

What is the function of the sysprep.inf file?

❍ a. It is used for remote installations.

❍ b. It is the answer file for **Sysprep** installations.

❍ c. It is used to configure custom parameters for **sysprep.exe**.

❍ d. It is the settings file for custom keyboard layouts.

Question 18

You want to deploy Windows 2000 Professional to network clients by using a remote installation server. However, when the clients attempt to boot their computer from their network adapter, the client cannot connect to the remote installation server. How else can the client connect to it?

❍ a. Use the Network Client Administrator to create a network boot disk to connect to the remote installation server.

❍ b. Use **rbfg.exe** to create a network boot disk to connect to the remote installation server.

❍ c. Use **dcpromo.exe** to create a network boot disk to connect to the remote installation server.

❍ d. Use Recovery Console to create a network boot disk to connect to the remote installation server.

Question 19

A computer on which you want to install Windows 2000 Professional has 96MB of memory, a Pentium II 400MHz CPU, and a 4GB hard drive with 500MB of free space. You attempt the installation but it fails before the graphic phase of the process. What must you do to install Windows 2000 Professional on this computer?

❍ a. Install a Pentium III 500MHz CPU.

❍ b. Install 128MB of memory.

❍ c. Configure the hard drive with at least 650MB of free space.

❍ d. Install an AGP video adapter.

Question 20

You have eight Windows 2000 Professional computers in your company's Art department. They all have built-in USB controllers. You install a USB tablet-pointing device, as well as the manufacturer's 32-bit tablet software on each machine. A Tablet icon shows up in the Control Panel, but none of the tablets works. You examine the Device Manager and notice no device conflicts. What should you do to get the USB tablets to work?

❍ a. Enable the USB ports in the system BIOS, and then reinstall the USB tablet device drivers.

❍ b. Enable the USB root hub controller, and then reinstall the USB tablet device drivers.

❍ c. Disable USB error detection for the USB root hub controller, and then enable the USB tablet device in each machine's hardware profile.

❍ d. Reinstall the USB tablet device drivers, and then disable the USB error detection.

Question 21

You plan to install Windows 2000 Professional on a new computer with two monitors. All of the hardware is Windows 2000 compatible. You want to accomplish the following:

- Provide the user to place items on either monitor.
- Configure the display adapter built into the motherboard as the secondary display.
- Provide the user with the ability to start applications from the primary display.
- Allow the resolution for each display to be configured separately.

You perform the following tasks:

1. Install the additional display adapter in an available slot.
2. Attach the cable from each monitor to the appropriate display adapter.
3. Run Setup to install Windows 2000 and allow Setup to detect and configure the display adapters.

Which result or results do these actions produce? [Check all correct answers]

❑ a. Provides the user with the ability to start applications from the primary display.

❑ b. Provides the user with the ability to place items on either monitor.

❑ c. Configures the display adapter built into the motherboard as the secondary display.

❑ d. Allows the resolution for each display to be configured separately.

Question 22

You back up PRO1 each morning using the following backup strategy:

Monday: Incremental

Tuesday: Differential

Wednesday: Differential

Thursday: Incremental

Friday: Normal

On Wednesday afternoon, PRO1 crashes and you must recover the hard drive. Which backup sets must you restore, and in which order?

Monday

Tuesday

Wednesday

Thursday

Friday

Question 23

You are deciding on specifications for 50 new computers your company will purchase for the Engineering department. They will run Windows 2000 Professional. You want Windows 2000 to be able to use all the hardware that comes in the computers. What is the maximum amount of memory you could have in your new Windows 2000 computers?

❍ a. 2GB

❍ b. 4GB

❍ c. 8GB

❍ d. 16GB

Question 24

Your original network adapter card fails. You replace the network adapter card on your computer, which is running Windows 2000 Professional. What utility should you use to make sure that the device driver for the original network card is removed from your machine?

❍ a. Device Manager

❍ b. Add/Remove Programs

❍ c. Network and Dial-up Connections

❍ d. System applet in Control Panel

❍ e. Add/Remove Hardware Wizard

Question 25

You are dual-booting Windows 98 and Windows 2000 Professional on your computer. You upgraded the second hard drive in the machine from basic to dynamic, and you are using it to store business records. The next time you boot the machine to Windows 98 and try to access your business records, you cannot read the files at all. What is most likely to be the cause of this problem?

❍ a. You formatted the partition(s) on the second drive to NTFS 5, so now Windows 98 cannot read the data on that drive.

❍ b. You forgot to convert the second disk from dynamic back to basic before booting to Windows 98.

❍ c. The data on the second drive is either encrypted or corrupt.

❍ d. Only Windows 2000 can read data stored on dynamic disks.

Question 26

Your Windows 2000 Professional machine has a shared compressed folder on drive D called Sales. The D: drive is formatted as NTFS. You move the Sales folder into an uncompressed folder called CompanyData on drive D. Which of the following statements most accurately describe the Sales folder now?

❍ a. The Sales folder is uncompressed because it resides in an uncompressed folder.

❍ b. The Sales folder is uncompressed because it was removed from its original location.

❍ c. The Sales folder is still compressed because it was moved within the same NTFS volume.

❍ d. The Sales folder is still compressed because it was moved between two NTFS volumes.

Question 27

You want to dual-boot your computer using Windows 98 and Windows 2000 Professional. You are going to be using resource-intensive CAD applications while booted to both of the operating systems, and you need to be able to access all files on the machine regardless of which operating system you are using. What file system should you select for this single partition, single disk, machine?

❍ a. FAT16

❍ b. FAT32

❍ c. NTFS

❍ d. HPFS

Question 28

You are viewing the status of all disks and volumes using Disk Management on your Windows 2000 machine. You notice that all the disks and respective volumes have their status listed as Healthy, except for one. One disk shows each of its volumes status listed as Healthy (At Risk). What does this mean, and what step(s) should you take, if any?

- ❍ a. The volume is initializing and is displayed as Healthy once initialization is finished. You do not need to take any action.
- ❍ b. The volume is accessible but errors have been detected on this disk. You can return the disk to Healthy and Online status by reactivating the disk. Right-click the disk and select Reactivate Disk. Make sure you have a recent backup of the data on the disk.
- ❍ c. This status indicator has appeared because this disk is on the verge of failure. Make sure you have a recent backup of the data on the disk, and replace the disk before failure occurs.
- ❍ d. This status indicator appears when the underlying disk is no longer online. Right-click the disk and select Bring Online.

Question 29

On a Windows 2000 Professional computer, which type of volume includes areas of equal size on multiple physical disks to which data is written at the same time?

- ❍ a. Mirrored volume
- ❍ b. Spanned volume
- ❍ c. Simple volume
- ❍ d. Striped volume
- ❍ e. RAID-5 volume

Question 30

In Windows 2000, how do you change or convert a hard disk from dynamic to basic?

❍ a. Use Disk Management to right-click the disk and select Revert To Basic Disk.

❍ b. Use the Storage snap-in to right-click the disk and select Revert To Basic Disk After Rescan.

❍ c. Remove all the volumes from the disk. Then use Disk Management to right-click the disk and select Revert To Basic Disk.

❍ d. You cannot do this in Windows 2000—you can convert only from basic to dynamic.

Question 31

You need to delete a quota entry defined for a user's account on drive F of a computer running Windows 2000. What utility should you use to locate the files owned by the user and move the files to a shard folder on another server?

❍ a. **ntdsutil**

❍ b. Windows Explorer

❍ c. Active Directory Users And Computers

❍ d. Disk Management

Question 32

What happens to encrypted files that are made available offline?

❍ a. Nothing happens; the files are available and are still encrypted.

❍ b. Encrypted files can't be made available offline.

❍ c. The user who encrypted the file must decrypt the file for offline usage.

❍ d. Encrypted files are not encrypted in the offline cache.

Question 33

Users report that when they access the Presentations share on a Windows 2000 server named \\server1, they can select files from this share to be available while offline. However, when users select files located in the Finance share on \\server1 the Make Available Offline option does not appear. What do you need to configure to allow files in the Finance share to be available while users are offline?

- ❍ a. Configure the caching properties for the Finance share to allow caching of files.
- ❍ b. Ensure that the users have the share permission to the Finance share on \\server1.
- ❍ c. Enable Offline Files on the users' computers.
- ❍ d. Create a logon script that maps \\server1\finance for all users.

Question 34

Users in the **corp.com** domain require that the settings and configurations that have been established on their computer to be available on any computer they may log on to. How do you accomplish this task? [Check all correct answers]

- ❑ a. Configure the local user account to use the local profile on every client computer.
- ❑ b. Rename ntuser.dat to ntuser.man.
- ❑ c. Create a profile share point.
- ❑ d. Configure the users' Profile option with the UNC path for their profile.

Question 35

You have created a Group Policy software package to assign an office suite package to all domain users. You want to prevent the office suite from appearing in the Add/Remove Programs applet. How do you configure this?

- ❍ a. Configure a Group Policy to hide the Add/Remove Programs applet.
- ❍ b. Configure the properties of Software installation Group Policy to display the office suite in a Category.
- ❍ c. Enable the Uninstall This Application When It Falls Out Of The Scope Of Management feature.
- ❍ d. Configure the properties of the office package in Group Policy.

Question 36

Alice has enabled files located on the network to be available for offline usage. She wants to configure synchronization to occur every day at 4:30 P.M. How should Alice configure synchronization to occur each day at a specific time?

- ❍ a. Configure Synchronization Manager to synchronize during an idle period.
- ❍ b. Use Synchronization Manager to force synchronization before leaving.
- ❍ c. Use the Scheduled Task Wizard to configure when synchronization will occur.
- ❍ d. Use Scheduled Synchronization Manager to configure when synchronization will occur.

Question 37

A user requires that the Narrator Accessibility tool be launched automatically when Windows 2000 starts. How do you configure this option?

- ❍ a. Use the Accessibility Options applet to configure the Narrator Settings to start when Windows starts.
- ❍ b. Select the Start Narrator Minimized option.
- ❍ c. Add a registry entry to enable the Narrator to run when Windows starts.
- ❍ d. Use Accessibility Utility Manager to enable the option to start automatically when Windows starts.

Question 38

A user needs to move the mouse pointer by using the numeric keypad on her keyboard. What feature of Windows 2000 Professional do you need to enable to provide this functionality?

- ❍ a. ToggleKeys
- ❍ b. FilterKeys
- ❍ c. MouseKeys
- ❍ d. StickyKeys

Question 39

You need to configure a user's Windows 2000 Professional computer to display a virtual keyboard. This will allow the user to type data using the mouse pointer. What utility must you enable?

- ❍ a. ToggleKeys
- ❍ b. FilterKeys
- ❍ c. StickyKeys
- ❍ d. On-Screen Keyboard

Question 40

You are using a 32-bit Windows word processing application. You have added the French input locale. You have been typing documents in English and now want to start typing in French. How do you do this?

- ❍ a. Change to the French input locale within the word processor.
- ❍ b. Close the application and select the French user locale from the Regional Options applet and restart the application.
- ❍ c. Close the application and log off the computer and then log on and choose the French input locale.
- ❍ d. Select the French input locale using the Language icon in the system tray.

Question 41

You work for a large multinational company with offices in Europe and the United States. Users in Europe regularly need to read and write documents in several different languages and work with the interface of the required language. You need to deploy Windows 2000 to support a Multilanguage configuration while keeping to a minimum the administrative overhead of the deployment and ongoing administration of these computers. How should you deploy Windows 2000 to achieve these goals?

- ❍ a. Deploy a separate version of Windows 2000 for each needed language.
- ❍ b. Deploy the Multilanguage edition of Windows 2000 and install language User Interfaces as needed.
- ❍ c. Deploy Windows 2000 with all required language groups.
- ❍ d. Deploy Windows 2000 with all the required input locales.

Question 42

A user accidentally pressed the Shift key five times. The computer made a high-pitched sound when this occurred. Why did the computer make this sound?

❍ a. MouseKeys was enabled.

❍ b. FilterKeys was enabled.

❍ c. StickyKeys was enabled.

❍ d. ToggleKeys was enabled.

Question 43

You have lost the Setup Disks that come with Windows 2000 Professional and you need to recreate them. You boot a Windows 2000 Professional computer and put the Windows 2000 Professional installation CD-ROM in the computer. What command do you use to create the Setup Disks?

❍ a. **winnt32.exe /ox**

❍ b. **makebt32.exe**

❍ c. **makeboot.exe**

❍ d. **winnt.exe /ox**

Question 44

You want to create a remote installation image of a Windows 2000 Professional computer and its installed applications. What utility is required for this task?

❍ a. **risetup.exe**

❍ b. **rbfg.exe**

❍ c. **sysprep.exe**

❍ d. **riprep.exe**

Question 45

A computer on which you want to install Windows 2000 Professional has 28MB of memory, a Pentium II 400MHz CPU, and a 500MB hard drive with 50MB of free space. You attempt the installation but it fails. What must you do to install Windows 2000 Professional on this computer? [Check all correct answers]

- ❑ a. Install a Pentium III 500MHz CPU.
- ❑ b. Install 32MB or more of memory.
- ❑ c. Configure the hard drive with at least 650MB of free space.
- ❑ d. Install a 2GB hard drive or greater.

Question 46

You want to deploy Windows 2000 Professional with an RIS server. The client computers have a PXE-compliant network adapter. You have installed a Windows 2000 domain controller as well as Domain Name System (DNS) and Dynamic Host Configuration Protocol (DHCP) on a Windows 2000 server. You have installed and configured RIS. However, when clients boot from their network adapter, they fail to connect to the RIS server. What is the problem?

- ❍ a. Verify that DHCP has been authorized in Active Directory.
- ❍ b. Create reserved TCP/IP addresses for all RIS clients in the RIS scope.
- ❍ c. Configure the clients with a static TCP/IP address.
- ❍ d. Create a host record in DNS for the RIS server.

Question 47

Which of the following operating systems can you directly upgrade to Windows 2000 Professional? [Check all correct answers]

- ❑ a. Windows 95
- ❑ b. Windows 98
- ❑ c. Windows 3
- ❑ d. Windows NT 4
- ❑ e. Windows NT 3.51
- ❑ f. Windows 3.11

Question 48

Which two protocols work with the Multilink feature to dynamically add or remove Dial-up Connections as needed? [Check all correct answers]

❑ a. Bandwidth Allocation Control Protocol (BACP)

❑ b. EAP

❑ c. Bandwidth Allocation Protocol (BAP)

❑ d. Remote Authentication Dial-In User Service (RADIUS)

Question 49

Where do you configure encryption settings for both passwords and data for a Dial-up Connection?

❍ a. Open the Network And Dial-up Connections window. Right-click the Dial-up Connection and choose Properties. Click the Networking tab. Select Client For Microsoft Networks and choose Properties.

❍ b. Configure a remote access policy.

❍ c. Open the Network And Dial-up Connections window. Right-click the dial-up connection and choose Properties. Click the Options tab.

❍ d. Open the Network And Dial-up Connections window. Right-click the dial-up connection and choose Properties. Click the Security tab.

Question 50

What IP address range does ICS use by default?

❍ a. 10.0.0.2 through 10.0.0.254

❍ b. 169.254.0.1 through 169.254.255.254

❍ c. 192.168.1.2 through 192.168.1.254

❍ d. 192.168.0.2 through 192.168.0.254

Question 48

[illegible]

Question 49

[illegible]

Question 50

[illegible]

12

Answer Key

1. c
2. d
3. a, b
4. a
5. b
6. *
7. b
8. a
9. c
10. a
11. c
12. d
13. b
14. d
15. b
16. c
17. b
18. b
19. c
20. a
21. a, d
22. *
23. b
24. e
25. d
26. c
27. b
28. b
29. d
30. c
31. d
32. d
33. a
34. c, d
35. d
36. d
37. d
38. c
39. d
40. d
41. b
42. c
43. b
44. d
45. b, d
46. a
47. a, b, d, e
48. a, c
49. d
50. d

This is the answer key to the sample test presented in Chapter 11.

Question 1

Answer c is correct. Security Configuration And Analysis allows you to apply security templates, including the High Security Workstation template created by Microsoft. Local Policy and Group Policy would require more "guesswork" and Domain Security Policy applies only to domain controllers, making answers a, b, and d incorrect.

Question 2

Answer d is correct. A Group Policy for the OU of your laptop overrides a domain policy. The registry entry and local security policy are overridden by the domain policy, so answers a and b are incorrect. A security database is used to evaluate security settings, so answer c is incorrect.

Question 3

Answers a and b are correct. You can use Local Security Policy to configure user rights on any Windows 2000 Professional system. You can use Group Policy to configure user rights for Windows 2000 Professional systems that are members of a domain. You cannot use User Manager (a Windows NT 4 tool) or the Users and Passwords applet to manage user rights. Therefore, answers c and d are incorrect.

Question 4

Answer a is correct. The right to format a hard drive partition is given to administrators only. Therefore, you would have to put Cory into the Administrators group, which you can do with the Users And Passwords applet. The other tools do not let you manage the Administrators group. Therefore, answers b, c, and d are incorrect.

Question 5

Answer b is correct. Template accounts are generally disabled so that they are not active accounts. When you copy the account, you should ensure that the Disabled attribute is cleared for the new user. Answer a is not a setting of a template account, and answers c and d would not be causing the logon problem. Therefore, these answers are incorrect.

Question 6

The correct order is Friday, Monday, Tuesday, and Wednesday. Normal backups are "complete," so you can begin with Friday's backup. Incremental backups back up only what has changed since the last incremental or normal backup, so you must restore each incremental backup since the normal backup.

Question 7

Answer b is correct. You must back up the system state so that you can back up the registry in Windows 2000. The ERD no longer contains a backup of the registry. Therefore, answer a is incorrect. You cannot "copy" the registry while the system is running, and the user profile does not contain machine-specific registry settings. Therefore, answers a, c, and d are incorrect.

Question 8

Answer a is correct. Memory: Pages/sec over 20 indicates too much paging activity, which itself contributes to processor and disk usage. Lack of memory is therefore the bottleneck on this system. Enhancing the processor or disk subsystem would not address this bottleneck, so answers b, c, d, and e are incorrect.

Question 9

Answer c is correct. This system's processor is at capacity, and the queue length is above 2, indicating that threads are waiting to be processed and a second processor could alleviate the bottleneck. Answers a, b, d, e, and f would not be the best solutions to address this bottleneck.

Question 10

Answer a is correct. From the Properties sheet of a drive volume, you can launch defragmentation from the Tools tab. You cannot perform defragmentation using the tools in answers b, c, and d.

Question 11

Answer c is correct. Task Manager allows you to monitor at what priority an application is running. Computer Management, System, and Add/Remove Programs will not allow you to change an application's priority, so answers a, b, and d are incorrect.

Question 12

Answer d is correct. The local profiles on a Windows 2000 Professional computer are found in %SystemRoot%\Documents and settings. However, if the computer had been upgraded from Windows NT to Windows 2000 then the profiles would be found in %SystemRoot%\Winnt\profiles.

Question 13

Answer b is correct. If a share point is not configured to allow caching of files, then you cannot cache files from that share point. Also, the option to make files available offline is not available until this option is selected, so answer a is incorrect. Answer d is not an available option until the share point has been configured to allow for caching of files; therefore answer d is incorrect. Answer c is incorrect because it is the wrong computer. The problem is on \\server1 not of the sales staff's computers.

Question 14

Answer d is correct. If you restart the Windows Installer service, the service release is installed the next time the client logs on to his or her computer. If there had been a problem with the service release msi file, it would not have installed on any computers. However, it did install on all but one of the client computers. This indicates that the failed install of the service package is an issue with the client computer. Therefore, answers a and b incorrect. Restarting the Windows Installer service would only be an appropriate answer if the application couldn't be installed on the domain controller. The domain controller is simply being used to deploy applications; therefore answer c is incorrect.

Question 15

Answer b is correct. Jerry can use Synchronization Manager to synchronize on the fly by clicking the Synchronize button. Doing so forces a synchronization of all files that have been changed. Copying the file to the share point could potentially overwrite the existing files. Therefore, answer d is incorrect. Answer a would require the user to wait until an idle period before the files were synchronized. The user must disconnect the computer from the network before the idle period sets in, therefore answer a is incorrect. If answer c were chosen the user may not have synchronized files before removing the computer from the network. The user must synchronize files before logging off the network. Answer c doesn't synchronize files until the users logs back on to the network, which is too late; therefore answer c is incorrect.

Question 16

Answer c is correct. You use the Narrator accessibility option to read aloud on-screen text, dialog boxes, menus, and buttons that are selected in Windows 2000 Professional. SoundSentry generates visual warnings when the computer generates sound alerts, whereas ShowSounds tells applications to display captions for sounds the application may make. Therefore, answers a and b are incorrect. Windows Media Player cannot speak aloud written text, but it can display text in Close Caption. Therefore, answer d is incorrect.

Question 17

Answer b is correct. The sysprep.inf file is the answer file for **Sysprep** installations of Windows 2000. It is not used for remote installations. It could be if it were renamed and placed in the correct location. Therefore, answer a is incorrect. This file is not used to configure **sysprep.exe**, nor could it ever be used to adjust settings for keyboard layouts. Therefore, answers c and d are incorrect.

Question 18

Answer b is correct. The only utility that you can use to create network boot disks to connect to a remote installation server is **rbfg.exe**. The Network Client Administrator is a Windows NT 4 server utility that creates generic network boot disks; you can't use it to find and connect to a remote installation server. Therefore, answer a is incorrect. You use **dcpromo.exe** to promote a member server to a domain controller, and the Recovery Console is a Windows 2000 troubleshooting tool. Therefore, answers c and d are incorrect.

Question 19

Answer c is correct. Windows 2000 Professional requires at least 650MB of free hard disk space to complete a successful installation. You can install Windows 2000 Professional on a computer with only 32MB of memory and a Pentium 166MHz CPU, so this system meets minimum requirements, which makes answers a and b incorrect The installation fails before Plug and Play would attempt find the video adapter, so that is not the issue. By process of elimination, an incorrect configuration of the hard drive is the best answer.

Question 20

Answer a is correct. The operating system is recognizing the tablets, but they do not work. You need to enable the USB ports in the system's BIOS, and then reinstall the drivers for the tablets. Having the single USB tablet device on each machine does not necessitate having a USB root hub controller, nor would answers b and c solve the problem unless the USB ports were enabled in the BIOS. Therefore, answers b and c are incorrect. Answer d is a distracter, so it is incorrect.

Question 21

The correct answers are a and d. You have to install Windows 2000 before you install a display adapter other than the one that is built-in. Otherwise, Setup will disable the built-in adapter when it detects another one present. The order that you completed the tasks results in only one display adapter and monitor being enabled. So, the user can start apps from the primary display and configure each display's settings separately—but that's it. Answers b and c are incorrect.

Question 22

The correct order is Friday, Monday, and Wednesday. Normal backups are "complete," so you can begin with Friday's backup. Incremental backups back up only what has changed since the last incremental or normal backup, so you must restore each incremental backup since the normal backup (Monday). Differential backups back up all files that have changed since the last normal or incremental backup, so Wednesday's backup includes all files that have changed since Monday morning.

Question 23

Answer b is correct. Windows 2000 Professional can address up to 4GB of RAM.

Question 24

Answer e is correct. You must use the Add/Remove Hardware Wizard to ensure that drivers are removed from your hard disk. You can use Device Manager to uninstall drivers, but it does not remove the driver from your machine—it just makes sure the driver is not loaded during system's startup. Therefore, answer a is incorrect. From Network and Dial-up Connections, you can disable a Local Area Connection for a network adapter card, but the drivers are not removed from the hard disk. Therefore, answer c is incorrect.

Question 25

Answer d is correct. Down-level operating systems (Windows versions before Windows 2000) cannot read the Windows 2000 dynamic disks. Answer a is incorrect because you have no information about the file systems in use in this scenario. You do not convert dynamic disks back to basic solely for the purpose of reading them once you've rebooted to a down-level operating system. Therefore, answer b is incorrect. You have no evidence to support the assertion that data on the second drive is missing or corrupt, so you cannot select answer c.

Question 26

Answer c is correct. When you move an object within the same NTFS volume, it retains its compression attribute. This is a golden rule to remember.

Question 27

Answer b is correct. Windows 98 cannot read NTFS or HPFS. FAT32 uses smaller cluster sizes and is more efficient than FAT16, plus both Windows 98 and Windows 2000 can use FAT32. FAT16 would work, but it is not the best choice because it uses larger cluster sizes and less efficient use of disk space. Therefore, answer a is incorrect. Answers c and d are incorrect because Windows 98 cannot read them.

Question 28

Answer b is correct. When the disk is Healthy (At Risk), it is not simply offline. "At Risk" means errors have been detected on the disk. Healthy (At Risk) does not display when a volume is initializing, so answer a is incorrect. There is not enough information to conclude this disk is on the verge of failure, so answer c is incorrect.

Question 29

Answer d is correct. This questions deals with the straight definition of a striped volume. A striped volume has areas of equal size on multiple disks to which data is written at the same time. Just as a side note and something to keep in mind—Windows 2000 Professional does not support mirrored volumes or RAID-5 volumes. Therefore, answers a and e are incorrect.

Question 30

Answer c is correct. You *must* remove all the volumes from the disk before you convert or revert a dynamic disk back to basic. You do not use the Storage snap-in for this. Therefore, answer b is incorrect. Answer d is preposterous—of course you can convert a disk from dynamic back to basic. Therefore, answer d is incorrect.

Question 31

Answer d is correct. You use the disk quota management system within Disk Management. When you delete the user's quota entry, a dialog box that allows you to move, delete, or take ownership of files owned by the user on drive F appears. **ntdsutil** is a command-line utility that manages the Active Directory database, so answer a is incorrect. Windows Explorer has no feature to expose files owned by a specific user. Therefore, answer b is incorrect. Information about individual files owned by a user is not available in Active Directory Users And Computers. Therefore, answer c is incorrect.

Question 32

Answer d is correct. Files that have been encrypted can be made available while a user is offline, so answer b is incorrect. However, the encrypted files are not encrypted in the offline cache, so answer d is correct. Answer c is not a required action. Files are encrypted and decrypted in the same manner whether or not they are tagged for offline usage. No, user action is necessary to decrypt a file that has been encrypted. This action is performed automatically by the security subsystem.

Question 33

Answer a is correct. The caching properties for the Finance share have been disabled, and you need to enable them before the clients can cache files contained in this share. Because the users can get to the files in the Finance share, we know that there is nothing wrong with the permissions. Therefore, answer b is incorrect. We know that the users' computers have enabled the Offline Files option because they can make files in the presentations share available for offline usage; therefore answer c is incorrect. Answer d wouldn't correct the problem. A drive mapping would be created but the files would not be cached, therefore answer d is incorrect.

Question 34

Answers c and d are correct. To allow a user profile that has been created on a user's computer to be available on any computer the user logs on to, there must be a central profile share that the user's profile is uploaded to. In addition, you must then enter the UNC path to the share for each user account that needs roaming profiles. Answer a would not use a central profile that would be available on every computer a user might log on to. Instead the local profile would be used, thus answer a is incorrect. Answer b would simply make a profile mandatory, but it does not enable a profile to roam, therefore answer b is incorrect.

Question 35

Answer d is correct. You can configure assigned applications not to appear in the Add/Remove Programs applet. This configuration is simply a software policy option that you can use for either assigned or published applications. However, you should use it just for assigned applications. You don't want to hide the entire Add/Remove Programs applet, just the presence of the office suite within the applet, therefore answer a is incorrect. Answer b doesn't solve anything as the Category option is found within the Add/Remove Programs applet. The policy had instructed the package not to appear in the Add/Remove Programs applet so placing the software within a Category won't make the application appear, therefore answer b is incorrect. Answer c does not control whether or not a software package will appear in the Add/Remove Programs applet. It is used to remove the entire application from a computer when a user account is moved from on Organization Unit (OU) to another.

Question 36

Answer d is correct. The Synchronization Manager can be used to control synchronization to occur during an idle period, or at a scheduled interval. In this case the user Alice needed to schedule synchronization to occur at 4:30 each day. Answer d provides this capability. You can use Synchronization Manager to synchronize on the fly by clicking the Synchronize button. Doing so forces a synchronization of all files that have been changed, but requires the users to be present to manually push a button. This option doesn't allow for synchronization to be configuration at a specific time, therefore answer b is incorrect. The Scheduled Task Wizard doesn't control when offline files can be synchronized, therefore answer c is incorrect.

Question 37

Answer d is correct. You can use Accessibility Utility Manager to configure the Narrator to start automatically when Windows starts. The other options do not provide this capability. Therefore, answers a, b, and c are incorrect.

Question 38

Answer c is correct. You use the MouseKeys accessibility option to control the mouse pointer with the numeric keypad. The other options do not allow for this functionality. Therefore, answers a, b, and d are incorrect.

Question 39

Answer d is correct. The On-Screen Keyboard is a virtual keyboard that is displayed on a user's desktop. Users can use a pointing device such as a mouse to enter data with this keyboard. ToggleKeys plays a high-pitched sound when the Caps key is pressed. Therefore, answer a is incorrect. FilterKeys adjusts the keyboard repeat delay. Therefore, answer b is incorrect. StickyKeys allows users to select keystrokes such as Ctrl+Alt+Delete individually. Therefore, answer c is incorrect.

Question 40

Answer d is correct. You can select an input locale by using a keyboard shortcut or by selecting the Language icon in the system tray. Changing the user locale to French would not affect the input locale. French characters do not appear until the input locale is selected. Therefore, answer b is incorrect. Answer a is not even possible. The input locale has to be switched either by using hot keys or the system tray. At that point an application could then type characters from different languages. Therefore answer a is incorrect. It is not necessary to log off the computer to invoke different input locales. They can be changed on the fly, therefore answer c is incorrect.

Question 41

Answer b is correct. If you use the Multilanguage edition of Windows 2000, you don't need to use separate SPs, hot fixes, and upgrades. If you deploy a separate version of Windows, you increase the administrative burden because these computers do require separate SPs, hot fixes, and upgrades. Therefore, answer a is incorrect. While the Multilanguage edition can use the same service packs, answers c and d do not provide enough options for the user.

Question 42

Answer c is correct. By default, pressing the Shift key five times enables StickyKeys Pressing Left Alt+Left Shift+Num Lock enables MouseKeys, thus answer a is incorrect. Holding down the Right Shift key for eight seconds enables FilterKeys, thus answer b is incorrect. ToggleKeys can be invoked by holding down the Num lock key for five seconds, which makes answer d incorrect.

Question 43

Answer b is correct. The user booted into a Windows 2000 computer, so **makebt32.exe** is the correct executable. Therefore, answer a is incorrect. **Winnt32.exe /ox** is not a viable command. This switch provides no functionally at all with this executable, therefore answer a is incorrect. If the user had booted to a DOS prompt, **makeboot.exe** would have been the right executable to use. Therefore, answer c is incorrect. **winnt.exe /ox** is the method to create setup floppy disks for Windows NT 4. The **/ox** switch does not create the Setup Disks for Windows 2000. Therefore, answer d is incorrect.

Question 44

Answer d is correct. **riprep.exe** creates remote installation images of Windows 2000 Professional computers. These images are automatically placed on a RIS server. In contrast **risetup.exe** is used to configure a server to be a remote installation server, thus answer a is incorrect. The **rbfg.exe** utility is used to create remote boot disks for RIS clients to connect to a RIS server, thus answer b is incorrect. **Sysprep.exe** is used to prepare a computer to be imaged with third party imaging software by removing unique parameters from the computer. Therefore answer c is incorrect.

Question 45

Answers b and d are correct. The minimum requirements for Windows 2000 Professional are 32MB of memory, a 2GB drive with 650MB of free space, and a Pentium 133MHz or higher CPU.

Question 46

Answer a is correct. Active Directory needs to authorize a Windows 2000 DHCP server to give TCP/IP addresses. If the server has not been authorized, it does not give out IP addresses and the RIS clients cannot connect to the RIS. Unless the DHCP server has been authorized created reserved TCP/IP addresses for the RIS clients still won't obtain a TCP/IP address, thus answer b is incorrect. Answer c is incorrect as the client must obtain a TCP/IP address from a DHCP server. A static TCP/IP address can't be used; therefore answer c is incorrect. Answer d is not related to the problem. Unless the DHCP server has been activated clients won't get a TCP/IP address and cannot connect to the RIS server. RIS could be completely configured unless there was a host record for the RIS server in DNS. Therefore answer d is incorrect.

Question 47

Answers a, b, d, and e are correct. You can upgrade only Window 95, 98, NT 4, and NT 3.51 to Windows 2000 Professional. You cannot upgrade Windows 3 or 3.11. Therefore, answers c and f are incorrect.

Question 48

Answers a and c are correct. BAP and BACP work together in conjunction with Multilink to combine multiple communications devices (modems and ISDN terminal adapters) for achieving higher throughput. BAP and BACP can dynamically drop or add lines based on pre-determined usage rates as specified in remote access policies. EAP is the Extensible Authentication Protocol, which is an authentication protocol, not a bandwidth protocol. RADIUS is a set of remote access accounting services, which do not concern bandwidth.

Question 49

Answer d is correct. The Security tab displays the settings necessary for configuring password and data encryption. Encryption settings are not configured from the Networking tab, the Options tab, nor from remote access policies.

Question 50

Answer d is correct. By default, ICS uses the IP address range of 192.168.0.2 through 192.168.0.254 for clients, with 192.168.0.1 reserved for the Windows 2000 computer sharing its Internet connection. Although the IP scheme 10.x.y.z is a private nonroutable set of addresses; ICS does not use it, so answer a is incorrect. The range of 169.254.x.y is used by APIPA, not ICS. Therefore, answer b is incorrect. The range of 192.168.1.x is also private and nonroutable; it is not the default IP scheme that ICS uses. Therefore, answer c is incorrect.

Glossary

A (address) resource record

A resource record used to map a Domain Name System (DNS) domain name to a host Internet Protocol (IP) address on the network.

Accelerated Graphics Port (AGP)

A new interface specification (released in August 1997) developed by Intel. AGP is based on peripheral connection interface (PCI) but is designed especially for the throughput demands of 3D graphics. Rather than using the PCI bus for graphics data, AGP introduces a dedicated point-to-point channel so that the graphics controller can directly access main memory. The AGP channel is 32 bits wide and runs at 66MHz. This translates into a total bandwidth of 266Mbps, as opposed to the PCI bandwidth of 133Mbps. AGP also supports two optional faster modes, with throughputs of 533Mbps and 1.07Gbps. In addition, AGP allows 3D textures to be stored in main memory rather than in video memory. AGP has a couple important system requirements: The chipset must support AGP, and the motherboard must be equipped with an AGP bus slot or must have an integrated AGP graphics system.

access control entry (ACE)

An element in an object's discretionary access control list (DACL). Each ACE controls or monitors access to an object by a specified trustee. An ACE is also an entry in an object's system access control list (SACL) that specifies the security events to be audited for a user or group.

account lockout

A Windows 2000 security feature that locks a user account if a certain number of failed logon attempts occur within a specified amount of time, based on security policy lockout settings. Locked accounts cannot log on.

Active Directory

The directory service included with Windows 2000 Server. It is based on the X.500 standards and those of its predecessor, Lightweight Directory Access Protocol (LDAP). It stores information about objects on a network and makes this information available to users and network administrators. Active Directory gives network users access to permitted resources anywhere on the network using a single logon process. It provides network administrators with a hierarchical view of the network and a single point of administration for all network objects.

Active Directory Users And Computers snap-in

An administrative tool designed to perform daily Active Directory administration tasks. These tasks include creating, deleting, modifying, moving, and setting permissions on objects stored in the directory. These objects include Organizational Units (OUs), users, contacts, groups, computers, printers, and shared file objects.

Address Resolution Protocol (ARP)

A Transmission Control Protocol/Internet Protocol (TCP/IP) protocol that translates an Internet Protocol (IP) address into a physical address, such as a MAC address (hardware address). A computer that wants to obtain a physical address sends an ARP broadcast request onto the TCP/IP network. The computer on the network that has the IP address in the request then replies with its physical hardware address.

Advanced Configuration and Power Interface (ACPI)

A power management specification developed by Intel, Microsoft, and Toshiba. ACPI enables Windows 2000 to control the amount of power given to each device attached to the computer. With ACPI, the operating system can turn off peripheral devices, such as CD-ROM players, when they are not in use. As another example, ACPI enables manufacturers to produce computers that automatically power up as soon as you touch the keyboard.

Advanced Power Management (APM)

An application programming interface (API) developed by Intel and Microsoft that allows developers to include power management in Basic Input/Output Systems (BIOSes). APM defines a layer between the hardware and the operating system that effectively shields programmers from hardware details. Advanced Configuration and Power Interface (ACPI) will gradually replace APM.

ARPANET

A large wide area network (WAN) created in the 1960s by the U.S. Department of Defense (DoD) Advanced Research Projects Agency for the free exchange of information between universities and research organizations.

Asynchronous Transfer Mode (ATM)

A networking technology that transfers data in cells (data packets of a fixed size). Cells used with ATM are relatively small compared to packets used with older technologies. The small, constant cell size allows ATM hardware to transmit video images, audio, and computer data over the same network as well as ensures that no single type of data consumes all of the connection's available bandwidth. Current implementations of ATM support data transfer rates from 25 to 622Mbps. Most Ethernet-based networks run at 100Mbps or below.

attribute
A single property that describes an object; e.g., the make, model, or color that describes a car. In the context of directories, an attribute is the main component of an entry in a directory, such as an email address.

auditing
The process that tracks the activities of users by recording selected types of events in the security log of a server or workstation.

authentication ticket
A permission to access resources indirectly that a Kerberos Key Distribution Center (KDC) grants to clients and applications.

authorize
To register the Remote Installation Services (RIS) server or the Dynamic Host Configuration Protocol (DHCP) server with Active Directory.

Auto Private IP Addressing (APIPA)
A client-side feature of Windows 98 and 2000 Dynamic Host Configuration Protocol (DHCP) clients. If the client's attempt to negotiate with a DHCP server fails, the client automatically receives an Internet Protocol (IP) address from the 169.254.0.0 Class B range.

backup domain controller (BDC)
In Windows NT Server 4, a server that receives a copy of the domain's directory database (which contains all of the account and security policy information for the domain). BDCs can continue to participate in a Windows 2000 domain when the domain is configured in mixed mode.

Bandwidth Allocation Protocol (BAP)
A protocol that dynamically controls the use of Multilinked lines. BAP eliminates excess bandwidth by allocating lines only when they are required. You can control dynamic links with remote access policies, which are based on the percent of line utilization and the length of time the bandwidth is reduced.

baselining
The process of measuring system performance so that you can ascertain a standard or expected level of performance.

basic disk
A Windows 2000 term that indicates a physical disk, which can have primary and extended partitions. A basic disk can contain up to three primary partitions and one extended partition, or four primary partitions. A basic disk can also have a single extended partition with logical drives. You *cannot* extend a basic disk.

Basic Input/Output System (BIOS)
Built-in software that determines what a computer can do without accessing programs from a disk. On PCs, the BIOS contains all the code required to control the keyboard, display screen, disk drives, serial communications, and a number of miscellaneous functions. A BIOS that can handle Plug and Play devices is known as a Plug and Play BIOS. A Plug and Play BIOS is always implemented with flash memory rather than read-only memory (ROM). Windows 2000 benefits if your machine has the latest Advanced Configuration and Power Interface (ACPI)-compliant BIOS.

boot partition
The partition that contains the Windows 2000 operating system and its support files.

Challenge Handshake Authentication Protocol (CHAP)
An authentication protocol used by Microsoft remote access as well as network and dial-up connections. Using CHAP, a remote access client can send its authentication credentials to a remote access server in a secure form. Microsoft has created several variations of CHAP that are Windows specific, such as Microsoft Challenge Handshake Authentication Protocol (MSCHAP) and MSCHAP 2.

Client-Side Caching (CSC)
See *offline file*.

compression
The process of making individual files and folders occupy less disk space with the NT File System (NTFS) 5 file system in Windows 2000. Compressed files can be read and written to by any Windows- or DOS-based program *without* having to be decompressed first. They decompress when opened, and recompress when closed. The NTFS 5 file system handles this entire process. Compression is simply a file attribute that you can apply to any file or folder stored on an NTFS 5 partition.

computer account
An account that a domain administrator creates and that uniquely identifies the computer on the domain. The Windows 2000 computer account matches the name of the computer that joins the domain.

container
An object in the directory that contains other objects.

counter
A metric that provides information about particular aspects of system performance.

daily backup
A backup of files that have changed today but that does not mark them as backed up.

Data Recovery Agents (DRA)
A Windows 2000 administrator who has been issued a public key certificate for the express purpose of

recovering user-encrypted data files that have been encrypted with Encrypting File System (EFS). Data recovery refers to the process of decrypting a file without having the private key of the user who encrypted the file. A DRA may become necessary if a user loses his or her private key for decrypting files, or if a user leaves an organization without decrypting important files that other users need.

default gateway

An address that serves an important role in Transmission Control Protocol/Internet Protocol (TCP/IP) networking by providing a default route for TCP/IP hosts to use when communicating with other hosts on remote networks. A router (either a dedicated router or a computer that connects two or more network segments) generally acts as the default gateway for TCP/IP hosts. The router maintains its own routing table of other networks within an internetwork. The routing table maps the routes required to reach the remote hosts that reside on those other networks.

Device Manager

The primary tool in Windows 2000 used to configure and manage hardware devices and their settings.

dial-up access

When a remote client uses the public telephone line or integrated services digital network (ISDN) line to create a connection to a Windows 2000 remote access server.

differential backup

A backup that copies files created or changed since the last normal or incremental backup. It does *not* mark files as having been backed up (in other words, the archive attribute is not cleared). If you are performing a combination of normal and differential backups, restoring files and folders requires that you have the last normal backup as well as the last differential backup.

digital signature

The use of public key cryptography to authenticate the integrity and originator of a communication.

digital versatile disc or digital video disc (DVD)

A type of CD-ROM that holds a minimum of 4.7GB, enough for a full-length movie. The DVD specification supports disks with capacities from 4.7 to 17GB and access rates of 600Kbps to 1.3Mbps. One of the best features of DVD drives is that they are backward compatible with CD-ROMs. This means that DVD players can play old CD-ROMs, CD-I disks, video CDs, and new DVD-ROMs. Newer DVD players can also read CD-R disks. DVD uses Moving Picture Experts Group (MPEG)-2 to compress video data.

Direct Memory Access (DMA)

A technique for transferring data from main memory to a device without passing it through the CPU. Computers that have DMA channels can transfer data to and from devices much more quickly than can computers without a DMA channel. This is useful for making quick backups and for realtime applications. Some expansion boards, such as CD-ROM cards, can access the computer's DMA channel. When you install the board, you must specify the DMA channel to be used, which sometimes involves setting a jumper or dual in-line package (DIP) switch.

discretionary access control list (DACL)

A list of access control entries (ACEs) that lets administrators set permissions for users and groups at the object and attribute levels. This list represents part of an object's security descriptor that allows or denies permissions to specific users and groups.

disk group

A Windows 2000 term for multiple dynamic disks that are managed as a collection. All dynamic disks in a computer are members of the same disk group. Each disk in a disk group stores replicas of the same configuration data. This configuration data is stored in a 1MB region at the end of each dynamic disk.

Disk Management

A Windows 2000 MMC snap-in that you use to perform all disk maintenance tasks, such as formatting, creating partitions, deleting partitions, and converting a basic disk to a dynamic disk.

disk quota

A control used in Windows 2000 to limit the amount of hard disk space available for all users or an individual user. You can apply a quota on a per-user, per-volume basis only.

domain

The fundamental administrative unit of Active Directory. A domain stores information about objects in the domain's partition of Active Directory. You can give user and group accounts in a domain privileges and permissions to resources on any system that belongs to the domain.

domain controller

A computer running Windows 2000 Server that hosts Active Directory and manages user access to a network, which includes logging on, authentication, and access to the directory and shared resources.

domain forest

A collection of one or more Windows 2000 domains in a non-contiguous DNS namespace that share a common schema, configuration, and Global Catalog and that are linked with two-way transitive trusts.

Domain Name System (DNS)

The standard by which hosts on the Internet have both domain name addresses (for example, **rapport.com**) and numerical Internet Protocol (IP) addresses (for example, 192.33.2.8). DNS is a service that you use primarily for resolving fully qualified domain names (FQDN) to IP addresses.

domain tree
A set of domains that form a contiguous DNS namespace through a set of hierarchical relationships.

driver signing
A method for marking or identifying driver files that meet certain specifications or standards. Windows 2000 uses a driver signing process to make sure drivers have been certified to work correctly with the Windows Driver Model (WDM) in Windows 2000.

dynamic disk
A physical disk in a Windows 2000 computer that does not use partitions or logical drives. It has dynamic volumes that you create using the Disk Management console. A dynamic disk can contain any of five types of volumes. In addition, you can extend a volume on a dynamic disk. Dynamic disks can contain an unlimited number of volumes, so you are not restricted to four volumes per disk as you are with a basic disk.

Dynamic Host Configuration Protocol (DHCP) server
A Windows 2000 server that dynamically assigns Internet Protocol (IP) addresses to clients. Along with the assignment of IP addresses, it can provide direction towards routers, Windows Internet Naming Service (WINS) servers, and Domain Name System (DNS) servers.

dynamic volume
The only type of volume you can create on dynamic disks. There are five types of dynamic volumes: simple, spanned, mirrored, striped, and RAID-5. Only computers running Windows 2000 can directly access dynamic volumes. Windows 2000 Professional machines *cannot* host, but *can* access, mirrored and RAID-5 dynamic volumes that are on remote Windows 2000 servers.

Emergency Repair Disk (ERD)
A disk created by the Backup utility that contains information about your current Windows system settings. You can use this disk to attempt to repair your computer if it will not start or if your system files are damaged or erased.

emergency repair process (or repair process)
A feature that helps you repair problems with system files, your startup environment (if you have a dual-boot or multiple-boot system), and the partition boot sector on your boot volume. Before you use the emergency repair process to repair your system, you must create an Emergency Repair Disk (ERD). You can do this using the Backup utility. Even if you have not created an ERD, you can still try to use the emergency repair process; however, any changes you have made to your system, for example service pack updates, may be lost and might need to be reinstalled.

Encrypting File System (EFS)
A subsystem of NT File System (NTFS) that uses public keys and private keys to provide encryption for

files and folders on computers using Windows 2000. Only the user who initially encrypted the file and a recovery agent can decrypt encrypted files and folders.

Extensible Authentication Protocol (EAP)

An extension of Point-to-Point Protocol (PPP) that provides remote access user authentication by means of other security devices. You may add support for a number of authentication schemes, including token cards; dial-up; the Kerberos v5 protocol; one-time passwords; and public key authentication using smart cards, certificates, and others. EAP works with dial-up, Point-to-Point Tunneling Protocol (PPTP), and Layer 2 Tunneling Protocol (L2TP) clients. EAP is a critical technology component for secure Virtual Private Networks (VPNs) because it offers more security against brute force or dictionary attacks (where all possible combinations of characters are attempted), and password guessing than other authentication methods, such as Challenge Handshake Authentication Protocol (CHAP).

fault tolerance

The ability of a computer or operating system to ensure data integrity when hardware failures occur. Within Windows 2000 Server, Advanced Server, and Datacenter Server, mirrored volumes and Redundant Array of Independent Disks (RAID)-5 volumes are fault tolerant.

file allocation table (FAT) or FAT16

A 16-bit table that many operating systems use to locate files on disk. The FAT keeps track of all the pieces of a file. The FAT file system for older versions of Windows 95 is called virtual file allocation table (VFAT); the one for Windows 95 (OEM Service Release—OSR—2) and 98 is called FAT32. Windows 2000 can use the FAT file system; however, it is often not used on Windows 2000 and NT machines because of its larger cluster sizes and inability to scale to larger volume sizes. The FAT file system has no local security.

file allocation table (FAT)32

A newer, 32-bit version of FAT available in Windows 95 OEM Service Release (OSR) 2 and 98. FAT32 increases the number of bits used to address clusters and reduces the size of each cluster. The result is that it can support larger disks (up to 2 terabytes) and better storage efficiency (less slack space) than the earlier version of FAT. The FAT32 file system has no local security. Windows 2000 can use and format partitions as FAT, FAT32, or NT File System (NTFS).

FireWire or Institute of Electrical and Electronics Engineers (IEEE) 1394

A new, very fast external bus standard that supports data transfer rates of up to 400Mbps. Products that support the 1394 standard go under different names, depending on the company.

Apple originally developed the technology and uses the trademarked name FireWire. Other companies use other names, such as i.link and Lynx, to describe their 1394 products. You can use a single 1394 port to connect up to 63 external devices. In addition to its high speed, 1394 supports time-dependent data, delivering data at a guaranteed rate. This makes it ideal for devices that need to transfer high levels of data in realtime, such as video devices. Although extremely fast and flexible, 1394 is expensive. Like Universal Serial Bus (USB), 1394 supports both Plug and Play and hot plugging as well as provides power to peripheral devices. The main difference between 1394 and USB is that 1394 supports faster data transfer rates and is more expensive. For these reasons, it is used mostly for devices that require large throughputs, such as video cameras, whereas USB is used to connect most other peripheral devices.

forward lookup

In Domain Name System (DNS), a query process in which the friendly DNS domain name of a host computer is searched to find its Internet Protocol (IP) address.

forward lookup zone

A Domain Name System (DNS) zone that provides host name to Transmission Control Protocol/ Internet Protocol (TCP/IP) address resolution. In DNS Manager, forward lookup zones are based on DNS domain names and typically hold host (A) address resource records.

Frame Relay Permanent Virtual Circuit (PVC)

A protocol where messages are divided into packets before they are sent. Each packet is then transmitted individually and can even follow different routes to its destination. Once all the packets that form a message arrive at the destination, they are recompiled into the original message. Several wide area network (WAN) protocols, including Frame Relay, are based on packet-switching technologies. Ordinary telephone service is based on a circuit-switching technology where a dedicated line is allocated for transmission between two parties. Circuit switching is best suited for data that must be transmitted quickly and must arrive in the same order in which it is sent. Most realtime data, such as live audio and video, require circuit-switching technology. Packet switching is more efficient and robust for data that can withstand some delays (latency) in transmission, such as email messages and Web content.

global group

A group that can be granted rights and permissions and can become a member of local groups in its own domain and trusting domains. However, a global group can contain user accounts from its own domain only. Global groups provide a way to create sets of users from inside the domain that are available for use both in and out of the domain.

Group Policy
The mechanism for managing change and configuration of systems, security, applications, and user environments in an Active Directory domain.

Group Policy Editor (GPE)
A Windows 2000 snap-in that allows customers to create custom profiles for groups of users and computers.

Group Policy Object (GPO)
An object created by the Group Policy Editor (GPE) snap-in to hold information about a specific group's association with selected directory objects, such as sites, domains, or Organizational Units (OUs).

Hardware Abstraction Layer (HAL)
A component of an operating system that functions something like an application programming interface (API). In strict technical architecture, HALs reside at the device level, a layer below the standard API level. HAL allows programmers to write applications and game titles with all the device-independent advantages of writing to an API, but without the large processing overhead that APIs normally demand.

hardware profile
A profile that stores configuration settings for a collection of devices and services. Windows 2000 can store different hardware profiles so that users' needs can be met even though their computer may frequently require different device and service settings depending on circumstances. The best example is a laptop or portable computer used in an office while in a docking station and then undocked so that the user can travel with it. The two environments do require different power management settings, possibly different network settings, and various other configuration changes.

Hash message authentication code (HMAC) Message Digest 5 (MD5)
A hash algorithm that produces a 128-bit hash of the authenticated payload.

hibernation
A power option in Windows 2000 Professional portable computers that helps to conserve battery power. Hibernation is a complete power down while maintaining the state of open programs and connected hardware. When you bring your computer out of hibernation, your desktop is restored exactly as you left it, in less time than it takes for a complete system restart. However, it does take longer to bring your computer out of hibernation than out of standby. Put your computer in hibernation when you will be away from the computer for an extended time or overnight.

home directory
A location for a user or group of users to store files on a network server. This provides a central location for files that users can access and back up.

HOSTS file
A local text file in the same format as the 4.3 Berkeley Software Distribution (BSD) Unix /etc/hosts file. This file maps host names to Internet Protocol (IP) addresses. In Windows

2000, this file is stored in the \%SystemRoot%\System32\Drivers\Etc folder.

incremental backup

A backup that backs up only those files created or changed since the last normal or incremental backup. It marks files as having been backed up (in other words, the archive attribute is cleared). If you use a combination of normal and incremental backups, you need to have the last normal backup set as well as all incremental backup sets to restore your data.

Infrared Data Association (IrDA) device

A device that exchanges data over infrared waves. Infrared technology lets devices "beam" information to each other in the same way that your remote control tells the TV to change the channel. You could, for example, beam a document to a printer or another computer instead of having to connect a cable. The IrDA standard has been widely adopted by PC and consumer electronics manufacturers. Windows 2000 supports the IrDA standard.

input locale

The specification of the language you want to type in.

input/output (I/O) port

Any socket in the back, front, or side of a computer that you use to connect to another piece of hardware.

integrated services digital network (ISDN)

An international communications standard for sending voice, video, and data over digital telephone lines or normal telephone wires. ISDN supports data transfer rates of 64Kbps. Most ISDN lines offered by telephone companies give you two lines at once, called B channels. You can use one line for voice and the other for data, or you can use both lines for data, giving you data rates of 128Kbps.

integrated zone storage

Storage of zone information in an Active Directory database rather than in a text file.

Internet Connection Sharing (ICS)

A feature that is intended for use in a small office or home office where the network configuration and the Internet connection are managed by the computer running Windows 2000 where the shared connection resides. ICS can use a dial-up connection, such as modem or integrated services digital network (ISDN) connection to the Internet, or it can use a dedicated connection such as a cable modem or digital subscriber line (DSL). It is assumed that the ICS computer is the only Internet connection, the only gateway to the Internet, and that it sets up all internal network addresses.

Internet Printing Protocol (IPP)

A standard that allows network clients the option of entering a Uniform Resource Locator (URL) to connect to network printers and manage their network print jobs using a Hypertext Transfer Protocol (HTTP) connection in a Web browser. In Windows 2000, IPP is fully supported. The print server is either a Windows 2000 server running Internet Information Services (IIS) 5, or a Windows 2000 Professional system running Personal Web Server (PWS). PWS is the "junior" version of IIS. All shared IPP printers can be viewed at **http://servername/printers** (e.g., **http://Server2/printers**).

Internet Protocol (IP)

One of the protocols of the Transmission Control Protocol/Internet Protocol (TCP/IP) suite. IP is responsible for determining if a packet is for the local network or a remote network. If the packet is for a remote network, IP finds a route for it.

Internet Protocol (IP) address

A 32-bit binary address used to identify a host's network and host ID. The network portion can contain either a network ID or a network ID and a subnet ID.

Interrupt Request (IRQ)

A hardware line over which a device or devices can send interrupt signals to the microprocessor. When you add a new device to a PC, you sometimes need to set its IRQ number. IRQ conflicts used to be a common problem when you were adding expansion boards, but the Plug and Play and Advanced Configuration and Power Interface (ACPI) specifications have helped to remove this headache in many cases.

Internet Protocol Security (IPSec)

A Transmission Control Protocol/Internet Protocol (TCP/IP) security mechanism. IPSec provides machine-level authentication, as well as data encryption, for Virtual Private Network (VPN) connections that use Layer 2 Tunneling Protocol (L2TP). IPSec negotiates between your computer and its remote tunnel server before an L2TP connection is established, which secures both passwords and data.

ipconfig

A command that allows you to view, renegotiate, and configure Internet Protocol (IP) address information for a Windows NT or 2000 computer.

Kerberos v5

A distributed authentication and privacy protocol that protects information on a network between devices and enables Single Sign-On (SSO). Kerberos v5 is used in the Windows 2000 security model.

language group

A Regional Options configuration that allows you to type and read documents composed in languages of that group (e.g., Western Europe and United States, Japanese, and Hebrew).

Last Known Good Configuration

Starts Windows 2000 using the registry information that Windows saved at the last shutdown. Use this only in cases when you have incorrectly configured a device or driver. Last Known Good Configuration does not solve problems caused by corrupted or missing drivers or files. Also, you will lose any changes you made since the last successful startup.

Layer 2 Tunneling Protocol (L2TP)
An industry-standard Internet tunneling protocol. Unlike Point-to-Point Tunneling Protocol (PPTP), L2TP does not require Internet Protocol (IP) connectivity between the client workstation and the server. L2TP requires only that the tunnel medium provide packet-oriented point-to-point connectivity. You can use the protocol over media such as Asynchronous Transfer Mode (ATM), Frame Relay, and X.25. L2TP provides the same functionality as PPTP.

local group
A group account that is stored in the Security Access Manager (SAM) of a single system. You can give a local group access to resources only on that system.

local user
A user account that is stored in the Security Access Manager (SAM) of a single system. A local user can belong only to local groups on the same system and can be given access to resources only on that system.

logical drive
A simple volume or partition indicated by a drive letter that resides on a Windows 2000 basic disk.

logon script
A file that you can assign to user accounts. Typically a batch file, a logon script runs automatically every time the user logs on. You can use it to configure a user's working environment at every logon, and it allows an administrator to influence a user's environment without managing all aspects of it. You can assign a logon script to one or more user accounts.

makeboot.exe or makebt32.exe
The command that you use to create a set of four setup boot disks for Windows 2000. You use **makeboot.exe** on 16-bit operating systems and **makebt32.exe** on 32-bit operating systems. To create the setup disks, you'll need four 3.5-inch floppy disks; the disks will be formatted before they are created.

Microsoft Challenge Handshake Authentication Protocol (MSCHAP) 1
A special version of Challenge Handshake Authentication Protocol) (CHAP) that Microsoft uses. The encryption is still two-way and consists of a challenge from the server to the client that is made up of a session ID. The client uses a Message Digest 4 (MD4) hash to return the username to the server.

Microsoft Management Console (MMC)
A set of Windows 2000 utilities that allow authorized administrators to manage the directory remotely. The MMC provides a framework for hosting administrative tools, called consoles.

mirrored volume
A fault-tolerant set of two physical disks that contain an exact replica of each other's data within the mirrored portion of each disk. It is supported only on Windows 2000 Server versions.

mixed mode domain

A migration concept that provides maximum backward compatibility with earlier versions of Windows NT. In mixed mode domain, domain controllers that have been upgraded to Active Directory services allow servers running Windows NT versions 4 and earlier to exist within the domain.

mounted drive, mount point, or mounted volume

A pointer from one partition to another. Mounted drives are useful for increasing a drive's "size" without disturbing it. For example, you could create a mount point to drive E: as C:\CompanyData. Doing so makes it seem that you have increased the size available on the C: partition, specifically allowing you to store more data in C:\CompanyData than you would otherwise be able to.

Moving Picture Experts Group (MPEG)

A family of digital video compression standards and file formats. MPEG generally produces better-quality video than competing formats. MPEG files can be decoded by special hardware or by software. MPEG achieves a high compression rate by storing only the changes from one frame to another, instead of each entire frame. There are two major MPEG standards: MPEG-1 and MPEG-2. The MPEG-1 standard provides a video resolution of 352x240 at 30 frames per second (fps), which is video quality slightly below that of conventional VCR videos. A newer standard, MPEG-2, offers resolutions of 720x480 and 1,280x720 at 60 fps, with full CD-quality audio. This is sufficient for all the major TV standards, including NTSC and even HDTV. DVD-ROMs use MPEG-2. MPEG-2 can compress a two-hour video into a few gigabytes. Currently, work is being done on a new version of MPEG called MPEG-4 (there is no MPEG-3). MPEG-4 will be based on the QuickTime file format.

Multilink

An extension to Point-to-Point Protocol (PPP), that allows you to combine multiple physical connections between two points into a single logical connection. For example, you can combine two 33.6Kbps modems into one logical 67.2Kbps connection. The combined connections, called *bundles,* provide greater bandwidth than a single connection.

Multiple Processor Support (MPS)-compliant

Windows 2000 provides support for single or multiple CPUs. If you originally installed Windows 2000 on a computer with a single CPU, you must update the Hardware Abstraction Layer (HAL) on your computer so that it can recognize and use multiple CPUs.

name resolution

The process of translating a name into an Internet Protocol (IP) address. This could be either a fully qualified domain name (FQDN) or a NetBIOS name.

namespace
The method or conventions by which objects in a group of cooperating directories or databases are hierarchically structured and named.

native mode domain
A migration concept in which all domain controllers are running Windows 2000. The domain uses only Active Directory services multimaster replication between domain controllers, and no Windows NT domain controllers can participate in the domain through single-master replication.

network directory
A file or database where users or applications can get reference information about objects on the network.

network interface card (NIC) or network adapter
A piece of computer hardware called an adapter card that physically connects a computer to a network cable.

normal backup
A backup that copies all files and marks those files as having been backed up (in other words, clears the archive attribute). It is the most complete form of backup.

NT File System (NTFS) 5
An advanced file system designed for use specifically within the Windows 2000 operating system. It supports file system recovery, extremely large storage media, and long file names.

NT File System (NTFS) permission
A rule associated with a folder, file, or printer to regulate which users can gain access to the object and in what manner. The object's owner allows or denies permissions. The most restrictive permissions take effect between share permissions and NTFS permissions on an object.

object
In the context of performance monitoring and optimization, a system component that has numerous counters associated with it. Objects include Processor, Memory, System, Logical Disk, and Pagefile.

offline file
A new feature of Windows 2000 that allows users to continue to work with network files and programs even when they are not connected to the network. When a network connection is restored or when users dock their mobile computers, any changes that were made while users were working offline are updated to the network. When more than one user on the network has made changes to the same file, users are given the option of saving their specific version of the file to the network, keeping the other version, or saving both.

Open Systems Interconnect (OSI) model
A layer architecture developed by the International Organization for Standardization (ISO) that standardizes levels of service and types of interaction for computers that are exchanging information through a communications network. The OSI

model separates computer-to-computer communications into seven layers or levels, each building upon the standards contained in the levels below it.

optimization
The process of tuning performance for a particular system component.

Organizational Unit (OU)
A type of container object used within the Lightweight Directory Access Protocol (LDAP)/X.500 information model to group other objects and classes together for easier administration.

Packet Internet Groper (Ping) utility
A utility that determines whether a specific Internet Protocol (IP) address for a network device is reachable from an individual computer. It works by sending a data packet to the specified address and waiting for a reply. You use it to troubleshoot network connections in the Transmission Control Protocol/Internet Protocol (TCP/IP) network protocol.

paging file
Formerly called the swap file or virtual memory file, an extension of memory space stored on the disk drive as a kind of virtual memory.

partition
The information area beginning at a branch of a directory tree and continuing to the bottom of that tree and/or to the edges of new partitions controlled by subordinate Directory System Agents (DSAs).

Password Authentication Protocol (PAP)
The protocol that allows clear-text authentication.

peripheral connection interface (PCI)
A local bus standard developed by Intel. Most modern PCs include a PCI bus in addition to a more general Industry Standard Architecture (ISA) expansion bus. Many analysts, however, believe that PCI will eventually replace ISA entirely. PCI is a 64-bit bus, though it is usually implemented as a 32-bit bus. It can run at clock speeds of 33 or 66MHz. Although Intel developed it, PCI is not tied to any particular family of microprocessors.

Personal Computer Memory Card International Association (PCMCIA)
An organization of some 500 companies that developed a standard for small, credit card-sized devices called PC Cards. Originally designed for adding memory to portable computers, the PCMCIA standard has been expanded several times and is suitable for many types of devices. There are in fact three types of PCMCIA cards, along with three types of PC slots the cards fit into: Type I, II, and III, respectively.

Plug and Play
A standard developed by Microsoft, Intel, and other industry leaders to simplify the process of adding hardware to PCs by having the operating system automatically detect devices. The standard's intention is to conceal unpleasant details, such as

Interrupt Requests (IRQs) and Direct Memory Access (DMA) channels, from people who want to add a new hardware device to their system. A Plug and Play monitor, for example, can communicate with both Windows 2000 and the graphics adapter to automatically set itself at the maximum refresh rate supported for a chosen resolution. Plug and Play compliance also ensures that devices will not be driven beyond their capabilities.

Point-to-Point Protocol (PPP)
A method of connecting a computer to a network or to the Internet. PPP is more stable than the older Serial Line Internet Protocol (SLIP) and provides error-checking features. Windows 2000 Professional is a PPP client when dialing into any network.

Point-to-Point Tunneling Protocol (PPTP)
A communication protocol that tunnels through another connection, encapsulating PPP packets. The encapsulated packets are Internet Protocol (IP) datagrams that can be transmitted over IP-based networks, such as the Internet.

policy
A configuration or setting that is specified for one or more systems or users. Policies are refreshed at startup, logon, and after a refresh interval, so if a setting is manually changed, the policy refreshes the setting automatically. Policies provide for centralized management of change and configuration.

primary domain controller (PDC)
In a Windows NT Server 4 or earlier domain, the computer running Windows NT Server that authenticates domain logons and maintains the directory database for a domain. The PDC tracks changes made to accounts of all computers on a domain. It is the only computer to receive these changes directly. A domain has only one PDC.

primary master
An authoritative Domain Name System (DNS) server for a zone that you can use as a point of update for the zone. Only primary masters can be updated directly to process zone updates, which include adding, removing, or modifying resource records that are stored as zone data. Primary masters are also used as the first sources for replicating the zone to other DNS servers.

primary monitor
The monitor designated as the one that displays the logon dialog box when you start your computer. Most programs display their window on the primary monitor when you first open them. A Windows 2000 computer can support multiple monitors or displays.

privilege
The capability to perform a system behavior, such as changing the system time, backing up or restoring files, or formatting the hard drive. A privilege used to be, and often still is, referred to as a user right.

public key cryptography
An asymmetric encryption scheme that uses a pair of keys to code data. The public key encrypts data, and a corresponding secret key decrypts it. For digital signatures, the sender uses the private key to create a unique electronic number that can be read by anyone who has the corresponding public key, thus verifying that the message is truly from the sender.

Recovery Console
A command-line interface (CLI) that provides a limited set of administrative commands that are useful for repairing a computer. For example, you can use the Recovery Console to start and stop services, read and write data on a local drive (including drives formatted to use NT File System—NTFS), repair a master boot record (MBR), and format drives. You can start the Recovery Console from the Windows 2000 Setup disks or by using the **winnt32.exe** command with the **/cmdcons** switch.

Redundant Array of Independent Disks (RAID)-5 (or striped set with parity) volume
A fault-tolerant collection of equal-sized partitions on at least three physical disks, where the data is striped and includes parity data. The parity data is used to help recover a member of the striped set if one of its members fails. Windows 2000 Professional cannot host a RAID-5 volume but Windows 2000 Server versions can.

Remote Authentication Dial-In User Service (RADIUS)
A protocol used by Internet Authentication Services (IAS) to enable the communication of authentication, authorization, and accounting to the homogeneous and heterogeneous dial-up or Virtual Private Network (VPN) equipment in the enterprise.

Remote Installation Service (RIS)
A RIS server provides Windows 2000 Professional operating system image(s) that can be downloaded and installed by network clients using network adapter that comply with the Pre-boot eXecution Environment (PXE) boot read-only memory (ROM) specifications. RIS requires Active Directory, Dynamic Host Configuration Protocol (DHCP), and Domain Name System (DNS) to serve clients.

reverse lookup zone
A Domain Name System (DNS) zone that provides Transmission Control Protocol/Internet Protocol (TCP/IP) address to host name resolution.

route
A Windows 2000 command-line utility that manipulates Transmission Control Protocol/Internet Protocol (TCP/IP) routing tables for the local computer.

Safe Mode startup options
The options you get at startup when you press the F8 function key. Safe Mode helps you diagnose problems. When started in Safe Mode, Windows

2000 uses only basic files and drivers (mouse, monitor, keyboard, mass storage, base video, and default system services, but no network connections). You can choose the Safe Mode With Networking option, which loads all of the above files and drivers plus the essential services and drivers to start networking. Or, you can choose the Safe Mode With Command Prompt option, which is exactly the same as Safe Mode except that a command prompt is started instead of Windows 2000. You can also choose Last Known Good Configuration, which starts your computer using the registry information that Windows 2000 saved at the last shutdown. If a symptom does not reappear when you start in Safe Mode, you can eliminate the default settings and minimum device drivers as possible causes. If a newly added device or a changed driver is causing problems, you can use Safe Mode to remove the device or reverse the change. In some circumstances, such as when Windows system files required to start the system are corrupted or damaged, Safe Mode cannot help you. In this case, the Emergency Repair Disk (ERD) may be of use.

sampling (or update) interval

The frequency with which a performance counter is logged. A shorter interval provides more detailed information but generates a larger log.

scalability

A measure of how well a computer, service, or application can grow to meet increasing performance demands.

Security Account Manager (SAM)

The database of local user and local group accounts on a Windows 2000 member server or Windows 2000 Professional system.

Security Identifier (SID)

A unique number that represents a security principal such as a user or group. You can change the name of a user or group account without affecting the account's permissions and privileges, because the SID is what is granted user rights and resource access.

Serial Line Internet Protocol (SLIP)

An older remote access communication protocol used in Windows 2000 for outbound communication only.

service (SRV) record

A resource record used in a zone to register and locate well-known Transmission Control Protocol/Internet Protocol (TCP/IP) services. The SRV resource record is specified in Request for Comments (RFC) 2052 and is used in Windows 2000 or later to locate domain controllers for Active Directory Service.

Setup Manager

Used to create answer files for Windows 2000 unattended installations. Setup Manager can create answer files for an unattended, Sysprep or RIS installations.

share permission

A rule associated with a folder, to regulate which users can gain access to the object over the network and in what manner.

Shiva Password Authentication Protocol (SPAP)

A protocol that third-party clients and server typically use. The encryption for the protocol is two-way, but it is not as good as that for Challenge Handshake Authentication Protocol (CHAP).

simple volume

In Windows 2000, the disk space on a single physical disk. It can consist of a single area on a disk or multiple areas on the same disk that are linked together. You can extend a simple volume within the same disk or among multiple disks. If you extend a simple volume across multiple disks, it becomes a spanned volume.

slipstreaming

The process of integrating a Windows 2000 Service Pack into an existing Windows 2000 installation share. Subsequent installations of Windows 2000 will then include the service pack that you have slipstreamed into the installation share.

smart card

A credit card-sized device used to securely store public and private keys, passwords, and other types of personal information. To use a smart card, you need a smart card reader attached to the computer and a personal identification number (PIN) for the smart card. In Windows 2000, you can use smart cards to enable certificate-based authentication and Single Sign-On (SSO) to the enterprise.

smart card reader

A small external or internal device, or even a built-in slot, into which you insert a smart card so that it can be read.

spanned volume

In Windows 2000, the disk space on more than one physical disk. You can add more space to a spanned volume by extending it at any time. In NT 4 and earlier, a spanned volume was called a volume set.

spooler service

The primary Windows 2000 service that controls printing functionality.

standard zone storage

Storage of zone information in a text file rather than in an Active Directory database.

standby mode

A power-saving option in Windows 2000. Your computer switches to a low-power state where devices, such as the monitor and hard disks, turn off and your computer uses less power. When you want to use the computer again, it comes out of standby quickly, and your desktop is restored exactly as you left it. Standby is useful for conserving battery power in portable computers. Standby does not save your desktop state to disk; if you experience a power failure while on Standby, you can lose unsaved information. If there is an interruption in power, information in memory is lost.

static pool
A range of Internet Protocol (IP) addresses configured on the remote access server that allows the server to allocate IP addresses to the remote access clients.

striped volume
A volume that stores data in stripes on two or more physical disks. Data in a striped volume is allocated alternately and evenly (in stripes) to the disks of the striped volume. Striped volumes are *not* fault tolerant. Striped volumes can substantially improve the speed of access to your data on disk. You can create them on both Windows 2000 Professional and Server machines. Striped volumes with parity, also known as RAID-5 volumes, can be created *only* on Windows 2000 Server machines. In NT 4 and earlier, a striped volume was called a striped set.

subnet mask
A filter used to determine which network segment, or subnet, an Internet Protocol (IP) address belongs to. An IP address has two components: the network address and the host (computer name) address. For example, if the IP address 209.15.17.8 is part of a Class C network; the first three numbers (209.15.17) represent the Class C network address, and the last number (8) identifies a specific host (computer) on this network. By implementing subnetting, network administrators can further divide the host part of the address into two or more subnets.

suspend mode
A deep-sleep power-saving option that still uses some power.

Symmetric Multiprocessing (SMP)
A computer architecture that provides fast performance by making multiple CPUs available to complete individual processes simultaneously (multiprocessing). Unlike with asymmetric processing, you can assign any idle processor any task as well as add additional CPUs to improve performance and handle increased loads. A variety of specialized operating systems and hardware arrangements support SMP. Specific applications can benefit from SMP if their code allows multithreading. SMP uses a single operating system and shares common memory and disk input/output (I/O) resources. Windows 2000 supports SMP.

Sysprep
A tool that prepares a Windows 2000 computer to be imaged using third-party disk image software. It does this by removing unique identifiers such as computer name and Security Identifiers (SIDs). **Sysprep** adds a service to the image that generates a unique local domain SID after the image has been applied.

system state
In Backup, a collection of system-specific data that you can back up and restore. For all Windows 2000 operating systems, the system state data includes the registry, the Component Object Model (COM)+ Class Registration database, and the system

boot files. For Windows 2000 Server, the system state data also includes the Certificate Services database (if the server is operating as a certificate server). If the server is a domain controller, the system state data also includes the Active Directory directory services database and the Sysvol directory.

Sysvol
A shared directory that stores the server copy of the domain's public files, which are replicated among all domain controllers in the domain.

ticket
A feature of the Kerberos security model by which clients are granted access to objects and resources only indirectly, through services. Application servers use the service ticket to impersonate the client and look up its user or group Security Identifiers (SIDs).

tracert
A Windows 2000 command-line utility that follows that path of a data packet from a local computer to a host (computer) somewhere on the network (or internetwork). It shows how many hops the packet requires to reach the host and how long each hop takes. You can use **tracert** to figure out where the longest delays are occurring for connecting to various computers.

universal group
A security or distribution group that you can use anywhere in the domain tree or forest. A universal group can have members from any Windows 2000 domain in the domain tree or forest. It can also include other universal groups, global groups, and accounts from any domain in the domain tree or forest. Universal groups can be members of domain local groups and other universal groups but cannot be members of global groups. Universal groups appear in the Global Catalog and should contain primarily global groups.

Universal Serial Bus (USB)
An external bus standard (released in 1996) that supports data transfer rates of 12Mbps. You can use a single USB port to connect up to 127 peripheral devices, such as mice, modems, and keyboards. USB also supports Plug and Play installation and hot plugging. It is expected to completely replace serial and parallel ports.

User Datagram Protocol (UDP)
A connectionless protocol that runs on top of Internet Protocol (IP) networks. Unlike Transmission Control Protocol/Internet Protocol (TCP/IP), UDP/IP provides very few error recovery services and does not guarantee delivery of data. UDP is a direct way to send and receive datagrams over an IP network. It's used primarily for sending broadcast messages over an IP network.

user locale
Controls the date, time, currency, and numbers on a per-user basis. These settings are used by all applications and can be configured via the Regional Options applet in the Control Panel folder.

user profile

The collection of desktop and environmental settings that define the work area of a local computer.

user right

See *privilege*.

video adapter

The electronic component that generates the video signal sent through a cable to a video display. The video adapter is usually located on the computer's main system board or on an expansion board.

Virtual Private Network (VPN)

A private network of computers that is at least partially connected using public channels or lines, such as the Internet. A good example would be a private-office local area network (LAN) that allows users to log in remotely over the Internet (an open, public system). VPNs use encryption and secure protocols like Point-to-Point Tunneling Protocol (PPTP) and Layer 2 Tunneling Protocol (L2TP) to ensure that unauthorized parties do not intercept data transmissions.

Windows Backup

A Windows 2000 utility that helps you plan for and recover from data loss by allowing you to create backup copies of data as well as restore files, folders, and system state data (which includes the registry) manually or on a schedule. The Windows 2000 Backup program allows you to back up data to a variety of media types, not just tape.

Windows Installer Packages

Files with the .msi extension that install applications. These files contain summary and installation instructions as well as the actual installation files. You can install Windows Installer Packages locally or remotely through Windows 2000 Group Policies.

Windows Internet Naming Service (WINS)

A service that dynamically maps NetBIOS names to Internet Protocol (IP) addresses.

Windows Management Instrumentation (WMI)

An initiative supported in Windows 2000 that establishes architecture to support the management of an enterprise across the Internet. WMI offers universal access to management information for enterprises by providing a consistent view of the managed environment. This management uniformity allows you to manage your entire business rather than just its components. You can obtain more detailed information regarding the WMI Software Development Kit (SDK) from the Microsoft Developer Network (MSDN).

Windows or Win32 Driver Model (WDM)

A 32-bit layered architecture for device drivers; it allows for drivers that Windows 2000, NT, and 98 can use. It provides common input/output (I/O) services that all operating systems understand. It also supports

Plug and Play; Universal Serial Bus (USB); Institute of Electrical and Electronics Engineers (IEEE) 1394 bus; and various devices, including input, communication, imaging, and digital versatile disc or digital video disc (DVD).

winnt32 /cmdcons
The command and switch used to install the Recovery Console onto a Windows 2000 computer. This command uses **winnt32** on the installation media, or in the distribution source.

workgroup
A peer-to-peer network in which user accounts are decentralized and stored on each individual system.

X.25 Virtual Circuit (VC)
A connection between two devices that acts as though it's a direct connection although it may physically take different routes. X.25 connections involve at least two hosts in a packet switching network. With X.25 VCs, two hosts can communicate as though they have a dedicated connection, although the data packets might actually travel very different routes before arriving at their destinations. VCs can be either permanent or temporary.

ZAP
A file that you use to allow applications without an .msi file to be deployed via Windows 2000 Group Policy.

zone
In Domain Name System (DNS) standards, the namespace partition formed by each domain within the global namespace or within an enterprise namespace. Each zone is controlled by an authoritative DNS server, or in the case of Active Directory services, by a group of domain controllers.

zone transfer
Copying of Domain Name System (DNS) database information from one DNS server to another.

Index

Bold page numbers indicate sample exam questions.

A

Access permissions, 46-48, **98**
Accessibility options
Accessibility Options applet, 129-131
Accessibility Wizard, 131-132
Display tab, 130
FilterKeys, 129-130
High Contrast, 130
Keyboard tab, 129-130
Magnifier, 132
Mouse tab, 131
MouseKeys, 131
Narrator, 132
On-Screen Keyboard, 132
SerialKey, 131
ShowSounds, 130
Sound Tab, 130
SoundSentry, 130
StickyKeys, 129
ToggleKeys, 130
Utility Manager, 132, **324**
Accessibility Options applet, 129-131
Accessibility Wizard, 131-132
Account policies, 89-90
ACLs, 34-36
Active Directory, 86-88, **161**
Add/Remove Hardware Wizard, 170, 173, **199-200, 320**
Add/Remove Programs, 115, **120-121**
Administrators group, 30, 78, **95**
Advanced permissions, 37-41
Append Data permission, 41
Change Permissions permission, 41
Create Files/Write Data permission, 40
Create Folders/Append Data permission, 41
Delete permission, 40
Delete Subfolders and Files permission, 40
Execute File permission, 40
Read Attributes permission, 40
Read Data permission, 40
Read Extended Attributes permission, 40
Read Permissions permission, 41
Take Ownership permission, 41
Traverse Folder/Execute File permission, 40
Write Attributes permission, 40
Write Data permission, 40
Write Extended Attributes permission, 40
Anonymous Logon built-in group, 31
APIPA, 235, 242, **260-261**
Application performance, managing, 284
ARP, 240
Attended installation
CD-ROM installation, 146-147
hardware requirements, 146
installation methods, 146-147
network installation, 147

overview, 146
setup disks, installation with, 147
Audit policies, 90-91
Auditing, 50-51, **70**
enabling, 51-52
specific files and folders, enabling auditing for, 52-53
Authenticated Users built-in group, 31
Authentication
automating logon, 86
overview, 85
security dialog, 85-86
Authentication protocols
BAP, 244, **326**
EAP, 243-244
IPSec, 242-243
L2TP, 243
RADIUS, 244
Automated installation
launching, 151
RIS, 153-157
Setup Manager utility, 148-151
switches, 151
System Preparation Tool, 151-153

B

Backing up and restoring data
backup marker, 265
backup strategies, 266
backup types, 265
Backup Wizard, scheduling backups with, 267-268
configuring file and folder backup, 266
copy backups, 265
daily backups, 265
differential backups, 265
incremental backups, 265
normal backups, 265
permissions, 264
restoring files and folders, 268
Scheduled Jobs tab, configuring jobs with, 268
scheduling backups, 267-268
system state data, backing up, 267
user rights, 264
Windows Backup, 264
Backup marker, 265
Backup Operators group, 30, 78, **95**
Backup strategies, 266, **317**
Backup types, 265
Backup Wizard, scheduling backups with, 267-268
BACP, 244, **326**
Bandwidth Allocation Protocol. *See* BAP.
BAP, 244, **326**
Baseline, creating, 279-280
Basic disks, 204, **224, 229.**
See also basic volumes.
detecting disk errors, 214
diagnosing problems, 213
Disk Cleanup Wizard, 216
Disk Defragmenter, 215
diskperf.exe, 214-215
dynamic disks compared, 205
monitoring disk performance, 213-214
repairing disk errors, 214
troubleshooting, 213-216
upgrading to dynamic disks, 206-207
Basic permissions
files, 36
folders, 37
Basic volumes
extending, 213
logical drives, 209
overview, 208
partitions, 209
spanned volumes on basic disks, 208
striped volumes on basic disks, 208-209
troubleshooting, 213-216
BIOS, **165,** 183, **196-197**
Boot disk, 154, **319**
Built-in groups, 30-31
Administrators group, 78
Backup Operators group, 78
Guests group, 79
Power Users group, 78
Replicator group, 79
Users group, 78-79
Built-in system groups
Anonymous Logon group, 79
Authenticated Users group, 79
Creator Owner group, 79
Dial-up group, 79
Everyone group, 79
Interactive group, 79
Network group, 79
Built-in user accounts
Administrator account, 77
Guest account, 78

C

Caching files, 27-29, **318, 322**
CACLS.exe utility, 36
Cameras
  installing, 179
  overview, 178
  testing, 179
CD-ROM installation, **162**
Certificates, 178
Chdir command, 273
Chkdsk command, 273
Cls command, 273
Copy backups, 265
Copy command, 273
Counter logs, 278
Creator Owner built-in group, 31

D

Daily backups, 265
Debugging Mode, 270
Default gateway, 238
Default permissions, 41-42
Delete command, 273
Desktop settings
  Display applet, 109-110
  Keyboard applet, 109
  Mouse applet, 110
  overview, 109
  Quick Launch Pad, 111
  Sound applet, 110
  Start menu, customizing, 110-111
  toolbars, 111-112
Device conflicts, 173
Device Manager, 170, 172–173, **195**
DHCP, 234-235, **325-326**
DHCP servers, **161,** 235, **254, 260**
Dial-up built-in group, 31
Dial-up Connections, 242, **326**
  BACP, 244
  BAP, 244
  EAP, 243-244
  Internet connections, creating, 249-250
  IPSec, 242-243
  L2TP, 243
  RADIUS, 244
  RAS servers, connecting to, 245-248
  VPN connections, 248-249
Differential backups, 265, **320**
Dir command, 273
Directory Services Restore Mode, 270
Disable command, 273
Disk Cleanup Wizard, 216
Disk Defragmenter, 215
Disk Management, **228-229, 322**
  accessing, 206
  basic volumes. *See* basic volumes.
  dynamic volumes. *See* dynamic volumes.
  moving disks, 207-208
  offline disks, reactivating, 208
  troubleshooting disks and volumes, 213-216
  upgrading disks, 206-207
Disk performance, managing, 282
Disk quotas, 220-221
Diskperf.exe, 214-215
Display applet, 109-110
Display settings, 186, **320**
Display tab, 130
DNS server, 56, **72, 161,** 235, 238
Domain accounts, 76-77, **99, 121**
Domain controllers, 77
Domain security, 31-32
Domain user accounts
  copying, 84
  creating, 83-84
  deleting, 84
  disabling, 84
  local groups, adding to, 85
  managing, 83-85
  modifying, 84
  template user accounts, creating, 84
DRAs, 55, **67**
Drive letters
assigning, 218-219
changing, 218
removing, 218
Driver signing, 173-174
Driver updates
  device conflicts, 173
  driver signing, 173-174
  Group Policy Object (GPO), 174
  overview, 172
  Signature Verification tool, 174
  system files, Windows Update used for updating, 172-173
  updating individual drivers, 172
DVD devices, managing, 222-223
DVD drives, 223, **226**

Dynamic disks, 204-205, **229**, **321**. *See also* dynamic volumes.
- basic disks compared, 205
- conversion to basic disks, 207, **322**
- detecting disk errors, 214
- diagnosing problems, 213
- Disk Cleanup Wizard, 216
- Disk Defragmenter, 215
- **Diskperf.exe**, 214-215
- limitations of, 212-213
- monitoring disk performance, 213-214
- troubleshooting, 213-216

Dynamic volumes
- extending, 211, 213
- limitations of, 212-213
- overview, 210
- RAID-5 volumes, 212
- simple volumes, 210
- spanned volumes, 210-211
- striped volumes, 212
- troubleshooting, 213-216

E

EAP, 178

EFS
- accessing encrypted files, 55
- copying encrypted files, 56
- moving encrypted files, 56
- overview, 53-54
- Windows Explorer, encrypting file or folders from, 54-55

Emergency Repair Disks. *See* ERDs.

Enable Boot Logging, 269

Enable command, 273

Enable VGA Mode, 269-270

Encrypted files, 54-56, **67**, **70**, **322**

ERDs
- emergency repair process, 274-276
- Fast Repair option, 275
- Manual Repair option, 275
- overview, 274
- repair process, starting, 276
- restarting computer, 276
- Setup, choosing repair options during, 275
- type of repair, choosing, 275

Everyone built-in group, 31

Exit command, 273

Extensible Authentication Protocol. *See* EAP.

F

FAT, 216

FAT32, 216, **225**, **227**, **321**

Fax service
- configuring, 132-133, **138**
- Fax Service Management console, 133-134
- sending faxes, 132
- support for, 181

Fax Service Management console, 133-134, **137**

Fdisk command, 273

File compression, 42-44

File systems
- conversion between systems, 217-218
- default NTFS permissions, reapplying, 218
- FAT, 216
- FAT32, 216
- NTFS 5, 216-217
- NTFS partition, converting from FAT partition to, 217

Files
- basic permissions, 36
- copying compressed, 45-46
- moving compressed, 45-46
- offline files. *See* offline files.
- optimizing access to, 48-50
- ownership of, 49-50
- permissions and copying, 48-49
- permissions and moving, 48-49
- permissions used to control access to, 46-48

FilterKeys, 129-130, **138**

Finger, 239

Fixboot command, 273

Fixmbr command, 273

Folder compression, 44-45

Folders
- basic permissions, 36–37
- copying compressed, 45-46
- moving compressed, 45-46
- offline folders. *See* offline folders.
- optimizing access to, 48-50
- ownership of, 49-50
- permissions and copying, 48-49
- permissions and moving, 48-49
- permissions used to control access to, 46-48
- shared folders. *See* shared folders.

Format command, 273
FTP service, 58, 236, 239

G

Group accounts, local.
  See local group accounts.
Group Policy, 92-93, **96–97, 99, 118-119, 122-123, 316, 323**
    application of, 93
    OU design and, 93-94
Group Policy Object (GPO), 174
Guests group, 30, 79

H

Hard disk management
    basic disks. *See* basic disks.
    dynamic disks. *See* dynamic disks.
    guidelines for relocating disks, 207-208
    missing disks, reactivating, 208
    moving disk to another computer, 207-208
    offline disks, reactivating, 208
    troubleshooting, 213-216
Hardware
    configuring, 170
    driver updates, 172-174
    I/O devices, 174-184
    IrDA devices. *See* IrDA devices.
    keyboards, 176
    mice, 176
    mobile computer hardware.
      See mobile computer hardware.
    mobile users, 177-178
    modems, 179-181
    monitors. *See* monitors.
    network adapters, 184
    non Plug and Play devices, installing, 171
    overview, 170, 174
    Plug and Play devices, installing, 171
    printers. *See* printers.
    scanners, 178-179
    smart card readers, 176-177
    smart cards, 176-177
    tips on installing devices, 171
    wireless devices. *See* wireless devices.
Help command, 273
Hidden network shares, 26-27
High Contrast, 130
Home folders, 103
HOSTNAME, 240

I

ICS, 184-186, **257, 326**
    configuring, 251-253
    overview, 250-251
    troubleshooting, 253
IIS
    administration, 56-57
    installing, 56
    Internet Web sites, problems connecting to, 59
    intranet Web sites, problems connecting to, 59
    settings, viewing and modifying, 57
    troubleshooting, 58-59
Incremental backups, 265, **287, 320**
Input locale, 126-127, **142**
Installation
    attended installation, 146-147
    automated installation.
      See automated installation.
    dependency failures, 160
    domains, problems joining, 160
    drive space, lack of, 160
    errors, 160
    halts, 160
    hardware requirements, 146
    media errors, 159-160
    memory requirements, 146, **319**
    noncompatibile CD-ROM drive, 160
    troubleshooting, 159-160
Interactive built-in group, 31
Internet Connection Sharing. *See* ICS.
Internet Printing Protocol. *See* IPP.
I/O devices
    IrDA devices. *See* IrDA devices.
    keyboards, 176
    mice, 176
    mobile users, 177-178
    modems, 179-181
    network adapters, 184
    overview, 174
    printers. *See* printers.
    scanners, 178-179
    smart card readers, 176-177
    smart cards, 176-177
    wireless devices. *See* wireless devices.
IP addresses, 237, **256, 261**
IPCONFIG, 240
IPP, 66, **200**
IPSec, 236

IrDA devices
bandwidth allocations for USB host controllers, viewing, 183
described, 181-182
enabling receiving files, 182
preventing receiving files, 182
USB controllers, improper installation of, 183-184
USB hubs, viewing power allocations for, 182-183

K

Keyboard applet, 109, **118**
Keyboard tab, 129-130
Keyboards, 176

L

Languages, multiple.
See multiple language support.
Last Known Good Configuration, 270, **286-287, 287-288**
Local group accounts
built-in local groups, 78-79
built-in system groups, 79
configuring account properties, 80-81
creating, 79-80
deleting, 82
managing, 77-79
membership, 81
overview, 76-77
passwords, 80
renaming, 81-82
Local groups, 30-31
Local Policy, 89, 92
Local profiles, 102, **318**
Local Security Policy, 92, **96, 316**
Local user accounts, 76-77, **98**
built-in user accounts, 77-79
configuring account properties, 80-81
creating, 79-80
deleting, 82
disabling, 82
enabling, 82
managing, 77-79
passwords, 80
renaming, 81-82
Users and Passwords applet, 82-83
Logical Drives, 209, 220
LogicalDisk counters, 282
Logon command, 273
Logon scripts, 103
LPQ, 240
LPR, 239
L2TP, 236

M

Magnifier, 132
Map command, 273
Memory, 146, **201,** 280, **319–320**
Memory:Available Bytes, 280
Memory:Pages/sec, 280, **289-290**
MFT, 215
Mice, 176
Microsoft Certification exams
adaptive exam strategy, 17-18
adaptive testing format, 13-14
build-list-and-recorder question format, 6-8
case study exam strategy, 15-16
case study testing format, 13
create-a-tree question format, 8-10
drag-and-connect question format, 10-11
exam situation, 3-4
exam-readiness, assessing, 2
fixed-length exam strategy, 16-17
fixed-length testing format, 13
layout and design of exam, 4-12
multiple-choice question format, 5-6
practice exams, 19
preparing for, 19-20
question formats, 5-12
question-handling strategies, 18-19
select-and-place question format, 11-12
short-form exam strategy, 16-17
short-form testing format, 14
testing formats, 13-14
test-taking strategies, 14-18
Web sites, 20-21
Microsoft Certified Professional Web site, 20
Mkdir command, 273
Mobile computer hardware
ACPI, 190-191
airplanes, using portable computers on, 192
APM, 190
battery power, managing, 192
hardware profiles, managing, 189-190

hibernation mode, 191-192
overview, 189
Plug and Play devices, managing power when installing, 192
power options, 191-192
standby mode, 191
Mobile users, 177-178
Modems, **137-138,** 179-181, **198-199**
installing, 179
multilinking, 180-181
troubleshooting, 181
Monitors
arranging multiple monitors, 187
configuring, 186-188
display settings, 186, **320**
moving items between monitors, 188
multiple-display support, 186-188
primary monitor, changing, 187-188
troubleshooting multiple displays, 188
viewing same desktop on multiple monitors, 188
More command, 273
Mounted drives, 219
Mouse applet, 110
Mouse tab, 131
MouseKeys, 131, **324**
Multilanguage edition, 128-129, **140, 324**
Multilink
configuring, 180
overview, 180
tips for, 180-181
Multiple language support
input locale, 126-127, **142, 324**
installing multiple language settings, 128
language options, 126
locales, 126-127
Multilanguage version of Windows 2000, 128-129
user locale, 126-127
Multiple processors, 193-194
Multiple-display support
arranging multiple monitors, 187
configuring, 186-188
moving items between monitors, 188
primary monitor, changing, 187-188
troubleshooting multiple displays, 188
viewing same desktop on multiple monitors, 188
My Documents folder, 103, **122**
My Network Places, 25-26, 107

N

Narrator, 132, **139, 319**
NBSTAT, 240
Net use command, 26
NETSTAT, 240
Network adapters, 184
Network built-in group, 31
Network cards, **197**
Network performance, managing, 283
Network protocols. *See* TCP/IP.
Normal backups, 265, **320**
NTFS, 5, 29, 216-217, **225, 321**
copying compressed files and folders, 45-46
denying access to a resource, 47-48
file compression, 42-44
folder compression, 44-45
moving compressed files and folders, 45-46
optimizing access to files and folders, 48-50
ownership of files and folders, 49-50
permissions, 46-48, 48-49, **228**
security. *See* NTFS security.
NTFS compression, **69,** 221, **228**
copying compressed files and folders, 221
guidelines, 221-222
moving compressed files and folders, 221
NTFS security
ACLs, 34-36
Administrators local group, 30
advanced permissions, 37-41
Anonymous Logon built-in group, 31
Authenticated Users built-in group, 31
Backup Operators local group, 30
basic permissions, 36-37
built-in groups, 30-31
CACLS.exe utility, 36
Creator Owner built-in group, 31
default permissions, 41-42
Dial-up built-in group, 31
domain security, 31-32
Everyone built-in group, 31
Guests local group, 30

Interactive built-in group, 31
local groups, 30-31
Network built-in group, 31
permission conflicts, 42
permissions, setting, 31-32
Power Users local group, 30
Replicator local group, 30
Users local group, 30
Windows 2000 logon process, 33-34
workgroup security, 31

O

Offline files
accessing, 108
managing, 108-109
overview, 104-105
setting up, 105-106
share points, configuring, 105-106
steps for making files available offline, 106-107
synchronizing, 107-108
Offline Files and Folders, 104-105, **120**
Offline folders
accessing, 108
managing, 108-109
overview, 104-105
setting up, 105-106
share points, configuring, 105-106
steps for making files available offline, 106-107
synchronizing, 107-108
On-Screen Keyboard, 132, **324**

P

Paging file, managing, 280-282
Partitions, 209, **225-226**
Passwords, 80, **96, 98**
Performance
application performance, managing, 284
baseline, creating, 279-280
configuring alerts, 277-278
configuring logs, 278
counter logs, 278
disk performance, managing, 282
LogicalDisk counters, 282
managing, 278-284
memory performance, managing, 280
network performance, managing, 283
paging file, managing, 280-282
Performance Logs And Alerts, 277-278
PhysicalDisk counters, 282
processor performance, managing, 283-284
System Monitor, 276-277
Task Manager, 284
trace logs, 278
VMM, 280-281
Performance bottleneck, 280, **317**
Performance Logs And Alerts, 277-278, **291**
Permission conflicts, 42
Permissions, 264
access to files and folders, 46-48
copying files and folders, 48-49
moving files and folders, 48-49
setting, 31-32
shared folders, 29
PhysicalDisk counters, 282, **288**
PING, 240
Point-to-Point Protocol. *See* PPP.
Policies
account policies, 89-90
audit policies, 90-91
group policy. *See* Group Policy.
Local Policy, 89
local policy, 92
overview, 89
Security Options node, 91-92
user rights, 91
Power Users group, 30, 78, **95**
PPP, 178, 236
PPTP, 236
Preferred and alternate DNS servers, 238
Print device, 60, **69**
Print jobs, 60, **71**
managing, 65-66
Print queue, 60
Print resolution, 60
Print server, 60
Print spooler, 60
Printer driver, 60
Printer port, 60
Printer Properties sheet
Advanced tab, 64-65
Device Settings tab, 65
General tab, 64
Ports tab, 64
Security tab, 65
Sharing tab, 64
Printers, 59, **71**
Availability setting, 175

command line, connecting to network printer via, 63
IPP, 66, 175
local printer, adding, 60-61
managing, 65-66
network printer, connecting to, 61-63
Print Pooling setting, 175
Print Priority setting, 175
printer ports, 175
printer property settings, 175-176
properties, configuring, 63-65
Restart setting, 176
Separator Pages setting, 175
Spooler Service, 176
Processor performance, managing, 283-284, **290**
Processors, multiple, 193-194

Q

Quick Launch Pad, 111

R

RAID-5 volumes, 212, **321**
RAS, 242
RAS servers, **198,** 245-248
Rbfg.exe, 154
RCP, 239
Recovery Console
chdir command, 273
chkdsk command, 273
cls command, 273
commands, 273
copy command, 273
delete command, 273
dir command, 273
disable command, 273
enable command, 273
exit command, 273
fdisk command, 273
fixboot command, 273
fixmbr command, 273
format command, 273
help command, 273
launching, 272-273
logon command, 273
map command, 273
mkdir command, 273
more command, 273
overview, 271-272
rename command, 273
rmdir command, 273
system that won't start, running Recovery Console on, 272
systemroot command, 273
type command, 273
Remote Installation Options, 270
Rename command, 273
Repairing Windows 2000 system
Debugging Mode, 270
Directory Services Restore Mode, 270
Enable Boot Logging, 269
Enable VGA Mode, 269-270
Last Known Good Configuration, 270
Remote Installation Options, 270
Safe Mode, 268-269
Safe Mode with Command Prompt, 269
Safe Mode with Networking, 269
Replicator group, 30, 79
Restoring files and folders, 268
REXEC, 240
Riprep.exe, 156-157, **325**
RIS
clients, configuring, 153-154
configuring, 154-156
downloading images, 157
images, creating additional, 156-157
installing, 154-156
overview, 153
requirements for, 154
RIS server, 153-157, **162**
Rmdir command, 273
Roaming user profiles, 103-104
ROUTE, 240
RSH, 240

S

Safe Mode, 268-269, **286**
Safe Mode with Command Prompt, 269
Safe Mode with Networking, 269
Scanners
installing, 179
overview, 178
testing, 179
Scheduled Jobs tab, configuring jobs with, 268
Scheduling backups, 267-268
Security
auditing. *See* auditing.
authentication. *See* authentication.

encrypted files. *See* encrypted files.
NTFS security. *See* NTFS security.
Security Options node, 91-92
SerialKey, 131
Service packs. *See* SPs.
Setup disks, 147, **325**
Shared folders. *See also* NTFS.
access, 24-25, **68**
automatically generated hidden shares, 26-27
caching of files, 27-29
controlling access to, 27-29
permissions, 29
properties, modifying, 27-29
Shared network resources
connecting to, 25-26
My Network Places, 25-26
net use command, 26
ShowSounds, 130
Signature Verification tool, 174
SLIP, 235
Slipstreaming, 159, **165**
Smart card readers, 176-177
Smart cards, 176-177, **255**
SMTP, 237
Sound applet, 110
Sound Tab, 130
SoundSentry, 130
Spanned volumes, 208, 210-211
SPs, **318**
applying, 159, **166**
deploying, 159
slipstreaming, 159
Start menu, customizing, 110-111
StickyKeys, 129, **139, 325**
Striped volumes, 208-209, 212, **230**
Subnet mask, 238
Synchronizing offline files and folders, 107-108, **117, 318, 323**
Sysprep.inf, 153, **163, 319**
System files, Windows Update used for updating, 172-173
System Monitor, 276-277
System Preparation Tool, 151-153
System state data, backing up, 267, **317**
Systemroot command, 273

T

Tape devices, managing, 222
Task Manager, 284, **289, 317**
Task Scheduler, 134-135, **141**
creating a task, 135
opening, 135
troubleshooting tasks, 136
TCP/IP, 234, **254-255**
APIPA, 235, 242
ARP, 240
configuring, 238-239
default gateway, 238
DHCP, 234-235
DNS server, 235
Finger, 239
FTP, 239
FTP service, 236
HOSTNAME, 240
IP addresses, 237
IPCONFIG, 240
IPSec, 236
LPQ, 240
LPR, 239
L2TP, 236
NBSTAT, 240
NETSTAT, 240
PING, 240
PPP, 236
PPTP, 236
preferred and alternate DNS servers, 238
RCP, 239
REXEC, 240
ROUTE, 240
RSH, 240
SLIP, 235
SMTP, 237
subnet mask, 238
Telnet, 240
TFTP, 240
TRACERT, 240
troubleshooting, 239-241
WINS, 235
WINS addresses, 238
WWW publishing service, 236
Telnet, 240
Template account, 84, **316**
TFTP, 240
ToggleKeys, 130
Toolbars, 111-112
Trace logs, 278
TRACERT, 240
Transmission Control Protocol/Internet Protocol. *See* TCP/IP.

Troubleshooting
- basic disks, 213-216
- basic volumes, 213-216
- dynamic disks, 213-216
- dynamic volumes, 213-216
- hard disk management, 213-216
- ICS, 253
- IIS, 58-59
- installation, 159-160
- modems, 181
- service fails, recovery actions for when a, 271
- system stopping unexpectedly, 270-271
- tasks, 136
- TCP/IP, 239-241

Type command, 273

U

Update packs, 158, **163**
Updating individual drivers, 172
Upgrades, **326**
- disk utilities, 158
- drive compression, 158
- hardware compatibility, 158, **164**
- operating systems, supported, 157-158
- pre-upgrade checklist, 158
- software compatibility, 158, **164**
- update packs, 158, **163**

USB, 182-184, **196, 320**
User accounts, local. *See* local user accounts.
User profiles, 102, **119, 323**
- home folders, 103
- local profiles, 102
- logon scripts, 103
- roaming user profiles, 103-104

User rights, 91, 264
Users and Passwords applet, 82-83, **96, 316**
Users local group, 30
Utility Manager, 132, **324**

V

Video adapters, 189
VMM, 280-281
VPN, 248-249, **258–259**

W

Web sites
- Microsoft, 21
- Microsoft Certified Professional, 20
- search tools, 21

Windows 2000 logon process, 33-34
Windows Backup, 264, **285**
Windows Installer Service Packages
- assigning applications, 115
- Group Policy, creating, 114-115
- installing packages, 113
- .msi files, 114
- overview, 112-113
- publishing applications, 115
- ZAP files, 113, **123**

WINS, **72,** 235, 238
Wireless devices
- bandwidth allocations for USB host controllers, viewing, 183
- described, 181-182
- enabling receiving files, 182
- preventing receiving files, 182
- USB controllers, improper installation of, 183-184
- USB hubs, viewing power allocations for, 182-183

Workgroup security, 31
Workgroups, 77
WWW Master Service Properties, 58
WWW publishing service, 236

Z

ZAP files, 113, **123**

A+
AUDIO REVIEW

Routing and Switching

Routing and Switching